12

DATE DUE

Van 7/29/13	
APR 0 8 2016	

GAYLORD   PRINTED IN U.S.A.

'CARA has truly made a difference through its invaluable work. Due to its principled commitment to academic freedom it provides life changing support to individual academics who are under threat in their own countries. Alongside this it also upholds the principle of freedom of inquiry by acting as a beacon for academics around the world committed to intellectual freedom.'

Bill Rammell, Minister of State, Life Long Learning, Further and Higher Education, UK Government

'CARA has not only greatly enriched my country through their assistance of well known exiled South African academics during the apartheid years but also many other academics in the rest of Africa and elsewhere. Academic activity is vital for any nation and, by preserving intellectual capital, they are doing the world a great service.'

Lindiwe Mabuza, South African High Commissioner

The **Council for Assisting Refugee Academics (CARA)** was founded in 1933, to save academics from the onslaught of Nazism and to preserve the wealth of knowledge under threat at the time. Throughout the 20th century, conflicts, civil wars, repressive regimes and rogue factions have led fleeing academics to CARA in search of solidarity and practical support. CARA is currently assisting over 180 refugee academics through its Grant Programme, Campaign of Action for Iraqi Academics, Fellowship Scheme and UK University Network, helping them to re-establish their lives and careers.

For further information about CARA, or to make a donation, please contact:

CARA
London South Bank University
Technopark
90 London Road
London SE1 6LN
www.academic-refugees.org
Tel: 020 7021 0880   E mail: info.cara@lsbu.ac.uk

COUNCIL FOR ASSISTING REFUGEE ACADEMICS

cara

The Refuge and the Fortress

Britain and the Flight from Tyranny

Jeremy Seabrook

palgrave
macmillan

First published 2009 by
PALGRAVE MACMILLAN

Palgrave Macmillan in the UK is an imprint of Macmillan Publishers Limited,
registered in England, company number 785998, of Houndmills, Basingstoke,
Hampshire RG21 6XS.

Palgrave Macmillan in the US is a division of St Martin's Press LLC,
175 Fifth Avenue, New York, NY 10010.

Palgrave Macmillan is the global academic imprint of the above companies and
has companies and representatives throughout the world.

Palgrave® and Macmillan® are registered trademarks in the United States,
the United Kingdom, Europe and other countries.

ISBN-13: 978–0–230–21877–2   hardback
ISBN-10: 0–230–21877–6   hardback
ISBN-13: 978–0–230–21878–9   paperback
ISBN-10: 0–230–21878–4   paperback

This book is printed on paper suitable for recycling and made from fully
managed and sustained forest sources. Logging, pulping and manufacturing
processes are expected to conform to the environmental regulations of the
country of origin.

A catalogue record for this book is available from the British Library.

A catalog record for this book is available from the Library of Congress.

10   9   8   7   6   5   4   3   2   1
18   17   16   15   14   13   12   11   10   09

Printed and bound in Great Britain by
CPI Antony Rowe, Chippenham and Eastbourne

Contents

List of Illustrations

Foreword

Jon Snow

One of the most critical elements that has made the United Kingdom the totemic multi-cultural society that it has become in the twentieth and twenty first centuries is the vast pool of intellectual capacity brought to this country by academics in flight from war and repression elsewhere in the world. From Austria to Zimbabwe they have come in their thousands. Sometimes singly, sometimes in their hundreds – as in the flight from Nazi Germany – these refugees have often had to struggle both to enter and remain in Britain. Our arms have not always been enthusiastically open. The ameliorating force combating this inconsistency of welcome and support for these academics for three quarters of a century has been CARA, the Council for Assisting Refugee Academics.

I first came across CARA when working as a reporter on the long Eritrean war of independence from Ethiopia. My best and most constant informants were refugees from assorted universities from Newcastle to London. When it came to wars in Central America in the early 1980s it was again people from the refugee academic community such as Dr Salvador Muncada at London University who led me to the critical contacts that informed my work on the ground in the region. Since then wherever I have travelled to universities, schools and colleges I have met academics who have continued to play the same role. As I write amid the media shut down in Zimbabwe the intellectuals who have fled to Britain are again at the forefront of the struggle to inform the world of what is happening 'back home'.

Of course I write as a journalist, but as a member of wider British society I am more than aware of the huge role played by refugee academics in fields from economics to medical research, and much in between. This book celebrates the diversity of contribution that the many thousands of refugee academics have played over the past three quarters of a century. It is largely thanks to CARA that we have so detailed an account of the scale and reach of that contribution. In leafing through CARA's history one is obviously struck by the sadness that the need for such an organization should still be so urgent so many years after its founding.

It's remarkable to note that of the more than ten thousand refugee academics CARA has helped since 1933, eighteen have gone on to win Nobel Laureates; sixteen received Knighthoods and over a hundred have become fellows of the Royal Society and the British Academy. For the most part it has been CARA that has enabled these men and women to re-connect with their studies from their countries of origin and continue them in British institutions and their home countries, when the time is right to return.

CARA deserves particular recognition for its 'Campaign for Iraqi Academics', a programme launched in 2006 to support a group which is the target of a systematic campaign of kidnap, torture and assassination. In continuing Sir William Beveridge's work, this initiative also carries forward key elements of Albert Einstein's 1933 vision of a university in exile for those fleeing Nazi Germany. Through the CARA-Scholars at Risk Universities Network and other core partners, CARA is endeavouring to sustain Iraq's academic capital in the region and build bridges back in support of an increasingly young and inexperienced teaching cohort on whom the future of Iraq's higher education sector depends.

But this book is also a tribute to Britain and those who made these refugees welcome, providing support and inspiration to enable so many to put repression and war behind them, and lead fulfilling lives during which they were able to put so much back. I am genuinely honoured to be allowed to be part of the celebration of CARA's work, and of people they have served.

Jon Snow
Newscaster, Channel 4 News

Acknowledgements

This book is the result of the co-operative work of scores of people, to whom I would like to express my warmest thanks, particularly to the staff of CARA and especially to Laura Wintour and John Akker. (Contact details for CARA are given in the bibliography.) I am indebted to many of the descendants and relatives of scholars who came to Britain in the 1930s, particularly Professor Lewis Elton, Ben Elton, Professor Gustav Born, Dr Ralph Kohn, Vivien Perutz, Lord Krebs, Professor Richard Gombrich and Marcia Saunders. I am grateful to Lore Segal, William Lanouette, Ania O'Brien and Barry Davis, who have all written or spoken of exile. I would like to thank all the refugees I have met, past and present, who received help from CARA, and who have repaid it a thousandfold to the country that offered them sanctuary. I have learned much from some remarkable individuals who exemplify the endurance and resilience of human beings in the face of injustice, oppression and torture. I am grateful for the research of Dr Amanda Bergen, Ruth Boreham, and to all the members of the council of CARA, in particular Professor Shula Marks, Professor Sir Robert Boyd, Professor Paul Broda, Professor Paul Weindling, Professor Michael Yudkin, Dr Peter Warren and Anne Lonsdale. Thanks, too, to Courney Stern, Liz Fraser, Alan Angell, Alan Phillips, Benny Pollack, Adrian Sington and John Murray. I am especially indebted to my editor, Andrew Maxwell-Hyslop, himself a descendant of Huguenot refugees, and his particular understanding of the issues.

I owe a special debt to several publications dealing with some of the issues raised in this book. I am grateful to Louise London for her remarkable and myth-dispelling study, *Whitehall and the Jews 1933–1948*; to Bernard Wasserstein for his melancholy *Britain and the Jews of Europe, 1939–1945*; to Daniel Snowman for his inspirational *The Hitler Emigres* and to the editors of the extraordinarily wide-ranging *Second Chance: Two Centuries of German-speaking Jews in the United Kingdom*. I owe much to the insights of David Zimmerman, the author of a forthcoming book on the Academic Assistance Council.

I would also like to thank the following for permission to reproduce material in the text: PEN International for Soleiman Adel Guémar's poem; Jack Mapanje for the 'The New Platform Dances'; Marta Zabaleta; and the Association of Jewish Refugees.

The author and the publishers would like thank the following for their kind permission to reproduce illustrations: Figure 1, Mrs Ilse Eton (Assistant Secretary, SPSL 1944–45 and Secretary, April 1946–51); 2, LSE Archives; 3, Cavendish Laboratory, University of Cambridge; 4, CARA Archive, London; 5, Egon Weiss Collection; 6, MRC (Medical Research Council) – Laboratory of Molecular Biology;

7, Gustav Born; 8, University of Sheffield; 9, Pevsner – Getty Images; 10, Popper – Lucinda Douglas-Menzies/National Portrait Gallery, London; 11, Leonie Gombrich; 12, International Spinal Cord Society (ISCoS); 13, John Wiley & Sons Ltd; 14, National Archives; 15 and 16, Wiener Library, London; 17, Albie Sachs; 18, Sarah Lee (*Guardian* photographer); 20, United Nations High Commissioner for Refugees. Appendices: Bodleian Library, Oxford.

Finally, I should like to acknowledge the support and instruction from friends who have helped me understand the position of refugees in contemporary Britain, including Murtaza Shibli, Ghias Aljundi and especially Ayache Khettar.

Jeremy Seabrook

April 2008

A Note on the Text

The names of a substantial number of individuals in this book have been changed to protect their identity and shield them and their families from possible harm in their country of origin. In certain cases, in the interests of anonymity, the details surrounding their arrest, imprisonment and subsequent treatment have also been slightly altered. Their stories are, for the most part, told in their own words and the record they give is sometimes a little confusing, since they have suffered greatly, and they do not always tell a story that can be broken down into clear sequences. Many of their accounts are not, and cannot be expected to be, impartial, since they articulate experiences which, to a majority of people in Britain, are horrible beyond belief. Their story of home is as they experienced it; and they have spoken with an admirable candour and openness, although some of what they say may not always chime with official or 'objective' versions of events they describe.

In the section on the 1930s, the individuals discussed are only a few examples of the vast pool of talent that came here from central Europe, with or without the help of the Academic Assistance Council or the Society for the Protection of Learning and Science. They are not intended to be a representative sample, but suggest something of the scope and depth of our indebtedness to those who came to Britain as refugees.

Academic refugees are predominantly male. This was especially true of the 1930s although I have tried, whenever possible, to use the testimony of the women on whom they depended. Even today, most academic refugees are still men, since this reflects the personnel in the universities of the countries they have fled; but, of course, gender balance is scarcely a priority in the minds of torturers and oppressors in their assault upon the human person.

Jeremy Seabrook

Introduction

One of the most puzzling questions of recent times is why the asylum seeker and the refugee have become objects of widespread scorn and suspicion in Britain. It is not simply that the popular press has claimed that people have singled Britain out as a 'soft touch' or an 'easy ride'; there are clearly dynamic forces at work, which have transformed 'asylum seeker' (with its suggestions of persecution and exile) from an expression arousing not compassion, but abuse. It has also attracted the disparaging qualifier 'bogus', which delegitimates in advance claims upon our scarce sympathy.

In cases where the authorities have refused asylum, another equally negative word has been coined, namely the 'failed' asylum-seeker, as though asylum were an arduous examination which people must pass. The aggregate of 'bogus' and 'failed' suggests that the opportunists and chancers of the earth are finding passage to Britain, to take advantage of our legendary kindness, tolerance and softness of heart. This, in turn, nourishes one of our most persistent myths – that we are too easy, that we 'bend over backwards' to accommodate the mistreated and abused, who are secretly laughing at our gullibility – 'taking the piss' in the popular expression.

Governments proclaim the rising numbers of 'deportations' a measure of success. This, too, has a long and ugly history. An elderly Jewish woman in north London said, 'Whenever I hear governments utter the word "deportation", it sends a shiver down my spine. For me it will always be associated with the "deportations to the East" of the Hitler regime, with all that implied. I wonder how many of these "successes" will be subject to arbitrary arrest, imprisonment and torture? They have become, in the word of the Hungarian Nobel literature laureate, Imre Kertesz, "fateless".'

British refugee organizations regularly publish denials of the myths surrounding refugees and asylum-seekers. The latter are not given priority over people on accommodation waiting lists, for they are usually housed in hard-to-let and rundown property. They do not take our jobs, are not offered mobile phones, televisions or cars and are unlikely to commit crimes. They do not come here because of rumours of our generosity – indeed they know nothing of the welfare system – and cannot work until they have waited more than a year for a decision on their case. The income they receive is a mere 70 per cent of income support, hardly extravagant living.

The Refugee Council says that 1,000 medically qualified refugees are recorded on the British Medical Association database. Retraining a refugee doctor is about one-twentieth of the cost of training a British doctor from scratch. Many refugees have academic qualifications. There are more than 1,500 refugee teachers in England. It is estimated that 30,000 jobs have been created in one city, Leicester, since Ugandan Asian refugees arrived in 1972.

This suggests that refugees represent a particular stratum of people: they are often educated, socially committed, economically active and politically involved in their country of origin. Indeed, this is often why they suffer, singled out by dictatorial or ideologically-driven regimes as 'threats' to stability and order. Such people's fate is this book's concern, its primary focus being the contribution over the past 75 years of academic refugees to the social, intellectual, economic and cultural life of Britain. This is the work of CARA (the Council for Assisting Refugee Academics), whose origins go back to 1933 when it was founded as the Academic Assistance Council to assist Jewish academics dismissed by the Nazis from German universities. The organization was originally seen as a temporary arrangement. That the need it sought to meet persists three generations later suggests that Hitler's Germany was no isolated aberration, while CARA'S work, both past and present, has encountered considerable resistance, official and popular.

A particular contemporary problem, although not entirely new, is the result of the degradation of the very idea of refugee or asylum seeker. A reluctance to admit persecuted people into this country was also evident earlier in our history, notably during the Tsarist pogroms at the end of the nineteenth and early twentieth centuries, and in the rise of Nazism in the 1930s. Indeed, that unhappy period provides an important insight into the psychology of indifference. At a time of great stress and distress, governments of the free world – itself a smaller realm then than now, bounded by the grim ideological boundaries of Nazism and Communism – sought places far from sight to locate Europe's unwanted. In the 1930s and well into the Second World War, Britain and the United States undertook a doomed search among what Bernard Wasserstein called 'the waste places of the world' for suitable destinations for Jewish refugees from Nazi Germany. These included Angola, Madagascar, Mauritius (a few actually wound up there), the Dominican Republic (an agrarian settlement financed by the USA was started, but fizzled out for want of support), Eritrea, Ethiopia, Kenya and Mindanao in the Philippines, all outside the territories of Britain, its white dominions or the USA.

Britain, at that time of extreme urgency, extended a modest and selective help to a minority of Jews. Those admitted were absorbed effortlessly; their special talents and abilities acknowledged, they and their families recognized for their unique contribution. But a majority of European Jewry were destined to take the most malignant journey undertaken by the persecuted of the earth across the unpoliced frontier between life and death. Before this, they were banished to another moral universe from that of the majority, built from the calloused feelings and exhausted sympathies, the flint in the heart and iron in the spirit of other human beings.

Nazi Germany targeted a distinctive population with ferocious energy and industrial efficiency. Today, refugees come from far and wide, the great majority from countries torn by conflict, civil strife, war or ethnic cleansing – Iraq, Afghanistan, Iran, Somalia, Sudan, Democratic Republic of Congo, Sri Lanka. These people are, in their way, refugees of globalization. Where will such asylum-seekers beg refuge?

This, perhaps, offers a clue to why antagonisms remain, notwithstanding the efforts of agencies, charities and voluntary bodies. Despite their fact-sheets with myth-busting arguments and truths about refugees, the opposing view – we are being exploited, refugees steal our labour and come as 'benefit-shoppers' or 'health-tourists' – will not go away. At its most benign, the argument that there is simply 'no room in this overcrowded island' is usually offered as the last word.

Integrating (to a varying extent) virtually every country's economy into a global system has had profound repercussions. It isn't just a question of the great movements of humanity from rural to urban areas, involuntary migrations away from traditional patterns of living and loss of livelihood through development projects; it is also about reactions to this process, the search for identity in a return to traditional religious, ethnic or linguistic groups, and the defensive shelter these may offer people disoriented by globalization. A whole world has been set in movement, certainly not initiated by the victimized and persecuted. Yet these become scapegoats, doubly blamed for events beyond their control.

The reluctance of countries whose people have seen an access of modest privilege to open their doors to those who have suffered (partly to further the good fortune of people in the 'developed' world) helps explain a general hostility to, and rejection of, refugees. The rich Western countries, in any case, absorb only a small fraction of them; Britain takes less than one in 2,000. The vast majority shelter in neighbouring countries, often in miserable conditions. Over a million Iraqis are in Syria, and half a million in Jordan. Burmese refugees spill over into Thailand. People fleeing the Sudanese militias are trapped in the wastes of Chad. Civilians caught up in the wars of the Democratic Republic of Congo look for a refuge in Rwanda and Uganda, while those fleeing the catastrophe of Zimbabwe enter South Africa. Poor countries, not rich ones, bear the burden of assisting refugees. But it makes no difference. People's ability to believe what they want to believe has long been known; the triumph of unreason has its own function, as many of those whose stories figure in this book testify.

The formulation of a more joyful, liberating narrative than the narrow fables of a sullen exclusion is the only way to fight myths presented as self-evident truths.

The story is not about exploiters and opportunists, but rather the immeasurable riches, diversity and practical contribution which refugees have made to this country. While there is no guarantee that such a humane story will gain ground against its more malignant competitor, that is scarcely an excuse for remaining silent. CARA exemplifies this story of our better selves.

1
Academic Refugees

Why it matters

Is the idea of the 'scholar' an archaism today? The word evokes someone (almost invariably male) secluded, preoccupied with esoteric knowledge and not quite of this world.

The academic, a later offspring of this stereotype, bridges to some degree the gap between the caricatured scholar and the contemporary world while remaining slightly out of touch, inhabiting the ivory tower rather than the airless, musty study.

However, in the popular imagination the academic is now being superseded by the expert; the practical, no-nonsense provider of statistics, comment or facts required by our 'need to know' – not in a way that necessarily requires energetic effort, but in order to remain 'informed' on the issues of the hour. The expert is a functionary, whose place of study is dominated by the flickering screen, shadowless white light, and plants which have no habitat outside the desiccated atmosphere of offices that produce more data than wisdom.

Although exaggerated, this captures something of changing social attitudes towards the academy. On the one hand, it furnishes ideas and knowledge which generate open and democratic debate. While safeguarding research, innovation and inquiry, it must also defend places of higher learning against government direction and ideological intrusion. Academics appear daily in the media, for they have become interpreters of events whose significance would otherwise escape us. In a growing division of labour, theirs is a language of translation. They also have a high responsibility, as they are entrusted with the intellectual formation of a new generation that will take its place in the expected evolution of the economy and society.

These multiple functions often engender friction. Societies change, but also resist it. Those working at the frontiers of knowledge pose a danger to Authority: if their discoveries challenge received wisdom, they may become dissidents, subversives, even enemies of the state. There is no settled relationship between those dedicated to learning and the society which is the beneficiary – or otherwise – of the knowledge that results from their studies.

Much of the debate in the democratic Western world hinges upon the degree to which institutional independence and academic freedom are compatible with the demands of growing global integration: are we 'producing' enough scientists, technicians and innovators to face the challenge, not merely from the rest of Europe and the developed countries, but from China, India and other emerging powers? The pursuit of knowledge for its own sake may be at odds with the need to 'turn out' a given number of young people equipped to confront technological change. Which has primacy? Are they compatible? If so, what kind of institutional arrangements can best create this best of all possible worlds?

Academics are, in general, no different from other social actors, representing the diversity of opinion to be found in any other group of people, although perhaps more adept at arguing their case. They should not be considered a class apart as regards values and beliefs; although in terms of erudition, they usually are.

Most intellectuals, like most of us, desire a 'quiet life', in order to focus on personal priorities – human relationships, bringing up children – while performing a useful social function that provides them with livelihood and security. They do not want the disruption of war, violence, crime, political upheaval or ideological interference, but wish to exist in what Albie Sachs calls 'the beautiful mundane'.

He should know. Imprisoned and tortured by South Africa's apartheid regime, he was later the victim of a bomb planted by the South African Intelligence Services in 1988 in Maputo, Mozambique, when he sustained multiple injuries. He is glad now that the moment of struggle is over. Such intense emotion, the dread and the hope, cannot be maintained for long. He speaks of a shift 'from the epic to the everyday' as a deliverance.

The epic, however, rarely leaves human societies alone. Our values and the practices of daily life are fashioned according to forms of belief and social organization in a state of perpetual flux, and sometimes, violent change. And although conflict, the fight for power and ideological dominance may remain in abeyance for decades, they reappear usually as ideology, or those conformities of religion, language or ethnicity which define others as barbarians, outsiders, evildoers – or even 'expendables'. The world changes far less than we think, whereas our perceptions of it are constantly changing. 'It was Hitler who taught me I was a Jew,' said many of the assimilated of Germany in the 1930s. Refugees from the Soviet Union were defined by others as 'bourgeois', 'class traitors' or 'undesirable elements'; while 'the military junta defined me as an enemy of the state' is the testimony of people escaping dictatorship from Argentina to Pakistan, from Indonesia to Chile.

Certain categories of people are more likely than others to be entangled in these momentous shifts: artists, writers, journalists, political activists and academics. All whose work involves sensitivity to change, whose understanding or knowledge disturbs authority, usually figure in any wave of imprisonment, persecution, torture or killing. Situated at the point where sudden shifts in ideology and its underpinning power-structure meet daily life, they are disproportionately represented among those fleeing oppressive regimes – victims of 'new brooms', dictators or the application of ideologies of revelation, both secular and transcendent.

Even when catastrophe approaches, it can strike with unpredictable force, as Luis Munoz says when describing the 1973 coup in Chile. 'The world so far had been one with values, morals and principles that seemed to have been in place for ever, not only in the fibre of our society, but in the whole of human kind. "Things" were taught without words – tenderness, respect, fraternity, solidarity, tolerance, love were things that emanated purely from the act of living.'

At such moments, resistance becomes inevitable, for who will silently permit themselves to be cast as the spoiler of the people's wellbeing or an agent of social destruction? When Hitler declared the Jews to be polluters of Aryan purity, Stalin stigmatized kulaks as class enemies, Pinochet called Leftists enemies of the nation, South Africa classified people according to their skin colour; when the Kinshasa mob hunts child witches and the dictators of Cameroon or the Congo Republic abuse minority ethnic or linguistic groups as a threat to stability, when Islam and terror become identified in the minds of the confused, getting on with life as if nothing was happening ceases to be possible. Events compel opposition and refusal.

'Private life' is in part an illusion, an undefended country always at risk of invasion. Yet how easy to leave the protection of this fragile territory to those more powerful, perhaps more wise, than we are! How tempting to retreat into a daily routine untainted by external concerns.

This book focuses on academic refugees. These, however, form only a part – highly conspicuous, very articulate and often distinguished – of a wider population forced to escape violence or persecution of one kind or another. Academics should not be artificially detached from the wider flow of injured humanity driven from home by tyrannies or intolerant regimes, and compelled to seek a life of dignified freedom elsewhere; and the presence of this broader population, its abilities and its gifts to our society, is part of the same story of involuntary migration and banishment.

Academics, involved as they are with independent inquiry and research, are among the most sensitive monitors of shifts in the ideological wind in any society. This does not mean that the same academic disciplines always run against prevailing orthodoxies. These vary according to the regime in place. All whose stories differ from the dominant narrative are susceptible to being silenced.

Theocratic states threaten secular ideologies. The Central and South American dictatorships hated social scientists for highlighting inequalities which their power sought to maintain. In 1971, on the eve of an independent Bangladesh, the Pakistani army shot hundreds of intellectuals – writers, poets, university teachers and activists – devoted to Bengali language and culture. The Soviet Union and its satellites set their face against a ubiquitous but vague enemy that spread 'bourgeois' ideas or values. In the contemporary world, academics may fall foul of the idiosyncratic world-view of authoritarian or military leaders, as in Burma, North Korea or the dictatorships of Paul Biye in Cameroon or Gaddafi in Libya.

This book examines the waves of refugees who have sought shelter in Britain over the past 75 years. It is concerned with the complex interplay of attitudes between the British government (and its degree of hostility towards the ideology of the sending regimes), public opinion (an amorphous, sometimes 'manufactured', but potent concept), and the voluntary organizations which were sympathetic and welcoming to the persecuted and displaced. In particular, this means the Academic Assistance Council (AAC) – founded in 1933 soon after the National Socialists took power in Germany – which subsequently became the Society for the Protection of Science and Learning (SPSL) in 1936, and from 1998 CARA (the Council for Assisting Refugee Academics).

Threats to independence

There are, broadly, three major threats to independence of thought: people may be punished for who they are, for what they believe (and say) or what they do. These categories are highly permeable, and many persecuted academics cross the divide between them.

National Socialism was a supreme example of the first. People were evicted unceremoniously from German universities simply because they were Jewish, a definition determined by the Nazis, even when it contradicted people's own perception of their identity. It is ironic that the modern idea of academic freedom arose with the growth of the independent research-based university in nineteenth-century Germany, a development the Nazis abjured as speedily as they did so many other attributes of a decent society.

Today's worldwide repression against ethnic groups – and especially national minorities – shades into discrimination against individuals because of what they believe. This is – sometimes mistakenly – considered less damaging than the assault on people for what and who they irreducibly are. But it is an uneasy distinction. Many consider faith as an equally indivisible part of the self as ethnicity; and some of the most violent attacks on whole populations are based upon 'alien' ways of worship or belief.

The work of discovery undertaken by individuals – particularly if original, creative and critical (overtly or implicitly) of mainstream values – is the most pervasive perceived threat to established power in society, prompting, perhaps, the most common efforts by governments or majorities to stifle voices that bring disturbing news from distant intellectual frontiers. This has particular resonance in a world in which 'knowledge-based industries' have a higher salience than ever before.

Some ideologies will target a particular group of 'enemies': historians, when falsification of the past is required; economists querying official accounts of wellbeing and progress; lawyers and judges, when governments wish to demonstrate their power over all state institutions; social scientists, who know about mechanisms of dominance; physicists, who suggest the laws by which we have conventionally measured nature are more variable than we imagined. And always in the frame are writers, artists and musicians, who speak a deeper wisdom than the revelations of scripture, theological or secular.

Past, present and future

The Soviet Union valued its scientists highly, particularly those involved in the competitive military and economic race with the United States. Academics falling foul of 'socialist' orthodoxies were different from those evicted by Nazism. The Party's tortuously shifting edicts, the increasingly mystical exegesis of the writings of Marx and Lenin, provoked resistance from writers and activists, since Communism, with its theoretical notions of internationalism, did not single out those stigmatized by Hitler's racial obsessions; and their fate – 'liquidation' – in the labour camps of the gulag, or in exile, is well known. 'Socialist' science, which would dethrone its outworn capitalist predecessor, also claimed its victims. For four decades from the late 1920s, Trofim Denisovich Lysenko's biological and agricultural theories in pursuit of an agricultural revolution were enthusiastically embraced by the Soviet authorities. Rejecting Mendel's work, Lysenko insisted that plants could be modified to grow according to the needs of the state, with new characteristics being bred into them. In his way a theorist of future genetic modification, he was devoid of the practical ability to realize it.

The widespread application of his theories led to incalculable suffering, hunger and environmental ruin. Critics of Lysenko's pseudo-science were silenced; academics were dismissed, removed to labour camps or shot.

The Cold War sent refugees out of Europe after the Hungarian uprising of 1956, the Prague Spring of 1968 and a recurrence of anti-Semitism in Poland in 1969–70. At the same time, military regimes and dictatorships in central and Latin America, in Asia and Africa, often with Western support as a 'bulwark' against Communism, displaced thousands of university teachers and students to seek sanctuary in Western Europe and North America. One particularly significant group of expellees was from South Africa, marking a return to the politics of race. In the apartheid regime everyone was graded according to skin colour. There had been, of course, no dearth of 'scientific' justifications adduced by white supremacists in the nineteenth and early twentieth centuries, and the echoes of Nazism so soon after the Holocaust were offensive and repellent. The bureaucratic contortions required by the classification process now appear archaic and absurd; yet such 'principles' were applied with sufficient energy to drive thousands of scholars out of their homeland. An Office for Race Classification 'refined' the broad categories into which people were divided – white, mixed race, Indian and Bantu (black). Officials devised pseudo-scientific tests to determine race, by examining an individual's eyelids, gums, nostrils and fingernails. The outcome determined whether people could vote or not, where they might live, work, eat, spend their leisure, and whom they could love, marry or have a sexual relationship with. 'A white person', stated the Population Registration Act, 'is one who is in appearance obviously white – and not generally accepted as Coloured – or who is generally accepted as White and is not obviously non-White, provided that a person shall not be classified as a White person if one of his natural parents has been classified as a Coloured Person or a Bantu.'

This drove tens of thousands into exile, and led to imprisonment, torture and execution of those who defied the race laws, finally repealed in 1990–91. As Nelson Mandela wrote in *A Short Walk to Freedom*, 'where one was allowed to live and work could rest on such absurd distinctions as the curl of one's hair or the size of one's lips'.[1] Yet he was not embittered by the years of incarceration on Robben Island. A characteristic of apartheid's opponents, both those who remained within the system or who found refuge abroad, was a uniquely humane legacy, suggested by Albie Sachs' memorable phrase, the 'soft vengeance' of the freedom fighter. Each wave of academic (and other) refugees to Britain left a unique residue in the country that received them. If the Jews of central Europe brought scientific innovation and intellectual passion, the Latin Americans opened us up to an exultant internationalism.

After the demise both of apartheid and the totalitarian regimes in Russia and Eastern Europe, it is relatively easy to enumerate those countries where freedom to study and to learn are compromised. The model of the university in colonial territories, for instance, was usually taken from the metropolitan power, and often devised to serve its interests. Following the wave of colonial independence in the mid-twentieth century, not only the university, but also the government apparatus – and not infrequently a considerable amount of law – was 'inherited' from the former colonial powers and subsequently employed to sustain those who took over the governing function from earlier elites.

That so many highly qualified and competent people chased from a livelihood in learning remain in need of refuge suggests that the world is not as stable as the fall of totalitarian ideologies has led us to believe. The Western democracies are certainly the preferred destination of displaced and professional personnel, although most ousted scholars remain, like the overwhelming majority of refugees, academic and others, in countries neighbouring those from which they have fled.

In most Western countries, it seems, academic freedom is assured; and although never absolute and unconditional, threats to it appear contained and manageable, for example constraints on spending, the neglect of research for which there is no 'market', or a hostility to the pursuit of knowledge for its own sake, to name a few. Even the threatened boycott of places of higher learning in Israel, initiated by the enemies of the international free circulation of knowledge does not seriously erode the basic principles of academic freedom.[2]

The essence of the free exchange of learning and instruction is that it is mutable and fluid. Yet the moment freedom is considered 'secure', it may be in danger of being undermined, the menace sometimes coming from an unexpected source. Even in the relative security of the liberal democracies, which permits a majority to disengage politically and pursue their own individual concerns, new sources of dispute and uncertainty are clearly discernible. The epic has not deserted the world, but is merely biding its time, stirring on the margins of awareness. The war on terror, for instance, and the 'with-us-or-against-us' mentality it generated, certainly frightened many people into silence, or at least gloomy acquiescence. The power to harness that amorphous, but powerful creature, public opinion, to stifle criticism and proscribe the 'unthinkable' is always in the armoury of power, ready to be wielded against the questioner and the dissenter.

We can, perhaps, predict from where future long-term threats to academic – and wider – freedoms will come, even though we cannot foretell what forms restriction on thought, research or knowledge might take. What, for instance, will be the consequences of the end of oil, the loss of biodiversity, desertification and the depletion of water or other resources indispensable to sustain life against a background of global warming? What of the spread of nuclear weaponry, perhaps among 'non-state actors'? What is lurking in the deep shadows cast by the perpetual artificial sunshine of the technosphere? What political formations will these potential sources of future conflicts throw up, and what might they take from cherished freedoms?

When the epic irrupts once more into our lives, it will demand that we alter once more what we thought, briefly, was reality. And the most sensitive auditors of these changes, the insights of the artists and the attentiveness of the academy, are no doubt already busy forewarning the world. Upon our response to the news they bring much depends. Will they be heeded as messengers of truth, or will they be silenced as emissaries of what we do not wish to hear?

The outspoken and the silent

Academics persecuted by tyrannical regimes for their independence of thought are, rightly, valued for their courage. But there is no dictatorship, no repressive regime, no ideology of intolerance which fails to call forth hundreds of competent and intelligent supporters, ready to avow that this or that ruling elite embodies the only possible ordering of human affairs. Scepticism, an important attribute of scholars, does not exempt them from the suspension of disbelief which affects a majority of people in the world. German universities continued to function under the Nazis. Some scholars who remained truly believed they could – and indeed, did – mitigate some of the cruelties of the regime. Soviet scientists took seriously the rivalry with the United States, created nuclear weapons and rocketry, and pushed the frontiers of space exploration. Graduates continued to be produced under the military dictatorships of the 1960s and 70s; and although students have always been monitored by authoritarian regimes as a potential source of unrest, most obtained their degrees and were absorbed into structures of injustice of totalitarian regimes of one kind or another. There is no aberrant ideology, no monstrous system of belief that cannot find clever adherents and apologists. Laurence Rees reminds us that the Wannsee Conference of January 1942 which elaborated the 'final solution' was attended by fifteen people, eight of whom held academic doctorates.[3]

Perhaps penitence is more common among the more thoughtful and reflective of the population, and scholars regret in later life their commitment to this or that malignant ideology – gods that failed, faith disconfirmed by events. But we should not think that those who say nothing are impartial, nor that silence implies acquiescence.

In his 1983 book, *The Death of Utopia Reconsidered*, Leszek Kolakowski, a philosopher removed from his post in the University of Warsaw, offers a good definition of academic freedom when he writes of the cultural role of the philosopher which 'is not to deliver the truth but to build the spirit of truth, and this means never to let the inquisitive energy of mind go to sleep, never to stop questioning what appears to be obvious and definitive, always to defy the seemingly intact resources of common sense, always to suspect that there might be "another side" to what is taken for granted, and never to allow us to forget that there are questions beyond the legitimate horizons of science that are nonetheless crucial to the survival of humanity as we know it.'[4]

2
Then

'My first thought when I arrived in Britain was "Now I'm safe." I could sleep through the night, I could walk through the streets without anyone following me with intent to do me harm. I could make phone calls. Of course I was disoriented. Nothing was familiar. It was December, cold and dark. But I had had a burden lifted. I was grateful. I still am, and it's been more than thirty years.'

Woman refugee from Chile

Leo Szilard

Among those who found refuge in Britain in the early 1930s, the figure of Leo Szilard is emblematic of the restless brilliance of a generation of intellectuals banished from central Europe by the graveyard ideology of Nazism.[1]

Born in Hungary in 1898, after the First World War he fled the fascist Horthy regime to study engineering in Berlin – a fateful destination for a refugee from Fascism. Soon he was caught up at the Kaiser Wilhelm Institute for Physics in a group that included Erwin Schrödinger, who developed wave mechanics, Max Born, who published his paper on probability and causality, and Werner Heisenberg, originator of the uncertainty principle. His PhD was on thermodynamics, a problem he had resolved on his own. This would be a characteristic of Szilard – he did not belong. Dynamic and inventive, this classic outsider was always ahead of his contemporaries, enthusiastically embracing and then abandoning an idea when overtaken by another. Einstein was impressed by Szilard, with whom he eventually filed a patent for a refrigerator pump they jointly designed, inspired by hearing of a whole family asphyxiated by gas from a domestic refrigerator.

In 1931, Szilard foresaw Hitler's rise to power and two years later left for Vienna, where, according to one account, he met William Beveridge because they were staying at the same hotel. The latter convinced Szilard that his projected 'university in exile' was less practical than the placement of exiled academics in existing universities. In his work with the Academic Assistance Council in

1933–34, Szilard characteristically operated outside Beveridge's organization, often finding places for ousted German scholars on his own initiative. He appeared and disappeared in European capitals, a kind of Scarlet Pimpernel of the intellectual aristocracy.

Szilard moved to the United States in 1938, living mainly in hotels – the archetypal refugee with the constantly packed suitcase. Towards the end of his life, at the time of the Cuban missile crisis in 1962 and the stand-off between the USA and the USSR, he shocked friends by leaving the USA for Switzerland, convinced that the world was about to witness the nuclear apocalypse he had both helped to render possible, and fought so hard subsequently to prevent.

Szilard was a major player in displaced European Jewry in the 1930s. His mind worked at amazing speed; he foresaw answers to questions that took others years of thought. It was he who first conceived the 'chain reaction' that could release the enormous destructive force of the atomic bomb, an idea that came to him in London while watching the traffic lights in Southampton Row turn from red to green.

Szilard was instrumental in conveying Einstein's letter to President Roosevelt in 1939, urging the US government to expedite research on the atomic bomb, to prevent Germany – whose scientists he feared were already far advanced in the research – perhaps getting there first. In a less publicized second letter in 1945, he urged President Truman to demonstrate to the Japanese the annihilating power of the A-bomb rather than drop it on innocent civilians and sought in vain to prevent its use.

Rebuffed by politicians, he helped in June 1945 to draw up the Franck Report which repeated the arguments of his second Truman letter. This was ignored, so Szilard organized a petition to Truman with 155 signatories of Manhattan Project scientists, urging the President to consider his moral responsibilities. It was rejected.

Afterwards, Szilard tried to undo the damage he believed he had helped bring about, by campaigning tirelessly for disarmament. Szilard had, with Enrico Fermi, built the first nuclear reactor; he also conceived the 'fast breeder' reactor, which created more fuel than it used. He became bitterly remorseful about this, and when the experiment with Fermi succeeded, announced that it was 'a black day for humanity'.

After the A-bomb was dropped, Szilard and other scientists lobbied Congress for civilian control of the atom, advocating talks between US and Soviet scientists to prevent an arms race. In 1946, he, Einstein and others formed an Emergency Committee of Atomic Scientists, to warn of the dangers of atomic weapons and in 1962 he established the Council for a Liveable World to raise money for Senate candidates in favour of arms-control treaties. Szilard never lost faith in what he called the 'slim margin of hope' for humanity.

Characteristically Szilard cured himself of bladder cancer in 1961. He later turned to biology, and Monod, Jacob and Lwow, whose work on DNA won them a Nobel prize in 1965, publicly expressed their debt to Szilard in their speech. His biographer William Lanouette believes his most lasting influence may lie in his doctoral thesis, which provided the basis for information theory.

Szilard never deserted his liberal, humanitarian views, while some of his compatriots – notably Edward Teller – went on to work on the H-bomb, and advise President Reagan on his 'Star Wars' initiative. Szilard and his fellow-scientists directly bequeathed to the world the phrases 'critical mass', 'chain reaction', and 'fallout', their origin in weaponry of destruction which Szilard first encouraged and then sought to control.

'Racial pollution' and the search for saviours

The world watched disbelieving as Hitler persuaded a significant proportion of the German people that the Jews were not only at the root of economic collapse, but also a source of 'racial pollution'. With a Jewish population of a mere 1 per cent, 25 per cent of Germany's Nobel prizes between 1900 and 1932 had gone to those of Jewish descent. This only fed the paranoia of Hitler, in thrall to the seductive idea that reason was a dangerous diversion from the supremacy of instinct.

Many in Europe and the wider world were swift to perceive the damage to Germany caused by the dismissal of Jewish academics soon after Hitler's takeover of power in January 1933, namely that this would irreparably harm the foundations of Germany's industrial and commercial power. A policy that exalted irrationality over reason was bound to reduce scientific criticism to impotence: into the void the Nazis poured the corrosive vitriol of manifest untruth. Their proposition that 'Jewish science' was subversive and inaccurate showed that no aspect of life was immune from ideological penetration. The physicist Professor Philipp Lenard of Heidelberg University scorned claims that 'German Physics' was international. 'In reality, science, like every other human product, is racial and conditioned by blood.' Professor Rudolph Tomaschek, Director of the Institute of Physics in Dresden, said: 'Modern physics is an instrument of Jewry for the destruction of Nordic science ... In fact, all European science is the fruit of Aryan, or better, German thought.' Jewish intellectuals in Germany were more rooted in society than Jews anywhere else in Europe, regarding the humanistic values of the country of Beethoven and Goethe as an earnest that Germany was indeed the supreme site of civilized values. Many had forsworn, been converted from, or allowed their Jewish heritage to lapse. Amos Oz, writing much later from Israel, captures the sensibility of his family, whose psyche had been shaped by Europe. 'So there they were, these over-enthusiastic Europhiles, who could speak so many of Europe's languages, recite its poetry, who believed in its moral superiority ... who had loved it unconditionally and uninhibitedly for decades, since the beginning of the Jewish Enlightenment, and had done everything humanly possible to please it, to contribute to it in every way and in every domain, to become part of it ...'[2]

This Jewish sense of security and belonging was decisive in the vibrant environment of scientific innovation and research, a flowering unparalleled elsewhere. The list of those removed from their posts comprises a reservoir of talent and ability which in situ would certainly have altered the course, and possibly the outcome, of the Second World War.

The presence in Germany of this concentration of ability was, in part, a result of the liberation in the second half of the nineteenth century from disabilities imposed by the state and from the straitjacket of religion. This released the energies of Jews who swiftly became part of the intellectual middle class. Jewish scholars were liberated from the rabbinical tradition of minute exegesis of Jewish texts, although the disciplines could be applied to new and secular areas of academic and scholarly concern.

The assimilated Jews engendered both admiration and resentment in Germany. That the latter prevailed in the 1930s was certainly a consequence of the humiliation felt by Germans at the terms of the post-First World War settlement, and of the economic catastrophe after the 1929 Wall Street Crash. This affected Germany with particular violence. In addition, as J.D. Bernal notes in a faintly superior tone, 'There had always been a strong undercurrent of mystical irrationality in German thought ... From the German mystics to the philosophers of the eighteenth and nineteenth centuries, the tendency to confuse the obscure with the profound had never disappeared ... This mode of thinking, or rather refusing to think, was seized on by the Nazis and turned in the direction of glorifying the twin ideas of race and war.'[3] Bernal was not wrong, but wrote animated by a belief in 'scientific socialism', that other twentieth-century dogma of salvation, which would also strew the world with corpses.

Many refugees offered sanctuary in Britain had long ceased to be religiously observant. It was a common observation that their Jewish identity was bestowed as a kind of malign gift by Hitler. Gustav Born was typical. 'I had been christened. We saw ourselves as Lutherans.' Nikolaus Pevsner converted at the age of 19 to Evangelical Lutheranism. Ernst Gombrich's parents were also Lutheran converts. 'They were deists,' according to Richard Gombrich. 'My father's mother believed in God in a vague sort of way. Neither of my parents was brought up to be Jewish. My father said that whether or not he was Jewish was a preoccupation for the Gestapo, suggesting that it was not his concern.' Sir Hans Krebs said: 'I was not a Jew until Hitler made me one.' Otto Frisch said that his father 'had a strong feeling for right and wrong. He was not religious in the conventional sense, but with his profound respect for life he might have been called a Buddhist and indeed took a great interest in Buddhist writings.'[4] The last practising Jew in Engelbert

Broda's family was his grandmother, who left the community in 1879, when she married someone who had already converted to Catholicism.

At the same time, an afterglow of faith remained, although projected onto secular activities. People said, 'music was my religion'; 'the university was our church'; 'Goethe was god in our house'; 'learning was sacred'; 'science was our guide'. Scars, as it were, of religious belief.

The causes of the rise of Nazism have been exhaustively analysed and argued over, including the political and economic failures following the First World War, the punitive visitations of the Allies upon Germany and the Great Depression. Bernard Wasserstein writing of the 'endemic grip of anti-Semitism on the popular mentality', says it may be understood as 'a relic of the ancient hatred of the different; as a mutation of Christian beliefs in a post-Christian society; as part of the debris of romantic nationalism; as a product of the social and intellectual upheaval resulting from rapid and uneven industrialization; as a collective psychopathy in which the Jew is identified with the devil; or as a modern version of the witch craze.'[5] But even this cannot explain a phenomenon which haunts the world like few others, emanating as it did from the heart of what has been thought of as civilization itself.

The victorious First World War powers – like all who triumph – had little insight into the likely consequences of their actions. Perhaps they treated Germany in the way they had dealt with the peoples they had subdued in the previous several hundred years. Imperial powers rarely show any great concern for the social and moral arrangements they disrupt in their progress through the world; for example, the conquistadores in the Americas or the East India Company's merchant-warriors took for granted the inferiority of the inhabitants in the trackless worlds they had 'discovered'. Their incursions ought, perhaps, to have alerted them that cultures do not submit meekly to alien values, even when presented as liberators, or bringers of truth or freedom.

In extreme circumstances – like those in Germany after the First World War – peoples *in extremis* turn to myth and magic. The history of vanquished cultures shows a desperate reliance on supernatural rescuers and the appearance of messiahs is often accompanied by upheavals and cataclysms. But if it was believed that Europeans were proof against appeals to such 'primitive' unreason, Nazism would tell another, chastening story, not of imaginary wish-fulfilment, but grimly material, industrial and military efficiency.

The British response

Britain's response to the plight of Jews of central Europe from 1933 onwards was complex, and must be detached from myths that have subsequently crystallized around the events of the time.

There are at least four groups of refugees from central Europe in the 1930s that had a lasting impact upon Britain and indeed, the wider world. First, the significant academic figures to whom the British government extended a welcome. Others, less celebrated, were aided by voluntary organizations, both religious and secular, Jewish and Christian; they entered Britain through the pressure of individuals, often despite government obstruction, sometimes through the pulling of strings and private influence.

Secondly, those who came for reasons of their possible economic usefulness to this country. The Home Secretary, Sir Samuel Hoare, opposing a more open policy towards Jews, said in a Cabinet minute of 1938, that we were 'going as far at present as public opinion would allow …' He thought, however that we might agree to admit a number of young Jews for the purpose of agricultural training, with a view to their ultimate settlement elsewhere. He was also in favour of admitting a number of Jewish maidservants. These were areas of employment to which the people of Britain were showing increasing aversion in the 1930s, despite high unemployment.

Thirdly, the children who came – in one of the spectacular acts of generosity by the British government – on the Kindertransport of 1938.[6] Many of these proved invaluable to the wellbeing of Britain in subsequent decades, intellectually, artistically, politically and morally.

Finally, there is another group, more difficult to quantify: those who came or remained illegally. These, too, deserve to be rescued from the shadows, since many of their children and descendants, absorbed silently and without fanfare into Britain, have also served the country well.

British reaction to the 70,000[7] or so Jews who were granted refuge in the country between 1933 and the outbreak of war, was equivocal and disturbs all settled convictions about what 'we' did in the great human emergency with which National Socialism confronted the world in 1933. A distinction must be made between official government attitudes and those administering restrictive refugee policies with discretion and sensitivity. Similarly, there was also a gulf between the attitude of voluntary organizations dedicated to the rescue and placement of refugees, and that of a wider public.

While government remained hostile to what was referred to, even then, as an 'influx', or 'wave' of Jewish immigrants, bureaucratic flexibility combined with the kindness of influential individuals permitted the evasion of the tightest regulations. The feeling of the British people was also not clear-cut. While a minority, understanding the nature of the threat to European Jewry, worked for a more generous admissions policy, a negative 'public opinion', frequently invoked by politicians, certainly existed. Xenophobia, hostility to strangers and a minority of organized Fascists unsettled the authorities.

Most academic refugees, who found a place in British universities, met with a warm welcome and some understanding of what they and their families had suffered. Others found themselves in a chill and unfamiliar environment, to which it was difficult to adapt, the more so since many had been granted temporary residence, en route to a more permanent destination, usually the USA. Those arriving as domestic servants or as children fared more unpredictably – some found friendship, protection and love, while others met duty, incomprehension and a cool impatience of people with little imaginative understanding of the trauma they had been through.

The work of the Academic Assistance Council was not conducted in an atmosphere of tolerance, since the fate of the distinguished individuals who readily avow their debt to Britain, can only be fully appreciated in the context of British immigration policy of the times. This was itself inflected by the experience of Jewish immigration at the turn of the century, although the earlier newcomers were a markedly different social group from those seeking refuge in the 1930s. The victims of Tsarist pogroms had been generally poorer, people of the shtetl, far from the urbane (and more urban) population of Europe's most sophisticated cities. And although British Jewish organizations pledged that no Jewish refugee would become a charge upon the state, there was an element of misgiving among British Jews that German and Austrian refugees were of a higher social class, and consequently that their rather superior presence and high expectations of life might engender an anti-Semitic backlash. Harmonious absorption required a limit on numbers.

This same argument was, of course, used by the British government to justify its restrictive immigration policies, and has been reiterated ever since. In our time, in the interest of good race relations, as few Caribbeans, South Asians or foreigners as possible should be allowed to settle here. Such restrictive general policies also have serious implications for today's academic refugees and asylum-seekers.

There is also widespread anxiety, cast in terms of what Britishness or Englishness is, since there remains considerable nostalgia when a 'nation' meant an ethnically and culturally homogeneous population. This, however, ignores the considerable, often violent fault-lines in the past that divided class from social class, separations scarcely less acerbic than ethnic and religious divisions conspicuous in our time.

Contemporary anxieties also echo those of the 1930s, when government was concerned to stem the 'flow' of would-be refugees. This had historical roots, repeating the response to Jews who had fled the pogroms of Tsarist Russia. Then, the British government had passed the Aliens Act in 1905 – a highly symbolic precedent and the first legislation designed to prevent a 'flood' of migrants into a Britain then emphatically not a country of immigration.

The Aliens Act was introduced by an embattled Conservative administration, destined to fall the following year in the great Liberal landslide which laid the foundations for the welfare state. The government had responded to popular panic which anticipated both the anxiety of the 1930s and more scares over 'asylum seekers' in our time.

Until 1905, a foreigner might spend a lifetime in Britain without official permission and without having to register with the authorities. In this lies one source of the British 'myth' of our tolerance and hospitality; 'myth', not in the sense of untruth, but of an informing belief about ourselves and who we are. Certainly Britain had been open to political refugees throughout the nineteenth century; people fleeing Tsarist oppression, nationalist or anti-Socialist sentiment in Europe had found sanctuary here; and the lengthy presence of Karl Marx in the British Museum Reading Room is a dramatic emblem of the relative serenity and stability of Britain during its high imperial moment, undisturbed by ragged continental intellectuals living on the margins of a city open to the world.

The arguments provoked by the arrival of at most 100,000 Jews from Eastern Europe in the 1880s–90s have a contemporary ring. Foreigners, supported by the Poor Law at public expense were dubbed 'invaders' who brought 'crime and disease'. A Royal Commission on Aliens, reporting in 1903, found that a mere 1 per cent of the population received Poor Law assistance. They 'send their children regularly to school, and are rewarded by the quickness with which the children acquire knowledge and the number of prizes gained by them'. Notwithstanding this, the Commission advised immigration controls, the government interpretation of popular sentiment prevailing over a painstaking investigation of the facts.

The 1905 Act gave officers the power to turn away 'undesirable' immigrants, and those without visible means of support. It applied only to 'steerage' passengers, and exempted those fleeing political or religious persecution. There was also a right to appeal. It remained fairly liberal and humane.

The inter-war years and government dilemmas

By comparison with what was to come, this legislation was benign. During the First World War, the internment of 'enemy aliens' was both symptom and consequence of popular anger, although not all those of German origin were interned. Mobs attacked businesses and homes belonging to German nationals; newspaper accounts of suicides by foreigners and injuries to aliens were widespread. The sinking of the liner *Lusitania* by a German U-boat in 1915 raised Germanophobia to a new intensity.

The Aliens Restriction Act of August 1914 removed the right of appeal and passports were introduced in 1915. The Act, extended at the end of the war, was consolidated in the Aliens Order 1920. Further limitations followed. Anti-German popular feeling continued well into the 1920s, partly due to disillusionment with the peace and the elusive 'land fit for heroes' promised to the survivors; while the 1917 Bolshevik Revolution in Russia was also associated with the work of specifically German Jews. In the 1920s, the dramatic publication of the fraudulent *Protocols of the Elders of Zion* furthered belief in an international Jewish conspiracy. The presence of 'aliens' in the country exercised both people and parliament in the 1920s, particularly in the light of continuing economic turbulence. Thus Stanley Baldwin in October 1924: 'I want to examine the laws and regulations as to the entry of aliens into this country, for in these days no alien should be substituted for one of our own people when we have not enough work at home to go round.'

In 1925, Sir William Joynson-Hicks, the Home Secretary, expressed the view that would prevail for the following 15 years, when he said 'The dominating factor … is the well-being of my country, and not the well-being of aliens who desire to come into it from other quarters.' In the same year, William Greene, MP for Worcester, said in a debate on aliens that it was essential 'to preserve the purity of our race and to prevent contamination with the riff-raff of Eastern Europe, the stiffs (sic) of the Mediterranean and the dead-beats of the world'. No new legislation was enacted against refugees in the 1930s, but existing laws were interpreted more restrictively.

Yet the desire to relieve suffering of the persecuted also expressed itself in an outpouring of sympathy from voluntary organizations, Gentile and Jewish, religious and secular. The coexistence of parochialism with humanitarianism suggests a continuous battle, in which the latter, although often eclipsed was never defeated. Britain provided a haven to many uprooted people in spite of itself rather than as a consequence of determined policy. It was in this atmosphere of low-level but pervasive anti-Semitism that the events of January 1933 occurred together with the demands refugees were to make upon the compassion of the people. This is also the context in which the achievements of the AAC/SPSL should be understood.

Perhaps it was Britain's insularity that prevented part of the majority from comprehending the experience of abused and persecuted others. Maybe people here just felt too safe. Many refugees who did settle were astonished at British complacency, the 'it-couldn't-happen-here' mentality, which desensitized many ordinary citizens to the events on 'the continent', that remotely incomprehensible elsewhere.

On the other hand, as well as the liberal intelligentsia, religious groups – Quakers in particular – Socialists and Communists quickly understood the peril in which German Jews stood; and alongside a stony indifference arose a wave of fellow-feeling, manifested in spontaneous organizations formed to help those seeking shelter here. The history of Britain is again a tale of two countries. This was not new, as Disraeli's *Sybil, or the Two Nations*, written in 1845, shows; and it remains the case today.

British attitudes are neither this nor that. We are not cruelly deaf to the cry of strangers, nor do we enthusiastically welcome the afflicted. We are not uniquely tolerant, nor are we coldly disdainful of foreigners. We can be insular in our prejudices while displaying great individual kindness; indeed these qualities readily exist together within the same individual. The relationship is complex: a generous action after a tepid welcome, a superficial hostility and live-and-let-live acceptance.

In a 1936 lecture the Home Secretary, Sir Samuel Hoare, expressed 'gratitude for all the services that the Jewish intellect has rendered to humanity'. He saw no reason why, in admitting refugees, 'the world of thought should differ from the world of industry', but stressed that very careful selection 'was necessary in order to harvest the capital in the form of skills, knowledge and foreign technical processes' that emigrants could supply. The government was in a bind: it could not repudiate the British reputation for tolerance and liberal hospitality to political refugees; conversely it would not permit the indiscriminate passage into Britain of all who sought protection here.

Indeed, these precedents also had fateful consequences for European Jews. The British preference was for 'political' refugees, since it was hospitality offered to victims of political persecution that underpinned the British belief in our generous openness to ideas. Discrimination on grounds of people's espousal of a cause seemed to present more urgent grounds for offering asylum than what were, even in the 1930s, described as 'racial or economic migrants' – a significant conflation, intended to downgrade their claims on public sympathy. In our time, the distinctions have been further elaborated; and efforts made to invalidate the claims of refugees by referring to them as '*bogus* asylum-seekers'.

These ambiguities are still far from being settled; and echoes of 1930s arguments are being re-articulated with even sharper insistence. The desire of Joynson-Hicks to 'put the country first' has been heard again in debates on government immigration policies from the 1960s to the present day: labour shortages relaxed controls; hostility and demonstrations, riots and racism retightened them. Restricting the numbers of incomers in the interests of communal harmony is the characteristic compromise in these later debates: whether the economy is enriched or the social fabric stretched by migrant admissions remains a constant source of dispute.

Growing pressures: foreign arrivals, British reactions

Louise London places the ambiguities of the 1930s in context.[8] Following the break-up of the Ottoman and Austro-Hungarian empires after the First World War, the consolidation of European nation-states brought about significant movements of population. The nation-state thereby became more homogeneous in population, language and culture, a culmination of the nineteenth-century European independence movements; diverse, multi-ethnic populations were seen as remnants of dissolving empires. This contributed to the growing intolerance of minorities within national boundaries, an attitude shared by a Britain so convinced that it was not a 'country of immigration', that it became obsessed with the temporary nature of the stay of refugees it admitted, seeking anxious assurances that their onward migration would follow – to the United States, South America, or the 'dominions'. A plan to settle European refugees in British Guiana lapsed, largely because the cost of preparing the north coast of South America for this was too daunting.

There are other reasons for the British government's determination not to mount any significant rescue attempt of Jews from Nazi control. The recurring fear of 'floods' or 'waves' likened migration to unstoppable forces of nature, which it would be folly to resist. Recourse to this imagery has not ceased in more recent times: Mrs Thatcher referred, in the curious semaphore of the half-uttered of which British politicians are such accomplished practitioners, to the popular fear of being 'swamped' by strangers. Governments also suggested that Nazi spies might infiltrate refugee populations, with disastrous consequences for sabotage, the establishment of a 'fifth column', or later, the betrayal of secrets that might damage the war effort – an anxiety not entirely without foundation, as the experience of Klaus Fuchs shows.

It is easy with hindsight to see how short-sighted many of these misgivings were. Clearly, the removal of the physicists, chemists and mathematicians, and the other Jewish and Gentile opponents of Nazism in the universities, deprived Germany of crucial brainpower of which the Allies were beneficiaries. Research that led to the creation of the atomic bomb was carried out by Germany's rejected academics. This has often been described as Hitler's gift to his enemies; and their presence on British, and later, American soil, certainly robbed Germany of the pre-eminence it had enjoyed in scientific discovery in the pre-Nazi era.

There were three moments when pressure intensified on foreign governments to receive German academics: first, in the immediate aftermath of the Nazi seizure of power in 1933, after the 'Nuremberg laws' in 1935, and following the annexation of Austria in March 1938 and Kristallnacht in November of the same year.[9] Britain accepted a proportionately greater number of displaced scientists than the USA, particularly early on, when American universities were still suffering under the impact of the Depression. Links between the Academic Assistance Council and government (two MPs were particularly active – A.V. Hill, member for the University of Cambridge 1940–45, and Eleanor Rathbone) ensured that the issue stayed before the public. Indeed, in the more restricted world of government, press, the civil service and industrial and academic life, an idea of *noblesse oblige* had not yet quite faded; much could be achieved by a word in the appropriate ear. What is now scorned as elitism was certainly important in the recognition of what the displaced scientists were doing, its potential advantage to Britain being well understood. Lord Rutherford, first President of the AAC, stated the organization's fundamental outlook when he spoke of 'the conviction that the Universities form a kingdom of their own whose intellectual autonomy must be preserved'.

The government was sympathetic to dismissed academics; although it had little time for less prominent victims of persecution. Immigration rules were restrictive: a mere 10,000 refugees from Germany were admitted between 1933 and 1938, and only after the events of 1938 were rules relaxed. In that year, more than 40,000 were admitted, and 10,000 children came with the Kindertransport. The fiction was maintained throughout that most refugees were in Britain temporarily and would move on as soon as possible – as indeed, many did. But by September 1939, it was clear that the majority would remain in Britain, at least for the war's duration. The Academic Assistance Council itself encouraged onward migration and provided grants for travel to the United States, where the academics might find employment in universities. Many took advantage of this scheme, and were rewarded with academic posts.

Throughout the 1930s and the first 18 months of the war, the Nazis' primary objective was to get rid of the Jews through emigration. The 'final solution' was not immediately articulated; and, although not permitted to take property or wealth with them, Jews were free to leave until 1941. But there was simply nowhere for them to go, particularly with Britain's low limits for admissions to Palestine, then under the British mandate. 'Migration' did not have the connotations which later 'deportations to the East' were to assume. Courtney Stern, a young researcher from the United States working voluntarily at CARA in 2007–08, tells how her grandfather, who had migrated to the USA and was studying at Penn State University, had been able to get his parents into the USA, even though his father was in Buchenwald. Bruno, her great-grandfather was detained in 1938. His wife sent a telegram to their children in the US to tell them that their father was 'away from home' – code for imprisoned. His son got the president of Penn State University to draft a letter, stating that Bruno would be welcome at the university. The letter was taken to Germany in a diplomatic pouch. Bruno was released, and he and his wife Frieda, were allowed to go, first to Britain, and then to the USA. 'He was broken by it. He had a tattoo from the camp. He had been decorated in the First War, and didn't leave because he considered himself a German first, a Jew second. He knew no English. She had been to finishing school, and knew how to cook. She started a bakery, and Bruno delivered the items. She died of breast cancer and Bruno died 3 months later in 1957, deaths most likely hastened by the Nazi trauma.'

Otto Frisch's father was seized by the SS and sent to a concentration camp in November 1938. 'The next two months are a confused nightmare in my memory ... My father's boss, Dr Bermann, had managed to escape to Sweden before Kristallnacht and restart his business; he offered his father his old job back if he could come. On the strength of that offer a high Swedish official, Justizierad Alexandersson, promised that my father would get a labour permit, should he reach Sweden.' Non-political prisoners in concentration camps were often released if they had somewhere to emigrate to; after the war, Otto Frisch's parents joined him in Cambridge.

Such stories were exceptional. For most, the way out was barred. This is no surprise. It is not easy to recapture the sense of siege which affected the British psyche early in the war, particularly with the westward sweep of the Nazis. All the wartime iconography – standing alone, this small island, Britain can take it, pluck in the Blitz and potential invasion – grew from the deepest anxieties about survival. The fear of being overwhelmed by Germany was intensified by older invasion scares – the Napoleonic Wars, even the Spanish Armada. Understandably the government saw in Hitler's defeat the best hope for European Jewry; and who knows how far a subconscious fear of refugees – particularly from enemy territory – combined with all the accumulated determination to resist foreign invasion of any kind, and hardened the resolve to bar entry into the beleaguered citadel?

Another factor, more deeply buried and vehemently denied, is the relationship between anti-Semitism – always present in Britain, although never, of course, approaching the levels of malignancy seen in Germany – and racism, the dominant ideology of the ruling classes in imperial governance. The anti-Semitism of many MPs and even members of the government in Britain is well known. Chamberlain himself said: 'No doubt Jews aren't a lovable people; I don't care about them myself; but that is not sufficient to explain the pogrom.'[10]

The official British view of its colonial possessions remained firmly supremacist – all the values so spectacularly forsworn subsequently were still at their florid imperial noon. Yet when a version of that grisly ideology burst forth in the heart of Europe, (significantly, in a country without the extensive imperial hinterland of Britain or France), Britain's leaders were appalled. Did they recognize a distant kinship between it and their own practice elsewhere? Were they unable to assess accurately the temper of the people they governed here, and did they fear these might also be tempted, if not by the powerful exaltations which had seized the imagination of many in Germany, then by other destructive ideologies of liberation articulated by the leaders (if not the population) of Russia?

Coexisting with these dark fears and possibilities, however, there has always been a zealous, reforming, even radical, Britain – the conscience of a significant liberal minority whose influence exceeded their numbers, since they espoused the cause of oppressed majorities, both among the poor and excluded of early industrialism, and the oppressed and humiliated of colonial possessions. A heartening aspect of British life is that no oppression, atrocity or injustice happens in the world which does not call forth some group, however small, dedicated to righting the wrong. This has remained undiminished with time;

for what is often ridiculed at first later becomes a matter of common decency. The issues range from the slave trade and the excesses of the first industrial era – hours of labour, the employment of children, living conditions in city slums and so on – down to the iniquities of imperialism, racism, apartheid, dictatorship and human rights abuses, mass hunger and human trafficking. Such campaigns have often been initially reviled: our competitors and rivals will steal a march upon us should we yield. Yet over time, the views of radicals and dissenters have become tomorrow's humanitarian axioms. The coexistence of apparently incompatible values is one of Britain's least noticed virtues, lying nearer the heart of a reputation for tolerance than more strident myths about our unique sympathy for the underdog and innate sense of fairness. These worlds rarely intersect, but when they do, they are in dialogue, occasionally acrimonious, but rarely erupting in violence.

Refugees, now as then, is such an issue. Pleading the sanctity of national borders and invoking 'this crowded island' appears to make the admission of the persecuted an impossible prospect ('much as we might like to …'). Yet the disruptions of a globalism of which Britain and all the rich countries are both the principal initiators and the main beneficiaries impose other imperatives: who supports tyrannies or aids regimes that abuse their people, and what suspensions of morality does this involve? The answers may one day appear as self-evident as doing away with slavery or the folly of believing one ethnic group of human beings superior to another; yet such was the conventional wisdom of only the day before yesterday.

There is a link between the tumultuous, conflicting forces at work in the 1930s and 40s and those of the present day. It is not surprising that racism, even when officially repudiated by Authority, has shown a tenacious afterlife in the popular psyche. The population's more conservative elements – notably the poorest – are slower to adapt to a changing world than their rulers. Publicly we are opposed to racism, although its subterranean yet pervasive odour of nostalgia still permeates official attitudes to strangers and foreigners, despite overt abhorrence of such sentiments distasteful to contemporary sensibilities. Anti-Semitism – although it made a brief and ugly re-appearance in Britain just after the war (as a result of attacks on British forces in Palestine) – has faded in recent decades. The focus of prejudice shifted, first to blacks, and then Muslims. However anti-Semitism was merely sleeping; it stirs from time to time, most recently in a Left unholy/holy alliance with radical Muslims, Israel's policies towards Palestinians having become the screen on which anti-Semitism can project its re-awakened nightmares.

The spectre of public opinion

A word of explanation about 'public opinion'. This amorphous concept was – and is – widely used by the Authorities as a useful alibi for doing nothing, when something clearly should be done. 'Our hands are tied' is a bondage politicians relish when invoking those vigilant majorities always ready to hold them to account for irresponsible humanitarianism.

The animosity expressed to those requesting assistance here is common; people often articulate an ideology of uncompromising exclusion. Yet when encountering genuine need, they show a remarkable capacity for fellow-feeling, sympathy and goodwill. Prejudice and intolerance flourish behind the invisible walls of separation. Remedies for this may be simpler than apologists for the status quo sometimes maintain, although they certainly are not 'dispersal policies' which send refugees to crumbling tower-blocks or short-life housing in decaying urban areas.

Three years into the Second World War, Louise London says that 'decrypts' of enemy wireless telegraph messages made the British government and senior officials 'aware that the German regime was carrying out a programme of wholesale killing of European Jews. About half the estimated total of 5.1 million murders of Jews by the Nazis were committed in the year 1942.'[11] The 'public opinion' which government had used to show its powerlessness, mobilized on behalf of spontaneous pity and compassion through meetings, demonstrations, organization and an avalanche of letters to government ministers. Early in 1943, a group of MPs, writers and intellectuals pressed the government to offer at least temporary refuge to those Jews who still might be able to escape. They commissioned a survey, which showed that 78 per cent of people supported admission of Jews from occupied Europe. But the British government continued to insist that only those who could make some demonstrable contribution to 'the war effort' would be admitted. Action on humanitarian grounds was ruled out. 'Public opinion' which today also paralyses governments and inhibits acts of commiseration and sympathy, is clearly not an immovable monolith. Through direct contact, hostility is eroded; that a challenge to the shrill assertions of the popular press is absent is an aspect of failed leadership, not of the cruelty of the British people.

Anne Lonsdale spent much of her early childhood in the care of refugees, Karl and Lena Weissenberg, whose warmth and tenderness were a substitute for parents busy with war work. The Weissenbergs arrived at her parents' house in Southampton – often the arrival point of refugees, before war began. She spent time with them later in their flat in Manchester with their two old Yiddish-speaking aunts. She says: 'My childhood would have been miserable without the Weissenbergs. They brought a humanizing quality. However eminent they were, refugees were also people loved as teachers and scholars.' The successful insertion of a majority of academic refugees into British life shows how a common purpose, a shared social and intellectual function, can easily overcome perceived differences.

This prefigures debates heard in Britain today. Nothing said now has not been spoken before, as loudly and eloquently enunciated as any vituperative declaration made by the *Daily Mail* or *The Sun* in the present time. The fate of refugees in the 1930s reminds us of both continuity and change in British social and moral attitudes over three-quarters of a century.

A very British rescue mission

The distinction could not be clearer between official reaction and the swift, spontaneous response of the academic community to Hitler's baleful view of the world. When Sir William Beveridge decided to do something about those removed from the universities of Nazi Germany in 1933, he could utilize a network of highly-placed luminaries prepared to devote themselves to the rescue of dispossessed intellectuals.[12] Beveridge tells how in a Viennese cafe in March 1933, only a few weeks after the Nazis had taken power, he read a newspaper report that German-Jewish professors had been ousted from universities all over Germany. In his version, told in *A Defence of Free Learning*, he makes no mention of Leo Szilard who played such a major part.[13] Later, in a sermon at Carrs Lane Church in Birmingham in 1935, Beveridge expressed the puzzlement of liberal progressives, when he said: 'There are things today all over Germany as lovely as music, youth and human affection can ever be, but there are also things so ugly and savage that we thought mankind had put away 300 years ago. We can only ask "What has gone wrong with this great and gifted people?"' Not content with rhetoric however, characteristically he urged his listeners not simply to ask questions, but to deeds against 'the challenge to the two great civilizing principles of science and religion'.

Beveridge and his colleague Lionel Robbins decided to create a scheme to aid the dismissed teachers immediately.[14] Within weeks the Academic Assistance Council (AAC) came into existence under the Presidency of Lord Rutherford, the Cambridge physicist. It would support refugee academics chased from their jobs and homeland by interference in their work, the withdrawal of their means of livelihood, and threats of violence and death.

This may now be seen as a matter of common sense, but in the turbulent early thirties, a significant proportion of informed opinion in both Britain and Europe believed either that the Nazi regime would be short-lived, or that it was a bulwark against Communism. Together with a background murmur of anti-Semitism, economic disruption and high unemployment in Britain, this could have offered a persuasive justification for inaction.

Beveridge and his colleagues accepted no delay. The initial declaration of the Council, in May 1933, was signed by over 40 of the most prominent academics in Britain. Beveridge used his own personal contacts to enlist their support, including the President of the Royal Society, Sir William Bragg, Cambridge economist John Maynard Keynes, Regius Professor of Greek at Oxford, Gilbert Murray, former Governor of Bengal, the Second Earl of Lytton, physiologist and future MP, A.V. Hill, and the Director of the British Museum, Sir Frederic Kenyon.

The influence a few individuals were capable of exercising shows how clearly it was a different world from that of today. For one thing, the sphere of scholarship and learning was far more restricted, both numerically and socially. Those who lent their support to the AAC all knew each other. Many had attended the same schools and universities. A word in the right place, the lifting of a telephone, a friendly note could galvanize like-minded others into action. Their friendships, family relationships and a common experience ensured they would be heard. It was, no doubt, patrician and elitist; but it was effective. One can admire their energy and commitment, without necessarily approving of the hierarchies of privilege, to which, in part, they owed their capacity to get things done.

The establishment of a relief fund was given impetus by the coming together of three refugee organizations at a meeting at the Albert Hall in October 1933 when Albert Einstein addressed 10,000 people. Einstein had become a Swiss citizen in 1901. He based himself in Germany in 1913, when he joined the Prussian Academy of Sciences, and accepted a post at the University of Berlin. In the USA in January 1933 when the Nazis gained power, he resolved never to set foot in Germany for the duration of their regime. Visiting Oxford in October 1933, he was eager to address the gathering. The meeting created an atmosphere of intense expectation, but also of anxiety, because of rumours that there was a plot to assassinate Einstein. An extremist group was reported to have offered £1,000 to kill him: in 1933, he had renounced his German citizenship and resigned from the Prussian Academy of Sciences. In Britain, the host of Einstein the pacifist was Commander Locker-Lampson, barrister, MP and belligerent imperialist, who also spoke at the meeting. He said: 'The task of the League of Nations is so enormous that some people think it cannot help Jews in their distress. Ladies and gentlemen, if that League of Nations cannot help the Jews, there is another, greater league of nations, the British Empire, that shall and will.'

In a memorable contribution to the occasion, Dr Maude Royden, suffragist, preacher and social reformer, in a request for funds, said: 'The scientists have put us in command of a wealth of which the world of a generation ago never even dreamed. I do not therefore ask you *in forma pauperis* (as a pauper), and I do not ask for your charity. I ask you to discharge a debt which the world owes to these distinguished scientists, who are represented by the greatest of them all tonight, Professor Einstein.'

Einstein's speech, on 'Science and Civilisation', was electrifying and prescient. He expressed his gratitude to the work of the AAC 'as a man, as a good European and as a Jew … You have shown that you and the British people have remained faithful to the traditions of tolerance and justice which for centuries you have upheld with pride. It is in times of economic distress such as we experience everywhere today, one sees very clearly the strength of the moral forces that live in a people. Let us hope that a historian delivering judgment in some future period when Europe is politically and economically united, will be able to say that in our days the liberty and honour of this Continent was saved by its Western nations, which stood fast in hard times against the temptations of hatred and oppression; and that Western Europe defended successfully the liberty of the individual which has brought us every advance of knowledge and invention – liberty without which life to a self-respecting man is not worth living …

'We are concerned not merely with the technical problem of securing and maintaining peace, but also with the important task of education and enlightenment. If we want to resist the powers which threaten to suppress intellectual and individual freedom we must keep clearly before us what is at stake, and what we owe to that freedom which our ancestors have won for us after hard struggles.

'Without such freedom there would have been no Shakespeare, no Goethe, no Newton, no Faraday, no Pasteur and no Lister. There would be no comfortable houses for the mass of the people, no railways, no wireless, no protection against epidemics, no cheap books, no culture and no enjoyment of art for all. There would be no machines to relieve the people from the arduous labour needed for the production of the essential necessities of life. Most people would lead a dull life of slavery just as under the ancient despotisms of Asia. It is only men who are free, who create the inventions and intellectual works which to us moderns make life worth while …'

Einstein's address to the audience in the Albert Hall was followed by a singing of 'God Save the King', and a spontaneous rendering of 'For He's a Jolly Good Fellow'. Four days later, Einstein left for the U.SA. This was his last visit to Europe.[15]

Einstein's commitment generated great enthusiasm. A special fund was set up at the London School of Economics, and the staff donated between 1 and 3 per cent of their annual salary to persecuted German colleagues.

The AAC assumed two main tasks: firstly, to provide a register of possible employment opportunities for temporary or permanent posts at British universities; and secondly, to provide modest maintenance grants – £250 for a married couple and £182 for a single person. Each refugee completed a questionnaire, detailing possible alternatives to an academic career, and a list of countries to which they were prepared to go.

By 1938, it is estimated that one-third of the teaching staff at German universities had been dismissed. Of these, about 2,000 had emigrated. More than half came to Britain, for many simply a halting-place on a longer journey. In the first two years of its existence, the AAC helped about 60 German lecturers procure a permanent post, while 148 others were placed in temporary research or teaching positions. The organization's effectiveness tells us much about the temper of the times. If the academic world was smaller then than now, it was paradoxically also more spacious, in the sense that both the commitment and the resources could be found from within to assist persecuted colleagues abroad. There was then, perhaps, a more ample sense of time for reflection before action, a luxury now forfeited. And the sense of duty should not be underestimated among university staff of the period, who were, in general, from a privileged background and more likely than most to grasp the significance of the ideologies sweeping Europe at a time of mass unemployment, economic depression and dramatic social change.

Although the British government applied immigration laws stringently, it delegated substantive responsibilities to voluntary bodies. The Jewish Refugees' Committee, set up by Anglo-Jewish leaders as soon as the refugee crisis first appeared in 1933, underwrote the costs of settling refugees. This absolved the government from any accusation that the public purse might be called upon for this, thereby giving the Committee considerable control over who was admitted. Similarly, the AAC approved displaced scholars and undertook to place those it rescued and provide basic sustenance for them during an adaptation period.

The AAC's work has to be understood in this context: it sought to rescue individuals of considerable attainment, of considerable promise, and sometimes of international renown. The government certainly would accept any credit it might receive for its cost-free generosity in extending hospitality to people of outstanding ability. A Cabinet minute of April 1933 reflects government thinking. It stated that British policy was 'to try to secure for this country prominent Jews who were being expelled from Germany, and who had achieved distinction … in pure science, applied science such as medicine and technical industry, music or art. This would not only obtain for this country the advantage of their knowledge and experience, but would also create a very favourable impression in the world, particularly if our hospitality were offered with some warmth.' This frank exposition is sobering, not least the calculating chill in its final phrase, and reveals the government's mixture of opportunism and generosity as regards the potentially most 'valuable' refugees; it was far less welcoming when it came to the humble and lesser-known.

The flight from Nazism

It is easy to imagine the apprehension that swept through Jewish communities when Hitler entered into a coalition with Von Papen after the election of November 1932, after which the more far-sighted Jews quickly made arrangements to leave Germany.

The informal arrangements between the British government and voluntary organizations allowed for flexibility in decisions about who might be admitted into the country. Richard Gombrich, son of the art historian Ernst Gombrich, says his parents were indebted to his grandmother, a celebrated piano teacher. 'Many of her pupils were daughters of the British aristocracy. She taught the

Asquith girls and other children of Liberal Party celebrities. They helped pull strings to get them to Britain. Lady Violet Bonham Carter had two daughters and two sons, and the elder daughter was my mother's closest friend. We knew them well. I am sure my father's family would not have been saved without these connections.'

The flight from Germany, and later Austria and Czechoslovakia, can still just be remembered by those young at the time. Professor Lewis Elton, son of Victor Ehrenburg, was a boy of 15 in 1939, when with his parents he left Prague. Although German, Professor Ehrenburg had been at Prague University for ten years. His family had a history of involvement in education reform – an augury, perhaps of Lewis Elton's activities in the same field in Britain.

Lewis recalls the urgency of the time. Like his father 70 years earlier, he remembers the anxiety and foresight of his family, especially his mother. 'Luckily, we were always one step ahead. After the Hitler–Chamberlain agreement of 1938 in Munich, my father was at a conference in Zurich. He made contacts there in case things became so bad we would have to get out. Apart from Chamberlain, everyone suspected Hitler's intention.

'At school we had to learn a foreign language. My father being a professor of Greek History, it was natural my brother and I should opt for Greek. Under our mother's influence, however, we presciently changed to the English class.

'We were not refugees, although none of us believed we would ever come back. My father had applied to a number of places, including the SPSL, and the latter awarded him a research scholarship for £250, which would have been enough for him and his wife, but not for his children.'

Without English friends, the boys could not have accompanied their parents to England. A chain of circumstantial friendships, starting with a former English teacher in Germany who had become acquainted with Eva Ehrenburg, led to the wife of the chaplain at Rydal School, through whom places were offered to both boys in 1939. 'The letter from Rydal School arrived in mid-January. We left Prague in mid-February and four weeks later, Hitler marched in.'

The Ehrenburgs' journey was more hazardous than it might have been, and for the most poignant of personal reasons. They took a last chance to see Victor's mother in Kassel and Eva's sisters in Frankfurt. Czechoslovakia was still – just – a free country. Because Hitler intended to invade without arousing suspicion, no one challenged them on their travels.

'We spent three days in Germany. There was a certain risk involved, the more so since the day we were in Kassel, Himmler chose the same day to pay a visit. We spent a day with my grandmother. She died two years later in her bed, in January 1941; and the way this happened was significant. I had a cousin who was adopted; a pure Aryan boy. When his father left Germany in 1934, this boy had the choice of staying or going with him. He was 15 years old and at agricultural school. He decided to stay. At the beginning of the war he joined the Mountain

Troops. In January 1941, he marched into the Gestapo HQ in Kassel and said to them, apropos of his adoptive grandmother, "Let the old Jewess die in her bed." They did. She died before the deportation. Her goods went to those who were looking after her, an Aryan family.

'After the war, my father was visiting Tübingen, and as he entered the house where he was to stay, he exclaimed *"Mein Gott!"* He found himself facing a painting which he recognized from his mother's house, a quite opulent painting of children, members of the family. The people he was staying with gave it to him. It now hangs in my house in Guildford.

'In Frankfurt, we tried to persuade my mother's sister to come with us. She said, "No, if they want to kill us they will." In 1941, she was taking a transport of Jewish orphans from Munich to Riga which, although they didn't know it, was the first step to extermination. In Riga, they were all shot.

'We travelled from Frankfurt to England via Belgium. At the Belgian frontier, there was no problem, because we had Czech passports. All those travelling with German passports were held back; I have no idea what happened to them.

'We crossed the channel in brilliant sunshine and saw the cliffs of Dover. We were met at Victoria by the family of an acquaintance of my father, who was a professor of classics. We stayed at their house and became firm friends.'

Many refugees had dramatic escapes. The biochemist Hans Krebs was forced to leave the University of Freiburg without being allowed to collect his possessions on 19 April 1933. His colleagues packed 20 crates with his scientific apparatus, and he left on the night train from Freiburg. He was welcomed, almost penniless, at Victoria station by Hermann Blaschko, but within a few weeks was working at the laboratory of Gowland Hopkins, which, he later recalled, 'sheltered six refugees from central Europe: Friedman, Lemberg, Chain, Malherbe, Bach and myself ... for the acceptance of one-time strangers into the family of biochemists I shall always be grateful'.

Ernst Boris Chain, a pioneer in the purification of penicillin, graduated in chemistry and physiology in Berlin and took a doctorate at the Institute of Pathology. His career was interrupted when, as he said, Europe 'was temporarily plunged into a darkness in which the darkest Middle Ages now appear as a blaze of light'. He left Berlin and arrived at Harwich in April 1933 with £10 in his pocket. Later he worked at Oxford with Sir Howard Florey on penicillin. Always overshadowed by Sir Alexander Fleming (who was presented as a hero: at school we heard nothing of Florey and Chain), he acknowledged his gratitude to Britain, and became a Fellow of the Royal Society in 1949, four years after he, Florey and Chain had jointly received the Nobel Prize.

Dr Gustav Born tells how his father was advised by Einstein in 1933 to leave Germany at once. Max Born, a pacifist, was not dismissed from his post at Göttingen, but was sent on indefinite leave on salary. The family decided to get out. Gustav was ten. 'I remember the date; it was 10 May 1933. They took a train to Munich, and from there to the South Tyrol, where they had rented a summer holiday flat. We crossed the border into Italy, where it was safer, because although Mussolini was in power, Italy had not yet passed race laws. I remember the journey well – it was a great adventure for a boy. In Bavaria, the train passed through a town where books were being burned. My father was wild with fury, and had to be restrained from leaving the train to intervene in this festival of destruction. We had a long summer holiday that year, and stayed until it was time for me to start school in Cambridge, where my father had been offered a job. I had no strong sense of menace at the time, although my parents had explained to me the circumstances we were in.'

Otto Frisch called himself 'apolitical'. Absorbed in his work, he scarcely noticed the coming to power of the Nazis. When he realized the danger, a friend, who was actually a Nazi, arranged for him to travel on a small freighter going to London.

'On that cockleshell on a windy day in October 1933, I left Germany with all my belongings in several trunks which kept sliding forth and back in my cabin as the ship rolled and pitched across the North Sea. Once we had entered the Thames the ship quietened, and I could sit on deck and watch the flat landscape and then the dockland and the City of London until we finally tied up somewhere near Greenwich. I had to wait until the immigration officer came on board.

'When I showed him my passport, he asked me, "Have you got a work permit? You must have one if you want to take a job in England."

'"I have no job," I replied. "I have a grant." (This was the AAC grant of £250 a year, which Otto Frisch judged "quite adequate".)

'"A grant is a high-class name for a job; you must have a work permit."

'"But how do I get one?" I asked him.

'"You give the steward half a crown and send him ashore to phone your professor; see what he can do."

'It worked like a charm; within two hours, the immigration officer was back with his stamp, ready to let me in.'[16]

Others had an even more dramatic escape. Some came on the last boat out of Holland in May 1940, when the Nazis were at the door of Amsterdam. According to a passenger: 'The British didn't know what to do with the ship. We were diverted and spent two days lying offshore from where we could see the coastline. We finally arrived at Liverpool, seven days after we set out.'

Entering, adapting, achieving, giving

For the family of Max Born, who knew where they were going, the transition was planned, almost leisurely, despite the drastic upheaval in their lives. A shock awaited many other émigrés, although few complained since their escape had often been by the skin of their teeth. Britain often appeared unwelcoming, and the chill greyness of the climate reflected the cool politeness of the people. The energy and exuberance of many exiles found little echo in the damp, depressed 1930s. 'London was grim, a dirty, smelly city,' said Ernst Gombrich, who arrived in the winter of 1935 and found lodgings in Pimlico. 'It was freezing cold. My landlady lit a tiny fire which was so weak that it didn't warm the room at all. I had very little money – a grant of £250 a year – which was very little, and usually ate in those Lyons or Express Dairy cafes which seemed very dirty and smelled of old fat.'[17]

Their reminiscences recall sooty air and mist-shrouded streets, trees with their buds of silver raindrops, the winter that required artificial light all day long; the busy preoccupation of people with their own worries of insecure employment, poor relief or, in higher social strata, whether the maid might have to be sacrificed in economically straitened times.

Their rented rooms were small and dusty, the windows uncleaned, while the wind whistled around the chimney-pots and sent clouds of smoke from the inferior coal back into the room; hot water, when available, gushed into the bath rust-coloured from ancient pipes; gas-fires fed with sixpences dried the air and made the eyes smart; and landladies in headscarves muttered anxiously about noisy foreigners talking into the night and disturbing the other tenants. A particular bane for many was the drab, puritanical Sundays – the absence of life from the streets and the curious languor which made the 'day of rest' even more oppressive than workdays. All this affronted the sensibilities of urbane and intelligent people, who came to realize that these unwelcoming circumstances represented home for a perhaps indefinite future.

Those who went immediately into a more receptive academic environment fared better. They discovered another Britain; the concerned liberal middle-class, often in rambling houses, where cat-hairs had to be removed from cracked Spode cups before tea could be poured, and vanilla slices remained on the table from yesterday or the day before, covered in dust. These were small inconveniences to set against the kindness and understanding of individuals, befrienders of the unhappy and the exiled who knew only too well what Hitler portended and the inevitability of war.

Molecular biologist Max Perutz arrived in Cambridge as a student of J.D. Bernal in 1936. His parents intended him for the family textile business, and had him tutored in English. His father had been trained in England and sent him to Cambridge 'kitted out with the accoutrements of an English gentleman: a bowler hat, white tie and tails for formal dinners, smart grey suit for work and tweed plus-fours for recreation'.[18] Although he had difficulty in finding a college to which he could affiliate, within the first week he decided he liked Cambridge. 'Like every visitor, he was bowled over by the beauty of the buildings, and impressed that they were still used for the purpose for which they were built. He was also struck that even though he was a lowly student, everyone treated him with great kindness and courtesy, from his academic superiors ... to the laboratory technicians and college servants.'[19] London, however, he found dirty and ugly. His daughter, Vivien, says, 'Britain was backward in some ways – my parents had grown up with central heating, so they found the cold uninsulated houses, where the pipes froze in winter, distinctly chilling. However, they were delighted with their first proper home, a tiny attic flat, and considered themselves lucky – they thought they had all modern conveniences, since it boasted electricity and an indoor loo.'

It was often the wives or children who recorded their mixed feelings about their new home. Hedwig Born, in an article praising Britain and its democratic system, describes how the sense of strangeness and longing were little by little transformed into affection and gratitude. She says: 'Homesickness averted my heart and eyes from everything new. However, the good and valuable that I didn't want to see has made itself forcefully noticed and I ultimately loved it. On first arriving in England I thought I was transplanted into a strange part of the world. Everything was different from the Continent – not only the door handles, light bulbs, bread and hedges along the road (instead of trees) – but the very atmosphere.'

An initial awkwardness was widespread. Some felt unwanted, but most saw the country as 'a foster-mother' in the words of Eva Ehrenburg, wife of Victor Ehrenburg, a classical scholar helped by the SPSL in 1938. Her touching tribute to Britain is an eloquent reminder of the thankfulness of those who found a refuge and whose skills were recognized and rewarded. Hindsight softened the asperities which had jarred on many when they first arrived. In her memoir, *Sehnsucht – mein geliebtes Kind*, published in Germany in 1963, she wrote: 'Our mother had only one name, she was called Germany. We, her children, were called after her: Germans. We were not only so called. Because we loved her devotedly, we believed that she loved us too. Though we might have known better, that is, worse. Germany never really loved us, but we could be happy there.'[20]

'I wanted to die in freedom', Sigmund Freud wrote from exile, 'but one had so dearly loved the prison.'

Other factors influenced people's ability to adapt, not the least the way they had been assimilated in Germany; this itself depended to a considerable degree, on temperament. Lord Krebs, remembering Sir Hans, his father, says: 'He was very dispassionate, not emotional. His character was formed in Germany by a Prussian-style discipline. His father's family was a little like one in Victorian England. They were rather formal. They lived with material austerity and intellectual elegance.' Such people clearly found it easier to adapt to the sometimes tepid, controlled sensibility of Britain than those who expressed feelings as easily as they articulated their ideas and opinions. Anne Lonsdale, speaking of her dearly loved Karli Weissenberg, found the opposite to be true: Karli, warm and affectionate, adapted well, but his wife, 'more Prussian, cool and controlled', always remained ill at ease.

For many refugees – and this is true everywhere – a certain loss of status accompanied the journey. When the physicist Max Born arrived in Cambridge in 1933, he dropped from full professor and head of department to a research student with one room, although within two years he was appointed to the Chair of Physics in Edinburgh. He did not feel this as demotion: relief at feeling safe overrode all other considerations.

Such was the impression of many scholars who found sanctuary in a university, a community of learning that, despite the persistence of patronage and connections of Oxbridge, was nevertheless open to people of original thinking. There was a considerable difference in the way Britain was perceived between those enthusiastically welcomed in academic society and people who had to depend, initially, on their own resources.

Eric Hobsbawm, came to Britain as an orphan to live with his aunt and uncle in a guest-house in Folkestone which, he said, 'could have stood for any of so many temporary staging-posts on the endless migrations of the twentieth century uprooted'.[21]

He saw London as a 'come-down' after the excitements of Berlin. 'Nothing in London had the emotional charge of those days, except – in a very different form – the music to which my viola-studying cousin Denis introduced me, and which we played on a hand-wound gramophone in the attic room of his mother's house in Sydenham, where the family first found shelter in London, and discussed with the intensity of teenage passion over tins of heavily sugared condensed milk ("Unfit for Babies") and cups of tea: hot jazz ...'

Hobsbawm encountered an England which those who went into an academic environment mostly avoided. 'Britain in 1933 was still a self-contained island where life was lived by unwritten but compelling rules, rituals and invented traditions: mostly class rules or gender rules, but also virtually universal ones, usually linked to royalty. The national anthem was played at the end of every performance in theatres and cinemas and people stood before it before they went home.'

The diversity of the contribution to Britain of expelled Jewish scholars is an inspiring episode in our recent history. The AAC was not instrumental in the rescue of all the eminent academics, but the particular atmosphere and moral tone it created became widely influential. It commanded the enthusiastic allegiance of many who came to Britain under their own auspices or with the help of other organizations. A number of those who found university posts here through their work in Germany or Austria, also helped the AAC in recommendations in making grants to younger, unknown colleagues.

Of those associated with the AAC – or its later incarnations – there have been 16 knighthoods, 18 Nobel laureates, 71 Fellows (or Foreign Members) of the Royal Society, and 50 fellows of the British Academy. Their contribution has been exhaustively documented elsewhere (Medawar and Pyke, Snowman et al.).[22] They and their descendants have left touching testimonies of their indebtedness to Britain, a relationship which has been reciprocal. Vivien Perutz says of her father Max, 'He was very happy to return to England after internment because it felt like home; even if it had been possible, which it was not, he was not keen to take up the offers he had received of jobs in the US. He had a great admiration for Britain and rather idealized it; he never felt English but was proud to be British.'[23] Richard Gombrich says his father 'was never nostalgic for Austria, apart from the mountains. He became very pro-British. He was grateful.' Of Sir Hans Krebs his son states: 'He adapted very well to Britain. When he came here, he was immediately integrated into the scientific community of Cambridge. He admired the fact that in Britain people could argue and disagree with each other without bearing grudges. That seemed very British and highly admirable.' Gustav Born, praising the AAC, says 'the British are marvellous people, and these were the best of them. I owe my life to two people – my father and Winston Churchill. Between them, they saved us.'

Some refugees sought to re-make themselves in the image of the host country; others, embittered by the rejection they had suffered, had no intention of being twice rejected. Many felt they remained here only provisionally, waiting for the war's end, the passage to the United States, the return home. But during and after the war years a majority saw the possibilities of making a life here; and set about this with diligence. Key to their sense of belonging to a land of tepid enthusiasms, cool tea and studied stoicism was a sense of *security*. All refugee testimonies, however unhappy, say that this silences all criticisms and smothers all other dissatisfactions. 'You cannot even begin to think of daily life, domestic habits, your professional future or the education of your children if you are thinking constantly about the knock at the door, the arbitrary arrest, the order to leave.' Even those uncomfortably aware of their alien status or who were greeted sympathetically by people who never doubted their own identity or their right to be where they were, acknowledge that they felt the violence in central Europe would not happen here – not it *could not* happen, only that it was far less likely.

Surprises, some very agreeable, awaited the central European academics. Sir Hans Krebs remembered in 1961, that 'it was in [Gowland] Hopkins' laboratory [in Cambridge] where I saw for the first time at close quarters some of the characteristics referred to as "the British way of life". The Cambridge laboratory included people of many dispositions, convictions and abilities. I saw them argue without quarrelling, quarrel without suspecting, suspect without abusing, criticize without vilifying or ridiculing, and praise without flattering ... What struck me, in particular contrast with the German scene, was the strong "social conscience" of Hopkins and his school, their deep concern for affairs of the world at large ...'

None espoused the values and sensibility of Britain more enthusiastically than Sir Geoffrey Elton. Geoffrey, younger son of Victor Ehrenburg, energetically embraced the qualities he perceived in the country in which he settled, achieving considerable distinction through his study of its historic virtues. Of his arrival in England as an adolescent, he wrote many years later: 'Within a few months it dawned upon me that I had arrived in the country in which I ought to have been born.' Having narrowly failed to get a history scholarship to Oxford, he worked for three years to get an external London BA, which was awarded with first-class honours in 1943. Seven years later, he was in Cambridge.

He became an authority on late medieval English history, 'bound', as he said sternly, 'by the authority of our sources (and by no other authority, human or divine)'. He hated historical theorists who generalized and propounded fashionable ideas taken from other disciplines like social or political science; nothing superseded the arduous labour of assembling primary evidence in an empirical whole. As Regius Professor of Modern History in Cambridge, he made the Tudor era central to English historical studies. According to an editorial in *The Times* of 7 December 1995, his work was 'a useful example of patriotic writing based upon meticulous scholarship'. His interest lay in administrative, political and constitutional history. His most famous contention was that in the 1530s, the government of England ceased to be 'medieval', dependent upon the will of the king, and changed into a modern, bureaucratic system rooted in the rule of law. His admiration for (and some exaggeration of) the role of Thomas Cromwell has been contested as an over-simplification, but his has remained the defining voice of the period. David Starkey has acknowledged his own debt to Sir Geoffrey Elton, admiring his 'slashing attacks on other historians, his caustic wit and passionate belief that history could be known with certainty and argued with clarity'.

Over time, after a spectacular career, public acknowledgment of their achievements and children growing up in Britain, most who remained became very attached to their adopted country. At a symposium in 1965, Sir Hans Krebs powerfully expressed the feeling of the émigrés who had prospered in Britain. In 1965, some of these successful people made donations to a Thank You Britain Fund, for which £90,000 was collected. When Sir Hans Krebs passed the cheque to the President of the British Academy, he said: 'What this country of our adoption gave us was not just a new home and livelihood. What we also found was a new and better way of life, a society whose attitudes to life were in many ways very different from what we had been accustomed to, and, I dare say, not only under the Nazi rule. Coming from an atmosphere of political oppression and persecution, of hate and violence, of lawlessness, blackmail and of intrigue, we found here a spirit of friendliness, humanity, tolerance and fairness ...

'If proof were needed that these attitudes which I have mentioned are prevalent traits of the British way of life, I would say: which other language uses in its everyday life phrases equivalent to "fair play", "gentleman's agreement", "benefit of the doubt", "give him a chance", "understatement", phrases indicative of a sense of justice, of a sense of perspective, of tolerance, of humility and above all, respect for humanity?'

They became 'naturalized'; a significant word, used both in Britain and the USA when individuals take on citizenship of the adoptive country. It carries a host of associations, not least, as Hungarian refugee George Mikes pointed out in 1966, a sense both of a previously irregular status and an earlier, scarcely legitimate identity, together with something even more telling.[24] For once the obstacles to becoming a citizen had been overcome, they received all the protection and privileges of this belonging. Many were honoured by Britain and by the wider world. They were secure in the land that had opened its doors to them; and it is only natural that Britain should have basked in their thankfulness.

Commitment to the country remains strong in the third generation. Ben Elton, grandson of Victor Ehrenburg, is explicit about his love of Britain, although he can also be critical.

'An Irish TV presenter once said to me, "You're no friend of Britain, are you?" I reacted very strongly to that. "I'm very fond of Britain." Of course as with any country some aspects of it are more worthy of celebration than others. When I was young and criticized the Thatcher government, I spoke out from a position of commitment to and affection for my country. In any case, Britain has long harboured a good-natured ability to take a long hard look at itself – ranting Lefties, speakers' corner. That is all part of a long tradition. My politics were pretty mild and welfare state social-democratic. I was well aware of the wickedness of the Soviet Union before a lot of students on the Left were.

'When Richard Curtis and I wrote *Blackadder Goes Forth*, my uncle Geoffrey wrote me a furious letter, saying I had ruined a good series through being so disrespectful to the British army. He said that Lewis, my father, owed his life to the British army. I wrote back saying I understood the sacrifices Britain had made and was respectful towards the army. It was sorted out. Actually we had appreciative letters from veterans of both world wars.'

The greatest fear of most refugees early in the war was that Hitler might invade. This contributed to their commitment to the war effort, and they found it all the more puzzling when they were interned as 'enemy aliens', since their only enemy was Hitler and the supremacist doctrines from which they had fled. Most were not embittered by the experience, and later admitted they understood the fear that swept through the country in early 1941, a feeling swiftly regretted, since the internment policy was soon reversed.

Gratitude was a two-way process. The most dramatic achievement of central European refugees was undoubtedly their work towards the creation of the atomic bomb, with which the war ended in 1945. But there were many other fields in which émigrés excelled, such as the arts and humanities, medicine and economics. The range of abilities of scholars and the enduring impression they have made suggests that apprehension about the stranger, voiced so stridently today, is rarely justified, since the vast majority of refugees seek absorption into the comfortable anonymity of belonging. Most swiftly adapt to the country that offers them shelter, and within a generation, all reservations about their presence here are dissipated. The example of Jewish intellectuals from central Europe should alert us today to the potential ability and talent of asylum-seekers, who ask nothing more than to follow illustrious predecessors by making the most of their talents and not be left in a limbo of unresolved cases, detention, or stateless impotence.

Max Perutz

Although Max Perutz had no need of direct help from SPSL, he was a lifelong supporter of its work, and advised it on the suitability of candidates for grants. His connection was strengthened through meeting his wife, Gisela, in the SPSL office where she worked. The SPSL helped create spaces in the 1930s in which exiled scientists could operate, sheltered from Europe's political storms. The beneficiaries of its modest grants were not the only ones who took advantage of the haven it represented against European extremism and British parochialism: a whole generation came under its benign influence on British intellectual life.

The son of a Vienna textile manufacturer, Perutz prevailed against his parents' ambition for him in the legal profession and enrolled at the University of Vienna. In 1936, familiar with the progress in biochemistry at Gowland Hopkins' laboratory in Cambridge, he was accepted by J.D. Bernal at the Cavendish Laboratory. Bernal encouraged him to pursue X-ray crystallography, which directed him towards the discovery of the structure and function of haemoglobin. Prompted by Bernal to understand the structure of proteins by the X-ray diffraction method, he began a lifelong study of proteins, beginning with haemoglobin: since all physiological reactions depend on enzymes, and all enzymes are proteins, the analysis of a protein molecule promised a significant breakthrough in the emerging discipline of molecular biology.

Perutz's work at the Cavendish led in 1962 to the setting up of the Institute of Molecular Biology. Many young researchers realized that the future for physics and chemistry lay in this field; Francis Crick arrived in 1949 and James Watson in 1951, both interested in the structure of genes, which were not proteins but deoxyribonucleic acid (DNA). In 1953, their celebrated model of the double helix, constructed of brass rods, aluminium plates and retort clamps, won them the Nobel Prize. Perutz's investigation of haemoglobin, a long and arduous process, earned him the Nobel Prize in 1962: not until 1959 had the first three-dimensional pictures of the haemoglobin molecule emerged from the Cambridge University computer. 'It was an overwhelming experience,' he wrote, 'to see a vital part of ourselves that is a thousand times smaller than anything visible under a light microscope, revealed in detail for the first time, like the first glimpses of a new continent after a long and hazardous voyage.'[25]

Perutz's research has led to a greater understanding of such diseases as sickle-cell anaemia and the transmission of inherited disorders such as Huntingdon's chorea. The value of the displaced scientists, not merely to this country, but to humanity in general, is incalculable. Most had an equally fateful impact upon the course of the twentieth century, that age of bones and ashes, but also a time of the most extraordinarily beneficial discoveries in the understanding and healing of disease.

Not that Max Perutz won his subsequent acclaim without struggle. Interned during the invasion scare of 1940, he was temporarily deported to Canada. His most extraordinary contribution to the war effort was in 1942 in a project code-named Habbakuk, an attempt to create landing platforms from an ice-fibre composite called pykrete for aircraft crossing the Atlantic. It was unsuccessful, and became unnecessary when aircraft could fly longer distances without refuelling.

His expertise spanned chemistry, physics and biology; this ability to create a new synthesis out of existing disciplines was characteristic of many exiled scientists, and something their host country was not always quick to recognize. It was only in 1947 that the Medical Research Council set up its research unit on the Molecular Structure of Biological Systems, and Perutz was appointed its head.

This humane, committed, and much appreciated man remained something of an outsider, particularly in his early years. Whether the innovative field in which he worked or discrimination caused the relative lateness of his recognition is difficult to say. The Unit's future location became uncertain; but ten years after its foundation it was re-named the Molecular Biology Research Unit – the first time an academic institution had officially been so designated. By observing similarities in the myoglobin of a whale with the haemoglobin of a horse, Perutz and his colleague Kendrew posited a common gene, from which they launched the idea of 'molecular evolution', which traces the unity of life through the family relationships of protein molecules.[26]

Perutz's role in an interlocking system of research enabled others to build on what he had done. Although often ill, and prevented from sharing his colleagues' social life, he was professionally generous over discoveries which he might have made in other circumstances. He vigorously defended the unity of purpose which drew scientists together in a common bond – 'to discover nature's secrets and put them to use for human benefit'. He said: 'My view of religion and ethics is simple: even if we do not believe in God, we should try to live as though we did.'

Max Born

Max Born was a major player in the development of 'quantum mechanics' that revolutionized the assumptions of Newtonian mechanics, accepted as given since the seventeenth century. In his Nobel lecture of December 1954, Max Born stated: 'Newtonian mechanics is deterministic in the following sense: if the initial state (positions and velocities of all particles) of a system is accurately given, then the state at any other time (earlier or later) can be calculated from the laws of mechanics. All the other branches of classical physics have been built up according to this model ... I asked myself whether this was really justified. Can absolute predictions really be made for all time on the basis of the classical equations of motion?'

Fifty years after Max Born received the Nobel Prize, his son, Dr Gustav Born, wrote in *Max Born – A Celebration*: 'He describes how he arrived at the necessity to abandon classical physics and the naïve conception of reality, which is to think of the particles of atomic physics as if they were exceedingly small grains of sand, with at each instance a definite position and velocity. For an electron this is not the case: [and] through investigations involving collision theory he reached the point of saying "One gets no answer to the question" "what is the state after the collision?" but only to the question "how probable is a specific outcome of the collision?" He proposed that electron waves were not continuous clouds of electricity as Schrödinger interpreted them, but instead represented the probability of finding a particle in a certain place after a collision. Born concluded that the motion of particles follows probability rules, but that the probability itself conforms to causality.'[27]

Since it was impossible to determine simultaneously both the position and velocity of electrons, only probabilities can be stated; concepts which correspond to no conceivable observation should be eliminated from physics. Einstein, whose friendship with Born lasted until Einstein died in 1955, tried unsuccessfully to measure both position and motion accurately at the same time; nevertheless he disagreed with Max Born, believing in the fundamental harmony of nature's laws.

Born said: 'I should like to say only this: the determinism of classical physics turns out to be an illusion, created by overrating mathematico-logical concepts. It is an idol, not an ideal in scientific research, and cannot, therefore, be used as an objection to the essentially indeterministic statistical interpretations of quantum mechanics.'

Max Born was the son of a professor of embryology at Breslau University. His mother died when he was four, and he suffered from poor health for most of his life. At university he ranged over mathematics, astronomy, physics, chemistry, logic, philosophy and zoology. In 1902 he went to the University of Heidelberg, and the following year to Zurich, increasingly drawn to mathematics. His PhD was from Göttingen in 1907. A brief period of military service – curtailed because of his health – led to revulsion against the army and militarism. In 1919 he was at Frankfurt and then back at Göttingen as Professor of Physics. He researched into crystal lattices – how atoms in solids hold together and vibrate.

Max Born left Germany in 1933. After 12 years at Göttingen his contribution to physics was well-known: he had reformulated the first law of thermodynamics (on the conservation of energy), had been identified with the quantum theory and Schrödinger's wave equation. He was offered a place in Cambridge. The altered circumstances of his life, the change of culture and of language, served as stimuli, and after two years he was appointed to the Chair of Physics at Edinburgh. He helped the SPSL with assessments of other refugee scientists, vouching for their ability and recommending them for assistance.

In 1936, he spent 6 months in Bangalore in southern India, where an English professor said that a second-rank foreigner driven from his own country was not good enough for them. Max Born confessed that he was so shaken that when he returned home, he simply cried.

He refused to work on the atomic bomb. Although, like Einstein, he abjured his earlier pacifist views in the light of the Nazi threat, and was a founding member of the Pugwash movement (the post-war initiative to halt the spread of nuclear weapons). Unlike Einstein, he returned to Germany in 1953, settling in Bad Pyrmont close to Göttingen, from where he continued to research, teach and write, and helped rebuild liberal democracy in Germany, although he maintained his British citizenship.

His son, Gustav, a biologist, speaks of his father's strong sense of moral responsibility, which Max absorbed from his own father. 'In my last year at school, my father advised me to study medicine because as a doctor I would not have to kill people in the War.'

Gustav Born believes his father expressed his most important intellectual legacy as follows: 'I believe that ideas such as absolute certitude, absolute exactness, final truth etc are figments of the imagination which should not be admissible in any field of science. On the other hand, any assertion of probability is either right or wrong from the standpoint of the theory on which it is based. This loosening of thinking (*Lockerung des Denkens*) seems to me the greatest blessing which modern science has given to us. For the belief in a single truth and in being the possessor thereof is the root cause of all evil in the world.'

There is a convergence in the thought of many of the great intellectuals of the first half of the twentieth century, among them Einstein, Heisenberg, Popper and Born. Impelled by a position which compelled them to exchange one society for another, they often came to a common view on the relativity both of the laws of physics, and of the values, beliefs and social organizations, which they considered as perishable as the certainties of mechanics, which, it had been assumed, had been established definitively and for all time.

Max Born expressed a characteristic humility towards his own achievement. 'The work for which I have had the honour to be awarded the Nobel prize for 1954, contains no discovery of a fresh natural phenomenon, but rather the basis for a new mode of thought in regard to natural phenomena.'

Hans Krebs

Hans Krebs was born in Hildesheim in 1900, the son of an ear, nose and throat specialist. The family were assimilated and the children sent to Protestant scripture classes. His biographer, Frederic L. Holmes, describes the household as 'secure and well-ordered'.[28] His son, Lord Krebs, principal of Jesus College Oxford, and first head of the Food Standards Agency, says his father's grandfather 'had a classic central European experience. They had a shop selling what would now be called soft furnishings in Gliwice in Poland, and his son, my grandfather, migrated from Silesia to Hildesheim. So the scientific tradition in the family started only with my grandfather.'

Hans Krebs enrolled as a medical student in Göttingen and Freiburg. He did his PhD at Hamburg, and in 1926 was taken on as research assistant to Otto Warburg at the Kaiser Wilhelm Institute for Biology in Berlin. In 1930 he was engaged on research at the university hospital of Altona, and in 1931 went to Freiburg, where he made the first of his discoveries, the synthesis of urea in the mammalian liver.

Holmes observes: 'For nearly 50 years he had stood at or near the forefront of the large subfield of biochemistry known as intermediary metabolism. His two most prominent discoveries – the ornithine cycle of urea synthesis and the citric acid or TCA cycle were viewed as foundations on which the modern science of intermediary metabolism has been erected. Thousands of other people who were not biochemists, but had taken at least an elementary course in biology had encountered the "Krebs cycle". The chemical reactions called the Krebs cycle elucidated a major source of energy in living organisms.'

When his post at Freiburg was cancelled by the Nazi government in April 1933 his growing international reputation generated an offer to work in Cambridge from Sir Frederick Gowland Hopkins. Krebs had already visited Britain on vacation, and with a grant from the Rockefeller Foundation, who would support him for three decades, he arrived in Cambridge in June 1933.

In keeping with its role in facilitating the dispersal of academic refugees, in March 1934, the AAC alerted Hans Krebs to the possibility of employment in Portugal through the Comité Internationale pour le Placement des Intellectuels Réfugiés in Geneva. He made enquiries, but was informed the post was already filled.

The delicacy of the employment situation in the academies of Britain in the early thirties was demonstrated by the controversy in some quarters over his Cambridge appointment. Even though he did not require financial help from the AAC, Lord Rutherford wrote to the general secretary in May 1934, saying that he had heard about 'a good deal of irritation among the younger men with reference to his appointment, and this may have some effect on future subscriptions' [towards the Council].

Gowland Hopkins, anxious to keep Krebs in Cambridge when the Rockefeller grant ran out, negotiated his appointment as Demonstrator in Biochemistry. The belief that Krebs had been preferred to an equally qualified British academic caused resentment among the staff. His occupancy of the post was justified on the grounds that the appointment was made on purely scientific grounds, and the general secretary observed: 'It is far better that first-class Germans should be appointed rather than second-class English scientists.'

These awkwardnesses, later seen as minor frictions, were at the time a matter of heated controversy. After three years, Krebs moved to Sheffield as Professor of Pharmacology, where the work on the Krebs cycle was completed. He became a Fellow of the Royal Society in 1947, received the Nobel Prize for Medicine in 1953 and was knighted in 1958. In 1947 he wrote to the SPSL: 'The work of your Society has no doubt been a very important instrument in paving the way for us refugees in this country. I think that apart from helping individuals directly by grants the Society considerably influenced public opinion and I for one shall always remember with gratefulness the moral backing we had through the Society.'

Sir Hans Krebs is recognized, as Dr Ralph Kohn, who knew him well, says, as 'a giant in his discovery of the oxidation cycle in the cell. He was one of the greatest biochemists in the world.' The biochemist Michael Yudkin also pays tribute to Hans Krebs, who was professor of the department in which he got his first academic post. 'In 1967, Krebs published, in the journal *Nature*, an article, in which he traces the professional genealogies of talented scientists, demonstrating the influence of eminent teachers upon their pupils through time; a kind of intellectual family tree, which shows the extent to which scientists of distinction have depended upon the pedagogic pedigree, as it were, or their scientific ancestry in their mentors and guides in their respective fields.'[29]

In the article Krebs places himself at the end of eight generations of inspiring teachers, whose power and ability was transmitted to their pupils, a 'lineage' going back to the early nineteenth century. He believed that the key to these fruitful lines of intellectual kinship involves 'close, prolonged association between teacher and pupil into the mature stage of the latter'. It is a question of attitudes of the distinguished teacher as much as knowledge – the virtues of humility, self-criticism, the ability to ask the right questions. He spoke of the importance of the aggregate skills of a team, and the importance of time to reflect and think. He believed that the universities were losing ground in Nobel awards, because of the growing pressure of work and lack of time. Even then, 40 years ago, he complained of 'too much equality, too little excellence'.

Lord Krebs says the key to the adaptability of the German scientists was the universality of their subject. 'My father was assimilated in Germany as medical doctor and researcher [and] he had highly portable skills which meant he could enter any academic community. So when he came to Britain, he was immediately integrated into the scientific community of Cambridge, and its welcoming nature made it easier for him than it must have been for many people.'

Sir Nikolaus Pevsner

One of the great boons of the exiles was the freshness of their vision, which helped us to look at ourselves in a different way. They enabled us to see our own virtues and the beauty of our land anew, thereby appreciating what had previously been taken for granted.

Nikolaus Pevsner was born in 1902 in Leipzig, son of a Jewish merchant. At 19, he converted to Evangelical Lutheranism. He studied in Munich, Berlin and Frankfurt. He was Assistant Keeper at the Dresden Gallery from 1924 to 1928, and was appointed lecturer at Göttingen University in the history of art and architecture. He visited England in 1930, and became interested in English art, scarcely anticipating how this would later influence his life.

In 1933, the Nazis removed him from his post in Göttingen. Like many assimilated Jews, he had been drawn to some of the values of German nationalism: he is reported as having told a refugee worker he met in Birmingham in 1933 that there was much that was 'Puritan and moral' in the Nazi movement. Germany, he said, had been humiliated by outside powers. He found it unsurprising that Hitler should appeal to the youth of the country; if they were united, Germany would no longer be the pariah of the world.[30]

His PhD thesis had been on the Italian Baroque. Once in England, he was helped by the AAC and became a research assistant in Birmingham into attitudes towards industrial design in British industry. Over time Pevsner was transformed from the immigrant who had entertained sympathetic attitudes to National Socialism into an enthusiastic Englishman. He was naturalized in 1946.

In his *Pioneers of the Modern Movement* (later republished as *Pioneers of Modern Design*) which appeared in 1936, he traced the development of modern architecture from William Morris to Walter Gropius.[31] Drawn to Modernism for its industrial efficiency and clear lines, his view of the Arts and Crafts Movement as a precursor, via Art Nouveau and Victorian engineering and architecture, of the Bauhaus in Weimar, suggests a synthesis of his original German sympathies and the sensibility of his adoptive country, these diverse influences in the production of Modernism being connected by the 'spirit of the age'. Architecture he held to be the most important of all the arts. Even when the new towns and tower blocks had fallen out of favour, he continued to admire the style of Gropius, which embodied the 'creative energy of this world in which we live and work and which we want to master, a world of science and technology, of speed and danger, of hard struggle and no personal security ...'

Pevsner was interned in 1940, and on his release undertook labouring work to make a living. Then, through a chance encounter, he was offered a part-time teaching post at London University's Birkbeck College, where he would later become a professor.

His greatest achievement was his monumental *Buildings of England*, a compilation of over 30,000 buildings most of which he visited personally between 1951 and 1974.[32] His clear, precise English helped a generation of British people look closely at their architectural heritage and a 'Pevsner' became a generic term for an architectural guide to the villages, towns and cities of Britain. His radio talks from 1945 graphically evoked the buildings he was describing. In 1955, invited to give the Reith lectures, he spoke on 'The Englishness of English Art'. He was drawn to the manifestation of 'national character' in art, in which he saw 'polarities' – the tendency of the British to be reflected in the 'practical, down-to-earth, detached, utilitarian and narrative tradition that responded to life as observed' (e.g. the Perpendicular style, the Elizabethan house, the paintings of Constable, the Crystal Palace) as opposed to the sinuous, the misty, the dreamy and visionary (the Decorated style, the paintings of Fuseli, Blake and the later Turner).[33]

Pevsner was, like Ernst Gombrich, a propagator of the history of art, a subject scarcely existing as an academic discipline in Britain before the arrival of the German-Jewish art historians. The first Slade Professor of Fine Art at Cambridge from 1949 until 1955, in 1959 he became Professor in the History of Art at Birkbeck College. A great speaker, he made his subject accessible to a wider public than ever before, opening British eyes to the importance of the built environment and the relationship between architecture, design and daily life. Pevsner helped Britain to look at itself, which he did with diligence, energy and great affection.

Karl Popper

The contribution of émigrés extended into every area of public life, including politics and governance. Karl Popper was one of the most influential philosophers of science of the twentieth century. An opponent of totalitarianism, and an advocate of the 'Open Society', he bridged the gulf between the highly specialized work of scientists and that of philosophers, moulded as he had been by the suffering and impoverishment that accompanied the breakdown of the Austro-Hungarian Empire, which 'destroyed the world in which I had grown up'.

Born in Vienna in 1902, his father was a lawyer with a keen interest in social and political ideas, while his mother's passion for music almost led him to a musical career. Briefly a Marxist at the University of Vienna, he was soon disillusioned by its ideological rigidity. He was also drawn to the theories of Freud and Adler, but it was Einstein's critical spirit which made him reject theories which could not be disconfirmed: Einstein's theory was testable in ways that could have shown it to be false.

Popper was a schoolteacher, but his interest in philosophy drew him into the Wiener Kreis (Vienna Circle);[34] although he criticized the main tenets of logical positivism, which alienated him from the group. He published *Logik der Forschung* (The Logic of Research) in 1935, which he later said undermined the basis of logical positivism; as a result of this, which became widely known, he was invited to lecture in England in 1935.[35]

Popper rejected the 'induction' method of scientific thought. Scientists, it was believed, should observe all available data and then build up a hypothesis which would remain valid until disproved by subsequent evidence. Popper said that, as abstractions, theories can be tested only by their implications. Scientific theory is conjectural, and is built up in response to specific problems that arise in particular context. No matter how many times experimental testings confirm the theory, if its implications can be falsified by a single example, the theory from which these derive must be false.

In 1936, Popper applied for an SPSL grant, although still working as a teacher in Vienna. His relationship with the SPSL offers insights into the organization and the imperfections in the discreet triage practised by those who held his destiny in their hands. Of course, it is easy in retrospect to appreciate the misplaced caution his application received; but the volume of correspondence it engendered, the doubts on his stature as an academic, the anxiety over the category into which he fell, now strike us as at odds with the urgency surrounding the fate of Jews in Vienna in 1936.

Even a reference from Niels Bohr, who knew Popper, did not allay uncertainties: '... his unusual power of tackling general scientific problems with his thorough knowledge of the modern development of the fundamental concepts of physics, justifies the greatest expectations as regards his future scientific and pedagogic activity in this field.'[36] A letter to the Secretary of the AAC on a meeting of the Mind Association and Aristotelian Society about the future of Karl Popper tells how '... about half a dozen people said they would be prepared to contribute to a special fund for one year if he were forced to leave Austria and were destitute: whether they would regard mere destitution as constituting compulsion to leave Austria I do not know ...'

Popper wrote to Professor Duncan Jones, who had invited him to Birmingham. 'Practising my post [as schoolteacher] I am unable to do scientific work at the same time. Besides this, anti-Semitism and Nazism are very common under Nazi schoolteachers and unfortunately especially under those of the school I am working at; and I don't feel myself able any longer to listen day by day to allusions and affronts concerning my Jewish origin equally made by nearly all of my colleagues and – under their influence – even by some pupils. ... Such more or less subjective difficulties must certainly not be compared with the brutal sufferings of Jewish people in Germany or of some of the German refugees (with whom I never wished to get into anything like a competition for support!).'

The SPSL was also preoccupied with its inability to give support to scholars who retained their positions in their own country, and could only help Popper if he resigned. This he did, and a grant at the rate of £150 per annum was made should he leave Austria. He was invited to Cambridge, but went instead to Canterbury University in New Zealand as lecturer in the Faculty of Education and Philosophy. At the end of the war, he returned to England to teach at the London School of Economics and became Professor of Logic and Scientific Method at the University of London in 1949.

Popper's early Marxism, and the Left's inability to halt Nazism (since the Left believed Nazism to be a necessary step in the self-destruction of capitalism and a precursor of the Communist utopia) led directly to his abhorrence of all totalitarian theories. The capacity of theories to explain everything was the source of their greatest weakness, since they defy falsification through empirical investigation. This was the problem with psychoanalysis, while Marxism had been subject to so many amendments to make it fit observable reality that it was not empirically falsifiable.

Such theories could not be called scientific. A theory is scientific only if it can be refuted by some exception. Nothing can be conclusively verifiable, but remains in a state of provisional acceptance until it can be shown to be false.

As with science, so with society: just as scientific theories are abandoned when falsified, so social science should be subject to similar scrutiny. The open society depends upon citizens judging critically the outcome of government actions, which should be modified in the light of such an examination. By elevating the right of individuals to criticize policies, just as falsified scientific theories are discounted, so damaging or harmful policies would be abandoned through critical discussion rather than force. Whatever the failings of such an objective, it avoids 'historicist' assumptions and predictions about social and political development which lead to totalitarianism.

Popper's views favoured liberal democracy, especially when the ruin of Nazism was replaced by the edifice of Soviet Communism; and his work encouraged those – including economists – who valued the aggregate of individual decisions and judgments over predictive systems of planning. He was a friend of his fellow-Austrian Friedrich Hayek, to whom he said he owed more than to any other living person, except Alfred Tarski. Hayek's work had a significant influence upon the economy and politics of the USA and Britain in the 1980s and beyond.

Klaus Fuchs

In the late summer of 1935 a young German woman arrived at Swarthmore College in the United States. She had been sent by her father, a Lutheran pastor in Russelheim, Germany, both to avoid the political disorder that threatened the country and because of a profound psychological instability in the family. Her mother had killed herself by drinking hydrochloric acid, and her sister had thrown herself under a train. Within two years, this young woman had married a young Jewish fellow-student. By 1944 they had three children.

The marriage was disastrously unhappy. Soon after, she had a breakdown and spent eight years in a psychiatric hospital diagnosed as a schizophrenic. Her daughter, now living in London, recalls a childhood in which she failed to bond with her mother. The parents were subsequently divorced. Some years later, this woman, released from hospital, re-married and became a well-known peace activist.

Her life was enlivened by the visits of her brother, who spent holidays with the children in New England. This brother was Klaus Fuchs, then working on the Los Alamos project on the atomic bomb.

The Nazis targeted Klaus Fuchs as a prominent Communist. He was not Jewish. An outstanding physicist and mathematician, the AAC helped him complete his PhD at Bristol in 1937. He then went to Edinburgh University and worked with Max Born. During the 1941 invasion scare, he was interned and sent to Canada with, among others, Max Perutz, who remembered him well. Internees used their time acquiring new skills from each other. 'Theoretical physics was taught to us lucidly by Klaus Fuchs, the tall, austere, aloof son of a German Protestant pastor who had been persecuted by Hitler for being a Social Democrat ... Having no inkling of the tortuous mind that later made Fuchs betray the countries and friends that had given him shelter, I simply benefited from his excellent teaching.'[37]

Following the intervention of the AAC and Max Born, Fuchs returned to Edinburgh, where he was approached by Rudolph Peierls (also a recipient of an AAC grant) to work at Birmingham University on the 'Tube Alloys' venture – the code name for the British-initiated atomic bomb project. He was granted

British citizenship in 1942, a time when he was first known to have had contact with the Soviet authorities. Fuchs and Peierls went to work on the Manhattan Project. From the summer of 1944, Fuchs was employed in the Theoretical Physics Division at Los Alamos under Hans Bethe, focussing on imploding the fissionable core of the plutonium bomb.

Between 1947 and 1949, Fuchs gave the Soviets the *theoretical* outline of the hydrogen bomb, together with information which enabled the USSR to assess how many atomic bombs the US possessed. In 1946, Fuchs returned to England as head of the Theoretical Physics Division of the Atomic Energy Research Establishment at Harwell. In 1949, he was challenged by intelligence officers, who had broken Soviet cyphers. In 1950 he confessed. Sentenced to 14 years imprisonment – the maximum for passing secrets to a friendly nation – he maintained in his defence that as a wartime ally, the USSR should not be excluded from secrets which had led to the allied victory. The value of the information which Fuchs gave the Russians remains unresolved.

Klaus Fuchs' niece is a neighbour of mine in north London. Her father studied at Harvard, and it was with them that Fuchs spent the summer holidays in New England. 'I remember him as a kindly uncle. He used to give us children presents like chemistry sets, which were wonderful, although perhaps in retrospect, a little provocative. The house was always full of people.

'My mother, Klaus's sister was diagnosed as schizophrenic. She was in and out of hospital. He wanted to help her, but at the same time, his involvement with us took advantage of her illness. They were a strange family. There was also something distinctly schizoid about his double life.

'I think he confessed to save himself from being deported to the US, where he risked the death penalty. He caused great problems for our family. My father could not find work. He had three children and a sick wife. It was devastating.

'I also remember at the time wondering how the Nazis, who had been our enemies, were suddenly replaced by the Communists. My uncle considered the Soviets our allies, which of course they were. I think he justified his actions on this basis. His motivations were entirely sincere.

'His years of imprisonment were served in Wormwood Scrubs. After ten years, he was released and went to East Germany. There he was able to work, and he died in Dresden in 1988. Of course, his case was followed by that of the Rosenbergs, who were executed, and the subsequent McCarthyite witch-hunts. This political atmosphere eliminated a whole generation of intellectuals like my father.

'In retrospect, this may be one of the reasons why I left the US and settled permanently in Britain. My mother is still alive. She is in a nursing home and is seriously infirm now.' Klaus Fuchs' niece says that whatever the public view of her uncle, he left her with an abiding feeling of affection and kindness.

Otto Frisch also wrote generously about Fuchs. 'I still believe that Fuchs acted entirely out of sincere motives. He was the son of a German clergyman and brought up to act according to his conscience. He felt that Communism was the nearest approach to Christianity to be found in today's world ...'[38]

The current panic over the loyalties of Islamic extremists in Britain has antecedents in the commitment of Communists to the former Soviet Union, the only difference being that Moscow was at least an identifiable place on earth. Lives articulated to eternity are even more difficult to control than those manipulated from the capital of the USSR.

The Warburg Institute and Ernst Gombrich

Not only individuals were rescued at the prompting of AAC; whole institutions were transferred when Nazism imperilled their existence. The Warburg Institute was founded by Aby Warburg, of the banking family, who was prepared to renounce all claims to the family business in favour of his younger brother, provided he could buy all the books he wanted. Preoccupied with the influence of antiquity upon the present, he built up his personal library based upon '*das Nachleben der Antike*' (the abiding influence of the classical tradition). The library, not limited to art history, covered philosophical, religious, cultural, administrative and literary aspects of antiquity, in an innovative, cross-disciplinary approach.[39] Aided by his colleague Fritz Saxl, the collection was established in a scholarly institute the Kulturwissenschaftliche Bibliothek Wearbur, affiliated to the University of Hamburg.

The Warburg Institute's 'escape' from the Nazis depended upon the ingenuity and foresight of Saxl, when in 1933 it ceased to function as a department of Hamburg University, and the staff were prevented from teaching. The staff agreed that both collection and personnel should be shifted to a place of safety, where research and learning might continue. The Nazi book-burnings provided an incentive to would-be rescuers. Interest from the USA, Netherlands and Italy was not followed through; but in July 1933, alerted by the AAC, a committee was formed in London. Support for its establishment in the capital was promised by Samuel Courtauld and the Warburg family. To prevent obstruction by the Nazis, this was presented as a temporary loan of the Institute's resources.

Astonishingly, the Nazis, appeased by a gift of some 2,000 volumes relating to the First World War, permitted the move, provided there was no publicity. In December 1933, two steamers were loaded with over 500 boxes containing 60,000 books, slides, photographs and furniture.

Samuel Courtauld extended support for a further seven years, and the collection was housed by Imperial College in South Kensington before being formally handed over to London University in 1944. The contribution this resource has made to the development of the study of art history in Britain cannot be overstated, particularly under the directorship of Sir Ernst Gombrich from 1959 to 1976. His vision altered the way art was perceived here, where he found, according to Daniel Snowman, 'too much preoccupation with detail … [and] the provenance and value of paintings. His approach was to ask broader philosophical questions, to encourage a wider discourse than can possibly be available to mere connoisseurship.'[40]

Ernst Gombrich was born in Vienna, the son of a lawyer and an accomplished pianist. Although his parents were Jewish, religion was not central to the family's life. He studied art and archaeology at the University of Vienna from 1928 to1935, where he also joined the Wiener Kreis.

Gombrich married Ilse Heller, one of his mother's pupils and settled in England in 1936. His son, Richard, born in England, remembers his parents' complex relationship, both with the past and with this country.

'My father spent some time in England in 1935. He returned to Austria to marry my mother, and they came back to London in 1936. My father was unpolitical, in the narrow sense, but he was under no illusion about the Nazis coming to power. Neither of my parents was brought up to be Jewish.

'He was a mixture of the innovative and inventive professionally, but conservative in personal habits and tastes. He insisted on wearing a waistcoat till late in life, and he wore a tie every day until he became incapable of tying it properly.

'They did find London depressing in the beginning. They had digs in Edgware Road. My mother told me the first time they went to Kenwood in Hampstead, what bliss is was to see that London had such beautiful places. She always said London smelled of mutton-fat.

'He was research assistant at the Warburg from 1936, assembling the papers of its founder, Aby Warburg. The director, Fritz Saxl, was to have written the biography, but he died and my father assumed the task.

'He used to tell how there was a crisis over where the books of the Warburg should go. The chief official of the Treasury would decide whether the funds could be found to accommodate them. This man was interested in neo-Latin poetry, so my father wrote him a poem in neo-Latin, requesting that he help find a place for them. It worked.

'He was employed between 1939 and 1945 at the BBC Monitoring Service. He was the first person in Britain to know Hitler was dead. He was monitoring the German broadcasts, and guessed that something dramatic was about to happen. He wrote down three or four probabilities, including that Hitler had died or surrendered. "Just watch," he said. Then the German radio played a movement from a symphony by Bruckner, which had been composed on the death of Richard Wagner, so he knew this presaged an announcement that Hitler was dead: "In the mighty struggle against Bolshevism, our great leader has fallen."

My father pointed with his pencil to "Hitler dead". The news was immediately relayed to Churchill.

'After the War, he went back to London. He thought war work important, but for him, academic and intellectual work was its own reward. His father was a lawyer, his uncle a doctor and he chose learning. In [such] households, Goethe was God, Lessing and Schiller were revered; the confluence of middle-class Jews and the Enlightenment marked the period of their highest attainment.

'He was a traditionalist, and of course the Warburg Institute was set up for the study of the classical tradition on our culture, including art. He was untroubled by the avant-garde in art. He kept to tradition in art as in music. That was his other abiding passion.

'He was interested in particular in the way artists learned from their predecessors, and his interest in the psychology of perception made his work uniquely innovative. He read enormously on the subject. There was J.J. Gibson, at Cornell, who said visual perception did not require inference or information processing, and Richard Gregory, Emeritus Professor of Neuropsychology at Bristol, who stated that perception is a predictive hypothesis based on knowledge stored from the past.

'When he came here, people in Britain had little interest in the history of painting or sculpture. They had more familiarity with the history of architecture. Some British experts were good at attributions, but he was not interested in that, let alone valuations. When he died, people expected him to have left a fine collection of paintings. They were disappointed. He always said it was better that paintings should be in public places where everyone could see them. He had no desire to own them. The pictures in his drawing-room were mostly only copies.

'He was an extremely close friend of Karl Popper. My father was not (politically) a Conservative and Popper was. We often went to their home. Popper was interested only in intellectual matters. He liked to talk, and he listened also, but he was unworldly. My parents were much more in tune with British society, partly through me, because of my school and growing up here. Popper never had that attachment to British society. Of course, he knew about all the important issues in world politics, but he felt he didn't require to know anything about day-to-day matters.

'It is easy to describe my father. He was a strong egalitarian, yet he measured people by their intelligence. He despised stupidity, but if the charlady said something intelligent, he would praise her and seek out her company. He also appreciated kindness. He had absolutely no interest in money whatsoever.

'My father's values were not political, but he was a liberal humanist. They never voted Conservative, although they were great admirers of Churchill as politician and leader. He was not ambitious, but some of his achievements delighted him.

He was made an honorary citizen of Mantua, since his dissertation had been on the architecture of the sixteenth-century artist, Giulio Romano. The mayor of Mantua came to the meeting held to commemorate him.'

Other institutions

The Warburg Institute was not the only institution that was transferred to Britain to evade the Nazis. The Wiener Library, set up by George Wiener in 1933 to inform the world of the persecution of the Jews, subsequently became one of the world's leading research institutions into the Holocaust and its aftermath. If publicity surrounding this collection was limited, this is because it was accurately monitoring the situation of European Jewry when it seemed 'floods' of refugees would be provoked by official recognition of their plight. Furthermore, the British government distrusted accounts of Jewish suffering published by Jews. The Wiener Library transferred to London in 1939 and has more recently become a major centre for the study of racism.

Another establishment was the progressive school of Anna Essinger, which she removed from Ulm to Britain with the help of the Quakers in 1933, 'when the Nazis had insisted that she should fly their flag from the building', according to Leslie Brent, a pupil at the school from 1939 to 1942. He arrived on the Kindertransport from Berlin in December 1938, and went to Dovercourt Camp near Harwich. 'The educational side of the camp was in the hands of Anna Essinger, whose school in Ulm was a co-educational progressive establishment with many Jewish pupils. Teachers saw themselves as friends and companions of the pupils.'

Many of the pupils and the staff came with her to Bunce Court in Kent, a beautiful, originally sixteenth-century building. Although initially the authorities were unimpressed by its untidy organization, she achieved in Britain what she had intended to do in Germany – to establish a school with 'advanced' values for those wanting neither state education nor the expensive conservatism of private provision. A Schools Inspectors Report in 1935 gave the school a glowing testimonial.

'Anna Essinger took 50 or 60 children from Dovercourt Camp, doubling the size of the school. I was befriended by one of the boys who had come to Dovercourt to help her manage the education of the refugee children.

'One day, I ran into this corpulent lady in the doorway. She said, "Who are you?"

'I told her, "Lothar Baruch" – a name that self-evidently expressed the mixture of Germanness and Jewishness of the family I came from.

'She said, "Would you like to come to my school?"

'It was deepest winter when we arrived at the North Downs. I was happy there as I could have been anywhere under the circumstances. Some children were not. I had already been through separation from my parents, when they took me out of school in the small town of Koslin in Pomerania because I was being beaten and tormented as the only Jew in the school, and placed in an orphanage in Berlin. Bunce Court seemed like heaven. It gave a good education, although there was little science, no chemistry and physics. There were biology, maths and English. It is surprising how many pupils later went into medicine or science. Before I was there from December 1938 until 1942, and it was a major formative influence.'

During the invasion scare the school moved to Shropshire, but returned in 1945. It closed in 1948, but its purpose had been fulfilled.

The industrialists

According to Austin Stevens, one-third of male refugees from Austria and Germany in the 1930s had been manufacturers, a category welcomed as early as 1935.[41] The government hoped they could address the intractably high levels of unemployment by investing their capital in depressed areas, particularly in the North East, West Cumberland, South West Scotland and South Wales. Assuming they could get their financial assets out of Germany, they would certainly fulfil the criterion, laid down in 1933, that no refugee should become a burden on the public purse.

Although the government lacked the powers of compulsion, after May 1937 applicants were given to understand that their application would be processed faster if they set up business in one of the Special Areas of extremely high unemployment. The main obstacle was the Reich itself: the Nazi authorities actively prevented the movement of significant funds, taking draconian measures against those who sought to evade the prohibition. Of those who set up manufacturing companies in Britain, many depended upon capital from friends or relatives, within Britain or elsewhere.

The government subsidized factories for light industry in the decaying cotton or mining areas. Of the 300 manufacturing companies established by refugees by February 1939, two-thirds were in depressed areas. The range of products was innovative, far from the declining industrial staples; it included boilers and radiators, adhesives, brushes, car accessories, chemicals, electronic controls, plastics goods, pumps, scientific instruments, spectacle frames, sports wear and toys. In 1974, Herbert Loebl estimates that surviving refugee firms employed more than 10,000 people in the North East and over 6,000 in Cumbria.[42]

The advantage to Britain of such companies suggests that the fears expressed that refugees might 'take away' jobs from people here were unfounded. Refugees could be net providers of labour.

The economists and Adolphe Lowe

Not all the well-known academic refugees came to Britain with the help of the AAC/SPSL, although the organization's existence alerted the country, and especially the educated classes, to the usefulness of admitting refugees, which was also the right thing to do. The AAC's tone was high-minded and virtuous, and the good relations it maintained with government made its influence greater than if it had opposed official policy.

Those who brought knowledge that transcended national or cultural borders had a distinct advantage over those who specialized in culture-specific disciplines. It was not easy to place lawyers, likewise historians expert in the history of central Europe.

Economic benefit to Britain is one thing, economists another. Of the 300 economists who left Germany and Austria, two-thirds finally reached the United States; but more than 50 remained in Britain. Others stayed long enough to exercise a significant influence on the issues arising from their studies.

Adolphe Lowe was already 40 when the Nazis came to power. Born in Stuttgart, he had studied in Berlin and Tübingen. He was a senior official in the Labour Ministry of the Weimar Republic, and subsequently Head of the International Division of the German Federal Statistical Bureau. In 1926, he became director of research at the University of Kiel's Institute of World Economics. His particular field was international trade cycles and international statistical economics.

In 1933, Lowe fled to Switzerland and thence to Britain, where, helped by the AAC, he researched at Manchester, and taught at LSE. He also advised the AAC on eminent German economists. Naturalized at the outbreak of war, he thereby avoided internment. In *Economics and Sociology* (1935) he argued for an interdisciplinary study of economic and social analysis, seeking to embed the former in the wider context of the social sciences and away from the realm of 'pure' economic theory, rejecting the existence of 'universal' economic laws.[43] Questioning whether economic man represented an adequate depiction of a universal human nature, he stressed the importance of socioeconomic and technological factors in shaping and determining expectations at any particular time and place. He distinguishes between early market society, dominated by small independent producers, and modern capitalism, whose capital-intensive methods and changing technologies lead to social and institutional transformations. His arguments in favour of interdisciplinary social science prefigure much later developments, including disciplines such as ecological economics and cultural studies.[44]

He was also preoccupied with the conflict between freedom and order, and in his 1937 pamphlet, *The Price of Liberty*, reflected on the British model of social conformity, which allied political freedom to personal self-restraint, as against

Germany, where individual self-realization depended on the external constraint of political autocracy.[45]

Adolphe Lowe left Britain in 1940 to become Director of the Institute of World Affairs at the New School for Social Research in New York. This 'University in Exile', much as conceived by Leo Szilard, was a graduate division of the NSSR, funded by the Rockefeller Foundation. Although its name was changed at the end of the war, its work continues to be liberal and internationalist. Among its teachers and students are political philosophers, Hannah Arendt and Leo Strauss, anthropologists Claude Levi-Strauss and Ruth Benedict, economist Thorstein Veblen, and Lewis Mumford, author of the *The City in History*.

Victims of prejudice – the medical refugees

Individuals varied in the degree to which they identified with Britain. Some never recovered fully from the cultural shock of rejection by Germany; but a majority, clearly focussed on their academic projects, and supported by the consolations of private and family life, were protected against some of the acerbities of British social life – class distinctions, snobbery or indeed, anti-Semitism.

Perhaps the most significant group of professional people denied the fullest expression of their powers were medical academics, researchers and teachers. Paul Weindling has documented the histories of around 5,200 people displaced from their countries of origin between 1930 and 1945, and charted professional resistance in Britain to the employment of medically qualified personnel. He says it is important to recognize that many lost their way, underwent hardship and poverty, fell sick or even, in some cases, committed suicide, although the overall balance is positive.

Home Office policy was permissive towards German-Jewish immigrants, provided they did not need work and had independent means. Since refugees had to leave everything behind, their portable skills and accomplishments were their only resource. The College of Physicians was particularly resistant to offering them work. Lord Dawson urged the Home Secretary in 1933 to limit the numbers, declaring, with a typically imperial parochialism, that 'The number [of foreign medical scientists] who could teach us anything could be counted on the fingers of one hand.'

Thus the true voice of British insularity: we have 'the best of everything', foreigners could teach us nothing – even against evidence to the contrary. The General Medical Council attitude was highly restrictive: Jewish practitioners with relatives in Britain might 'settle down in a practice in a Jewish district', or perhaps seek a career in the Colonies or Dominions or even Japan.[46] Home Office policy, not for the first time, was to reject the majority of doctors and dentists, while extending sympathetic consideration to 'leading persons' in the field.

Many went to medical research centres considered marginal by the British medical establishment, while a number of Jewish medical scientists moved into 'new' fields of expertise – psychoanalysis, and research in areas where biochemistry, physiology and pharmacology meet. In disciplines such as paediatrics and dentistry, Britain lagged behind its German and Austrian counterparts. Yet the professional medical elite opposed refugees, just as they opposed women practitioners in the 1920s and resisted the introduction of the National Health Service in 1948.

As in many other areas, the story tells of missed opportunities; for instance, in public and occupational health, research into industrial hazards and other ills that later needed attention in Britain. Paul Weindling notes that certain anti-Semitic GPs in the Medical Practitioners Union opposed the socialization of medicine as a Jewish conspiracy! A number with public health expertise moved on to the USA.

Many permitted to remain did so on the understanding that their sojourn here would be temporary. They assumed that they would soon re-emigrate, which some did. This led to Britain being regarded as a sort of superior employment exchange for emigrants en route to a more spacious – both professionally and physically – elsewhere. That meant mainly the United States; but others went to South America, Australia and Canada, not always voluntarily, as the events of spring 1940 showed.

The ability of the British authorities to single out those likely to achieve greatness in medicine – or who had already achieved it – was vindicated in the Nobel Prizes in medicine awarded to Ernst Chain in 1945, Hans Krebs in 1953 and Bernhard Katz in 1970. William Beveridge, surveying the impact of the SPSL in 1958, found that of 61 doctors who had sought to settle in Britain, 11 had gone on to posts abroad, 31 successfully followed their career in Britain and 19, unable to research, occupied a post more marginal than that they had previously enjoyed. A further 41 had been assisted to move overseas.[47]

Even though medical refugees had a more difficult time than their peers in other disciplines, the contribution of medical exiles to British health care is remarkable, including that made in less prominent fields such as psychogeriatrics, internal medicine and the modernization of medical education. Paul Weindling's assessment is that the refugees gave medicine a dynamism that changed its course, despite the setbacks of internment and a conservative medical establishment. There had been many radical providers of health care in health centres and polyclinics in Germany in the 1920s. In Vienna also, Professor Julius Tandler had been a pioneer in social medicine, running the Department of Social Welfare in Vienna, with birth control clinics and housing schemes associated with 'Red Vienna'. But when the Nazis turned on the Jews, 'German Jewish physicians were reduced from treaters of the sick to the treatment solely of Jews. Then university degrees were cancelled, on an individual basis, a process normally reserved for criminals. There was a terrible vindictiveness in this – if the Nazis couldn't strip people of their nationality because they had already left, they could rob them of their professional identity.' Degrees cancelled by the Nazis were revalidated in Britain. Interestingly, after the war, the degrees were never re-instated by Germany.

Paul Weindling had good reason to take an interest in the work of academic rescue and of medical history. His mother was on the Kindertransport, and was taken into the home of the physiologist A.V. Hill. 'It was January 1939, and she was at the upper limit of the age for the Kindertransport. She went to A.V. Hill, who, with Meyerhof, had won the Nobel Prize in 1922 for work on muscle physiology. A.V. Hill was a prime mover in the SPSL. My mother had already been in prison. She tried to escape to Rumania where she was detained, because the Rumanians no longer admitted their Jewish citizens from abroad. The family were of Rumanian background, and they spoke French at home. A.V. Hill's wife, Margaret, was the sister of John Maynard Keynes, and so my mother was thrust into a high-octane academic environment, quite unlike anything she had ever experienced. Her father was a commercial property investor, not at all academic. [Hill] was shocked when she told him how Jews had been made to get on their hands and knees and scrub the city pavements. He took her with him to Royal Society *conversazioni*, and he took her to meet Keynes.

'She had been thrown out of school in Vienna, so had to make a new start here. She went to Regent Street Polytechnic where she matriculated. Hill told her she could use his library. The family offered her genuine warmth and hospitality. She was expected to help around the house – nothing very arduous, make tea in the morning and so on. Mrs Hill tried to involve my mother in her schemes. She wanted her to go into children's nursing. She took her to child welfare clinics, where she was astonished to find children who had newspaper stuffed down their trousers because they couldn't afford underwear.'

She did not enter the nursing profession, although many women refugees did, since the biggest single category of migrants to Britain in the 1930s was women who came as domestic servants (see below). One of the most proficient figures in nursing was Annie Altschul, whose father died in a railway accident when she was five. She studied mathematics in Vienna, but fled Austria in 1938, and was admitted to Britain under the quota for domestic servants, working as a nanny with a well-to-do London family. According to her obituarist she 'was not struck by the hospitality of the British people'.[48] When the war started, she trained as a nurse and midwife, imagining that her exile would be brief. She gained experience of psychiatric nursing at Mill Hill Hospital, to where Maudsley Hospital had been evacuated. She stayed at the Maudsley until 1964, when she joined the Department of Nursing Studies in Edinburgh, becoming Professor of Nursing in 1976.

Annie Altschul was a pioneer of psychiatric nursing, both theoretical and practical. She brought innovative and irreverent practice to a profession which was highly conservative and regimented, valuing training above insight and understanding. She believed that people in emotional and mental distress needed more direct help than treatment according to theorists, and sought to comprehend rather than explain psychiatric illness. She later acknowledged her own kinship with the marginal and excluded, not only because of her exiled status but also because of her own experience of depression in the early 1980s, as a result of which she told her story in *Wounded Healers*, acknowledging the existence of the injured healer before this became as acceptable as it would later be.[49] She was an advocate of euthanasia, and her forceful and combative encounters with psychiatric nursing were profound and transforming.

Given the hostility of the British medical establishment towards their refugee colleagues, it is surprising that so many had such an impact on medicine here; or perhaps it is *because of* the sometimes abrasive environment in which they worked that they excelled. In any case, doctors are no different from any other social group, and where émigrés actually worked, they did so with British colleagues in a spirit of amity and cooperation. There is nothing like professional and personal contact for dispelling prejudice, as the achievements of Ludwig Guttmann show.

Ludwig Guttmann

Ludwig Guttmann is best known as director of Stoke Mandeville Hospital, which dramatically improved the treatment of paraplegics. Guttmann trained as a doctor in Breslau, where he specialized in neuro-surgery. When the Nazis came to power, Guttmann, like other Jewish doctors, was forbidden to treat 'Aryans', so he moved to the city's Jewish hospital, ultimately becoming medical director.

Guttmann worked on through the early years of Nazism, but with Kristallnacht in November 1938, the limit was reached. He insisted that all injured persons should be admitted. When the SS came to the hospital, and asked him to explain the medical condition of the 64 patients he had taken into the hospital that night, he persuaded the Nazi officers that all were suffering from conditions that pre-dated it. Four gave themselves away, but Gutmann saved the other sixty.

Jewish hospitals were permitted to continue working; and some Jewish doctors were even allowed to return from internment camps. Guttmann's passport had been impounded, but he went abroad twice to perform operations, the second time at the request of Dr Salazar, the Portuguese dictator. From there, he came to Britain, contacted the SPSL and secured a grant to work in Oxford. He then returned to Breslau to collect his wife and children.

For some time, Guttmann worked on nerve injuries, but was forbidden to practise neuro-surgery. His opportunity came when he was appointed Director of the Spinal Injury Unit in Stoke Mandeville, where he could deploy his skills without interference. Paraplegic numbers had increased as a consequence of war injuries. Guttmann overturned the conventional view that paraplegics were beyond help; and within two years had laid down the basic principles for the management of paraplegia, principles still observed today. He believed in immediate intervention, since most paraplegics died as a result of pressure sores or urinary infections and insisted on turning patients frequently to prevent the onset of sores.

He was also a passionate advocate of team work in the treatment of paraplegics – doctors, nurses, physiotherapists and occupational therapists. He initiated programmes of disciplined activity, to create a sense of both mobility and usefulness in his patients, and organized sports, and 'wheelchair polo'. The international paraplegic games, which he started in 1952, became the Paralympics for the first time at the Olympic Games in Rome in 1960.

Guttmann, dynamic, inventive and energetic, *inspired* people to recover; and his work has been influential internationally. Medawar and Pyke quote examples of some of his successes: paraplegics who could work and study. 'Woodwork and instrument-making in the hospital workshop were just the beginning. Some patients worked in a factory in Aylesbury, showing that it was possible to do a full day's labour. This led to the creation of government industrial rehabilitation centres. One army officer passed his law exam within a year of arriving at Stoke Mandeville. A jockey, who on arrival refused all treatment and simply wanted to die, took a correspondence course and qualified as an accountant.'[50]

Britain as a clearing-house

Although willing to take credit for humanitarian gestures towards some already eminent Jews, the British authorities made little effort to retain many capable people, most of whom went to the USA. The reasons were complex. The loosened criteria in the two years immediately preceding the war had depended upon the perceived temporary nature of the refugees' sojourn – Britain as clearing-house rather than destination, possibly a political concession to xenophobia, Germanophobia and anti-Semitism. Secondly, there was a degree of ignorance in officialdom about the intellectual treasures offered by people from abroad. Passing on the embarrassment at the presence of foreigners seemed logical and prudent in a country which was, in spite of earlier waves of Jewish migrants, overwhelmingly monocultural, even though its rigid class stratification astonished visitors.

Perhaps the most significant scientific departure westwards was of the researchers involved in the atomic bomb. Rudolph Peierls, offered a Rockefeller scholarship in 1932, went first to Rome to work with Enrico Fermi, who created the first chain reaction in 1942. Peierls subsequently moved to Britain, where he received help and advice from the SPSL. He later expressed thanks for the assistance he had received as an 'out-patient.' He also enlisted the support of Esther Simpson in bringing his father to Britain in 1938. He emphasized the urgency of this, 'particularly since the conditions for emigration seem to become harder and harder as time goes on'.

In 1936, he became Professor of Physics in Birmingham. There, he met with Otto Frisch in March 1940. Frisch had recently visited his aunt, the physicist Lise Meitner, in Sweden. They had discussed the work at the Kaiser Wilhelm Institute in 1938 of two physicists who had bombarded uranium with neutrons, which had split and produced further neutrons. Frisch informed Niels Bohr in Copenhagen of this discovery of atomic fission. It was assumed that the volume of material required to create a chain reaction for a bomb would be excessive.

Peierls and Frisch judged that the quantity of the uranium isotope 235 required to be separated from a mass of U238 would be only about 1 pound. They immediately foresaw the possibility of the bomb. Later, Otto Frisch admitted later they were 'frightened' by the realization. Peierls contacted the British government's chief scientific adviser, Frederick Lindemann, who spoke to Churchill. Churchill gave permission to start the project in August 1940, although the decision to construct an actual bomb was taken a year later. A plant to separate uranium was to be built in Mold, North Wales, but by that time the resources available in Britain and the need for secrecy and remoteness suggested that the large-scale development of the project should proceed in the USA. In 1943 Roosevelt and Churchill agreed to establish full cooperation in the USA-based enterprise, and the British efforts were subsumed in the Manhattan Project.

Although a considerable number of scientists from Nazi-occupied Europe remained in Britain, Medawar and Pyke say that in general, 'Britain rescued the refuge scientists and the United States received them'.[51] Otto Loewi, the Austrian physiologist, spent time in London and Oxford (as well as Brussels, until the Nazis invaded Belgium) before going to the USA; Hans Bethe, later awarded the Nobel Prize for his work on the sources of energy in the sun and the stars, spent an academic year in both Manchester and Bristol before leaving for Cornell; Edward Teller, to whom was ascribed the paternity of the H-bomb, was at University College, London, before Princeton. Sir Francis Simon also collaborated with Peierls and Frisch. He had been professor of Physical Chemistry in Breslau until 1933. When officials demanded he and his wife hand over their passports, he also returned the Iron Cross the Kaiser had awarded him after the First World War. Later, he would work at the Clarendon Laboratory in Oxford. Ironically, wartime prevented him and Peierls from working on the most top-secret research project – radar. Instead they applied their energies to the potential development of an atomic bomb.

This was the time that Leo Szilard and Edward Teller persuaded Einstein to write his famous letter to Roosevelt urging that work on an atomic bomb be urgently undertaken, for fear that Germany might do so first. Ever since 1939, when the possibility of atomic fission had become known to physicists worldwide, the refugee scientists foresaw the danger that the Nazis might create the weapon that would become decisive in determining the outcome of the war.

The transfer of atom bomb research to the USA is a metaphor for Britain's role in the pre-war refugee crisis: an enabling agent for the departure of the cream of German intellectuals to other shores. How should we interpret the eagerness of the British government to ensure that as many as possible of those seeking refuge should move on? Did a desire for freedom from foreign encumbrances override the consideration that the most extraordinary people of their generation might be slipping through the fingers of a myopic authority? Or was it that Britain lacked the resources and intellectual amplitude to accommodate the often restless psyche of those who in the first instance wound up here? Like so much else in the story, the answers are elusive.

It was a historic irony that Gustav Born, son of Max Born, who refused to work on the bomb, went to Hiroshima as one of two British pathologists in 1945. 'I was in Bombay, when the bomb was dropped on August 6th. The war ended about a week later. As a Royal Medical Corps captain, I was getting ready to take part in the invasion. After the bomb was dropped, it became an army of occupation under General Slim.

'We arrived late in the year. I don't quite know where we landed, because all the ports were destroyed. We convoyed to a place called Hiro, up the coast of the inland sea, about 5 miles from Hiroshima. All the Japanese towns had been destroyed, mostly wooden buildings. The hospital was intact, and that became the base for the British army. We started a laboratory with equipment we had brought for the diagnosis of malaria, syphilis, blood counts and so on. The army imposed strict conditions on fraternization and leave. The area, about 2 miles from the site of the explosion, was heavily contaminated.

'In the rubble people stood at the roadside, desperate, thin and starving, and very quiet. Thousands were still dying from the effects of radiation. This sight was one of the seminal influences that led to my later work on blood platelets. There was nothing we could do, because the cells in the bone marrow that form platelets had been destroyed. It was a vision you could never forget ... I remember the inland sea as a beautiful stretch of water. On the other shore at Mayajama is a famous Shinto peace shrine, the gates to which stand in the water. I was struck by the contrast between Hiroshima and this shrine – the thousands of people dying three or four months after the bomb, with no food and no medicine.

'I have to say, the British army was at its best. They shared their rations with the Japanese people. They came to the hospital and we did what we could. To the best of my knowledge, there was no epidemic at this time.

'I thought of my father's colleagues. They all admired him for his character as well as his intellect. They understood why he would not work on the bomb.

In Hiroshima, I was kept very busy as a clinical pathologist. I remember being tired all the time. What happened was on my mind constantly, and the shadow of it has not lifted to this day.'

National insecurities reflected in the AAC

Even the organization set up to help the threatened scholars was not exempt from the prejudices of the age. The same economic forces which had devastated Germany also created more poverty and unemployment in Britain. An anonymous AAC spokesman recognized the limits of what was possible in appealing for help for refugees. In an interview with the *Manchester Guardian* he stated that 'constructive relief ... is not an isolated refugee problem – it is intimately linked with the problem of the existing unemployed and with that of the ever-expanding intellectual proletariat. The task calls for the greatest constructive statesmanship; it demands national response and international initiative. It can be attempted only in a spirit removed from bitterness or political hostility; it need pass no judgment on the events from which the refugee problem originated ...'[52] This was very early in the Nazi regime; but ignoring the historical origins of Nazism and their implications soon became a moral and practical impossibility.

At that moment British universities were subject to funding pressures, with some departments facing the need to reduce numbers. Planning amidst instability and declining income led to a growing sense of insecurity. When the AAC asked universities to consider accommodating displaced scholars, some refused point-blank; others even implied an absence of sympathy with dispossessed German academics. Sheffield University pleaded poverty, and hinted at its own anti-Semitism. 'The opinion has ... been strongly expressed that, as there are many rich men of the Jewish religion whose individual incomes are larger than the whole income of the University, it would be appropriate that they be asked to support the teachers in the first instance.' They did, of course; as did the great majority of universities. Even those which offered no money freely provided facilities for the dismissed scholars.

David Zimmerman believes that historians have overlooked the role of the SPSL in politicizing the British scientific community.[53] Early on in Hitler's regime, AAC members were careful not to inflame the Berlin authorities. In the AAC's original appeal in May 1933, the authors said their 'action implies no unfriendly feelings to the people of any country; it implies no judgement on forms of government or any political issue between countries'.[54] Beveridge was at pains to state that the crisis was not solely a Jewish issue, since many academics hostile to the Nazi cause had resigned in sympathy with their Jewish colleagues as soon as the first dismissals took place. To win over the Royal Society, Beveridge said the AAC was 'overwhelmingly non-Jewish', and that it should be possible to nominate Professor Charles Singer – a medical historian – to the executive.

The Royal Society thought otherwise; and its support was won only when it was agreed to drop the idea. Whether this was because the AAC had received a number of hate letters in response to its first appeal for funds remains unclear. The Charter of the Royal Society specifically stated that its members should abstain from participating in politics. The AAC's remit was to assist those unjustly dismissed, not to take a political stand against the injustice itself.

The idea that science should be above politics influenced the early years – a position which became increasingly untenable over time. It was, perhaps, still expected that Nazism was a passing *coup de folie*. But when this was clearly not the case, the AAC/SPSL tone changed detectably.

The agency's non-political basis certainly helped recruit support from all political quarters. Frederick Lindemann (later Lord Cherwell), head of Oxford's Clarendon Laboratory, expressed anti-Jewish views, but nevertheless recruited Jewish scholars from Germany. Not for the first time, humane actions proved stronger than professed ideology. People are not the sum of their views; much more may be learned from what they do. A 'low profile' does not always indicate pusillanimity; it may achieve more than those who profess their ideals too loudly.

By the beginning of August 1933, the AAC had raised almost £10,000, much of it from British academics. Exactly who gave is significant: the City for example proved reluctant to open its tightly-drawn purse-strings. The chairman of Barclays Bank declared it could not devote its funds to this cause. The Carnegie and Rockefeller Foundations offered support, but ICI was the only large-scale corporate donor. This facilitated Lindemann's search for talent he could entice to the Clarendon.

By 1935, with the promulgation of the Nuremberg Laws (far more stringent in their prohibitions on Jews), political restraint on the rhetoric was relaxed. The government had agreed that the AAC should find places for refugee academics who could be deployed in British universities, provided this involved no charge to the taxpayer. (A refrain that echoes down the years: on almost no other issue is such tenderness shown over 'taxpayers' money' as the assistance given foreigners, migrants or other 'non-patrials'.)

That October, Beveridge adopted a different tone, speaking of the Nazis as 'a relentless persecution for which it would be hard to find parallel. Shadows of brutality and ignorance [are] returning from the past. The shadow lies not on Germany alone, but across the world. But the shadow looks deepest in Germany today, because in Germany before there was most light. The German people have been one of the great civilizing forces in the world – liberators of the spirit of humanity, liberators from ignorance and fear.'

The SPSL in 1935 expressed a feeling that has run through the decades until today: namely, how to reach out to a wider public than the liberal middle class and the politically active, already aware of the significance of what was happening in Germany. The question was – and remains – how to reach (to use a fateful term bequeathed to the language by the fugitive scientists themselves) a 'critical mass' of people, thereby raising both the profile and the issue to the status of a major campaign.

Zimmerman concludes that the AAC/SPSL was a major force in unifying British scholars in defence of academic freedom in general and of their threatened German colleagues in particular; and as such, deserves recognition for both its leadership and commitment.

In 1936, Lord Rutherford sent out a request for funds to the press and prominent individuals. He said the Academic Assistance Council had hoped its work might be required 'only for a temporary period, but is now convinced that there is a need for a permanent body to assist scholars who are victims of political and religious persecutions. The devastation of the German Universities still continues; not only University teachers of Jewish descent but many others who are regarded as "politically unreliable" are being prevented from making their contribution to the common cause of scholarship.

'The Council has decided to establish as its permanent successor a Society for the protection of Science and learning which will continue the Council's various forms of assistance to scholars of any country who on grounds of religion, race or opinion are unable to carry on the scientific work for which they are qualified.'

This generated significant donations, but also kindled the anger of those not in sympathy with the AAC's aims. 'Dear Lord Rutherford,' wrote one, 'I received a communication from you enclosing an appeal signed by various leading men (who ought to have known better) appealing to augment the £28,000 already being spent on finding jobs for exiles who seem to have been unworthy of their own country in the academic world of this country.

'I could have contemplated with equanimity the spending of £28,000 to keep them out, but I conceive it an act of treachery to spend a penny to bring them to deprive our countrymen of posts in an over-crowded profession.

'I must add that for members of the House of Lords, who should act as protectors of the people and guardians of tradition, to support this appeal for international iconoclasts in the name of science is debasing the peerage.'

Another said: 'May I ask you and those responsible what the feelings must be of the men burdened with the grave risk of ruling the new Germany (sic), when they see the direct insult embodied in such a phrase as "who find themselves in exile through no fault of their own?" Herr Hitler … considers that in the interests of the security of the country he has been called upon to govern, those persons who you call "exiled scholars" are undesirable citizens of that country … What right have we to publicly insult not alone the leader of the German people, but the people themselves, by appealing for funds for the purposes of assisting those who in these circumstances have been found by their own countrymen to be undesirable and unworthy of citizenship.'[55]

The pain of exile

Much is known of the high attainments of successful refugees of the 1930s. It may well be that the decline of anti-Semitism in Britain in recent decades owes a great deal to the benefits they have brought – in medicine, scientific and industrial innovation, the arts, humanities and psychology.

Their work has, at times, taken on an almost redemptive quality. The energy of their intellectual effort may have served to dull the pain of exile. This is rarely dwelt on in the heroic rescue stories. The emotional costs sometimes remain unspoken. On the other hand, the joyful absorption of scientists in their work is clear from the accounts they have left – Otto Frisch's delight in physics which emerges from his enthusiastic memoir must have proved a powerful distraction from separation and loss.

Occasionally we glimpse something of the disturbance that went with the famous 'portable' skills of those who arrived with their inner resources intact, but their feelings bruised by rejection by what they had regarded as home.

In some cases, hurt is covered by the most rigorous silence. The clean break, a refusal to look back, represents a kind of emotional self-cauterization, as if the disciplines of professional life were sometimes a self-anaesthetizing balm for psychic wounds. Otto Frisch, writing of his father's release from a concentration camp before he emigrated to Sweden, says: 'When he arrived in Sweden with my mother he seemed little changed, only a bit thinner. For a fortnight or so he was busy with the typewriter, and I saw some of what he wrote about his experiences; pretty gruesome reading in places. When he had finished he told me it was all in that envelope (which he sealed) and that he would never talk about the concentration camp again. And he never did.'[56]

Lord Krebs, says his father's autobiography tells what happens, but not how it felt. Many refugees would not talk about their life before exile, unless it related to their work. This served as an emotional bridge to what they had left behind. Ben Elton, speaking of his grandparents, Victor and Eva Ehrenburg, said that they were always a warm presence in his life, but they felt 'rather foreign to me as a child. They lived in Hampstead. They were rather stiff, with German accents. I was born in Catford: they lived in what seemed to me a dusty flat with pictures and books, and they talked of *Kaffee* and *Kuchen* (cake).' After Hitler entered Austria, Max Perutz's parents joined him in England. In order to bring in a little money and assist with the war effort, Max's father re-trained as a lathe operator. That position and later a job with Max's wife's uncle entitled his parents to a state pension, a godsend since they had come with little more than some jewellery.

Richard Gombrich says that when his parents arrived 'they knew English, but did not speak it well, although they soon acquired it. My father was rather shy, but my mother was warm and outgoing. They spoke English to me but German to each other.

'The wound inflicted by Nazism upon Europe exercised my father, who would talk about it in a general rather than a personal way. He was passionately opposed to totalitarianism, both Nazism and Communism.

'My father's immediate family survived – only one uncle remained in Austria, and he shot himself before they got him. A second uncle had died in time. My father could bring to Britain with the help [of the Bonham Carters] mentioned, his parents, two sisters, an aunt and her husband. My mother was less fortunate. Many of her relatives died. Her father was dead before the *Anschluss*, and her mother went to Palestine. The rest disappeared. They never spoke of her family. Only after my father died, my mother began to talk about it. It upset her a great deal. It was very sad and moving. She had always dreaded losing her mind. When she went into a nursing home, she suffered from a terrible paranoia that the Gestapo were in the next room. She would say, "*Was ist aus der Tante Marthe geworden?*" (What happened to Aunt Martha?) She was 96 when she died.'

I asked the 90-year-old widow of a university teacher in the North of England about her husband. 'He was an attractive figure, clever, with dark eyes and a charismatic manner; which he used to impress his students. Underneath, he suffered from a deep melancholy. Before I knew what had happened to me, I fell into the role of submissive wife. He said he would not bring children into such a cruel world; and in the aftermath of the war, the ruins of Europe, the camps and the displacement of people, I agreed with him, although I think I would have preferred to opt for life and hope. He was very demanding, and as he grew older, quite bitter. I was always a little afraid of him, his temper, his ability to find fault, especially with me. He enjoyed the company of men. He was a misogynist. I resented this because I am an intelligent woman. He died of a heart attack in 1970 in his early fifties. After that, I began to find myself. I became a teacher and I played music. I married again in 1977 and had twenty years of joyful companionship. I wonder how many more women paid the price for the dislocations of exile, how many men of achievement were helped by the ministrations of women? I merely wonder. Survival is the essential; perhaps these are small sacrifices when one looks at the heavy toll of Nazism, Communism and war in Europe. I never complained.'

Many such stories may be too painful to tell. Eva Hoffman, exiled as a young adolescent from Communist Poland following widespread anti-Semitism in the late 1950s (she went with her family to the USA), writes with great empathy and understanding of exile: 'In that first interval of uprooting and transplantation, I only knew that just as there is a different poetry of language, so I was now surrounded by a different music of selfhood, and that I was not attuned to it, could not sense its patterns and harmonies. I am not sure that the gaps between the two languages, and the two grammars of selfhood, can ever be completely closed.'

Insight into these awkward transitions among the distinguished refugees from the Nazis is oblique and often symbolic. What disturbance lay beneath the assertion of some exiles that they would not have children, since the world into which they would be born was too cruel and uncertain? The life of Leo Szilard, with his disavowal of emotional attachments, his compulsive mobility and emotional elusiveness (notwithstanding his later happy marriage) suggests something more than the protean movements of a quicksilver mind. Many spoke of 'cutting off', as though it had been an amputation. 'He never spoke of the past,' was a common reaction. A few – especially from the USA, returned to positions in West Germany after the war, Theodor Adorno and Ernst Fraenkel among them. More visited relatives, survivors of the Holocaust, but some, like Einstein, never returned to Germany again.

I asked Gustav Born about the silence of refugees on the traumas they had suffered. Was it because they were stoical or because the experience had been too terrible to speak of?

'It was almost certainly the latter. The Jews were not more stoical than anyone else. Indeed, they had been accustomed to expressing their feelings quite powerfully. If they remained silent, it was because they could not give voice to the unspeakable. They also came into the reticence and restraint of "don-land". The culture of the academy was not one that favoured the expression of emotion. It would have been considered bad form to make strong statements of feeling. Add to this the fact that many scientists invested their area of scholarship with profound emotional significance. The joys of discovery and learning showed the capacity of the intellect to generate powerful feeling. My father's autobiography exhibited little emotion, and Hans Krebs' likewise. They were biographies of intellect.'

Ernst Chain

Ernst Chain was a gifted musician; in his early life he might have become a concert pianist or a scientist. His father had come to Berlin from Russia to study chemistry, and established a chemical manufacturing business. When Ernst Chain left Germany in 1933 for the laboratory of Gowland Hopkins in Cambridge, convinced that Nazism would quickly burn itself out, his mother and sister stayed behind. They were last heard of in Theresienstadt. His friend and colleague, Dr Ralph Kohn, said he could never ask Ernst Chain about his family's fate as he never spoke about it and never appeared to want to discuss it.

Perhaps it was only natural that the well-known refugees were known for what they did rather than what they felt. After all, as Dr Kohn says of Sir Ernst Chain, he was an immensely practical man. Not only did he isolate and purify penicillin, he also took an active interest in its testing. In addition he advocated cooperation between the academy and industry when this was not fashionable. In general, a stoical silence cloaks the unspoken emotions of most refugees from the 1930s.

A powerful identification with Britain combined with immense gratitude for the security it extended is a very strong feeling. Secondly, absorption in work of great and concentrated seriousness can also anaesthetize. One senses little emotional space among the political urgencies of the time and the imminent war to look back on the trauma which many people had undoubtedly undergone. In any case, intellectual pursuits and academic quarrels often involved intense emotions: and passionate enmities arising from some abstract or theoretical dispute could become deeply personal.

This contrasts sharply with the highly personal and more emotional tone of refugee stories of our time. If this reflects the altered psyche of the age, Eva Hoffman exemplifies the transition.

Eva Hoffman had greater leisure to reflect and come to terms with her exile. She wrote of the difficulties she experienced: 'I ... do not disavow the acute sense of loss I felt at first, for I think it bespoke the strength of my attachments to my first language and home. And it is those attachments which, if you can successfully transport them from one place to another, are the source of later attachments which enable you to come to love new worlds, and to love the world in new ways.' Given that psychoanalysis had developed in central Europe, and that a number of psychiatrist refugees reached Britain, it is perhaps surprising that few scientists – who were, for the most part, also great humanists – found it difficult to look too closely at the personal pain. Perhaps music, a passion for many refugees, as Esther Simpson (long-term secretary of the SPSL) records, served also to assuage inexpressible loss and grief.

Sometimes, those close to exiles, children, husbands or wives, give a glimpse of the depth of sadness and disorientation of exile. I spoke with the daughter of a later refugee, also a Jew, who left Poland in 1969 in the wave of anti-Semitism unleashed by the Communists, keen to bolster their failing support at the time. Although this was not commensurate with the violence of the Nazis, Samuel Fiszman was in many ways characteristic of completely assimilated Jews, having become enamoured of Polish culture and poetry, and an eminent critic of the national poet, Adam Mickiewicz. Dismissed from the University of Warsaw for having signed a petition in favour of academic freedom, he declined a university post in Britain in favour of Bloomington, Indiana, where he remained for the rest of his life.

'His father and sister died in the camps. He spent most of the war in Russia in a refugee camp. There, he became a kind of unofficial doctor. After the war, he changed from science to literature. Polish and Russian literature became his life. He loved everything connected with Poland. Whenever he read in US newspapers about Polish concentration camps, he always said, "No, these were German camps on Polish soil." He acknowledged anti-Semitism in Poland, but many Poles saved Jews. It was his wish to be buried in Poland. It took him six years to get permanent residency in the US. And when he did return to Poland, his family remember him sitting in the apartment and weeping; and he didn't cry often.

'My father made friends and a career in the US, but his heart was in Poland. When he left, he never knew if he would return …'

Ania O'Brien suggests that nostalgia can be inherited. 'I have the same love of Poland. I brought my daughter up bilingually, but she sometimes says to me, "I can't talk to you because you are from Europe." My father was committed heart and soul to the Poland he loved. Leaving it was the tragedy of his life.'

The fame surrounding those successful in Britain should not obscure another story – that of the unacknowledged multitude who were rejected. Their fate, officially 'unknown' at the time, has been subsequently memorialized by the fathomless guilt of those who might have done more to help them.

Intellectual bequests

What is clear is that the presence of intellectuals from another cultural tradition in Britain produced a creative synergy between different sensibilities.

Many refugee scholars acknowledged, in retrospect at least, the stimulus provided by the new environment of their forced exile. The pharmacologist H.K.E. Blaschko said, 'I am certain that for Science and Learning my translation from Germany to England has been beneficial. Personally, the change of environment has brought me a definite line of research, which I have followed ever since I began, as a grantee of the AAC, to follow it in 1935. What little merit there is in my work, it has profited by the change and the coming together of my experience as a learner in Germany and the problems taken up here.'[57]

Paul K. Hoch, in an important article in 1986 wrote of three principal channels for the diffusion of information across international boundaries – the 'brain drain', the movement of informed people, and the temporary movement of scientists or technologists from one country to another.[58] He examines how émigrés with expert knowledge combined with the scientific skills of the host culture to produce spectacular advances. He compares the theoretical know-how of atomic scientists, Enrico Fermi and Eugene Wigner among others, with the technological know-how available in America in the development of the nuclear reactor. He refers particularly to the evolution of solid-state physics – 'a field which grew at the junction of chemistry, physics, crystallography and metallurgy only in the last half-century. In terms of its impact on solid-state electronics, luminescent lighting, magnetism, nuclear reactors and materials technology, it is far away the most technologically important part of physics.' The same is true in the growth of molecular biology.

The role of theoretical physics in the development of nuclear weapons is well-known, and applied mathematics was crucial to the development of aerodynamics; applied mechanics also intersects creatively with solid-state physics and metallurgy, especially in creating a sound scientific basis for mechanical and structural engineering. Pharmaceuticals and biomedical sciences were enhanced by Michael Polanyi and Fritz Paneth and others brought into Britain by scholarships offered by ICI. Hans Krebs and Ernst Chain were key biochemical émigrés. Hoch sees the pressure on central European refugees to synthesize the approaches of their original and adoptive cultures as a source of great creative inventiveness – 'the synthesis of "German" theory with "Anglo-American empiricism"'. The third factor was that in British or American universities, incoming scholars slid into the interstices between established disciplines to avoid displacing an indigenous applicant for work, their very marginality enabling them to cross what might have been regarded as disciplinary – as well as social and cultural – boundaries. 'Thus, the physicist turned physical chemist (e.g. James Franck) or applied mathematician (e.g. Peierls) or the chemistry student turned crystallographer (e.g. Max Perutz).' Hoch says the 'newly emerging interdisciplinary specialities in the natural sciences was thus in part the result of attempts by Central European émigrés to carve out niches for themselves by demonstrating the mathematical basis of physics, the physical basis of chemistry and the physical and chemical basis of life.' These laid the foundations for molecular biology, biotechnology and genetic engineering.

Much that we take for granted in our lives – from health care to travel, from household conveniences to home entertainment, from communications to the daily comforts of existence – owes an incalculable debt to émigrés and their interaction with the countries that gave them refuge. Yet society easily loses sight of the sometimes painful intellectual and material effort that went into their advances. Those forced into exile left a legacy too little appreciated by those who now repudiate the refugee and the asylum-seeker. Who knows what power and ability to transform our lives again may be sleeping in the spurned intellect and disdained qualities of those rejected as intruders at the gates of Europe and America? Self-interest, as well as common humanity, should prompt a more searching scrutiny of people who make their somewhat slender claims upon our sparing hospitality.

In *The Hitler Emigres*, Daniel Snowman traces the enduring effects upon Britain, intellectually, culturally and socially of the émigrés from central Europe throughout the whole post-war period in the media, academia, politics and society. After the war, 'most of the exiles would soon return whence they had come ... But most of the German-speaking refugees stayed; the world in which they had been raised had been utterly obliterated. ... Virtually every one of the Hitler emigres learned sooner or (more often) later, of friends and relatives lost in the anonymous barbarity of the death camps. How could they return to live in a country in which a genuinely popular government had wished to murder them?[59]

'When the emigres arrived, Britain, whatever its fissures and faults, was a nation "at one with itself". After the war this sense of national communality was, if anything, enhanced by the achievement of victory. The British had a clear sense of who they were and what they stood for. Their standing in the world was high. They were a people, a nation and a culture with whom anyone originating from elsewhere might be proud to identify.'

This is certainly reflected in what the surviving relatives and descendants have done, and how they regard the opportunities Britain gave them.

The impact of the refugees on society is manifold, particularly of those whose discoveries changed the way we view our lives. Secondly, those who specialized in the study of social and economic systems, and who pondered the economic collapse from which Nazism had emerged, bequeathed recommendations and policies for avoiding a repeat of the disaster. In addition, they also set in train a long process of change, in which some of the virtues of central European social life enriched the closed and inward-looking class divisions in Britain.

What Britain gained cannot be calculated solely in intellectual or economic terms, however significant these might be. Max and Hedwig Born, Victor and Eva Ehrenburg, Max and Gisela Perutz, Ernst Gombrich, for instance, gave the country a different pool of talent: children and grandchildren, whose commitment has enriched us in ways that escape academic, or even economic, calculus. The immediate descendants of those who remained have their own story to tell.

Professor Gustav Born, now in his mid-eighties, is a distinguished pharmacologist, whose family had a long history of contribution to European civilization before it was disrupted by Nazism. His great-grandfather had been an innovative physician in Gorlitz in Silesia working on the control of epidemics, while his grandfather was a well-known and original embryologist in Breslau (now Wroclaw).

'You must go back to the mid-nineteenth century to find practising Jews in the family, a heritage not significant until defined by a malignant ideology.' Gustav, who arrived in England aged 11, says, 'I didn't know what Jews were.' The family were Lutheran, and indeed, his mother, although three-quarters Jewish, traced the other part of her descent to Martin Luther.

Gustav Born's contribution to medical science has been remarkable. He graduated during the war in Edinburgh, did a PhD at Oxford, where he became

Demonstrator in Pharmacology, served in the British army and was one of only two British pathologists with the occupation force in Japan after the dropping of the A-bomb on Hiroshima. There he observed the effects of radiation on the circulatory system: many months afterwards, people were still dying of haemorrhages. He was for 12 years at the Royal College of Surgeons and then Professor of Pharmacology in Cambridge from 1973 until 1979. 'My main field has been in the circulatory system, especially thrombosis, haemostasis and atherosclerosis. My contribution has been work on the platelets in blood cells which are specifically important for stopping bleeding. This is, of course, connected to the causes of heart attacks and strokes. We discovered that aspirin stops the platelets from aggregating; this gave aspirin a second life as an anti-clotting agent. My generation who worked in biological science were very lucky: we bridged the generation that led to the development of molecular biology.'

Gustav Born has five children, three from his first marriage and two from his second to Faith, a retired GP. His daughter, Georgina, holds a Chair in Social Science in Cambridge; one son Sebastian is an Associate Director of the National Theatre, while another son became a journalist, and now runs a TV company founded by his partner that generates ideas for documentaries. Gustav Born is also the uncle of the singer Olivia Newton-John and a cousin of Lewis Elton.

There are no physicists or physicians in the present generation. The change in the family's direction illustrates how it has adapted to the changing temper of British life; as sensibilities shift, people direct their talents to where they may be best expressed. Gustav Born's family demonstrates the folly of making social predictions. The only constant is the principled moral purpose of his father, Max Born, and his forbears, a continuing commitment to liberal values and a critical openness to a changing world.

More humble émigrés

Was it the more egalitarian post-war outlook that made severe official judgments on categories of refugees that might be advantageous to Britain appear too narrow and elitist? Or were the achievements equally astonishing of those who had come into the country, as it were, at random – the arbitrary selections of the Kindertransport or those who had convinced potential employers that they would make excellent servants?

Whatever the cause, it was tacitly acknowledged that to view Britain as a beneficiary of the talents of only the most eminent refugees was mistaken. Divisions between the illustrious, the mediocre and the humble, although doubtless made in good faith at the time, now appear arbitrary and excluding. In truth most refugees from Nazism left a positive legacy, academically, socially and culturally. Some achieved academic distinction, others became writers and artists; almost all were great humanists.

Many were not welcomed with the fanfare extended to scientists already at the peak of their career before the Nazi era. The lesser known were often ill at ease with the British character, particularly if they were outside a place of learning. Non-academics were more exposed to the ambivalences of British attitudes to foreigners. Some found the British 'cold, undemonstrative, shy or so polite it was impossible to determine what they really felt and thought', (according to a former refugee, now living in New York).

Drawing the line between scholars whose merit 'qualified' them for SPSL assistance and those whose lower professional standing excluded them was always difficult; the Bodleian Library records hint at the heart-searching that took place beneath the polite official communications.

On the borderline were the crowds of refugees with nothing to convince the government that their presence in Britain would benefit the country. The same issue faces us today, in an even more aggravated form, given the diversity of forces expelling people from their homeland and driving them far from their roots.

One under-publicized aspect of refugees in the 1930s was that the largest single category at the outbreak of war comprised women admitted as domestic servants. In fact the overall number of women exceeded men. The servant problem, which had exercised the middle classes in the 1930s, was eased by issuing of permits to German-Jewish women provided they entered domestic service. This became a major source of escape, not so much for women who had been accustomed to domestic labour, as for middle-class women who, until the 1930s, had been mistresses rather than servants. Employment agencies in Berlin and later Vienna recruited women deemed suitable for this occupation.

Many were shocked by their duties when they arrived at their workplace. Lore Segal poignantly recalls her mother being shown round the house she was to clean. '"Ah," my mother exclaimed, "a piano! It is a Bechstein, no?" And she told Mrs Willoughby about her Blüthner which the Nazis had taken, and that she had studied music at the Vienna Academy. "Oh really," said Mrs Willoughby. "In that case, you must come in and play sometime when everyone is out."'[60]

Work was also available to male domestics, especially butlers and gardeners. Louise London tells the story of a British Passport Control Officer in Paris, who cited the example of a doctor, who offered to work as a butler.[61] "This is absurd," he wrote, "as butlering required a lifelong experience."'

Although many women were humiliated by the role reversals they underwent, many agreed they were fortunate to have survived. Their sense of dignity was scarcely enhanced when, in the invasion scare, Sir Neville Bland, British Minister at The Hague, said, 'the paltriest kitchen maid not only can be, but generally is, a menace to the safety of the country'. In the first weeks of May 1940, more than 8,000 women were dismissed – for many a blessing rather than a curse, since this led to more satisfactory employment in nursing, or what were later called the 'caring professions'. The mother of Louise London was taken on as a cook. One of the first things her employers in Bedford asked her to do was 'to make a summer pudding'. She had not the faintest idea what this meant.

Peggy Fink, now in her mid-nineties, daughter of a family of linen exporters in Belfast, was active on a committee set up to welcome refugees to Northern Ireland. She recalls one woman who went to London to collect two teenaged refugees. 'Our committee had taken them from a Jewish orphanage. When she got these two girls back to Belfast, she said, "You must call me Madam." One was to be cook, the other a house parlour-maid. She treated them badly. She never gave them enough to eat, and they often went hungry. She gave them five shillings a week, and they slipped the gardener sixpence to buy them a loaf of bread. One day, Madam's sister reminded the girls it was her sister's birthday, and the girls said, "Please buy her a bunch of flowers from us." She did; and their employer stopped their wages for a week. Our committee heard of the case. We took the children away and sent them to England to do nursery nurse training. The younger girl married a soldier. She now has two grandchildren – one just got a double first from Cambridge, the other is just starting at Oxford.'[62]

Peggy Fink's life crossed that of a number of refugees we have already met. Her future husband was working on the Warburg estate, which had been given to the Americans as a refuge for Jewish orphans released from the concentration camps. Her daughter, Michelle, studied molecular genetics, and worked in the laboratory of Max Perutz. When Peggy and her husband returned to Vienna after the war, Erwin Schrödinger was a neighbour.

Peter Pelz's father came, aged 16, to live in as a farm servant in Yorkshire. Despite high unemployment, Britons were deserting both agriculture and domestic service in the 1930s. The promise of work in Britain's depleted farms and fields was an exit route from Germany or Austria and allowed canny employers to get cheap – even free – labour. 'It was abusive. He was with another Jewish boy. They were overworked and underfed. They went on strike, because of inadequate food. He went from there to become a gardener in an Oxford college. That was where he met my mother. He fell in with some people from a Tolstoyan community of Leftish clergymen, including Paul Oesterreicher. They inspired him to go to Lincoln Theological College. He was ordained and served in Bolton in Lancashire, where he also wrote his books and articles.

'My father had been the repository of all the hopes of his parents. His father had cultural ambitions. He owned cinemas in Berlin. He raised his son to be what he would like to have been. Becoming a farm labourer was certainly a let-down, but he took it in his stride. He was glad to be alive.

'My mother's experience was traumatic. She came from a family of intellectuals, cultured and respected members of society. Her mother married the illiterate son of a poor peasant from Slovakia. She found the stresses of her marriage intolerable and committed suicide. Her daughter, my mother, then a ten-year-old, found the body slumped in front of the gas oven …

'My mother and step-grandmother were got out by the Quakers, who were a shining light for refugees at that time. They organized invitations to get people into Britain, and this meant offers of work. When my mother was interned on the Isle of Man, she always said this rescued her from a worse situation as domestic servant.

'My grandmother was a qualified pharmacist, but she accepted a job as housemaid in a middle-class household, where the husband and wife, who had been officials in the Indian empire, believed in keeping up appearances. It amused my grandmother that they would dress up for the most insignificant meals, such as a light super of cheese sticks and tomato soup. She coped with the humiliation, but one fine day, her new employers wanted to show her off to guests at supper, her fine Viennese cooking legendary in the district. They asked her to wear a dirndl for the occasion. Their fine manners clearly did not include sensitivity. Never a person to cross, my grandmother took pride in stoutly refusing and left.'

Peter Pelz's parents left a powerful mark on Britain. His father, the Reverend Werner Pelz, was a founder of the Campaign for Nuclear Disarmament. A man of radical views and great courage, he never went for the easy option. He wrote a book called *I Am Adolf Hitler*, which tried to imagine the subjective world-view of Hitler.[63] Unfortunately, it was misunderstood; *The Times* reviewer treated it as an apologia for Nazism.

'My father was at least 30 years before his time. He was ordained as a priest, but had little time for the church, which, he said had nothing to do with Christianity. This was the time of the 1960s God-is-dead controversy. He was interviewed for the position as vicar of a church in Hampstead. They asked him, a little apprehensively, "You do believe in God?" He said, "Of course not." He left the church. It was then he told me he went back to his Jewish roots and the poetry of the Old Testament. If it was the New Testament that made him go into the church, the Old Testament reminded him of his origins.'[64]

Peter Pelz is himself an artist and writer. The legacy of writers, scholars and thinkers who were either children themselves at the time, or were children of people who occupied menial positions in Britain at the time of their exile, has been scarcely less enduring than that of their more celebrated contemporaries.

The Kindertransport

One of the most poignant events was the Kindertransport, organized in the months leading up to the war, whereby Britain accepted some 10,000 unaccompanied children below the age of 17. Many – like Paul Weindling's mother – made a success of their life here. It is surprising, not that so many children adjusted with great difficulty to a new culture, and to their soon-to-be orphaned status, but that they proved so resilient and resourceful.

The wrenching of children from the security and love of a suddenly abridged childhood created the mixture of tragedy and hope of those who were saved. Survivors tell of tearful faces – adults themselves broke down as they saw the last of their children – in a blur of smoke, waved handkerchiefs and desperate valedictory kisses. (The film *Into the Arms of Strangers* about the Kindertransport, must be one of the most moving documents ever produced on separation and loss.) The epic nature of the journey cannot be overestimated; it must have seemed like a voyage to the other side of the world. The contrast, too, between the matter-of-fact reception by dutiful Britishers and the painful farewells from home, struck many of the children as a chilling presentiment of what lay in store for them. No-nonsense women who rejected the embrace even of little girls because this was 'cissy' or 'not done', was the first contact some had with dutiful hosts. Others became very attached to their charges, which resulted in many tender friendships. But often, as Lore Segal remembers, the children remained truculent and unforgiving to those who had opened their house, and sometimes, their hearts, to them. Although some had been placed in advance with families who received them at Harwich or Liverpool Street, others were dispatched to holiday camps and other institutions, where there would be a regular cull by prospective foster-families, a system later described as a 'cattle-market'. Some were even exchanged for others more tractable or obedient. One child, selected as she thought to be part of a family, discovered that she was expected to be a maidservant.

The request desperate parents made to departing children to try and arrange for them or their siblings to reach safety was a terrifying ordeal. A few children actually managed it, asking naively in well-to-do suburbs about work for a maid and a gardener. Occasionally the answer was positive. In this sense, some children became the guardians, as it were, of their parents, who found their status reversed when they arrived: their child knew so much more than they did, spoke the language and was more familiar with British ways. Lore Segal, in *Other People's Houses*, wrote of the eve of her departure from Vienna. 'I stood in the center of my circle of relatives, nodding solemnly. I said I would write letters to everybody and would tell the *Engländer* about everything that was happening and would get sponsors for my parents and grandparents and for everybody.' She was ten. It seems extraordinary to tell a child in such circumstances that it was her duty to rescue her parents. Lore Segal says, 'I took it very seriously. I thought it would be my fault if my parents were sent to a concentration camp.'[65]

Remarkably, she succeeded. An unhappy little refugee in Dovercourt Camp near Harwich, she sat in the freezing December cold. 'And then I saw something … in the middle of a semi-circle of snow that must in summer have been a flower bed in a grass plot behind the cottage, there grew a tall meager rosebush with a single bright-red rosebud wearing a clump of freshly fallen snow, like a cap askew. This struck me profoundly ... I would write it in a letter to Onkel (Uncle) Hans and Tante (Aunt) Trude in London, saying that the Jews in Austria were like roses left over in the winter of Nazi occupation. I would write that they were dying of the cold. How beautifully it all fell into place. How true and sad! They would say "And she is only ten years old!" I ran around the cottage and up the veranda steps ... I wanted to be writing. I was going to say "If good people like you don't pluck the roses quickly, the Nazis will come and cut them down."' Her aunt and uncle were duly impressed and showed the letter to members of various refugee committees. This, in turn, moved a family to sponsor Lore's parents for a married-couple visa, as maid and butler.

Although Lore Segal was the recipient of an unexcitable charity, her judgment on the ten years she spent in England is far from negative. She says that basic decency means a great deal, and is amazed that so many people accepted into their home a troubled and sometimes refractory child.[66]

She also recognizes the poignancy of middle-class Viennese, who had kept servants in their households, entering domestic service. While her mother became extremely competent, her ailing father was broken by the experience. 'It is difficult for people now to understand how improbable domestic life was for a middle-class man in the Austria of the 1930s. My father scarcely even knew there was a kitchen in the house. Food arrived and was cleared away by my mother and the maid. For him to have to start again in another country and in another profession was simply too much ...' As well as celebrating success, Lore Segal commemorates those who found in exile only lasting misery and unhappiness.

For many children, the provisional stay in Britain became routine, and at length accepted. The memory of parents remained, but the presence became distant. Postcards came telling that they were travelling to the East or were going away; children were exhorted not to worry if they didn't hear anything for a long time. For many, a laconic card or a terse telegram was the last they ever heard until the end of the war, when it was the fate of the majority to learn the worst.

Even those whose parents had survived or escaped found the reunion difficult: each remembered the other as they had been, but children had grown up and parents had aged, particularly those who had survived the camps. Sometimes, the common language was lost. It required time and effort for feelings, long hidden under the veil of English reserve, to be restored.

It was not the problems of reunion that preoccupied most people, but inconsolable, irretrievable loss. Some, unreconciled to British reticence, moved on after the war, usually to the USA. Palestine was too risky for people who had so narrowly escaped with their lives, and in any case there were strict quotas. A majority stayed here; their experience tells of cultural and linguistic adaptation and efforts to succeed, often to show absent parents that they had obeyed instructions to be good and grateful. They started families, made a career in medicine, law or business. Photographs of their children show them smiling in school uniform or the regalia of their degree ceremony. The reception by Britain of the thousands of children, amputated from their families, remains one of the most creditable and altruistic actions in the world at a dark time.

Leslie Brent arrived in Britain thanks to the Kindertransport. It remains a constant source of wonder to him that a child refugee should have become part of Peter Medawar's team researching skin grafts and tissue rejection which led to a Nobel prize in 1960. Leslie Brent's whole family died, except an uncle and a cousin, who were out of Germany at the time. His cousin, now 94, lives in the USA. 'My parents, sister, uncles, aunts, nephews and nieces, all died. We were from a small town in Pomerania on the Baltic coast called Koslin, now in Poland and renamed Koszalin.

'I lived there until I was eleven, when persecution at school became severe in the winter of 1936. The Headmaster also wanted me to leave, although I was the only Jewish boy in the school. I went into school one morning and written on the board was "All Christians are Liars and Cheats". I was punished, although of course I had nothing to do with it. There was stone-throwing and abuse from the other children. My parents didn't know what to do. I was taken in by a Jewish Boys' Orphanage in Pankow in Berlin. That was my salvation, because from there I was selected for the Kindertransport.

'My parents stayed in Koslin. My father lost his job. In 1938, they came to Berlin because it was easier to "disappear" there. They were deported in October 1942. I thought they had gone to Theresienstadt, and from there to Auschwitz. Once, when visiting Poland as a lecturer, I visited Auschwitz. I broke down. There was no grave or date, and I had never grieved for them properly.

'It turned out they were never there at all. They were sent to Riga in Latvia, where, three days afterwards, they were taken to the woods and shot. My sister was with them. She was a trainee nurse in the Jewish hospital in Berlin, which remained open throughout the war. Part of it served as a collection point for deportations. She insisted on going with her parents, and they died together.

'It has been a burden. I have always suffered from survivors' guilt. The orphanage is still there. It became the Cuban embassy after the war, and then was derelict. It is now restored, a fine building, used as library and nursery school.

'I felt safe there [the orphanage]. I was a peaceful youngster, able to accept more or less whatever came my way. Arrival at the orphanage was, of course, a shock after family life. But I never felt abandoned by my parents. I knew it was in my best interests.

'The director was from Koslin and knew my father. He was a very humane man, and ran a liberal educational institution. I was there two years. Parents nominated their children to go on the Kindertransport, and the director chose me. He nominated nine out of 100 boys. The ninth child could not get on the train because it had been overbooked. Another friend in the orphanage stayed in Berlin in the war, living underground. He survived, as a significant minority did, passing as Aryan or protected by friends.

'When we came to England, we had no idea it would be permanent. Most parents said, "We will see you soon." I kept up a correspondence with mine till just before they were deported. We were allowed to send messages through the Red Cross. They had to be anodyne, limited words. My last message from them told me they were going on a journey. I had no idea what it meant, but it must have been a week or two before they were deported. It was handwritten by my father – usually he typed the message – and his writing was rather wild. They understood their fate by then. I had had several letters about other members of the family, saying my aunt or uncle "*sind verreist*" (had gone on a journey). A euphemism for deportation ...

'My parents were very German. They loved German culture, music and literature. Their tragedy was that of hundreds of thousands of people. When Hitler came, they thought, "It can't last." They made no attempt to get out until it was too late.'

Leslie has a photograph – an iconic picture of a group of about ten children crowded in a railway carriage. Some are smiling, some look uneasy. Leslie appears apprehensive, his overriding feeling at the time.

His father was an Anglophile, and he learned English at the *Mittelschule* (secondary school), which proved very useful when he ended up in Dovercourt Camp near Harwich and, as already described, met Anna Essinger and went to her experimental school at Bunce Court.

'It was boarding and co-educational. I used to go back afterwards, whenever I was on leave from the army. I left after my School Certificate at fifteen. I had no one to pay for me to stay on. Anna Essinger arranged with a friend in Birmingham, a branch secretary of the Jewish Central Fund, and I was interviewed for a job in the Central Technical College as laboratory assistant. I also continued to study for Higher School Certificate, and took the exams in December 1943.

'Then I joined the army. For the next four years I was a soldier in the British army, although I remained a German enemy alien until naturalized in 1947. Until 1943, aliens were only allowed into the Pioneer Corps, but after 1943, it was possible to join the army even as an enemy alien.

'Internment came in 1940. Some were traumatized by it, but many were very forgiving. Having just escaped Germany, it was for most a very disagreeable experience. My friend Hans Meyer, critic and writer, was sent to Australia on the *Dunera*. He saw it as the panic measure it was, and was not embittered by it. Some of those sent to Canada and Australia shared quarters with Nazis. The internment camps saw a great flowering of culture – the Amadeus Quartet was founded, there were lectures, talks and courses.

'After training in Glasgow I went before the selection board. My father had been a stretcher-bearer in the First World War, and was awarded the Iron Cross, Third Class. I said I wanted to join the Royal Ambulance Corps, but they thought I was too intelligent. I was sent to a camp for officers in Kent, and I finished as Captain – a title I was told I could keep for life. After a spell in Northern Ireland, I was commissioned into the Royal Warwickshire Regiment. I joined the Fifth Division in Italy, just as the war was ending. I was part of the Army Bureau of Current Affairs. We were sent to Trieste to keep the peace between Italians and Yugoslavs at Pola. From there I went with the British Army on the Rhine to Luneborg Heath. Our job was to keep the Russians at bay over the Oder. My brigade was involved in Operation Woodpecker – cutting timber for British reconstruction. I had no compunction extracting resources from Germany.

'A friend of mine had a grant from the Ministry of Education for further study, since his studies had been interrupted by the war. It never occurred to me. But I applied and got a four-year grant to do a degree, graduating in Zoology 1951. My Head of Department was Peter Medawar, who offered me a place in his research team. In 1951, he moved to University College London, to the Jodrell Chair of Zoology. Although originally zoologists, we became immunologists.

'Medawar received the Nobel Prize in 1960 for his work on immunological tolerance.[67] He changed my life. For 30 years we worked together and became good friends. I was eventually invited to St Mary's Hospital [Paddington] Medical School; I stayed 20 years.

'I feel totally British. Germany is not my *Heimat* (home), nor Koslin either, although I enjoy going there. The army was very important to my experience – you had to become British pretty damn quickly. I first went to Mary Hill barracks in Glasgow, which they called Merry Hell. We were told we could go out only in pairs at night, because Glasgow was supposed to be very rough. I found Glasgow very friendly.

'The army led to my change of name. Going on leave during the war, the company commander said before I became an officer I should come back with an English name – for my own protection, because if caught by the enemy, with a name like that, I risked being persecuted as a Jew or shot as a traitor. I thought of Leslie because of Leslie Howard. I found Brent by flicking through the telephone directory.

'After the war I became naturalized. I decided not to go back to my original name, partly because it was unpronounceable and because I wanted to be assimilated. Some years ago, I did resume Baruch as a middle name.

'I have three children from my first marriage. My son is a forester in Devon. My older daughter is an aerialist, and has worked with the Cirque du Soleil and Archaos. My second daughter is an actor. She studied Drama at Hull University, and worked with some very creative theatrical companies.

'I regard myself as completely integrated into Britain – language, literature, music, politics. I never joined any political party until 1969, when I joined the

Labour Party. I was chair of a working party on social services in Haringey, and the recommendations we made then are only now being put into practice. Later, I became a founder member of the SDP. In fact, I became so committed, it was to the detriment of my career and family life.

'I am proud to have worked on immunological tolerance with Medawar and Billingham. It was a wonderful part of my life. The burns of war casualties led Medawar to investigate why skin grafts from donors were rejected. The immunological system of each individual is unique and the period for which a graft is accepted depends on how closely related the donor and recipient are. Grafting was possible between fraternal as well as identical twins. It was shown in animals that tissues are exchanged between twin foetuses. This suggests that the immunological system is acquired over time, not at conception.'

The team extracted from cells the antigens capable of calling forth transplant-ation immunity, setting the stage for the success of organ transplants. 'We showed that if you inject an animal with antigens from a potential donor before birth, the cells carry those antigens. It was believed that the resistance to genetically-different skin or organs created so profound a resistance that the barrier was insurmountable.

'The holy grail of immunology is to induce tolerance. We had to induce animals to be specifically tolerant to donor's tissues without crippling the immune-system. We found that our own immune-system doesn't destroy us because it is tolerant of our antigens.

'Understanding how rejection both by the recipient and the donor tissue works was the achievement, even though it still has not been totally overcome. The work we did then is coming to fruition now.

'After I retired I wrote a history of transplantation immunology, which was published in 1996. It is still a bible for transplant surgeons.[68]

'I went back to Berlin in 1946. It was a ruined city. It was the place from which my parents had been sent to their death. I hated it. It has changed now, and full of memorials to the events that took place.'

The image of the anxious child on the Kindertransport seems a million miles away from the warm, comfortable interior in north London; but he is still there, eloquent witness and tenacious survivor. The photograph suggests no sign of the achievements that would unfold, the benefits that this boy, plucked by chance from the ranks of doomed children, would offer to those who sheltered him.[69] In a moment of reflection in the cosy interior, with an indigo November gloom pressing against the window-pane, it was impossible to ignore the annihilated energies and aborted talents of the perished, and what the world might have become had they been allowed to express them. All the stories of survival and hope are shadowed by the absence of those in unvisited tombs in the charnel house that was Europe.

Those who failed

The story of those who lived to tell the tale is often heart-wrenching, but their voices were heard. Louise London estimates that of those who applied for refuge in Britain before the outbreak of war, about one in ten was successful. The British government saw the problem of Jews as essentially an issue of mass migration. They could not, perhaps, have foreseen the 'final solution' which Nazi Germany would later devise, although a more critical consciousness of their own imperial history and a closer reading of Hitler's intentions might have alerted them earlier; and a kind of willed unknowing greeted the stories that began to emerge from the camps in 1942. Louise London states that by August 1939, the population of confessional Jews in the Austrian provinces outside of Vienna had fallen from about 15,000 to 370. 'The Jewish death-rate – one-eighth due to suicide – was four times what it had been in 1937.'[70] Anne Lonsdale remembers the story of Karl Weissenberg's mother, who jumped out of the window and killed herself as the Germans marched down her Vienna street. These tragedies, which suggested how Jews left behind judged their probable fate, were overtaken in Britain by the urgencies of war.

Survivors' stories are bound to give an incomplete account of the world. When Peggy Fink arrived at Belsen in 1945, it had become a Jewish displaced persons' centre, with survivors arriving constantly. She found boxes full of unopened letters from all parts of the world, mostly search enquiries for missing relatives and friends; their undisclosed contents suggests a world of suffering lost in flames and forgetting. Although success in reuniting some families brought moments of joy, most were lost in the ashes of ideology. 'Sometimes a woman who had believed her husband to be dead had remarried. On such occasions, the rabbi would advise the woman to divorce both men and then choose one. Or occasionally we thought we had found a child for a mother, only to discover that, although the name was correct, just one day's difference in the birth date meant that it was not in fact the missing child.'[71] That so many testimonies of tenacity and endurance emerged serves as admonition to a humanity incapable of learning from what it routinely invokes as 'lessons of history', which has proved so melancholy and incompetent an instructor.

Only later did the psychic wounds of survivors begin to be understood. Many, haunted by the longings of exile, created, especially in those corners of London where they lived, the central European atmosphere of the inter-war years: the West Hampstead coffee-houses, the *Gemütlichkeit* (sociability) and openness, games of chess, conversations and arguments, attendance at lectures on science or art, philosophizing over the patisserie – strange customs to an austere 1940s and 1950s London. Some live on, now in their eighties and nineties – a warm afternoon in Golders Hill Park, West Hampstead, sees the very elderly, supported by their children, themselves no longer young, listening to the band and admiring the flowers in the late sunshine; reflecting upon journeys on which they carried the precious cultural paraphernalia of an urbane *Mitteleuropa*. They still carry the poignant aura of the elsewhere, unvisitable now as it is long vanished, although constantly revisited down the lengthening corridors of memory.

The stories of another group of Jews are suppressed or forgotten – the illegal refugees, the 'failed asylum-seekers' of their age, whose presence in Britain escaped Authority's stony vigilance. How many evaded the rigorous controls sustained even in the period of systematic extermination is unknown, but the story of Danny Marks' father was not an isolated example.

Danny has been my close friend for more than 30 years. 'My father was born into the unfriendly world of the Jews of the Russian Empire. Poverty was ever-present and violence periodically broke out. No wonder the German invaders of the First World War seemed a better option. He got on well enough with them to have learnt their songs, which he taught me. Germans were recruiting manpower among Poles, and of course, to ease labour shortages in Germany. Ludendorff, the German Commander, issued a proclamation in Yiddish – "*An mayne libe Yidn*" (to my dear Jews).

'My father, a baker, heeded the appeal, and went to work in Berlin. In 1918 he experienced revolution and economic disaster. When he visited his family in Poland, he could not stay there because he lacked Polish citizenship: all born in the territory which became Poland and who had not been there in 1918 were denied citizenship. My father, formerly a subject of the Tsar, became stateless.

'He went to Paris with his older brother, who, as a Russian soldier, had been a prisoner of war of the Germans. France, because of a low birth-rate and losses suffered in the war, was still fairly welcoming to migrants from Eastern Europe. Britain was less so. The brothers had three sisters living in Britain. Two had come before the First War, and the other had managed to join them as a widow after the war. The sisters were tough characters, and set up hairdressing businesses, one in the very un-Jewish area of Bermondsey, off the Jamaica Road.

'The brothers reached London, but as aliens their position was insecure, especially at a time of fear of Bolshevism, since Russian Jews were its supposed agents. They soon found out, however, that there were those in the metropolitan police who were, for a consideration, prepared to offer assistance. They obtained the appropriate papers, but lived in continuous fear of being "exposed". My father lied about his age, subtracting 15 years, so he could claim he had come to the country as a young child before the war. He did not swear allegiance to His Majesty King George VI until 1946, after the birth of his five children; but he never felt completely safe.

'He worked as a baker in the East End. He was a member of the London Jewish Bakers' Union, which was affiliated to the Arbiter Ring, (Workers' Circle) a Jewish friendly society and socialist cultural organization. I remember that going to make payments was an opportunity for warm social exchange (in Yiddish) in Leman Street, Aldgate, and the Sylvester Path, next to the Hackney Empire.

'My father could not retire with a pension because he was "too young", but he was overtaken by bad health and could no longer work.'

Danny's father would now be regarded as an 'illegal immigrant.' Nevertheless, Britain has been the beneficiary of his children, among whom are writers, an accountant and a historian; although two subsequently went to the United States. I have a particular interest in the fate of this family and its irregular status, since without them, I would never have known one of the most deep and enduring friendships of my life.

The journey between departure and the arrival may seem interminable to the traveller; but it is only a step from refugee to belonging. Is popular anxiety over refugees a result of their perceived 'difference', or because of the ease with which people are absorbed once they are accepted? Generosity towards refugees is usually repaid a thousandfold, since all they want is to offer their intelligence, labour and goodwill to the country that welcomes them. Have the cold North Atlantic winds chilled our compassion? Has a misty insularity convinced us that those unfavoured by being born here have come to take something from us?

Michael Yudkin was Honorary Secretary of SPSL/CARA from 1992 until 2003. His mother was a refugee from Germany in the thirties, and his father was the third child, and the first born in England, of grandparents who fled Tsarist Russia. Michael Yudkin speaks eloquently of the transition from petitioner to pride in achievement. 'My grandfather joined his cousin, who was already here, probably on the run from the Tsarist police. He [his grandfather] imported furs from Russia and they lived in Dalston. His cousin was a cabinet-maker. They were of the industrious artisan class. My father went to Hackney Downs school, got a scholarship to Chelsea College and a scholarship to Cambridge. He had a chair at London University before he was forty. He certainly would not have achieved that in St Petersburg. His next youngest brother became a consultant paediatrician. I worked in Sir Hans Krebs's Department and finished my working life as Professor of Biochemistry at Oxford.' Michael Yudkin's grandfather was an intellectual, although not in terms that were of immediate use to secular society. That, although Michael Yudkin does not say so, has been left to his descendants.

Internment

At the outbreak of war in September 1939, the government organized a review of the total of about 80,000 refugees in Britain who were, in theory, 'enemy aliens'. Those found by tribunals to have been victims of persecution in Germany were left at liberty. All academic refugees fell into this category, and continued with their work until May 1940. With the Nazi move westwards, invasion fears reached a peak, partly fuelled by newspaper scares of a 'fifth column', and the suggestion that spies might be smuggled into Britain disguised as refugees. An 'intern-the-lot' mood, reminiscent of 1914, seized the country, and Churchill decided to imprison all 'enemy aliens', including those who had fled for their life and previously designated as 'friendly aliens'.

Internment camps established on the Isle of Man included requisitioned hotels and boarding houses surrounded by barbed wire, turning part of Douglas into an ad hoc detention facility. Internee resourcefulness is legendary – the establishment of an informal university, where music was made, languages taught, physics and maths courses initiated and discussions on current events took place. Less happy was the fate of internees, 'transported' (a word with historic resonance) to Australia and Canada, notably those who died when the *Arandora Star*, crammed with Italians who were being deported overseas together with interned Austrian and German refugees, was sunk on its way to Canada in July 1940. Out of a total complement of 1,500, over 800 perished.

More than 27,000 'aliens' were interned in 1940, including many scientists and academics who had been helped by the AAC, or SPSL. The SPSL quickly mobilized to rescue its protégés from the country which had offered them refuge. Liberal opinion urged the government to reconsider its ill-advised action, since the great majority of the interned clearly presented no danger to Britain. The SPSL was prominent in advocating the release of people whose employment was unequivocally for the war effort. Following an initiative by A.V. Hill, a Vice-President of the SPSL and then MP for the University of Cambridge, a government White Paper defined categories of those who should be freed because of the national importance of their work.

By the end of the year, a Council of Aliens had been formed to deal with those eligible to be set at liberty. The latter included scientists, researchers and persons of academic distinction for whom work of importance in their special fields was available, as well as outstanding contributors to art, science or letters. In cooperation with the SPSL, tribunals were set up by the vice-chancellors of universities, the Royal Society, the British Academy and the Royal Society of Medicine to consider applications for release. The Royal Academy of Arts, the Royal Institute of British Architects, the PEN club and the musicians associations also set up committees to deal with applications from those professions. The SPSL prepared the applications for more than 550 individuals and many others who had been 'transported' to Canada and Australia in the autumn of 1940.

This was when Esther Simpson (see next section), then deputy secretary of SPSL, was at her energetic and proactive best. The government was clearly embarrassed that they had reacted too hastily to urgencies, real enough no doubt, but heightened by popular newspaper campaigns. The Home Secretary announced that anyone 'who is helping the pursuit of learning and science' would be eligible. It was Esther Simpson who drew up the list of over 550 candidates.

Some refugees have left vivid accounts of internment, none more so than Paul Jacobsthal, a scholar who specialized in Greek vase painting and Celtic art. He had left Germany in 1937, and was appointed lecturer at Christ Church, Oxford. In 1944 he would publish his *Early Celtic Art*, which examined the impact of Greek ornament on Celtic decorative arts.[72] He captured the irony and incongruity of the occasion, when he wrote: 'On Friday July 5 1940 in the morning when I was peacefully writing on Celtic Geometric Ornament a knock came at my door in Christ Church and a plain clothes police officer entered producing a warrant of arrest. Being an optimist by nature and wrongly believing in English "individualism" I was surprised; there had been a good many other scholars, loosely connected with the University, interned during the last weeks. But I had felt safe: had not the Public Orator in 1937 at the Encaenia mentioned me as *"huius Universitatis non inquilinum, sed insitivum"*?[73] And had not Judge Dale, presiding at the Tribunal, sifting Aliens, in 1939 addressed me "… it is an honour to have you here"? I saw the Dean who tried in vain to obtain from the Chief Constable a respite of six hours which would have enabled me to shelter my manuscripts and photos properly. I was driven home in the Black Maria, took my leave of my wife and fetched my case. On our way back to the police station we took my neighbour Dr Kosterlitz with his violin, a sympathetic, modest psychotherapist. In the police station my luggage was searched, my razor "temporarily impounded" – they were apparently afraid of suicide or murder (in other places they took more interest in boot-laces).[74]

'I found the following gentlemen already assembled: Dr Berkenau, neurologist, working in the Warneford Hospital, Oxford; Dr Brink, collaborator of the Oxford Latin Dictionary published by the Clarendon Press; Dr Forchheimer, Head of Department in the Austrian Ministry of Labour, attached to University College; Professor Gruenhut, formerly Professor of Criminal law in the University of Bonn, attached to All Souls; Professor Jellinek, Professor of Medicine in the University of Vienna, connected with Queens College; Dr Meinhart, formerly Keeper at the Ethnographical Museum, Berlin, Deputy Keeper at the Pitt-Rivers Museum, Oxford …' (There were many more.)

'We had our last normal lunch, served by friendly police officers; in the later afternoon we were driven in a hired Midlands bus to Cowley barracks. There was a detention room, locked up during the night, we were twelve people, bedded close together on the floor. We had a plain supper in a hall to which we were led by sentries with fixed bayonets. After supper we could walk in a cemented yard 25 by 35 feet and look into the country through barbed wire … Some of us were silent and depressed, others excited and talkative. Professor Jellinek lectured on his experiments on the influence of lightning on metal, illustrated by photos: he maintained that the Greeks as their representation of thunderbolts prove must have been acquainted with these phenomena, he told us that in his institute in Vienna he had pictures enlarged from a plate in some monograph

"The representation of the thunderbolt in antiquity" and he was delighted to meet the author.'

They were taken to Devon, where they received a prisoner number and were examined medically to see if they were suffering from venereal diseases. After two days, they went north. 'At 6 p.m. we arrived at an ugly town which we learned afterwards was Bury. We marched down a long road, Manchester Road, a clue to the part of England where we were – people stared at us with rather hostile looks. After 20 minutes we halted in front of a colossal disgustingly ugly factory showing all the symptoms of decay. Behind the wire fences old customers, reduced to looking like low-class refugees, grimaced and shouted at us newcomers – the whole thing a nightmare.

'We were taken upstairs to a huge hall, about 150 by 250 foot, the ceiling supported by cast-iron columns with Corinthian capitals, along it the remnants of cotton-spinning machinery, transmissions and crankshafts, partly dismounted, heavy pieces dangerously dangling. We had to line up, perspiring, penned together with our luggage: some people fainted. In a corner through the small windows some light still shone in, an officer and some sergeants were busy making lists and searching men and luggage till nightfall stopped them. They finished their job next morning, five captains, assisted by privates who had the manners and techniques of customs officers, were at work; they confiscated books, chocolate, cigarettes, writing paper, drugs: insulin was taken away from a diabetic, doctors had to give up their instruments; I personally managed to keep my Odyssey when I showed the Captain a certificate with the seal of the university. We stumbled through dark staircases and narrow catacomb-like corridors to a hall on the ground floor converted into a kitchen and had porridge and tea in tin vessels. Then we fetched palliasses and blankets and lay down on the floor in the hall upstairs well guarded by sentries with fixed bayonets.

'Next morning we learned the name of the Camp which now became our home for about a week: Warth Mill – or as some half-educated internee pronounced it Wrath Mill, which would have been a far more appropriate name.'

Paul Jacobsthal was transferred to Hutchinson Camp on the Isle of Man, maintaining a wry detachment and a highly graphic impression of his experiences, which he wrote with the same cool acuity. He was, perhaps lucky.

One former Professor of Chemistry, an international authority in dyestuffs and a former concentration camp inmate, escaped to England just before the war and was researching the use of sisal waste in submarines. As soon as the Release Orders were enacted, his employers applied for his exemption from internment. No answer came from the Home Office when the police arrived at his house. He begged them to wait until the Home Office replied. They wouldn't. Unable to face internment, he took poison.[75]

Max Perutz also wrote of his experience, not only of internment, but of deportation to Canada.[76] He was picked up in Cambridge in May 1940 and locked up with more than a hundred others in a school at Bury St Edmunds. From there, they were taken to a Liverpool housing estate and then Victorian boarding houses on the Isle of Man. 'A few days later, tight-lipped Army doctors came to vaccinate all the men under thirty – an ominous event, whose sinister purpose we soon learned. On July 3, we were taken back to Liverpool, and ... embarked on the large troopship *Ettrick* for an unknown destination. About twelve hundred of us were herded together, tier upon tier, in its airless holds. Locked up in another hold were German prisoners of war, whom we envied for their army rations. On our second day out, we learned about the Arandora Star ... After that we were issued life belts.'

When they arrived at Quebec ten days later, their status changed from internee to civilian prisoners of war, entitling them to army rations. Most assumed that internment would last for the duration of the war, which seemed an open sentence. Fear remained that if Britain lost the war, they would be sent back to Germany. 'To have been arrested, interned and deported as an enemy alien by the English, whom I had regarded as my friends, made me more bitter than to have lost freedom itself. Having first been rejected as a Jew by my native Austria, which I loved, I now found myself rejected as a German by my adopted country. Since we were kept incommunicado at first, I could not know that most of my English friends and scientific colleagues were campaigning to get the anti-Nazi refugees, and especially the many scholars among them, released. I had come to Cambridge from Vienna as a graduate student in 1936 and had begun my life's research work on the structure of proteins. In March of 1940, a few weeks before my arrest, I had proudly won my PhD with a thesis on the crystal structure of haemoglobin – the protein of the red blood cells. My parents had joined me in Cambridge shortly before the outbreak of war; I wondered when I would see them again. But, most of all, I and the more enterprising among my comrades felt frustrated at having to idle away our time instead of helping in the war against Hitler.'

Max Perutz entertained fantasies of escape to the USA, to join his brother and sister. More practically, he organized the camp university, along with mathematician Hermann Bondi, who later became chief scientist at the Ministry of Defence, and originated the steady-state theory of the universe. Klaus Fuchs also taught at this improvised institution.

When the camp commander told Max Perutz that the Home Office had ordered his release and that he had also been offered a professorship by the New School of Social Research in New York, he chose to return to England, where his research and his parents were. He learned that his father had also been interned on the Isle of Man. In New Brunswick, awaiting an escort back to Britain, 'we were met by one of Britain's prison commissioners – the shrewd and humane Alexander

Paterson sent out by the Home Office to interview any of the internees who wanted to return to Britain.' By the time a convoy had assembled to make the dangerous Atlantic crossing, it was already January. 'One gray winter morning, the entire convoy anchored safely in Liverpool Harbor. On landing, I was formally released from internment and handed a railway ticket to Cambridge, and I was told to register with the police there as an enemy alien ... Next morning, at the Cambridge station, our faithful lab mechanic greeted me, not as an enemy alien but as a long-lost friend; he brought me the good news that my father had been released from the Isle of Man a few weeks earlier and that both he and my mother were safe in Cambridge. That was January 1941.' His ordeal had lasted eight months.

In the journal of the Association of Jewish Refugees in September 2007, in response to two articles by Anthony Grenville, a number of correspondents wrote letters to the editor recalling their own and their relatives' experience of internment.[77] These show both the bitterness and tragedy of some lives; the comic absurdity of others. Max Sulzbacher, referring to his late father Martin Sulzbacher, said, 'In February 1940 he was hauled before a tribunal on trumped-up charges, laced in category A (that is those believed to pose the greatest "threat" to the security of Britain), and sent to a camp in Seton, Devon in that cold winter. In June he was sent to Liverpool on the Arandora Star bound for Canada ... Fortunately, my father was a strong swimmer and he found a raft from which he was eventually rescued by a Canadian destroyer. All this is beautifully described in two books: *Collar the Lot* and *A Bespattered Page* (by the late Ronald Stent).[78] The destroyer landed them in Greenock, Scotland, but a week later he was sent on the Dunera bound for Australia. There he was put into a camp in Tatura.

'To quote from Ronald Stent's book, "On erev Yom Kippur", he received a telegram that his house in north London had been bombed: his aged parents, his sister, his brother and sister-in-law had all been killed. Fortunately, my mother and my siblings had all been saved as they were interned on the Isle of Man.

'In November 1941 my father was allowed to return to England, but was sent to the Isle of Man before being released. His humorous remark was: "*Fur eine Nachkur*" (for an after-treatment).

'After these experiences he did not take up British nationality and it was left to me and my siblings to become naturalized individually when we came of age.'

Mrs Maria Blackburn wrote: 'My mother and I escaped from Vienna in March 1939 on her (non-Jewish) passport. My Jewish father had to acquire a forged passport in order to join us in England just before the war started.

'At the time I was eight years old and I remember very clearly how Father was taken away to the Isle of Man soon after his arrival. The next time I saw him he was dressed in the uniform of the British army – the Pioneer Corps actually. He served in Britain and France until the end of the war.

'Father never complained about internment but told us amusing stories about how the multinational internees chatted in 'Emigranto', a mixture of English, Yiddish and German. He was taught English and appreciated his intelligent, well-educated company.

'However, Father missed his family, so when he was told that he had two choices – to stay on the Isle of Man for the rest of the war or to join up – he quickly chose the latter ...

'Father's choice meant that Mother was given a work permit. So at last she was able to earn ten pence an hour, cleaning for some comfortably-off ladies living in our area of Yorkshire ... I never heard my father complain about his army service. He was very grateful to Britain for giving us shelter and saving our lives. So he was proud to serve and luckily came back to us without a scratch, living to a grand old age.'

Beveridge, in *A Defence of Free Learning*, also includes some testimonies of interned academics, including that of economist, Dr Leo Lipmann, who spoke of arrival in Douglas, Isle of Man, walking through 'streets lined by sullen crowds'.[79] The sociologist, Heinz Arndt, said internees were 'shoved across the Atlantic like cattle'. There were 450 Nazi prisoners of war on board the Motor Ship, *Estrick*. He kept a diary addressed to his fiancée, in which he says he spent much time trying to explain to the captain-interpreter the difference between Nazis and those oppressed by them. The internees were also expected to share huts with Nazis; they organized themselves in such a way as to avoid contact with their enemies. When they were at last given writing paper, it was stamped 'Prisoner-of-War mail', which they refused to use.

Most internees were released within a year. The events of 1940 came to be seen as a consequence of panic, a wasteful error, a detail in the monstrous mistakes of that violent and troubled era.

Helping hands

The well-known names who supported the Academic Assistance Council should not conceal the many less prominent people who gave professional and voluntary support, serving as counsellors, befrienders and initiators of sometimes bewildered strangers into the mysterious ways of the British. No one exemplifies this altruism and dedication better than Esther Simpson, employed by the AAC and SPSL for 45 years. Attentive to both the personal and professional wellbeing of all who passed through the organization, her tact and delicacy are still remembered, not only by those who received SPSL grants, but equally, by Council members or those acting as advisers and referees for exiled academics.

She was a significant figure, a rather enigmatic example of the Anglicized Jewish immigrant. She became a Quaker, and religious commitment combined with the wider horizons of the daughter of immigrants led to an early interest in international affairs (she read French and German at Leeds). She learned the violin from the age of six, and her relationships with émigrés were strengthened by a common and passionate interest in making music. Experience as a schoolteacher was followed by a spell as a governess in Germany, after which she became a secretary to a British aristocrat in Paris. She worked for the International Fellowship for Reconciliation, set up after the First World War and dedicated to understanding between former belligerents. In the background were the qualities of that particularly British view of 'good works' associated with pacifists, idealists, socialists and Quakers: earnestness, high-mindedness and a spirit of international-ism. She maintained regular contact with many rescued scholars and remembered birthdays and anniversaries. She often referred to them as her 'family'; and as she grew older, they frequently invited her to their home, club or hotel, where they looked after her as she had looked after them. In 1940 she admitted in a very British form of understatement, 'I faced one or two anxious moments last week. One naturally has something to worry about when one has a family of six hundred.'

Esther Simpson embodied altruism and duty, a combination far from joyless, since her kindness and patience have not been forgotten, any more than her formidable efficiency. She was the kind of woman of whose passing it was said that her like would not be seen again. This is true. But it does not mean that generosity and fellow-feeling have vanished. Today, these take a different form, no less dedicated, but perhaps more professional. Esther Simpson, born in 1903, was of that generation of women shaped by the slaughter of the First World War. Their devotion to the welfare of the injured and disabled, as to those less favoured than themselves, was in part the response of a bereaved generation and its sense of loss; the tenderness they bestowed was rooted, not only in culture and conscience, but also in the experience of a society amputated of so much youthful energy.

Esther Simpson became an idealized figure. But like many of those she aided, her inner life remains in shadow. She did, however, make something of a confidant of Engelbert Broda, the Austrian chemist who came to Britain in 1938. His son, Paul Broda, has a considerable correspondence between his father and Esther Simpson, in which she is less guarded than in the formal interviews she gave. From it a more idiosyncratic – and rounded – woman emerges, with a strong feeling of Englishness, although as she says in one letter (18 December 1950), her own parents were never really assimilated. 'England is full of faults, and these hurt me because I feel part of England in spite of my parents' origin.' She felt she had the advantage, as a child of refugees, of a more critical eye.

Her letters indicate that many of her standards were conventionally those of the upwardly mobile. In one, she reports that she had attended an excellent lecture, but that of course, she didn't understand it. If her admiration for her protégés would now be considered 'elitist', at the time this would scarcely have been thought worthy of comment. She would probably have agreed with E.M. Forster, who said if he had to choose between his friends and his country, he would choose the former. She wrote (18 December 1950): 'to me human relationships are the most important, because the most constructively creative factors operating in this world of woe. The human individual is what matters to me, not "humanity", and certainly not any Moloch of a "state" which purports to speak for "humanity".'

Tess Simpson and Engelbert Broda had an enduring friendship, despite political differences. In her letters, Esther appears to argue with his Communist allegiance without actually broaching the issue directly – another example of her tact. It does suggest a considerable degree of frankness between them. She wrote: 'What I cannot do is to let my idealism for this country – by which I mean my desire that it should be perfect and my consequent suffering that it is not – blind me to the beam in the other fellow's eye; I can't fall for another system simply because mine is not perfect, because I am only too conscious of elements in other systems which make for the destruction of the values which I believe in and without which no decent human intercourse is possible. Don't mistake me; when I say I feel part of England, it isn't out of any chauvinism – it's a mixture of the consciousness of privileges enjoyed during my childhood that my parents never had, the real affection I bear for what is best in the English character and institutions – but I believe that I have to belong to the world too; I do feel a citizen of the world. England so far allows me to be that – far too many countries would not.'

She was not above offering advice to her friends in personal matters. This emotional involvement in the lives of rescued scholars had its limitations. SPSL was, after all, as Paul Broda says, 'set up for European Jews who won Nobel prizes'. Engelbert Broda felt that the great and good of SPSL could never really understand people who had been imprisoned in central Europe and for whom escape was a matter of life and death.

At the end of *A Defence of Free Learning*, Beveridge says that by 1945, although Hitler was dead, intolerance was not. Of the 2,541 scholars on the register of the SPSL in 1945, 624 were in the USA, 612 in Britain, 80 in Central and South America, 74 in The Dominions and 66 in Palestine. He says that the SPSL was on the verge of closing down in 1956, when events in Hungary demonstrated that the need for such an organization was as urgent as ever.[80]

After the war, the great majority of scholars in Britain remained here. Nikolaus Pevsner, then Slade Professor or Fine Art at Cambridge, wrote to Beveridge 'Thanks to the generosity and the open-mindedness of this country, there was ... only a removal to more sympathetic surroundings. I have had two or three enquiries from Germany in the last few years, whether I would go back and occupy a chair, but our family is here, and our life and my job are here. We have after all lived in London longer than in any other single town.'

Max Born, then 75, did return to Germany. But he wrote: 'Through the generosity of the SPSL and the British Universities, in particular Cambridge and Edinburgh, I have found a second home in Great Britain and was able to give my children a good education. All my ten grandchildren have been born in Great Britain and have English as their mother tongue. I am deeply grateful for all this. After my reaching the age limit I have retired to my home country, partly for economical, partly for sentimental reasons. But I have retained my British nationality.'

The aftermath

Those who escaped – and the survivors of – the Holocaust appeared to herald a chastened society, which would be more just and learn to value people not only for their intellectual distinction, but because there are other forms of knowing, without which a civilized society is impossible: the informed spirit and the acuity of the heart, the insights of compassion and the far-sightedness of wisdom and watchfulness – not rhetorical abstractions, but the bonding of a common humanity, fragile and always threatened by the superior 'knowledge' of revelation, divine or of this world.

Esther Simpson became virtually the lone custodian of the SPSL's work, although, perhaps inevitably, satisfaction with work accomplished was overtaken by new urgencies. The mission of rescue would never be the same again as in the 1930s. It was not that racism and discrimination would disappear – far from it; human societies are rarely animated by reason, although are sometimes governed by it. Before long, other ideologies would send waves of dissenters to seek shelter in the shrinking sites of tolerance as much of the world succumbed either to Marxist or military dictatorships in the post-war era. By that time, other movements had emerged, which took over some responsibilities which the SPSL had made its own in the heroic years of the 1930s and 40s.

After the extraordinary talents of the 1930s generation, it is tempting to see a decline in the intellectual ability of subsequent refugees. But each fresh wave brings different qualities, and if we expect that early experience to be repeated, we are almost certainly looking in the wrong place. There is another shift in the contemporary world which Paul Broda points out. 'One element of that generation from the thirties that distinguished them from those who came later was that they really believed that they, personally, could change the world; and in many ways they did. I don't think any of us believes that now.'

Plate 1   Sketch of Albert Einstein
by Ilse Eton
With kind permission of Mrs Ilse Eton
(Assistant Secretary SPSL, 1944–45 and
Secretary, April 1946–51)

Plate 2   Lord Beveridge enjoying a glass
of wine
LSE Archives

Plate 3   Lord Rutherford
Cavendish Laboratory, University of Cambridge

Plate 4   Esther Simpson
CARA Archive, London

Plate 5   Leo Szilard
Egon Weiss Collection

Plate 6   Max Perutz with his
haemoglobin model
MRC (Medical Research Council) – Laboratory
of Molecular Biology

Plate 7   Max Born
With kind permission of Gustav Born

Plate 8   Sir Hans Krebs and his students
in the laboratory at Sheffield
University of Sheffield

Plate 9   Sir Nikolaus Pevsner
Photo that was published by the *Evening Standard* in 1954. Copyright © Getty Images

Plate 10   Sir Karl Popper
Copyright © Lucinda Douglas-Menzies/National Portrait Gallery, London

Plate 11   Sir Ernst Gombrich
With kind permission of Leonie Gombrich

Plate 12   Sir Ludwig Guttmann
With kind permission of the International
Spinal Cord Society (ISCoS)

Plate 13   Sir Ernst Chain at work in the
Sir William Dunn School of Pathology,
Oxford, 1939
John Wiley & Sons Ltd

Plate 14   Klaus Fuchs
National Archives

Plate 15   Kindertransport children in 1938
Wiener Library, London

Plate 16   Jewish refugees in Germany boarding a boat for England
Wiener Library, London

3
Until

Refugees, and not only the clever and celebrated, are a source of perpetual renewal and innovation in the societies that receive them; not only because they must re-invent themselves, but in so doing, they also creatively re-appraise the values of the host culture. This fundamental concept should not need to be fought for. While preparing this book, a number of people in the USA told me that such a simple truth should not even require enunciation. It does, of course, again, even in the USA, where the presence of an estimated 12–15 million 'undocumented', mainly Latino, newcomers, has also revived a debate still never quite settled in Europe.

Eva Hoffman observed of the late 1950s, 'I came to America at a moment when that country was on the cusp of enormous change. But at the time it still had a confident unified sense of itself and the conviction that it was not only a great power but that it represented progress, goodness and the desirable human norm. The ideology of emigration was still unequivocally assimilationist. The reigning metaphor was of the melting pot, and of course it was premised on the belief that new arrivals would be only too happy to do the melting, to leave their pasts behind and accept all that America had to offer gladly and gratefully. The imagination of difference, in other words, was neither nurtured nor strongly developed. [Thus] assimilation carried with it strong connotations of colonization, of having my first self, so to speak, undervalued and stifled by a very powerful force.'[1] Globalization is destabilizing fixed identities, even in the most exuberant and self-confident places. These uncertainties are reinforced by refugees who reach Europe and America, with stories of other forms of social organization and ways of living which, until now, had been only rumours on the outskirts of civilization.

EASTERN EUROPE

Hungary and Czechoslovakia

After the enormity of the Second World War and the realization of what had actually befallen Europe, it was understandable that the continent should focus on reconstruction. A work of ferocious expiatory economic repair took place which led within two decades to the *Wirtschaftswunder*, the German economic miracle. Because economic collapse had led directly to the social and moral catastrophe of National Socialism, it followed that economic growth would be the surest guarantor that the vow, 'Never Again', would be fulfilled.

The impulse to economic rehabilitation was also nourished by the competitive struggle with a Socialism which seemed, by force in Europe, and voluntarily by the independence struggles of former imperial territories, destined to dominate the future. But although the world had changed far less than was thought, and one form of totalitarian ideology in central and Eastern Europe had been exchanged for another, the persecution of academics in the Communist countries did not immediately seem to be of the same degree as under National Socialist regimes. For one thing, there was no crude repudiation of 'Jewish' science or physics and no expulsion of people on racial grounds. Communist ideological conformity demanded a different kind of tribute. In any case, the Soviet Union cherished its scientists, particularly those engaged in the rivalry with the USA for military and nuclear supremacy. Different categories of people were the primary targets of Communist orthodoxy – political dissidents, writers and artists, and all those who refused to accept the basic premise of a historically predestined proletarian future.

Refugees from Hungary after the 1956 uprising, and Czechoslovakia, following the crushing of the 'Prague Spring' in 1968, scholars who were victims of the junta in Greece and of the Liberation War in Bangladesh, all these would make fresh demands on the SPSL. When Jewish and anti-Communist refugees came from Poland, first in the late fifties and again a decade later, and the persecuted of South Africa brought their echoes of discrimination and hatred less than a generation after the end of the war, these were perceived as disturbing after-shocks of the convulsive events of the century, rather than evidence that other persecutions were on the march, dressed in new plumes and regalia, no doubt, but similarly devastating for their victims.

No one who heard the voice of Imre Nagy in 1956 as Soviet tanks entered Budapest could have doubted that the world had been changed by the convulsions of the war; and the Cold War represented a long coda of the unfinished business of totalitarianism in Europe. The violent reaction to the revolt in East Germany in 1953 and the Hungarian uprising in 1956 sent a different population in search of asylum.

The Jewish mathematician Imre Lakatos (born Imre Lipschitz) was caught up in these epic ideological conflicts. When in 1944, the year of his graduation, the Hungarian government collaborated with Hitler (thereby sending almost two-thirds of Hungary's Jews to their death) Lakatos changed his name to Imre Molnar. Both his mother and grandmother were to perish in concentration camps. He became a convinced Communist, and changed his name back to Lakatos, allegedly to avoid replacing the initials on his clothing. He worked in the Ministry of Education, involved with university reform. He came to believe that the Party should be governed by Science, and not science by the party, that censorship was unnecessary and that dissent and argument should be promoted. Arrested in 1950 for challenging the Russian authorities, he spent more than three years in jail and said he was partly saved by his faith in Communism. After his release he made a living translating mathematics books into Hungarian. When Hungary announced its withdrawal from the Warsaw Pact, Russia intervened and set up a compliant government. Many academics were among the 200,000 who escaped to the West. Lakatos went to Vienna, from where he was admitted to England and studied at Cambridge, supported by the Rockefeller Foundation. In 1960 he went to LSE, where he taught for 14 years until his sudden death in 1972. He revolutionized the philosophy and history of mathematics and science, seeing mathematics not as an accumulation of revealed truths but as evolutionary and concrete, permanently evolving new concepts and crystallizing old ones.

A number of academics were helped after the 'Prague Spring', when under Alexander Dubcek a modest reform of the Communist system was inaugurated, including freedom of the press, tolerance of new political parties and a concentration on the production of consumer goods. Brezhnev negotiated with Dubcek, but by August Warsaw Pact tanks had entered Prague. Many academics fled, among them G.J. Frankl, referred to the SPSL by the Jewish Refugee Committee. He wrote to the SPSL, telling his epic story in a few laconic, but heartbreaking words. 'I was born on 26th April 1921 at Hradec Kralove in Czechoslovakia. After my basic education I attended the Grammar School at Hradec Kralove (1932–1940). The Germans, who occupied Czechoslovakia in 1938 and 1939, closed all the schools of higher education in 1940. So I took a short intensive course for teachers and secretly taught Jewish children excluded from general school attendance. Soon afterwards, in 1941, I was put to forced labour, and in 1942 all my family – both my parents, my two sisters, their three children and both my brothers-in-law and I myself – were imprisoned by the Germans and sent to concentration camps. In Auschwitz in 1944 they were all executed. I alone left Auschwitz in July 1944 and was sent to other concentration camps. I spent most of the time in Schwarzheide-Ruhland and in Oranienburg in Germany. Later I took part in the so-called 'march of death' and was rescued in May 1945. I was fully exhausted – at the age of 24 I looked as if I were over 60 years old. It took nearly two months before I was able to be transported back to my country.'[2]

In 1962, Frankl was appointed a senior lecturer at the Prague School of Economics, where he remained until September 1968. He left because of the Russian occupation. His wife, daughter and son-in-law met him a week later in Vienna. They went on to London and rejoined their son Tom, who was studying at Holland Park school. Frankl secured a temporary teaching position at Starcross Comprehensive School in Islington.

SPSL in transition

SPSL's support of displaced academics was modest during the upheavals associated with the last part of the Cold War; and with dictatorships, military juntas and authoritarian regimes in much of central and South America, Africa and Asia, its resources could not possibly answer the demand.

SPSL's material assistance was limited by remit to post-doctoral students. As needs changed, the council provided academics not only with maintenance grants, but also allowances for travel, books and other forms of assistance. Its means were slender, even though an afterglow of the heroic age remained.

Esther Simpson's flat became the SPSL office until she was 75, when she officially retired. In 1978, her replacement, Liz Fraser was based in the office of the World University Service (WUS), where she had been working and continued to do so, since her SPSL appointment was one day a week. WUS had taken over many of SPSL's functions; it had more ample funding, a younger staff, and helped students and junior academics.[3] The energy had deserted the SPSL. Liz Fraser was also aware of the changing nature of refuge, which reverted to what, in the early days of Hitler, it was believed to be – a temporary sojourn, with academics expected to return home once the regime in question had been toppled, using the benefits gained from Britain to help rebuild their countries. At the same time, British influence would live on in the goodwill of people whose education had been completed here, and who would carry weight in the restored democracy at home. As time went by, younger students from different cultures and little-known education systems arrived, speaking unfamiliar languages; assessing their achievements and potential required a different yardstick from the stern standards of the pre-war academy.

Changes in academic life here also made a difference, especially the extension of higher education from the 1960s onwards. New social groups entered the universities, bringing an often truculent mixture of radicalism, pop culture and a refusal of deference, even, at times, to the idea of learning, while university staff brought a less exclusive openness to the world. Liz Fraser observes: 'When I started out as a university teacher in the late 60's, it was more or less expected that we would be involved in outside activities. These could be to do with, say, specific local issues, or more general academic campaigns.' This was not to last. Over the past two or three decades, governments have narrowed the duties of pedagogy to results, targets and access. Liz Fraser says, 'By the time I retired from CARA in 2000, the climate had changed drastically and the pressure and range of work demanded of lecturers made it much more difficult for them to give time to activities in the wider community.'

The World University Service took over something of the role of the SPSL. Representing a new time and culture, it was a product of a hopeful internationalism that had grown out of the ruins of destructive nationalisms in Europe.

SOUTH AMERICA

The role of the World University Service

Florid nationalisms appeared to have migrated. The military coup in Chile in 1973 created new needs and opportunities, as another generation of academics fled for their lives. Other organizations, new and existing, responded quickly to the imprisonment, torture and disappearances of prominent people who opposed the ousting of the democratically elected government of Salvador Allende.

The event had a profound international effect. It seemed – not for the last time – that democracy was conditional upon the right people being elected. Although Britain initially recognized the Pinochet regime, among the many voluntary movements of solidarity was Academics for Chile. Academics for Chile approached the World University Service to assist in finding places for those who could be released from the prison that Chile had become. WUS raised funds, and became a clearing-house and assembly point for university students and teachers, who began arriving in significant numbers, particularly when the government changed in Britain in February 1974.

The mobilization on Chile's behalf was one of the great successes of voluntary action to assist refugees in the era after the Second World War. Together with the apartheid regime in South Africa, people in Britain saw Chile as one of the most potent symbols of injustice, its attempt to construct a radical socialist regime by democratic means facing the opposition of the USA. Both countries had a particular relationship with Britain. Before Pinochet, Chile was held to be a model of South American democracy, the brutal coup arousing massive sympathy in Britain and indeed worldwide, according to Alan Angell, who founded Academics for Chile. South Africa had been expelled from the Commonwealth in 1953, as a result of an ideology unacceptable to the multiracial make-up of the international body; and London was the preferred destination of many academics, artists and activists, who found the administration of institutionalized racism objectionable.

With the help of Christian Aid, and a generous grant from the then Overseas Development Ministry for Chilean Scholars, in 1974 almost 100 scholars were helped, mainly young postgraduates, whose further study was widely expected to be of use to their country when democracy was restored. The number increased to 260 the following year. The largest single category helped were economists, followed by sociologists.

The demands of efficiency led to a certain professionalizing of the work, which became centrally organized and funded. The Chairman of WUS remarked in 1976 that this weakened contact between campus student activity on behalf of Chilean scholars and the London secretariat. This large-scale assistance also diminished the role of the SPSL, although it continued to assist prominent individuals. Its income could not match that of the more conspicuous – and politically more glamorous – WUS.

Chile's authoritarian militaristic nationalism, reinforced by the inspiration the Chilean army derived from the discipline and even the uniform of Bismarck's Germany, echoed the Fascism of the 1930s. The considerable migration of Germans, especially into the south of the country, added impetus to this.

Lucia Munoz, a Chilean refugee, worked for six years at WUS. Her brother, Luis, has produced a compelling account of the violence of the Pinochet years. He describes the torture and abuse practised by many military regimes in the 1970s and 80s – a bleak portrait of the fate of dissenters under authoritarian regimes, never short of highly-placed apologists during the last convulsions of the Cold War. His story – and touchingly, that of his sister's obsessive search for him and her role in securing his release – speak of the courage of thousands of young academics.

Luis Munoz, Chile

Luis was a student, and his sister was doing a Master's in Development Studies in 1973. Both belonged to a small left-wing party, and while they supported the socialist government, they were impatient with the pace of change. They were romantic idealists; and they paid a severe price for it.

When the coup was announced on Chilean TV on that other fateful 11 September, in 1973, Pinochet said, 'The glorious Chilean Armed Forces, in an attempt to save the country from chaos, have today taken control of the country. Salvator Allende refused to surrender, put up resistance in the presidential palace and died. Citizens should show restraint and go back to their homes to await further communiqués. Workers of essential services and utilities should remain in their posts until further notice. Anyone found to be committing acts of sabotage or resisting the armed forces will be executed.'

Luis Munoz describes the agitation following the coup. An insomniac energy seized those resisting the regime, as gunfire was heard all over Santiago, streets were occupied by patrol vehicles and armoured personnel carriers. Helicopters whirred overhead. The only hope lay in finding safe hiding-places, houses where opponents of the regime could lie low indefinitely. The junta broadcast the names of prominent people required to present themselves to the Ministry of Defence: public figures in the Allende government, union leaders, academics, journalists. Many people did indeed give themselves up.

'There were bodies lying in the streets. There were open municipal lorries collecting the corpses and piling them up on the back of the trucks for everyone to see. It was unbelievable. It was macabre. A few days before, everything had looked so normal. There were children playing in the streets, but they were now deserted apart from the personnel carriers, the municipal trucks and a few furtive pedestrians. And it felt cold, very cold.'[4]

Luis Munoz survived for about a year. Then he was picked up on the street in daylight, in full view of his fellow-citizens. He was taken to Villa Grimaldi, one of the most notorious interrogation centres of the Direcion de Inteligencia Nacional (DINA, the secret police). It contained 'all the sickening apparatus needed for extracting information. I would remain blindfolded, handcuffed, with my legs chained together the entire time I was there.'

After the men came to tie him up, naked, to the metal bed known as the *parrilla* (grill), they attached electrodes to the body's most sensitive parts. 'They do not miss any part: the toes, the penis, the anus, the nipples, the mouth and the ears. Then they proceed to apply high wattage electrical current, but they do not ask questions. The questions are shouted, rather than asked, by the most senior members of the team. In my case the man in charge was the infamous Captain Miguel Krassnoff. The others just shouted and screamed as if in a frenzy and made obscene remarks. The pain is unbearable; anyone who has not experienced this kind of torture is unable to imagine anything close to this amount of pain. Furthermore, the body suffers violent convulsions, which in turn help to cut open the flesh at the wrists and the ankles tied with wire to the metal bed, and sometimes even dislocate them.'[5]

Munoz later returned to Chile to give evidence at the trial of Miguel Krassnoff, his principal torturer, and his testimony helped secure his conviction. Luis Munoz was rescued by the British government, although it was never his choice to come here. 'They closed the camp where I was. Some prisoners were released, others expelled from the country. The rescue was done through an ecumenical church organization – the Council for European Migration. I was sponsored by Amnesty in Norway, and they asked the British to issue me a visa.[6]

'I didn't want to go to England. I pleaded, send me anywhere but England. They said, "You're going to England." I refused. Two days later an official from European Migration told me that some released detainees were being shot "at random", so it looked like a street crime; or the army announced they were killing "terrorists". He said, "We cannot protect you." I was taken to the Red Cross to get my passport. "You have to go, your visa and ticket are ready."'

He arrived in Britain in December 1976. 'It was cold, with snow on the ground. I was sent to a Home Office house in Shepherd's Bush, a former bed-and-breakfast hotel. We cooked for ourselves. I thought I would die of cold that first winter. I had left Chile in summer. I don't know what I expected. I gave away my winter clothing before leaving Chile.

'Because I had been expelled I couldn't get a grant to study. I got £17 a week, social security. The shock and the cold defeated me. I didn't want to go out. There were free English lessons, and for a short time, free transport. I got medical treatment, but not the psychological help I needed. I was told I was going to be sent to Birmingham, part of a policy of dispersal. I had already been dispersed. I spoke no English. I was in touch with friends in Paris, members of the Chilean Leftist Party to which I belonged. I said, "Get me out of here, I can't live here." [But] the Home Office had taken my passport. I had a travel card and could not leave the country for six months.'

For the first few years in Britain, Luis could not study. Only cleaning and restaurant jobs were available in the beginning. 'The cleaner may have a university degree but can find no other job because he or she is a foreigner. Let the refugee do the dirty work when the offices are empty in secret, without showing himself.

'I was involved in frenzied activity – meetings, SWP [Socialist Workers Party], Amnesty International, Vanessa Redgrave, Tony Benn, the miners, the unions. Later, another friend working for Amnesty got access to my file. She read it and found out I didn't qualify for Amnesty's grant towards medical help because I was not considered a prisoner of conscience, but a combatant. I had had a gun in Chile, yes; but from where did Amnesty get this information? It was a mystery. Later, at the time of the Malvinas [the Falklands War, 1982], I saw an interview with David Owen. He was talking about exiles from Latin America. Had British Intelligence vetted them? No. Where did their intelligence profile come from? Owen said, "Friendly agencies gave the information." Did that mean the CIA? Yes. It was a great irony – the CIA which had been instrumental in bringing about the coup in Chile had also been involved in our rescue.

'In 1977, relatives of the disappeared went on hunger strike in Chile and we did the same in sympathy. It lasted 16 days, the church of St Aloysius in Euston. I was weak, I lost weight, I must have been close to death. Sympathizers came, Cardinal Hume, Denis Healey. Helen Bamber, who started the Medical Foundation for the Victims of Torture, met me on the bus. She was from a Jewish family in Poland. She said, "How are you?" I said I was OK. She had told Amnesty she would see torture victims for free. Amnesty said that is not our job. She left and started the Foundation in an old hospital. I was partly the inspiration for this.

'In 1984, I was working part-time for the British Refugee Council. I had a heart problem, and Helen Bamber took me to a specialist. He wanted to give me an electric cardiogram. He placed the elements on me. I freaked out. He said, "It's all right, we are taking electrical impulses from your body, not giving you how and why they were forced into exile, and how their integrity was questioned or undermined, often by those who should have protected it. All are current or recent recipients of assistance from CARA.

THE ARAB WORLD

Mukhtar, Iraq

Mukhtar is a psychiatrist, who sees the culling of Iraqi professionals and academics as an ideologically driven assault upon the secular intelligentsia. This was a consequence of the short-sightedness of those who invaded the country in 2003, who thought they had to dissolve every system in Iraq – the army, police, intelligence services, the security and media systems. 'Saddam had done wrong, but to dismantle all functioning institutions was punitive. As to what the US expected when they came, that is a difficult question. On the ground, it is clear they encouraged division. What is their long-term plan? Is it to let the Islamists come to power, demonstrate their failure, and then replace them with secularists of their choosing?'

Mukhtar was involved in the modernization of Iraqi society, and specialized in child mental health. He studied in Britain in 2005 and returned to Baghdad to lecture in a post-graduate teaching department. 'Most paediatricians had no idea of the psychological afflictions of children. Mental health in any case had been generally neglected. I worked as part of a team, with a medical doctor, social worker, teacher, and nurses, to discuss each case, an issue that became crucially significant after the invasion and the trauma undergone by so many children.'

Mukhtar says British tolerance has been severely tested in its response to those fleeing violence and disorder in Iraq and sees Hitlerian echoes in today's Shia militias. Just as Hitler sought to remove 'Jewish' aberrations from 'Aryan' science, so Iraq's Shia militias have tried to destroy secular intellectuals in places of learning. Of course there is an important difference: the militias are not – officially – in power. But the pattern is clear. Over 200 academics were murdered between 2003 and 2007, while hundreds more fled. Most are in neighbouring countries – more than a million Iraqis are in Syria, at least half a million in Jordan.

'We cannot describe our grief and anger when our suffering is denied by those who have, in part at least, generated it. They have pushed us back to the Dark Ages, with the breakdown of society, murder in broad daylight, the destruction of electricity, water, health services and education.

'After I had studied here in 2005, I wanted to do something for the people of Iraq. It didn't occur to me I'd have to leave the country. Colleagues and friends said: "Take care, these people do not discriminate, whether you are a politician or a doctor." Every day I was hearing of colleagues kidnapped or killed. No one was immune.

'In April 2006, I received a threatening telephone call. I took my family to my mother-in-law. I asked colleagues in Britain if it was possible to find work here. My children finished their exams, and went to Amman. I got a visa to Britain. [In] Edinburgh, I discussed my position with a colleague. He arranged for me to meet his local MP, who advised me to go to the Home Office and apply for asylum. But I didn't do it.'

Through a friend, he contacted an immigration lawyer, who said, 'Your case is very strong. You will probably have little problem getting asylum status; it should be settled within six weeks.'

I met Mukhtar a year later. Nothing had happened. He could not work. After two months his money was exhausted. His application for help was refused, because at the time he was living with well-off friends. He says, 'In Iraq, I feel they cut off my legs. Here, they have paralyzed me.' He is prevented from using his skills to contribute to society: however much they might be required in Iraq, it is not as though the children of Britain have no need of psychiatric help.

'I didn't flee Iraq because of Saddam, but because of the mistakes made, among others, by the government of this country. When I sought protection I didn't find it.'

Mukhtar's wife and family returned from Amman to Baghdad. Soon after, they witnessed the murder of two people in a neighbouring house. An anonymous call told them to leave within 24 hours. They got a visa to go to Cairo where they are safe, although his daughter has lost a year in medical school. His 12-year-old son was traumatized by the killings he saw in Baghdad. His wife needs surgery, but they have no money to pay for it in Cairo.

Mukhtar feels imprisoned here. 'The whole of the UK is a prison. I asked the Home Office for my passport, but if I take the passport they will close my case. I am free to go to Cairo, but once I go, that is it.'

The British government is reluctant to admit that in 2007 Iraq is unsafe for academics. Since bringing order and democracy to Iraq has been a key coalition objective, the government are disinclined to shelter those with a different story, even though this is an open secret. The Home Office is also anxious to show the numbers of asylum-seekers is falling. One way to achieve this is simply by leaving applications pending, sometimes for years. In 2007, some 450,000 were set aside, with the promise that all would all be dealt with 'within 4 to 5 years'. Thus people's lives are frozen. In the end, frustrated, some withdraw their application and the figures control themselves. The misery this administrative sleight of hand induces is of no concern.

It should be; people goaded to the limit, become volatile, desperate. A government committed to reducing terror should not play with the emotions of people, particularly those already terrorized, tortured and betrayed in their own country. There is a large dose of hypocrisy here. Reducing the numbers is the principal objective; that the disaffection and resentment of those injured in the process may create greater problems is off the immediate agenda.

Sabreen, Iraq; the unintentional dissident

Those who escaped Iraq before Saddam's overthrow in 2003 have their own stories of terror and violence.

Sabreen is in her fifties and living in Birmingham, a refugee and teacher of dentistry marked by tragedy and loss, much of it directly attributable to the Saddam regime. One of four children born to a family from Basra, her father was a pilot, her mother a teacher. They moved to Baghdad, where life was smooth until Saddam assumed power.

'We were non-political; we just led our lives. I went to university [when] the Ba'ath Party was active in the universities, especially recruiting women. I was selected because I was active and quite prominent. When I told my father, he was furious. He said he wanted nothing to do with politics and I was not to join the party. I went back to university and said my parents didn't agree with my joining.

'From that moment, there was a question mark over me. They didn't allow me to work properly, they harassed me all the time. When I was studying dentistry they stole my instruments. I had been pressured to join: if it had been an error to say yes, it was an even greater mistake to say no afterwards.'

Arbitrary power is vindictive and unforgiving, with a capacity for extreme pettiness. Many of Sabreen's fellow-students, now in Dubai or elsewhere in the Middle East, used the privileges bestowed on them by Saddam to escape. They took his money, and abandoned the Ba'ath Party and Iraq, leaving people like Sabreen to suffer.

'My father was a principled man. The Ba'ath Party was rubbish, a bunch of criminals. Saddam was moody, but his moods were law – one day he said one thing, the next day something else. Three quarters of the population belonged to the Party, but in name only; otherwise they knew they would be punished.

'Saddam relied on other people who gave him a false impression of the world. They took the lead in killing and torturing. His henchmen did the dirty work, and he promoted himself as God.' This statement suggests much about the nature of contemporary tyrannies – in the absence of secular ideologies, the destiny of the 'strong man' becomes paramount, and is often elevated into a source of absolute wisdom. '[Saddam] knew how to frighten people. If anyone from your family committed a crime, the whole family would vanish. Saddam turned Iraq into a big prison. We didn't know what was going on in the world – everything was rigorously censored.'

Sabreen studied dentistry, and came first among the students of her year. 'I danced with joy. Next day they changed the results. "There has been an error.

You have come second." Whoever came first was entitled to a scholarship, but because I was not in the Party, I could not come first. I was not allowed to join the staff of the School of Dentistry [but] was sent to work in the Ministry of Health [in] a remote village on the boundary between the Kurds and what became known as the Sunni Triangle.'2

Sabreen was there for three years. In 1978, she decided to do her Master's in Britain. Her parents paid.

'I did my course in Birmingham and the Royal College exam, but after two years I went home because my father was ill. I returned to Baghdad in 1980, and stayed with him until he died. For the first six months I was happy to be with my family. My father was proud of me.'

The war with Iran began. Sabreen's oldest brother was a major in the army. 'Within six months my brother was killed. They said it was a sniper, a single bullet to the head. Then we heard another story. All his ammunition had run out and he asked his commander for more. He was told he was a coward. They brought his coffin to our house, and left it in the driveway. For three months my mother cried continuously. She couldn't accept she had lost her boy.'

Sabreen still puzzles over this war. It had nothing to do with Sunni/Shia conflict, but with old Persian/Arab enmities. She says Iran's proxies are now running Iraq. 'I feel there is a hidden agenda. Iran distributed its agents in the South through the holy city of Najaf. They want to destroy the Iraqi identity. The regional conflict comes from visions of past glory, Ottomans and Persians. How can the Americans and British not know this?

'Since the 1920s the British were trying to build up the nation – schools, universities, health facilities. Saddam was a devil, but he also established schools and universities. He gave scholarships for people to go abroad.

'There are 5,000 Iraqi doctors of all specialisms now in Syria. They were trained for six years. What a waste! The country has been depleted of its best brains, and is now ruled by thugs. Iraq had a strong army, police force, a vigorous academic life. Now there is nothing. People go for days without power and water, and you can forget about sewerage.

'At the funeral of my brother, my sister was crazy with grief. She went temporarily out of her mind and spoke words she should not have done. The house was full of security men. She said, "Why is this war being fought? It is all being fought because of Saddam." That was her big mistake.

'A few months later, she was killed in a car crash. It was a strange incident, the circumstances obscure. She criticized Saddam. She spoke in grief. A phone call. "Your sister has been involved in an accident. She is in hospital." When we reached the hospital, we were told we should go and identify her in the morgue. My father wept and wept. He became ill. He lost his sight.

'The family was broken. I tried to hold them together. My father was in and out of hospital. My mother used to lament: "If only my son or daughter were here." After that, I couldn't stand the Ba'athists.

'In 1982 I started work again, but stress brought on a form of paralysis. I simply collapsed from time to time. My mother thought I was going to die also. They decided to send me to England, where we had relatives. We contacted them. "Sabreen is ill. She needs a neurological specialist." They thought it might have been depression. I went to the Hospital for Neurological Diseases.

'The consultant said it was a rare disease, whereby the nerves fail to send the right impulse to the muscles; this leads to sudden paralysis. I was given medicine which stabilized my condition. I went home, but had to return to London, where a scan found a tumour behind my chest. I needed an urgent operation. This was successful, but lowered my immune system. I shall have to be on medication for the rest of my life.

'After the operation, I went home. It was two years before I regained strength and worked in the Medical Research Centre. I loved teaching. I stayed till the mid nineties. I realized this was what I most wanted to do. My father was very happy. He died in 1993.

'One day, I was with a colleague, waiting to go to the Dental School on the fifth [floor]. Some men were in the garden below, digging a hole, putting barrels in the ground. My colleague said, "Now we know where the chemical weapons are." I smiled. Within a week, she was dead.

'The Security Office called me. "You talked about chemical weapons. Get out as soon as possible. Get out, or you're next." I got a fake passport and fled to Jordan.'

A casual conversation became a fateful event. This, Sabreen says, is tyranny – arbitrary, pitiless. 'With ideologically driven governments, you know what you can say and what you can't. When there is only the naked power of a dictator, anybody can upset him without being aware of it. That is terror.'

Layla Almariya, Libya

The intolerance of the idiosyncratic beliefs formulated by military leaders or dictators can strike with great violence against those concerned with one or another aspect of truth. The imposition upon the Libyans of the thoughts in Gaddafi's Green Book echo the revelations of an even more destructive predecessor, Mao, and his little red book, which led to the death of millions in China in the 1960s. When Gaddafi overthrew the monarchy in 1969, he promised that 'revolutionary committees' would empower the people in a unique form of 'direct democracy'. This was the 'jamahiryya', or people's republic. Inspired by a mixture of nationalism and Islam, it would avoid all foreign influence, capitalism and Marxism alike. This soon degenerated into dictatorship, and the system allowed Gaddafi to retain total control.

Layla Almariya was arrested for criticizing the thoughts of Gaddafi as set out in the first three chapters of the Green Book. 'I was arrested in my office at the university.

I had no chance to talk to my family or the head of faculty. The phone line to my office was cut. They fabricated everything. For six months I was imprisoned and tortured. I was raped and told I was going to be executed on 7 April.'

On this day a gruesome secular festival in Libya takes place. It commemorates the killing of political opponents in 1976, after a student demonstration against Gaddafi. 'More than a hundred were publicly executed. It was the saddest day in our history. He listens to no one. For almost four decades, he has ruled by personal whim. Speak out and you'll find yourself in prison. You will be handcuffed and held for years, and a message will be sent to your family that you are dead.

'It is impossible to take seriously the contents of the Green Book. The first chapter explains why there is no parliament, just a president. Chapter Two is about economics and equality. Three is about society and the freedom of women. He says women must enjoy the same freedom as men. His bodyguards are female, but the purpose of this is so he can sleep with them.'

Layla's family was related to the wife of King Idris, deposed by Gaddafi in his 1969 coup. Her father had been in the king's administration. He died after having been arrested, imprisoned and tortured.

'We are from El Beida. But when Gaddafi came, his hatred of everything connected with the king was so great that he punished us and our area. Education, hospitals – cities in the East got the worst treatment. Other cities have become richer. Many people who prospered under the royal government have perished. When we were at university, public executions used to take place before our eyes as a warning.

'I was seven when my father died. We call Fatima, widow of Idris, auntie. She is still alive in Egypt. Other family members were arrested and released, but their names remain on a black list. They are not allowed to have a passport. We may have money and a big house, but we cannot spend anything because the government will question us. Gaddafi nationalized all businesses when he came to power. He had grand ideas for a pan-Arab federation of Syria, Egypt and Libya, but nothing came of it.

'I grew up seeing how people suffered under the regime. Gaddafi banned satellite TV and the Internet; then he restored them, but blocks some channels. You can't have the Internet at home. You have to go to an Internet cafe, and give your e-mail address and passport number. Gaddafi thinks he is immortal, and that his power will last for ever.'

Layla was a lecturer in international law and human rights at one of the Libyan universities. She was expected to teach within the framework of the Green Book. 'In other words, lies. I was forced to teach it, even though many students were not from Libya. The students asked embarrassing questions. I took their questions to the management committee of the university, because they are experienced professionals. I was a newly qualified teacher. I was swimming against the tide. I spoke out.

'I was still finishing the dissertation for my Master's, but couldn't finish it because of what happened. I was the youngest teacher in the university. I didn't stop to think. If you are aware of the outside world, you know the Green Book is damaging to society. TV satellite dish had showed us other countries. I had watched debates from the House of Commons on cable, and seen the practice of freedom. One student – I don't know who it was – reported me, and gave a copy of what I had written to the Security Services. In our classes, we never knew who was a spy and who was a student. I was arrested and my survival is a miracle.'

Latefa Guémar, Algeria

Algeria became an 'Arab-Islamic socialist' country in 1962 after its bitter war of independence from France that cost over a million lives as France tried to hold a colony it had occupied since 1834, where 10 per cent of the population were of French origin. In July 1962, Ahmed Ben Bella, head of the Front de Libération Nationale (FLN) became the first president. He was ousted in a bloodless coup by Houari Boumédienne in 1965, and the army displaced the FLN as the main source of political power. Boumédienne died in 1978, and in the succeeding years the army retained control, and the FLN was the only permitted party. Following the oil-price fall in the mid-eighties and Islamic reaction against a militarily enforced secularism, rioting broke out in 1985, and 1988. A new constitution in 1998 allowed other political parties to participate. This led to the rise of the Front de Salut Islamique (FIS – Islamic Salvation Front), which won the municipal elections in 1990, and was poised to win the national elections in 1991. But the army stepped in before the second round, and has ruled the country ever since. Anti-Islamist repression was resisted fiercely, and atrocities on both sides have led to more than 100,000 deaths. Abdelaziz Bouteflika, who assumed power as president in 1999, established an uneasy calm. While some have admired the 'Algerian model' of the control of extremists, the price paid, both in Algeria, and in external Islamist activities, suggests Algeria remains the site of unfinished business. Bouteflika was re-elected in 2005, with the continuing support of the army.

Latefa Guémar was a scientist in Algeria, researching the durability of industrial materials in the nuclear and aviation industries.

'In the late eighties the Islamists became powerful in the universities. For me as a woman it was worse, since women were their first target.

'In 1991 everyone knew [the FIS] would win the legislative elections. I was against the [army] coup, because we were sure there would be violence. We had to ask ourselves searching questions as feminists – we could not be against elections, the system encouraged the poor and the uneducated, and they had been told that a vote for FIS was a vote for God. Their [the FIS] first project would be to put women out of work; 74 per cent of teachers were women and 58 per cent of doctors. Their slogan was to put women in the home.

'After the first round we were apprehensive. A lot of the fundamentalists at the university had studied in the UK or USA. When I told them there was a mistake in my wage slip, they said, "Burn it, in a few weeks there will be no wage-slip."

'The Islamists were also divided, but it was all the same for women. After the coup most of my friends said, "*Vive l'armée.*"

'The elections saw the emergence of the uneducated. My mother, like many older people, voted for FIS, because it seemed a vote for God. For many it was a vote against the FLN, not for the FIS. In the process, the third tendency – secular, social democratic – was squeezed. The democratic tendency was represented by the FFS, the Socialist Front.

'Islamist politics was created by the regime. The democratic socialist tendency was destroyed partly by the Arabization of the university in Algeria. Historians were censored and couldn't write, sociologists were overtaken by the rise of Islamists. My generation was not familiar with the democratic tradition. When a people is prevented from learning its own history, there is bound to be a pathological reaction. Algeria banned books, it even banned French pop singers – you had no right to listen to Enrico Macias and Frank Adamo because they were Jews.

'At the time of the municipal elections in 1990, many families left. By the end of the first round of the legislatives, all our friends were in Paris. They invited me to work there, but FFS was still a force, especially in Algiers. The military was not scared of the Islamists but they were afraid of the FFS. The regime had introduced religious education, but there was no civic education at all.

'Democratic legitimacy does not exist in Algeria. Victims of the regime were human rights defenders, journalists and democratic politicians. The middle class was destroyed. It left the stark confrontation between the rich and the poor. The [remaining] professional middle class earn very little. My father is a surgeon, my brother a cardiologist. They earn about 800 to 900 euros a month. Of the students I supervised, most wanted to go abroad. Engineers went to Canada, journalists and doctors to France. Many young Algerians die in the Mediterranean trying to cross in unsafe boats. These are the *haraga* (illegal migrants). Mostly they are educated young people.

'I worked for the Comissariat, the National Research Institute, [on] a project awarded a prize for innovation. We created a densitometer which measured the density of X-ray film. A patent was required for it. My supervisor left, and a government official was now in charge of the innovatory process. I was supposed to have received an award; but after six months I was told they were sorry but all the papers had been burned. After a couple of years, a French company sold us the very same densitometer. They took the idea and because it had not been patented, they could copy it. It still hurts me, even though it was 20 years ago.'

Latefa Guémar's husband, Soleiman Adel Guémar, is a journalist and poet, forced to leave Algeria when he wrote an article about another journalist arrested after investigating links between the mafia and certain sectors of the state which had financed Islamic extremists. This journalist, arrested and imprisoned, committed suicide. The article was written in homage to this man.

Soleiman managed his own publishing house in Algeria. He visited Britain in 2001, negotiating with publishers here. His UK visa was valid, and he used it to travel here, and asked for asylum.

Latefa followed six months later. 'A few months before, in June 2002, we had been attacked. I came home early from work at about two o'clock in the afternoon. I saw the front door had been broken down. Nothing had been stolen; only our room had been turned upside down. A week earlier, a TV journalist had experienced the same thing, only the intruders were still there when he came home, and they killed him. Our unwelcome visitors had gone. The computer was there, but all the information on it had been taken. We are middle-class people, we had a DVD and a television, but nothing else had been touched. I panicked and called the local police.

'We had been there for about a year, just outside of Algiers. The police came, looked at the damage and asked, "What is your occupation?" I said I was a researcher at the Ministry of Higher Education, and my husband a journalist and publisher. Then they said, "That explains it." They refused to take fingerprints.

'"Why?"

'"We don't have the equipment."

'After 12 years of dirty war, it was inconceivable they didn't have the equipment to deal with terrorists. We could see how the police were working. We went to the local court, which registered a complaint against persons unknown. My husband's partner in the publishing house had been assassinated three weeks before they turned over our house.

'My daughter was one year old. I stayed with her for the summer vacation in my parents' house in Oran. In September I had to resume work. I went to a conference in Damascus, and when I came back, I stayed in my brother's house in Algiers. My husband returned to the flat to check our mail. But we never returned there to live.'

Soleiman's poetry is powerful and uncompromising.

'Illusions'

and we thought we were back together again
in a land of asylum
while others
lurking in the shadows
of all the frontiers
were already waxing

their nearly new boots
but you didn't know it yet

you were dreaming of a city where birds make their
          nests by every window
you were dreaming while others
were already marching
eager to trample over
the flowers of the garden
watered with your blood
but you didn't know it yet

you were getting ready to join
the jubilant crowd
while whole columns of others
were pouring through the city gates
and when you thought you heard
their nearly new boots
resounding
on the smoking tarmac
it was already too late.

'I'm involved in two projects here [Swansea]. One is in the Adult Education Department, looking at parenting in a multicultural European city. The second is in the Geography department, as assistant researcher at the Centre for Migration Policy Research. We are working with the Swansea Learning Partnership, and have developed a website to see how far new arrivals in Swansea can access e-learning to practise English. The Centre for Migration Policy Research is evaluating this e-learning project – how effective it is, how migrants use it, what kind of education may be available to migrants through e-learning. Are they using it to further degree studies? During the long wait for asylum, the one thing people can do is learn, improve their qualifications.'

AFRICA

Joseph Ndalou, Cameroon

Cameroon, on the West African Guinea Coast, has seen land invasions from the east, Portuguese slave-trading and British control of the palm oil and ivory trade. In 1884, it became part of Germany's limited overseas territories. After the First World War Britain and France divided it under a League of Nations Mandate, each half eventually becoming a UN Trust territory. French Cameroon became independent in 1960. The

British territory was split: the northern area became part of Nigeria following a 1961 referendum, while the southern portion was absorbed into Cameroon.

Old imperial rivalries between Francophone and Anglophone Africa have a malignant afterlife in Cameroon, so that the former French territory discriminates against the smaller, sometime British provinces. This colonial culture still influences the country's social and political life, almost half a century after independence. Formal decolonization did nothing to stop the internalization, at least among the elite, of the values of their former masters.

The North, where a majority of Muslims live, is poorer than the South, in which Christians dominate. The first president was Ahmadou Ahidjo, whose repressive regime lasted from 1961 until 1982, when Paul Biya, his designated successor and former Prime Minister, assumed power, despite being from the Christian South. Biya studied law at the Sorbonne. He subsequently accused Ahidjo of plotting a coup against him, and exiled him. Biya 'won' a presidential election as the sole candidate in 1984. He has held power for a quarter of a century. Elections have been boycotted by the Opposition.

Joseph Ndalou, studying for an MSc in Public Health and Health Promotion, lives with his wife and three children in Cardiff. He fled Cameroon because he was working for the South Cameroon Council (SCC), which challenges the ruling party, the CPDM (Cameroon People's Democratic Movement).

'I started as president of the youth wing of the ruling party in Bambili. I was a school prefect. All prefects are Youth presidents, and expected to campaign for the CPDM.

'When I left school, I enrolled in the University of Yaoundé, the only state university that gives a generalized education. Anglophone and Francophone young people studied together. Late in 1990, an uprising on the campus was provoked by conditions faced by English-speaking students. Ninety per cent of lectures were in French. I was in the Faculty of Natural Sciences, where 2,000 students were crammed into an amphitheatre in the open air. It was rough for English speakers, who had fewer chances in the labour market.

'This led to a bloody confrontation between students and the Gendarmerie. Two students were killed. The university was closed down.

'During the break I went to my home in Barminda province. I felt alienated from the ruling party. My father, a civil servant, decided that I should go to Nigeria. I went to Calabar University, close to the border with Cameroon. I took a course in Medical Laboratory Sciences. We had a union of Cameroon students there, most of whom had come because of the language problem. I became secretary of the Calabar branch of Cameroon students. During my four years in Nigeria, I went home only once.

'In 1992, there was another confrontation. Presidential elections had been rigged. We occupied the Cameroon consulate for a week. We entered into negotiations with the Cameroon authorities. In the end, things got worse. News from home was that there was an uprising in all the Anglophone areas. When we left the consulate, we had gained nothing.

'I then went home and worked as a lab technician. I couldn't get work in government hospitals or research institutes because of my linguistic disability. French speakers got the jobs.

'I moved out and lived alone. During that time, the leadership of the Opposition Social Democratic Front (SDF) became very autocratic. There was a power struggle, and people lost faith in them. Things looked dark. There was in effect no opposition.

'I joined the South Cameroon Council, a pressure group. It raised concerns of English-speaking people [and] did advocacy work with the United Nations and international organizations, trying to get mediation in the country between the two polarized groups. I saw it as more committed to development than to gaining political posts. It was a campaign to educate the people and create unity.

'The natural resources of Cameroon are in the English-speaking areas, and these have many cash-crops – tea, rubber, cocoa, coffee and palm products. The littoral area was also sympathetic to the Opposition, although not English-speaking.

'In 1999–2000, I came to prominence in the movement. I addressed meetings and became a founder member of a non-government organization in my home province called Health Impact. Its aim was to bring students and young people together to fight HIV/AIDS.

'The government accepts there is an HIV/AIDS issue. But the health care system also discriminates against English speakers. This became part of our discussion. We were helping people ignorant about the disease. We tried to get funding for affected individuals and their families.

'While campaigning, I was arrested and interrogated by the security forces at the Gendarmerie HQ, and told my activities were "raising dust". I was warned: if you are doing HIV, don't mix it with politics.

'I continued, and was arrested a second time. The SCC was celebrating its anniversary. The security forces made random arrests. For three days I was tortured. For the first day, there was no food, only water. Then I was interrogated under physical pressure, beaten with batons. On the second and third day, they made me watch the sun rise – if you closed your eyes, they beat you on the back. That burns the retina. Local leaders signed our bail. We were released when they promised to discipline us and oversee our activities.

'We did not stop. In March 2004 we were at a town hall in North-West province. It was market day. We were holding an HIV-sensitization programme. There was a big crowd. A security officer in plain clothes came to investigate. They wanted to know who had raised the issue in that community. I was arrested and locked up. The torture was unbearable. I had the scars for a long time. I was in detention a week.

'The ruling party said the SCC was sponsoring a military uprising, recruiting local and foreign fighters [and] acquiring weapons to use against the government. They claimed to be "clamping down on militants", and wanted information on arms and future plans of the movement. There had been a case in Barminda, an incident orchestrated by the government. A mobile police intervention unit was attacked by a group of masked individuals. The police were taken hostage, locked in a room with no windows. By morning, all the 'masked men' had disappeared. The SCC would gain nothing by attacking a single police unit. But that gave them an excuse to crack down on SCC militants.'

Matthew Douara, Cameroon

Matthew Douara is a teacher of educational psychology. His experience confirms what Joseph Ndalou said, but his conflict with the authorities came about quite differently. 'When English speakers voted to join la République du Cameroun, as French Cameroon was called in 1961, it was understood there would be a federal system. The values of each would be maintained, and the English-speaking areas protected.

'In 1986, four years after he came to power, Paul Biya declared a single Republic of Cameroon and the policy become assimilationist. The law, education, the whole system was articulated to the French model. This gave rise to secessionist groups, who wanted to keep the British system. One of such groups fighting today is SCNC (Southern Cameroons National Conference).

'Biya only asserted what was already happening. Cameroon had become increasingly homogeneous, and French values dominated. He was mimicking the colonial power, which said we are all French, only he was saying we are all Cameroonians. His policy reflected that of French colonialism – direct rule.

'Francophone Africa is characterized by wars, civil wars, coups d'état. Cameroon had its own war in 1984, after the coup of Paul Biya against Ahmadou Ahidjo, the first president. The military tried to overthrow Biya after he had plotted and stolen power from Ahidjo. French troops still operate in Cameroon. They never really left their colonies. The British instituted indirect rule. They put in place Africans they could trust to act on their behalf. If the British can get what they want from your country – resources and wealth – they leave you alone. The French want to get what they want and they want you as well.

'Ghana, Nigeria, Kenya – they have problems, but they are *their* problems. Most French colonies, post-independence, had their president approved by France. There is no economic independence. Cameroon is a rich country, but its top jobs in mining interests, agricultural interests, security industry are occupied by French people. Their physical presence remains.

'In Cameroon, democracy is shackled by diverse colonial legacies. We still have customs officers at internal borders between British and French sectors.

Language, culture, law, education – everything is different. Higher education is all in French, except for the single English university at Buea. Even there, its top people are French, and it has more Anglophone students than Francophones. But major faculties like Medicine have been confiscated by the Francophones. Two years ago, when the first entrance into the Faculty of Medicine was launched, the authorities published the list of successful candidates – mostly English speakers. But the presidency cancelled the list and sent names including French students who did not even sit for the exam. Students in Buea went on strike and six were killed, many imprisoned and dismissed and the rector of the university was sacked. Anglophone Cameroon now wants independence.'

'My father was a poor farmer. He had three wives and eighteen children. I struggled to go to school. Primary schools exist in the rural areas, but for secondary education, I had to go to the town, Wum, 27 kilometres away. There were always places available in school because most could not afford to go.' Matthew walked there and rented a room for 90 pence a month, but had to work to pay his fees – carrying water for 20 pence a day, cutting grass, looking after cattle, carrying head-loads for construction during the dry season, unloading goods from lorries and delivering them.

'For the first few weeks, my parents thought I'd gone off hunting. Children often went to kill squirrels and rabbits in the forest. Things have changed. More people send their children to school now primary education is free and NGOs also provide schools.

'My parents were very proud. At the beginning they didn't support children going to school. Education was the preserve of the rich. My father wanted his children to attend primary school and then go to work.

'I stood out at school. I vowed early on I would go to college. I got the idea from my teachers, because I was inquisitive and asked questions. They liked me.' He got his A-levels and went to university, 600 kilometres away from home. 'I had to pay fees for studying and rent. I offered tuitions and coaching. Everyone knows that to succeed you have to get an education. Then I trained as a teacher, still giving private lessons.

'It's a long way from there to here. In our school, they would beat us if we did wrong. Our former colonial masters give us aid, but it all goes into the pockets of the leaders. The Japanese government were wise – they constructed schools. They sent technicians and builders. They knew money would end up in Swiss bank accounts. Government, officials, bureaucrats save up millions for when they will lose their privileges. Transparency International found Cameroon the most corrupt country in the world three times. The President twice hosted African Union meetings, one for English-speaking, the other for Francophone Africa where billions were spent while three quarters of the people do not eat properly.'

In March 2007, there was a widespread one-week strike in protest against high inflation, large-scale poverty and unemployment, and increasingly high prices. 'Yet Mr Biya, who has been in power since 1982, wanted to change the constitution to give him two more terms of 14 years. The whole country was paralysed and about 36 people were shot dead. [There were] massive arrests and people sentenced to two years in prison without trial.

'The government has a divide-and-rule policy, an old colonial trick. There are 360 ethnic groups and over 300 languages in our country. I understand about 40 of them. Trade unions do not exist.

'What was my crime against these powerful people? We were involved in creating the first civil service trade union in 1993 out of a suggestion that we should form a group to express our grievances. We went for two months without salary. You went to the bank. No wages had been paid in. Civil service salaries had been slashed but we saw the police and army had not had their salaries cut – only doctors, nurses and teachers and civilian employees had 70 per cent of their income stopped. A friend said, "Let's see what we can do." When our salaries restarted, having been on about £240 a month, this was cut to £39.

'My friend, a senior teacher, went with a delegation to the Minister and asked for a 10 per cent restoration of what had been cut. Thus began the Cameroon Teachers' Trade Union. We had meetings. The news went out. Our salaries were suspended completely. There was little we could do. The police were monitoring discontent. We joined the Social Democratic Front, the opposition to the ruling CPDM.

'I became information secretary for the North-West province. My role was devising party slogans, galvanizing support – a high profile job. In the 1997 election – which Biya won again by means known only to himself and his cronies – I participated in a radio debate, with senior ministers. I asked direct questions.

'As punishment, I was transferred to a remote village – no road, radio, TV or computer. Nothing. It was a waste of resources. I returned to Yaoundé and said to the Minister, "Please send me where I can be used." I waited for his decision. Two weeks later, I went to the bank. No money had been paid into my account. Why? They would investigate.

'I had been sacked for "subversive behaviour". This only radicalized me more. I started a column in an independent newspaper investigating government officials who had killed, embezzled or committed other crimes. Only English-language papers were critical of the government. At the same time, I worked for the British Council. I thought this would offer me some protection. I asked people to boycott the celebration [on 20 May, National Day] since there was no shared nationality. What people needed was food, health care, education.

'I was working for the British Council in Douala when I was arrested. Fabricated charges were laid. They tell you why they want to kill you, not what you have done. I was told a link had been made between me and arms-smugglers from Nigeria, arms for use against the regime in Cameroon. You cannot prove them wrong. In an armed raid on my home my sister was tortured. They did terrible things to her, she still cannot talk about it. One activist died in the cell where I was locked up.

'After six months of mistreatment in jail, I was [told] I would be released if I would denounce the Opposition on the radio, call the chairman a dictator. They gave me a change of clothing and took me to the radio station. I did it. More problems. Now the SDF were also looking for me. I was a fugitive, with no job, no salary, no prospects.

'I stayed in Douala, where there was less chance of being identified. By 2003, I had had enough. I went to a newspaper and told them everything that had happened in jail. I was arrested again, and was soon awaiting trial on other charges. They said they had searched the house and found weapons. They accused me of conspiracy. The detention centre I was in was the worst, like Guantanamo. I thought I was doomed.'

Laurent Mpinde, Republic of Congo

The Republic of Congo is a small country with barely 3 million people. The French established control in 1880 and in 1910, together with Gabon, it became known as French Equatorial Africa. Its Bakongo kingdoms had traded with Europeans from the end of the fifteenth century and the littoral became a significant site of the slave trade. The kingdoms lost their power in the nineteenth century with the ending of the trade.

It declared independence from France in 1960 and after a brief military uprising in 1963, Alphonse Massamba-Débat was elected president for five years following publication of a Constitution in 1963. He declared a Marxist state, and was assassinated and replaced in a coup by Mariam Nguembi in 1977. He in turn was ousted by Denis Sassou-Nguesso in 1979. In 1981 Sassou-Nguesso signed a 20-year friendship pact with Leonid Brezhnev, but with the Soviet Union's disintegration, he renounced Marxism and opened up the country to foreign oil companies.

In 1992 elections took place and a return to democracy seemed possible under Pascal Lissouba. But in June 1997 civil war broke out which devastated large parts of Brazzaville and later that year Sassou-Nguesso regained power.

The Republic of Congo is unusual in Africa in that more than 80 per cent of its population is now urban. The country is effectively a dictatorship, but with oil and timber is courted by the oil companies. After his election as President of France, one of the first heads of state Nikolas Sarkozy welcomed was Denis Sassou-Nguesso.

Higher education has reflected the government's shifting ideological position. From the late seventies until 1990, this was Marxist; from 1990, private colleges have supplemented the single main state university. But education has stagnated, the number of students enrolled has fallen, and government maintains a vigilant watch on critical or independent thought.

Laurent Mpinde is in his mid-forties. He was studying sports science in Brazzaville. In Congo, individual sports – athletics and gymnastics – were well represented, but coaching for volleyball (Laurent's speciality) and other team sports were not integrated into the education system. He was teaching team-sports instructors in schools and colleges – work requiring knowledge of physiology, psychology, biometry and biology. His PhD was cut short by political violence.

'Congo is rich. But the administration polices people hard with an elaborate system of surveillance and control. There is no justice. The two main companies which extract oil are Elf, which is French and Agip, which is Italian. Our country is the private hunting-ground of France.

'Ethnic fighting broke out after the 1992 elections. The southern-based president, Pascal Lissouba, was in power from 1992 to 1997. Sassou's base is in the north of the country. France had begun to lose influence, and [supplied] arms to both belligerents. It seems almost every family lost a relative. People fled into the forests.

'I belonged to Lissouba's Union Pan Africaine pour la Démocratie Sociale. When we lost power, everyone fled. Elections were held in 2002. I set up a meeting at the university. We declined to participate, because we knew the outcome was a foregone conclusion. The president of our party was in England. He had been judged and condemned in his absence. The elections were a masquerade, although Europe saw fit to say it was fair. Whoever wins 90 per cent of the vote in a democracy? Democracy was confiscated.

'We were arrested at the university. We were beaten unconscious. When I woke up, I was in prison, where I remained for seven months. We often had to drink our own urine. I was physically violated. The country was in a state of war.'

Immanuel Samere, Eritrea

Immanuel Samere was born in 1978, in Asmara, capital of Eritrea, at that time still part of Ethiopia. His father was involved with the Eritrea People's Liberation Front, which subsequently became the government of independent Eritrea following a referendum in 1993. Eritrea, a former Italian protectorate, had been in a federation with Ethiopia before it was annexed in 1962 by Haile Selassie. This initiated the 30-year struggle for Eritrean independence. Haile Selassie was overthrown by Mengistu in 1977, who installed a brutal Marxist regime, which executed many officials of the imperial court.

Had the work of Immanuel's father for the Eritrean liberation movement become known, he would have been killed. He went with his wife to Sudan, and left Immanuel, an only child, behind with his grandmother because they travelled on foot. It was a two-week journey to Khartoum. Immanuel was three years old.

'Four years later, my grandmother took me to Khartoum to join the family. We couldn't find them. We heard they had gone to Europe. My grandmother and I stayed in Khartoum. She was elderly, and life was hard for her. She worked as a cleaner and domestic worker in a private house. I spent five years at school in Sudan. When Eritrea gained independence, we went back. I was 13.

'My grandmother was a mother to me. She loved and cared for me through a hard time. When we returned to Eritrea, she was sad, because we had lost hope of tracing the family. I studied in Asmara, till my grandmother died in 1994 [aged] 78. I have no feeling for my mother. I loved my grandmother dearly.

'Life became worse after she died. The only good thing [was] I had the little house in Asmara, but it was economically difficult. I was 15. I had some help from an uncle, a cousin of my father's. Otherwise, I would have been like the street-boys of Asmara, running wild. I had always been good at my studies, thanks to my grandmother's support. I won prizes in class. I studied in the morning, and worked in a shop in the afternoon.

'After ninth grade, I went to technical school. I studied surveying, and finished in 2000. I did well in the university exam. More than 10,000 apply each year for 900 places in the University of Asmara – the only one in Eritrea. It was very competitive. If you fell below 50 per cent in any exam, you were dismissed and had to go into the army.

'Eritrea became free in 1993. A Constitution, published in 1997, has yet to be implemented. A border war between Eritrea and Ethiopia lasted from 1998 to 2000. Tens of thousands were killed. I had to go for military training, because of the urgent need for fighters.

'Fortunately the war quietened down, so students could return to university. Many had been killed – three friends died early in 2000.

'On my return to university, I was elected student representative for my intake group. This meant by the end of my course, I would be president of the students' union. I was relieved and happy to be back.

'The problem began in 2001. The government ordered university students to go to villages affected by the border war and assess the damage in the region – two or three students to each village. We had to make our own way there, [but this] was not possible, because the border area was full of landmines. There was no transport. It was very remote. There was nowhere to stay, nowhere to eat. The government was offering a negligible sum of money, not enough to buy one meal, even if there had been anywhere to buy it. The villages were deserted.

'We called a meeting to discuss the situation. No one was happy. These were city students, unfamiliar with these distant areas. The government would not listen. They just gave the date we had to leave. We refused to go to the departure place. After a week, the students' union president was arrested. There were then two issues: unless he was released and our questions answered, we simply would not go.

'We were told to attend a court hearing on the student leader's arrest. The courtroom was soon surrounded by police. They forced us onto lorries and took us to a big stadium. We were kept in an open stadium for 48 hours without food or drink. It was raining. Relatives came to look for students, but were not allowed inside. There were 400 of us. We were accused of being against government policy.

'They brought trucks. Where are we going to? Why? We won't go. The students asked questions and were beaten into a huddle. Army personnel stood by, pointing guns, so that if we hit back, they could shoot.

'We were taken to Wia on the southern Red Sea coast, the hottest place in Eritrea. The temperature was 45 degrees. Two students died in the first two days. Everyone was sick. They sent tankers with water. We had no vessels to catch it, so we drank from our hands. We had to make a little shade against the sun by tying our clothes together on sticks.

'From there we were taken to Gelealo on the same coast. There were big hangars; it had been a military detention centre. They punished us, making us walk for one hour on foot to collect stones to build in a pile 6 feet high. It took hours, it was exhausting and pointless. Then we had to walk back to the detention centre. We were given lentils and flour to cook.

'They gathered the student representatives. Without us, they said, the students would have obeyed. We had to be punished. We were placed in separate cells, unable to communicate. These were underground, with a guard at the gate. They beat us every morning. We had to crawl on the sharp rocks.' Immanuel shows scars on his knees and arms. A deep cut from jagged rock left a cavity in his forearm. 'It just missed the artery. I asked for medical treatment. They said, "You're here to die, not to be treated." The pain and the swelling were terrible. It took months to heal. I still have scars on my back from the beatings.

'This went on continuously for three months. The others signed false documents, saying it was our fault for refusing to obey. They were allowed back to Asmara. I had to sign. I had no choice. You cannot win against the army.

'I went home. If I did anything against the government, there would be terrible punishment. I might be killed. I was not to give interviews.

'For the next couple of years. I was careful, and completed my degree in Geology in 2004. To earn money, I taught the son of my neighbours. I learned to live frugally. I did nothing but study. In the house I had no relaxation, no radio, only books. For relaxation I went to the library. More books.

'I did so well I was offered an assistant lectureship in the Geology Department. I had an income. It was very positive for me. I ran the laboratories for undergraduates, gave tutorials, led them in field work, helped analyse their field studies. I loved it.

'I was relaxed. I worked hard, and later, did research with an international team. We collected samples of petroleum minerals [from] the Danakil Depression in the East African Rift Valley, close to the Ethiopian border. The Depression, at 371 feet, is the lowest part of the landmass of the earth. We compared our results with those from Kenya, Sudan, Ethiopia. Our findings were published in papers in Uppsala and Florence.

'Everything was fine till 2005. There was a meeting between the university and the army to assess the situation in the country. A government official explained the political issues, economic and social questions, and asked what we could contribute. He said they wanted a democratic debate.

'I asked when the Constitution of 1997 was going to be implemented. This was provocative. Some former ministers, members of the G-15, were under arrest. I asked when they would come to court. No one knew if they were dead or alive.

'They said these were good questions. We will implement the Constitution as quickly as possible. The members of G-15 will be brought to justice soon. He answered very nicely. I thought that would be the end of it.

'Next day, five o'clock in the morning, a knock at the door. Who's that? Army police. I was in my pyjamas. Get in the police car. Why? Get in. Let me dress. No, come now. I was taken to the police station, then to a military training centre 400 kilometres away. Still in my pyjamas, I was thrown into military detention.

'My mistake was believing them when they said our opinion was important. After three days, an officer came. "You have not learned although you were warned. You raised questions in public. We will give you a lesson you will never forget."

'They beat me. They put me in the "helicopter" position – arms and legs tied together and thrown face down in the burning sun for hours. They also beat the soles of my feet. This happened every day for a month. They make sure you don't die. After such treatment, you cannot stand up. There were other detainees. Some had been there for three, four years. An indefinite sentence.

'I thought, "This is my fate. I'll end here." After four weeks of making you suffer, you do forced labour. There is agricultural work or stone-breaking for construction [and] a cotton plantation. All this is done in the heat, with inadequate food, a shower once a week. For the toilet, a guard accompanies you to a field.

'That continued two more months. I was taken to the cotton plantation by truck with other prisoners. I wondered how I might escape.

'One day, going to the plantation, a public bus collided with our truck. There were about 60 passengers. Some were injured, as were many guards in the truck.

'It was chaos. There was blood everywhere, crying and confusion. This was my chance to get away. Behind the road was a riverbed. I jumped down so I was below the level of the road. The river has no water for most of the year. I knew that to the West was Sudan. I followed the river for hours.

'Another prisoner had done the same thing. I thought he might be a guard. I hid myself. When he approached I saw he was also a detainee. He knew the area. We walked the whole day. We met some nomads. He spoke to them in their language, and they gave us milk and bread.'

Tirfe Etana, Ethiopia

Ethiopia witnessed the first defeat of colonial forces on the African continent by an indigenous army when Emperor Menelik II beat the Italians at the Battle of Adowa in 1896. To avenge this, Mussolini invaded Abyssinia in 1935. The Italian occupation was brief but violent: mustard gas was used against the people, public executions became commonplace, and following the attempted assassination of General Graziani in 1937, thousands of civilians were massacred.

The Emperor Haile Selassie ruled from 1930 to 1974, although he spent the war years in Britain. Promoting himself as progressive, he became a deity for Rastafarians. He was overthrown in 1974, partly as a consequence of a famine in 1973 in northern Ethiopia. Jonathan Dimbleby filmed this for TV; and the juxtaposition of images of starvation with the sybaritic indifference of the royal household is widely credited with preparing the ground for his fall in 1974, when an army junta under Colonel Mengistu deposed him.

Ryszard Kapuscinski interviewed surviving members of the Emperor's entourage immediately after the revolution.[3] One courtier recalled: 'It is true that some excesses were committed. For instance, a great palace was constructed in the heart of the Ogaden desert and maintained for years, fully staffed with servants and its pantry kept full, and His Indefatigable Majesty spent only one day there. But what if His Distinguished Majesty at some point had to spend a night in the heart of the desert? Wouldn't the Palace then prove itself indispensable? Unfortunately, our unenlightened people will never understand the Higher Reason that governs the actions of monarchs.'

At Mengistu's accession, Tirfe Etana, aged 14, was studying in a town 120 kilometres north of Addis Ababa. His life was determined by events which took place then; although he could not anticipate being caught up in conflicts, originating in Marxist ideology, but inflected by local ethnic and regional rivalries. Like many refugee academics, his personal fate is entangled with Ethiopia's destiny. 'Private lives' are rarely detached from social and political events, which permanently mark – or scar – individual experience.

'There was an ideological difference among the [revolutionary] forces. There was the army, which said it wanted to establish a peaceful democratic country. It wanted change "in which no drop of blood will be shed". That became a sad joke. How could you dispossess feudal landlords peacefully?

'The educated elements told the army it is all right to kill and destroy to bring about a better day – a day inspired by the USSR, which didn't have a very good record of better tomorrows. The educated class were well-read and well organized. They expressed anger at the landlords who controlled large tracts of the country. The Emperor had been slow to address the landholding issue.

'The army didn't have a clear vision but the intelligentsia wanted change. A hot-headed generation of students saw themselves like the Palestinian *fedayin*.

'I was 14, as radical as anyone else. We should have been learning, but we were fired up to kill and to die. It was a crazy time. Mature people who should have known better remained silent. Those who protested this was wrong were easily silenced.

'There were two main groups. The Ethiopian People's Revolutionary Party (EPRP) and the All-Ethiopian Socialist Movement (A-ESM). The latter wanted to work with the military to bring about gradual change, land reform. The EPRP wanted no compromise; they advocated a popular uprising to overthrow the army.

'In 1974 the army executed 60 officials of the Haile Selassie regime. The Emperor's regime was exhausted. He was 82. He died in mysterious circumstances, almost certainly killed by the army.

'The EPRP started a guerrilla movement. They began to kill members of the armed forces; a low-level civil war began.'

The great scholar, rights worker and humanist, Professor Mesfin Woldemariam, wrote: 'When eventually that traditional regime fell, it was hoped that Ethiopia would open new vistas for progress and development. But because [that] regime had concentrated power in one man and had, consequently, not allowed people to assemble and freely express their ideas and to organize, the regime as well as the people were outmanoeuvred by street-smart officers. As a result, the country fell under the rule of a regime worse than [the one] it replaced, so ruthless as to have not an iota of respect for human life whatsoever. Consequently, going into exile became the culture of Ethiopia. The quality of education degenerated under the pressure of a superficial belief in Marxist-Leninism.'[4]

'My father was a businessman. We were also landowners. On the morning when the decree on land reform was promulgated, I was jumping up and down on my bed in celebration. My father came to the door. He said, "What are you so happy about?"

'I said, "Don't you know? Land reform!" He said, "You are silly. This is your property. You are my only child. This is your land." My father was sad. He loved me. I was idealistic, thinking only of the kids I had seen without shoes. I didn't relate it to myself at all.

'Life changed. The army claimed that it wanted the students involved in developmental activities. In 1977, some 60,000 teachers and university students were sent into the rural areas. Some refused, saying it was a trick to get students out of the way, so the army could consolidate its power.

'The students did achieve something. They taught people the significance of the new land reforms. They helped with sanitation and literacy, planted trees and set up self-help groups [and] came back with greater support for the EPRP. It transformed many country people into activists, hostile to the military regime.

'In the south especially, the old feudal power had been very oppressive. The rural labourer had to give one-third of his produce to the landlord, and work on the landlord's [property]. They could be evicted at any moment, their children were forced into domestic service in the household of the landowners.

'Mengistu projected himself as a romantic revolutionary hero, like Che or Ho Chi Minh. He was kept in power by the All-Ethiopian Socialist Movement, but the EPRP intensified the guerrilla movement. At the same time, Mengistu was surrounded by other enemies – the Eritrean independence movement, the Oromo Liberation Front, the Tigrian Liberation Movement, Somalia – as well as the dispossessed landlords and their allies. The regime went on the "offensive" and eliminated thousands of people. This was the time of "Red terror" against the A-ESM. The two factions had been held together only by hatred of the Emperor: once he was gone, they fell upon each other.

'I joined the military academy, which saved my life. I did well and went to university. I studied Political Science and International Relations. I got a distinction in my studies and was offered a teaching job in the university politics department. The university was an island of relative freedom, but as soon as you stepped out of the campus, you risked arrest and imprisonment.

'Most lecturers discussed things freely. Professor Mesfin Woldemariam, who founded the Human Rights Council of Ethiopia, was in the same faculty with me. He wrote an article on the military regime, for which another academic had written a propaganda paper. Professor Mesfin poured scorn on the academic who could put his name to such nonsense. He said the army was fascistic and brutal. He expected to be arrested. Nothing happened. The army knew the university was not organized and posed no threat. Ironically, it was only under the present regime that Professor Mesfin was arrested and tried. He was released because he is known in the international peace movement.

'Perhaps the regime was wrong to neglect the university. A new generation formed by the university continued to ask questions on freedom, equality and justice.

'The famine of 1984, which had such an influence in the West, was downplayed in Ethiopia. Publicity about the famine of 1974 contributed to the Emperor's downfall; the Dergue was not going to let that happen to them.[5] Food was being exported to the West as the people starved. They imported 500,000 bottles of Scotch rather than wheat for the starving.

'The government brought bright people together to advise them, academics prominent among them. The academy is like any other cross-section of society. Mengistu set up a new organization called the Institute for Nationalities. There are more than 80 such groups in Ethiopia. He wanted to learn about them to devise policies for unity. In principle, the formation of the institute was a good idea – not everything the Dergue did was bad. Mengistu invited 25 intellectuals from the universities. He talked to them individually, asking them to join the Institute. Only Professor Mesfin refused. He told Mengistu to give back to the people their rights as citizens [so that] the country would be a better place. Again, he was not punished.

'I was a junior lecturer and expressed my views. My problem occurred later, after I had left for Moscow for my research and studies programme. I was at a conference on Ethiopia in Canada, and only then I began to understand how little we had learned from the events of the 1970s. As one of the speakers had said, the replacement of one army group by another would not improve anything. A civil administration was the only answer to the madness. I was attacked from all sides.

'We set up a group to talk of peace and reconciliation in 1987–89, intellectuals from Europe, Ethiopia, the USA. This coalesced into a movement. The US and USSR would come together to work for a resolution of frozen Cold War conflicts. In 1990, we had meetings with top US and Soviet officials. A communiqué was issued as a result of our efforts. When Gorbachev and Bush met in 1990, the Horn of Africa was to be included in the regional strategy to resolve outstanding problems amicably.

'We came under fire from all parties in Ethiopia – military and opposition. Mengistu said you are with the rebels, the rebels said you are bidding for power in the vacuum after the fall of the Dergue.

'Within a year, the rebels had overthrown Mengistu [in 1991]. They had power. They said we were trying to save him. The Eritreans and Tigreans came to Addis. We said, "Why dismantle the state? Why not federate?" The new regime sacked 43 university professors, five from the politics department. I could not survive in that atmosphere.'

Victor Abano, Sudan

Sudan, Africa's largest country, and tenth largest in the world, has significant fault-lines separating the Arab Muslim north from the Christian/animist south and the African/Muslim west.

Following Egypt's conquest of Sudan early in the nineteenth century, the British occupied Sudan from 1882 with a brief interregnum at the time of the Mahdi's revolt until the defeat of the Mahdists at Omdurman in 1899.

In 1942, the British divided Sudan into North and South, with movement restrictions between them to keep potential religious conflict at bay. After the British withdrawal from Egypt in 1936 (apart from the Canal Zone), Sudan remained under British control. In 1954 the British government signed an agreement with the Egyptians whereby Sudan would become independent in 1956.

From 1955 there was civil war between north and south until 1972, when the Addis Ababa Agreement allowed for considerable autonomy in the south. This was abrogated by Nimeiri in 1983; he wanted a federated state, and introduced sharia law. In response the Sudan's People's Liberation Army was formed in the non-Muslim area. In the ensuing 20-year civil war over 2 million people have died. Nimeiri was ousted in 1985, but after a short democratic interregnum, Omar al-Bashir's National Islamic Front seized power in 1989.

In 2005, following the Nairobi Peace Agreement, a joint North–South administration was established; a referendum is to be held by 2012 on independence for the south.

Meanwhile in Darfur there was a revolt by pastoralists against settled agriculturalists on the fragile eco-system of West Sudan and its border with Chad. The janjaweed, militias promoted by central government, killed and raped indiscriminately. Despite UN, Western and African Union pressure, the violence continues in Darfur and Chad. The conflict has killed 300,000–400,000 people and displaced more than 2.5 million.

Victor Abano grew up in Uganda, and then southern Sudan. 'I was at the University of Juba in the South, when the war became very intense in the late 1980s. My home village is 10 miles from the Ugandan border. My siblings and mother remained in the countryside. The rebel forces surrounded the town, and supplies of food had to be flown in. We shared our food with people in the hospital and the jail; otherwise they would have starved.

'It was difficult to keep the students in Juba, so the whole university was displaced to Khartoum. At that time, the government was becoming more fundamentalist. Islamic values were implemented very drastically. We had sharia law before – Nimeiri imposed it in 1983, but when he was out of the country in 1985, he was told not to return. A brief interval of democracy was overthrown by a coup, when Omar al-Bashir intensified sharia: alcohol poured into rivers, hands of criminals cut off. The National Islamic Front was behind Nimeiri, and supported al-Bashir. Life became difficult for people from the South.

'Emergency courts with military judges terrorized the population. Economic survival became difficult. Many women in the South distilled and sold alcohol. They risked 30 lashes as well as a jail term.

'I did well in my studies. I became a teaching assistant. I decided to visit Juba to see my family. When I returned, I visited friends at the university dormitory, with a message for someone whose relative had died. I was to take the information to a certain house. I took two friends with me. We stayed at the house till about eleven at night. On our way back to the dormitory we were stopped at gunpoint by men wearing Islamic *djellabas*.[6] We were jailed in the nearest police station – about 15 or 20 people in one small cell. There were criminals and drug addicts. It was a difficult night. Next day, ten of us were ordered into a truck at gunpoint, and driven to a military barracks in Khartoum.

'Close to the barracks was a school and a check-post, where they stopped vehicles to see if anyone had taken alcohol. Part of the school had been turned into a court. The army judge came at ten o'clock. People were accused of making alcohol, being drunk or violating the curfew. This was the charge against us. We came before the judge. "Did you violate the curfew?" We had to answer yes or no as a group. Officials told us that if we said "no", we'd be jailed until we said "yes". So we said "Yes." It was very humiliating. The curfew started at midnight. We had been picked up at 11.30.

'We were sentenced to 30 lashes. It is a horsewhip. They strike you twice each time, a forward and a backward stroke; in fact it is 60 lashes. You stand against a wall with your hands up. They administer the blows across your body, from top to bottom. It is extremely painful. Women are normally lashed in a tent, because women are thought to be weak, and it preserves their modesty. You can hear their screams.

'Then we were allowed home. The pain, although intense, was less than the psychological damage and humiliation. We couldn't tell anyone out of shame. I went to Uganda later and ran into my old friend in Adjumani, northern Uganda, by accident. I went with him to visit my mother, who was a refugee there. He said, "Oh, you are here. We are free. No one beats you here because of alcohol or because you walk at night." He fetched a crate of alcohol to drink in the street, to prove it. Of course, freedom is relative. In Uganda you don't get lashes for drinking or walking at night; but it has its own oppression.

'In 1991, I was to take up my responsibilities at the university, which was under Islamic administration. If they had known I had been beaten, I would have lost my job. I was embarrassed. It is difficult for people from the South. Luckily, I got a scholarship from the Ford Foundation, available for five Sudanese students, at the American University in Cairo. I was doing my MA there. We southerners had to get clearance from Sudanese security before a visa to Egypt was issued since we were regarded as rebel sympathizers. It was very difficult to get the clearance.

'I went to Cairo. In two years I completed my Master's in Public Administration. I decided to go back to my university in Khartoum. It was hard: the authorities thought I was connected with the rebels in exile, many of whom are in Egypt.

'When the fundamentalists came the second time, they wanted to do away with English, remove independent thinkers and put their people in place. They wanted to Islamize the system. We were pressured to learn Arabic. The Vice-Chancellor indicated that I could return provided I learn Arabic at an Islamic University. I thought, "OK, no problem, Arabic is a useful language."

'When I went to the course at the Islamic University of Khartoum, it was Arabic, but it was also indoctrination. It was about the Prophet, Islamic prayers. It was propaganda.

'I was frustrated and disappointed. The university is no longer a place of thinking, learning, contributing to knowledge. I could not live under these conditions.'

THE CAUCASUS, IRAN, CENTRAL ASIA AND THE FAR EAST

Ruslan Isaev, Chechnya

Chechnya, a Muslim area of about one million people, had a tragic history, especially under Soviet rule. In 1944 Stalin deported the entire population of around 600,000 – Chechens, Ingush, Kumyks and Bulkars – along with other 'unreliable elements', to Siberia because he thought them sympathetic to Hitler and Fascism. Almost half of them died. In exchange, many Russians from Siberia were resettled in Chechnya. After the collapse of the Soviet Union, Chechens – who had returned in 1958 – remained victims of Russian nationalism, and Chechnya's bid for independence in the chaos following its declaration of the same in 1991 was brutally crushed. The Islamist fighters coming to Chechnya from Afghanistan and Pakistan brought a sensibility quite alien to that of the Chechens, who paid dearly for their unsought allies. The Russians invaded and occupied Chechnya, reducing much of Grozny, the capital, to ruins. They are still regarded by a majority of Chechens as an illegitimate occupying force.

'My name is Ruslan Isaev. I was born in 1971 in a small town of about 40,000 people called Urus-Martan not far from Grozny. Chechnya is a beautiful piece of land in Caucasian mountains in the South of Russia. The total population of the country is approximately one million.

'My father was chief accountant within a state organization. He was well-read and a man of culture. My grandfather, although not officially an imam, advised people on religious and spiritual matters. My parents instilled an atmosphere of learning and culture in our home, and we were respected in the neighbourhood.

'In 1944 my parents were involved in the deportations to Siberia; my father was 14 years old, and my mother was only a child. It happened in January, when without warning, thousands of Russian soldiers came to the towns and were billeted with families. The official explanation was that this was only a temporary arrangement. But one morning in February, all male Chechens were ordered to assemble in the main square of our town Urus-Martan. The deportations began. The families were not allowed to take any belongings. My father later told me that the whole evacuation took one or two days. That is how long it took to wipe out a Chechen community which had flourished for hundreds of years.

'My mother's father was away at the time, and was probably caught up in the deportation system of the town in which he was staying. It was winter, and many people died of exposure and deprivation during the long journey to Siberia. Although they had been instructed that they must not leave their allocated areas in Siberia, my mother's mother decided to go and look for her husband. She and my aunt set off through the forests. They rarely saw any other human beings, the only life around them was a pack of wolves. Part of their journey was made by holding on to ice-floes which floated downriver. Eventually they found help, but too late for my grandmother; she died of pneumonia. My aunt survived, but never found her father. I knew nothing of this until I was 14 years old.

'In Siberia, my mother was brought up by her eldest brother. There was no help from the state. The exile lasted 13 years. Local people did not like them; they were told that these people were barbarians and enemies. It was during the time in Siberia that my parents met and married.

'Most Russians think themselves superior to Chechens. Chechens are open, generous and sociable. It was generally known that we Chechens could not really accept Communism. My grandfather had a good relationship with Russian aristocrats, who had dignity and civilized values, but times had changed.

'When they returned to Urus-Martan, they found that my father's old house, which was large, had been turned into a shop, apartments, and a sports club, and was occupied by Russian families. Like all other Chechens, they had to pay the Russians to get back their own houses – that is those who were able to raise the money.

'I grew up in a peaceful atmosphere. There were no killings, no crime. I saw no death except for old age. My grandfather died when I was seven and my great uncle when I was eleven. Our relatives who lived in Grozny had a harder time, because there were many Russian migrants who discriminated against Chechens. They were not even allowed to speak their own language. The schools which I attended were good, our teachers, mostly Chechens, were charismatic, but all teaching was done in Russian. We were given a wide general knowledge, far outside the standard curriculum. Teachers were encouraged to take extra classes, Saturdays from 3 to 7 p.m., sometimes later. These were very popular, although the teachers were not paid for extra work. I played basketball and volleyball. It was my dream to be in the Soviet Union basketball team. I had other dreams too; I wanted to be strong and outspoken, which is a characteristic of the Chechen people. I wanted to change society, only without revolution or violence. I admired the Communist ideal of equality, although I did not admire the regime. I would read in the Communist newspapers of the misery in capitalist countries but at the same time I enjoyed rock music and Western literature. I read in a magazine about an actor who performed on the streets of Paris, and slept on the banks of the river Seine. The idea attracted me.'

'From around seven or eight, I knew that I had no religious beliefs. My family were religious, but I could not find that type of faith within myself. It speaks volumes of the intelligence and liberality of my family that they allowed me to be comfortable with my free-thinking and scepticism. I felt secure and happy. We lived among intellectuals – teachers, artists, doctors, accountants, lawyers. My elder brother and sister, who were born ten years before me, discussed ideas and theories and they inspired me. But as I grew older I was disappointed to find that my own contemporaries seemed, by comparison, docile and conservative.

'But the Soviet Union was corrupt at every level. The children of high officials in the Party went to schools and universities to learn how to take their parents' place. They did not go on their own merit, nor get their positions honestly.

'I graduated from school with a silver medal, which is equivalent to good passes at A-levels in Britain [and] in 1988 I went to university in Rostov. My older brother is a lawyer, my sister studied literature in Moscow, another sister studied language and the other is a pharmacologist. My parents wanted me to become a doctor. I felt sad at their suffering during deportation, and didn't want to disappoint them. I wanted to be a scientist, but I accepted my parents' wishes.

'I loved every single day at university. I had independence. I always cherished freedom. I grew up in a fairly mono-ethnic area, but at Rostov there were Latin American, African and Asian students, Armenians, Georgians, Uzbeks, Jews, Tartars. I had many friends. After the collapse [in Chechnya] in 1992–93, there was no food. We suffered privations. Yet I remained optimistic. I was unhappy not to fulfil my ambition to become a scientist, but I wanted to give something to the country, and I was disgusted with corruption. My father, a traditional Chechen with a high sense of morality, wanted me to become successful by honest means.

'The government was very corrupt, especially after the collapse of the Soviet Union. The republics sought independence. Chechens were determined to have autonomy. There was chaos in Russia. People were not paid their salaries. Everyone was looking for someone to blame. Our leader, Dudayev, tried hard to settle things diplomatically, but failed. The conflict started and initially the Russians were repelled, but they then attacked Grozny with force and images were seen worldwide on television of the destruction of the city. The mufti also declared jihad against Russia, and soon after this, the extremists began to arrive in Chechnya. The local people supported them simply because they helped them to resist the Russians.

'I found that Chechens were being increasingly discriminated against. I remember once in Grozny with my older sister, a Russian woman shouted at her, "You should have been killed in 1944." Then my teacher at university gave me the lowest mark for what was obviously good work. I protested. He wanted money. I also did very well in Latin, which was part of my medical course. The teacher said I must have cheated, the implication being that stupid Chechens could not possibly succeed without cheating. With incidents like this as part of my daily atmosphere, it was not long before I started to support efforts for Chechen independence.

'The extremists in Chechnya made life hell. My father went to Moscow when he was threatened by militants. He was wise to do this – two of his friends were killed. I couldn't go back to Chechnya – it was a war zone. I went to Moscow, which seemed the only civilized place. I never thought of actual migration.

'I was very lucky to meet a brilliant professor of dermatology and venereology at one of the Scientific Research Clinical Institutes. I admired her, and she had a profound influence on me.

'She treated all patients, giving no preference to rich over poor. I told her I would like to do a scientific project with her. She offered me research into microsocial and clinical aspects of sexual abuse and sexually transmitted diseases. There had been no research into this in the Soviet period. In the medical academic circles many older professors resisted [her], but she was progressive, and wanted to expand our knowledge of the sociological aspects of venereology.

'It was harrowing. I met victims of abuse, both women and children. I was shocked and learned things I would prefer not to know. As part of the work I published several manuals to assist doctors in the techniques of examining victims. It was disturbing. I knew that in a stable society, you can change things, you can promote reforms. In the chaos of that time, we could do nothing. Criminals were in power.

'My professor asked if I would like to work in the institution. I was amazed. She said, "Don't you want to?" I replied, "Yes, of course I do! But can it be possible for me, a Chechen, to be offered a place at a central research establishment?" In fact I dreamt of working in this Institute which was full of prominent Russian dermatologists and venereologists. I accepted and the professor was wonderfully supportive. I worked from 1996 to 1999, doing further research and treating patients.

'In 1999, I finished my dissertation, and was awarded my PhD. Then, later that same year, the Russians invaded Chechnya. I was appalled at what I saw in the news media – they were inhumane, uncivilized. I wanted to go home.'

'I had a friend in Médecins Sans Frontières. I started to work with a Dutch charity organizing help for Chechen refugees in Ingushetia. I was a medical coordinator. It made me feel that I was really helping people in a direct tangible way. Eighty per cent of the people of Ingushetia were Sufis, devout, kindly people. My sister was also a refugee there. I was invited to stay with a family, who insisted that I should not live alone. I saw the sadness and suffering of the people of Chechnya. They lived in misery at that time, but they were my people.

'My mother died in Ingushetia in 2000 at five o'clock in the morning. I took her body to Chechnya where she wanted to be buried. We couldn't leave without an official letter. That took more than four hours. My youngest sister came with me. We had to cross 11 border controls to get home. They searched us and the body, to see if we were carrying drugs or weapons. They wanted money at each crossing point. We had to pay. My mother was such a lovely warm woman, it was disgusting to see the way she was treated in death. There was no word of condolence, only money.

'When we finally got to Chechnya, we did not have permission to bring in the body. We had to wait and could not bury her that day, in accordance with Muslim tradition. It was hot. My mother's body had started to decay. The next day we buried her. Many friends and relatives came. At the same time, Russian helicopters were flying overhead. They sometimes bombarded funerals.

'Five days later I went back. My older sister came with me. That saved my life. All the male passengers had their passports taken and checked, and were allowed to cross. I had to wait three hours. They took me to a room, and forced me to undress. They were looking for scars, which would indicate I was a fighter. It was disgusting. My sister wouldn't go without me. She became hysterical and started crying and shouting. They said, "Her tears show you are a rebel." I felt angry, but kept cool. They took money from her and let me go. After this experience, I decided I could not live like this.

'I got a flight from Ingushetia to Moscow. I stayed with a friend there and went to the airport. I still had a visa, because I had done an English course in Oxford. It was April 2003, and I felt a new life opening in front of me.'

Darius Zemani, Iran

Iran in the twentieth century has been the object of continuous external interference. If its desire to use nuclear power – whether for civilian or military purposes – is denounced as a threat to Middle Eastern stability, the abhorrence with which it is viewed is disingenuous. Its nuclear programme is not new. During the regime of the former Shah, Iran, with the USA's help, planned to produce 23,000MW of nuclear power by 2000.

Recent events in Iran are reported as though without antecedents. During the Second World War, Russian and British armies occupied the country which, although officially neutral, had shown Nazi sympathies. The Shah, Reza Pahlavi, abdicated in 1941 in favour of his son, Mohammad Reza Pahlavi, and in 1951 Dr Mohammad Mossadegh was elected to end external control of Iran's oil and terminate a foreign presence on its soil. In 1953, the CIA helped bring down Mossadegh which led to civil strife between monarchist and nationalist forces and the Shah's temporary exile from Iran. After his return, the Shah introduced a government favourable to the West. In the 1970s, Siemens began constructing nuclear reactors at Bushehr.

With rapid modernization and a growing divide between rich and poor, Leftists and nationalists were targeted by a repressive, authoritarian regime. The 1979 revolution disrupted the nuclear programme, because Khomeini – at least in the beginning – opposed nuclear technology. In any case, most nuclear scientists had left the country. In 1987 and 1990, however, Iran signed nuclear cooperation agreements, first with Pakistan and then with China.

Darius Zemani says that although the West supported the Shah, the US always considered him vulnerable to militant nationalist or Communist forces, preferring militant Islam as an opposition to nationalists or the Left. At the height of the Cold War, Islam appeared a solution to the Communist threat rather than a source of new problems.

Darius Zemani was a lecturer in the Engineering Faculty of Tehran University. 'Khomeini was in France until 1979. He was surrounded by Western-educated people, who thought they could control any Islamic administration. How wrong they were. The revolution executed about 200,000 people.'

'When I was teaching, young people asked me about the revolution or the war deaths, why the government had killed so many people. They asked me if it was wrong. How can you remain silent faced with such questions?

'I was called before the university authorities. I said I was only answering questions. They repeatedly told me this was not my job. The Ministry of Information has a branch in every university, to find out who is for and who against the government.

'I could not lie to students. I said there had been no gain in the war, since over a million people died [and] it left so many children without fathers. There are no state benefits for children: widows received a small pension, not enough to live on, and most had little education, no qualification to earn a living. The government insisted we won the war. Actually, no one won. Not Iran. Not Saddam because they wanted him to defeat the Islamic revolution. Not the West, because they strengthened the regime in Baghdad.

'War psychosis continues in Iran. A new generation is being prepared for war. In secondary schools, they study war, indoctrinated with the idea of an imminent American attack; and people see the destructive power the US has unleashed in Iraq.

'The media also teach that the US is controlled by Jews. People are frightened when the media say that behind the US government, rich Jewish people are manipulating the world. They even say bin Laden doesn't exist, but was an invention of the Jews. They will wipe out your family and children. How can you counter these distortions?

'Seventy million people are ready for war. Of these, perhaps five million seriously practise Islam. Some people say hatred is a result of extremism. I think hatred brings extremism. In the Koran, there are thousands of words of love. Nowhere is it said that people should kill themselves or others. Most people simply do not know enough about Islam. They pick up a few words from the Koran – the Prophet said wage war until the enemy is no longer in your land. It means support your country against invaders, not take war outside your country.

'The second mistake is to mix religion with politics. Religion is for eternity. Politics is of this world.'

'I grew up in Tehran. My two brothers are also civil engineers. My father was a senior official during the Shah's era. After the revolution, he lost everything. He finished up selling carpets to the West. He refused to leave. He said, "This is my land." He was upset that the West gave support to Khomeini. My father said the US would find out they were wrong to have allowed this to happen. He died ten years ago.

'If ignorance about Islam is fairly general in Iran, you can imagine how much worse it is here [the UK]. Some think Islam is violent. All religions teach peace and humanity, but all have been violent. Christianity has a very violent history. I believe we should leave religion in the mosque, church or temple. We need values to help us coexist. All religions speak of peace, but clerics, institutions, hierarchies abuse religion.

'In the faculty, people said repeatedly, "Why are you destroying your life? Why don't you stick to your job?" I said, "I don't know how to lie." I was eight years in post. Every six months I was questioned by Ministry of Information officials.

'In 1997–98, there was a movement of students for reform. I supported them, but it put me in a dangerous situation. In 1999 I was prevented from teaching. Students continued to ask questions. I couldn't refuse to answer.

'Other lecturers were in a similar situation. Some disappeared – you know, were eliminated. I finally decided my life was untenable. They said I was against God and against religion. In 2000, they took our house. I had no income and had to depend on other family members. They thought they had me in their power.'

Darius could have continued an untroubled career, had he accepted limits on his expression of opinions. There are doubtless many who, accepting the compromise offered by certain regimes, live without conflict. Those who cannot remain silent on political, and more importantly, moral, issues run foul of authority – a different experience from those fired or silenced because of ethnicity or some other unalterable aspect of their being. It requires from academics a particular courage, for when they do so, they are exposed to risks which people in more obscure walks of life can more easily avoid.

Behzad Mehrzad, Tajikistan

Tajikistan is a mountainous country in central Asia whose language is similar to Farsi. Part of the Persian Empire until conquered by Arabs in the eighth century, it was subsequently ruled by Tamurids, Uzbeks and then the Russians as an 'autonomous' Soviet Republic. When the Soviet Union disintegrated, the ensuing civil war between Islamists and the former Communist party cost more than 60,000 lives. The population of about seven million is around 80 per cent Tajik, and 15 per cent Uzbek. The autocratic President Rahmanov took power in 1992; two years later the Supreme Soviet metamorphosed into the Supreme Assembly. Rahmanov remains in charge, although elections have been unfair and fraudulent. There has also been a recurrence of anti-Semitism since the last Jewish synagogue, which served the small Bukharan Jewish community, was demolished in 2006. Tajikistan hosts a number of Russian bases, and is authoritarian and socially conservative. Standing on the narcotics trade route from Afghanistan, it remains, despite recent improvements, corrupt and, in places, lawless.

Behzad Mehrzad is from Khudjand (known in the Soviet era as Leninabad), founded in the fourth century BC by Alexander the Great as a Greek settlement close to the Silk Road. Behzad grew up in a village near the city, where his father was an engineer and his mother a doctor. His father died of cancer in 1998, and his mother no longer works. His sisters and brother live in Moscow – one sister is a biochemist, the other owns a cafe. Behzad's brother is a civil engineer.

'I went to university in Dushanbe. After graduating, I wanted to enter the diplomatic service. I did post-graduate study in international law. I was assigned to research and analyse the language and style of international treaties. After Soviet rule, international documents had to be drawn up in Tajik, not Russian. I had to look for terms in English or other languages that could be transliterated into Tajik.

'I did three years research. In my last year, I contended for a scholarship, which was open to any young researcher. I won the award, a high honour. My mother still has the official notification of my academic achievement. She is very proud of me.

'Parallel to my success there lurked a skeleton in the closet. I'm a gay man, and in Tajikistan it is very tough to be gay morally, culturally and legally. The country is heavily influenced by Islam, and the criminal code still states that sodomy is punishable with three years imprisonment. Sexuality in general was denied in the Soviet Union, and gay sex even more so.

'Muslims believe it the duty of every man to marry and have a family. If you delay marriage beyond the age of 25, people ask questions. It gets very insistent; Tajikistan is a small country, both in population and in what people know about one another.

'I am the youngest in my family. All the others are married. My father, critically ill in 1998, wanted to see his youngest son married before he died. I married in 1998 and tried to cope with living with my wife. At the same time, I had a boyfriend, also secretly gay. After I married, we split up, because he couldn't bear my being with someone else, a woman at that.

'I left my family in Khudjand to pursue further studies in Diplomacy in Dushanbe. I left my wife and baby daughter at home, under pretext of studying.

'After a year in Dushanbe, I had a new boyfriend. We shared a flat, living as students to the outside world. My career took off. I was supervised in my PhD by a professor in the law department of the national university.

'While studying I also got a part-time lectureship in social law. I published two or three books under my own name and co-authored others. After my PhD it was suggested that I might enter the diplomatic service.

'My ex-boyfriend was jealous, both of my success and my new partner. He was also jealous that I was married. He thought I should not be allowed to get away with it. We had a conversation. I didn't know he was taping me.

'Something else happened. In 2001, the students were due to take end-of-term exams. One demanded that I pass him, even though he was not up to standard and had not attended lectures. I refused him. He threatened me and we had an argument. Half an hour later the phone rang. It was the National Security Forces, the new incarnation of the old KGB.

'I was summoned to the office and accused of accepting bribes from students. I was told I'd wind up behind bars if I didn't obey the Security Forces. They place people in each class as their ears. The student who had demanded I pass him felt confident, because he assumed I'd understand. I had trodden on their toes without knowing it.

'With these two events – a brush with the security forces and my boyfriend having taped me – life became complicated. The part-time lectureship, renewed each year, was stalled. My publications were stopped and it was hard to get a viva to complete my thesis. I was due to finish it in this year; it was already June.

'By September my contract was totally blocked by the bureaucracy. The university also cancelled the last months of my scholarship. My supervisor did nothing. As he admitted, he was powerless.

'I called a friend of mine studying in London. He said, "Come over, and see how it goes." I applied for a language study course, which was also an introduction to UK, living with a family. The authorities thought I was going for a vacation. I got a visa.

'I prolonged the visa to do an advanced language course. I thought I'd wait till things cooled down. After a few months, I missed my boyfriend and wanted him to join me. The solicitor said, "I can help you apply for asylum, but I cannot help anyone outside the country."'

'I said "OK" and took the first flight home. I met my boyfriend in Dushanbe. We got a flat together. I told [my family] things had changed, I was moving to Dushanbe and wanted a divorce. One summer evening, the doorbell rang and there was my wife. She asked why I never came home and didn't spend time with her, and why I was living here with this man.

'I said, "I'm gay. This is my partner. Please leave." She started yelling. The neighbours came, and it threatened a scandal. I forced her out. We locked up the flat and disappeared into town, so if she called the police they wouldn't find us.

'We asked friends to accommodate us for a few days. We said we had locked ourselves out and our landlady was away. Eventually we went back. I phoned my mother. She said my wife had created a big scandal, so the whole town knew. I called a colleague at the university who said, "She has been here, don't come. Don't show up." I lost my job, my friends, my flat. If the story got out, the security services would know and put me behind bars.'

Abdul Lalzad, Afghanistan

'I was born in Badakhshan in the far north-east of Afghanistan, where my father was a farmer. The land was mountainous but we produced barley, wheat and rice. It is remote, 400 kilometres from Kabul. I went to primary school there, but for secondary education I went to Kabul. It was a US-sponsored technological school. It was established in the 1960s and the instruction was in English.

'After that there was a competitive system to go to university. I was admitted to the Faculty of Engineering in Kabul University. There were 15 faculties. Engineering and Agriculture were funded by the US, Pharmacy and Medicine by France, Economics by Germany, and there was a Soviet-backed polytechnic. Each was influenced by the country that sponsored them.

'On graduation and having high marks you are accepted as assistant professor, and then you would expect to go to the US for a Master's and PhD, returning to become a Professor. In December 1977, I became assistant professor, but in April 1978, the Communist coup occurred and relations with the US collapsed. I could not go, since the official relationship was now with USSR. In 1982, I went to Russia for a Master's at Kharkov in Ukraine, where I studied thermal engineering. I returned to Afghanistan in 1984, and taught at the University of Kabul. After the collapse of the Russian occupation, the mujahidin were fighting in Kabul, and our conditions of work became very difficult.

'In 1996, the Taliban took control of Kabul, and they closed all educational establishments. Women were not allowed to work or study – at the university 60 per cent of the students and 40 per cent of the teachers were women.

Professor Lalzad has written extensively on Afghanistan, and is exasperated with NATO's short-sighted approach to the country. Two years ago, he highlighted two issues – one external, the other internal – which, if not addressed, would prevent peace in Afghanistan.

'The first is with Pakistan. Why is Pakistan interfering in our affairs? Because the government of Afghanistan does not recognize the border with Pakistan. The border agreement was signed by the King of Afghanistan and British India in 1893. Pakistan was established in 1947. Afghanistan did not recognize the North West Frontier Provinces and Baluchistan as part of Pakistan. There are more Pashtuns in Pakistan than in Afghanistan – 15 million compared to 5 million. There is no such problem with the northern and north-eastern borders with Uzbekistan and Tajikistan.

'Pakistan wants to prevent the emergence of a greater Afghanistan that would claim two provinces of Pakistan to be part of Afghanistan. The border, known as the Durand line (after the Foreign Minister of British India in 1893), is uncontrolled, and stretches for more than 2,600 kilometres. It needs to be determined by Afghanistan, Pakistan and the international community. Afghanistan is dependent on Pakistan for most daily necessities. If the border is closed, there will be no food; the country will starve.

Afghanistan is a tribal society. Each group has its tribal pride. But what good is that if Pakistan is laughing at us? All we produce is opium. The Taliban was a mutation of tribalism. Tribalism is exclusive and totalitarian. It is fascistic.

'That is the external problem. Internally, after the collapse of Communism, there was civil war supported by Pakistan, and based on the dominant ethnicities – Pashtun, Tajik, Uzbek and Hazara. Each group constitutes a minority. When one rules, its thinking is purely tribal: Pashtun kill Hazaras who kill Uzbeks who kill Tajiks. If the international community were not present there would be ethnic fighting, as there was between 1992 and 1996. That is why people said the Taliban was better than anarchy, because they did impose order. "A prison is better than slaughter." Anarchy is the worst dictatorship. Only the Western presence prevents descent into tribal lawlessness.

'My proposals were that the Afghan government recognize the Durand line and internally, that each province elect its own administration. Each ethnic group should elect its own governor at the local level. Hamid Karzai [a Pashtun] sends governors from Kabul, which brings a culture repugnant to local groups and ethnicities. Afghanistan is seen as being dominated by Pashtuns. Tajiks, Uzbeks, Hazaras will not accept this. The main internal problem is minorities [and] the rights of minorities, because all groups in Afghanistan are minorities.'

'After the Taliban closed the universities, I was employed by the International Committee of the Red Cross as relief coordinator. We were responsible for delivering food and non-food aid to widows and the disabled, victims of the Soviet occupation – about 40,000 people in Kabul.

'During the civil war, between 1992 and 1996 I worked in Pakistan for a German NGO, GTZ, an organization that gave technical support to projects. Then I worked with a UN project in Kabul. In the last 30 years I have seen the manipulation of Afghanistan by outside forces.

'There had been two factions in the Afghan Communist party, the Parcham (mostly non-Pashtuns) and Khalq (mostly Pashtuns). They were simply tribally driven. It is impossible to export democracy after the fashion of the US or Europe to such a context. After the Soviets left in 1989, for three years Najibullah remained in power. He defended the regime against the mujahidin, which were also divided into many factions – Iranian, Pakistani, as well as ethnic divisions. The Khalq faction joined Hekmatyar (a Pashtun), and the Parcham joined Massoud who led the Tajiks, the Northern Alliance.

'For 250 years the Pashtuns had been in control of Afghanistan. They had never been a majority [and] have convinced the world using the wrong data that they are a majority.

'Massoud was Minister of Defence from 1992 to 1996, and then the leader of the resistance to the Taliban. The Pakistanis invested in Hekmatyar. When the ISI, the Pakistan Security Forces, saw that Hekmatyar was finished because Massoud was established in Kabul, they sponsored the Taliban [who were Pashtun]. They trained and armed the students who, starting in Kandahar, worked their way through the country, taking Kabul in 1996. They never conquered the Northern provinces.

'Massoud was killed two days before 9/11. Two terrorists had filled a videocamera with explosives. They said they wanted to interview Massoud, and exploded the videocamera. Massoud was the last resistance.

'I was on the scene in the region until 1998. My salary stopped when the Taliban came. I had six children. What was I to do? They said I was not a Muslim, because if I were, I would depend on God for my salary. That was when I joined the ICRC [International Committee of the Red Cross]. The Taliban undertook ethnic cleansing – getting rid of all non-Pashtun elements in the government. Because I was from Badakhshan, they thought I was an agent of Massoud. One day I was driving in the Red Cross car, and we were stopped on the road by Taliban brandishing Kalashnikovs. I was taken to prison. I was lucky, because I had radio contact, a communication system that linked up with the Red Cross. I told HQ. The Taliban denied they had taken me, but the ICRC knew exactly where the car had been stopped. They said if I was not released immediately they would cease all operations in Afghanistan. I was set free the next day. The Head of ICRC said, "So far we have supported you. This is your last chance. They will certainly kill you. You must decide what to do." I said "Thank you," and decided to leave the country.'

Hua Chan, China

The economic liberalization, which has transformed China in the past two decades into the world's manufacturing hub has not been accompanied by democratization. The Communist Party retains the monopoly of power. After 1978, Deng Xiaoping's economic reforms introduced a market economy, accompanied by an associated loosening of the rigidities left by Mao. The reformist Hu Yaobang (the Party's general secretary) resigned in 1987 following Party pressure. His death in 1989 provoked the students, who believed he was their protector, to mount large-scale demonstrations in Beijing. The main protagonists were students and intellectuals, who wanted political as well as economic reforms, and urban workers, who saw economic changes threatening their security and livelihood. The demonstrations gained momentum, despite official exhortations to abandon them. On 20 May, martial law was declared, and on 4 June the army opened fire in Tiananmen Square. The official death toll was two or three hundred, but student organizations estimate the casualties at ten times that number at least. The event had global repercussions; in China thousands were arrested, and sympathizers in the Party were purged.

At that time Hua Chan was a university lecturer in Wuhan City. His subject was originally History, but he also taught Economics and Politics. Having expressed sympathy with the Beijing demonstrators in 1989, he was passed over for promotion. At a demonstration in Wuhan, he was secretly filmed, which he discovered many years later, in 1996, when the same thing happened. 'My only crime was to say what everyone knew – that the government was corrupt. There was no freedom of the press; no private publishing house, TV, broadcast or newspaper can exist. You had to be a Party member to make progress in any institution – from factory to university. Bribery is general in China since Mao's death, especially to get a promotion.

'In 1989, my flat was searched by police and security forces. They also stole money. They wanted to find a video of the Tiananmen Square demonstration and tapes of speeches students had made. I was forced to live in the basement of the building. It was full of water. I went to a hotel [until] the water had been pumped out.

'I was invited abroad – Germany, France Holland. I applied for a passport but the authorities didn't give me a form.

'I was dismissed from the university in 1993, and not allowed to go abroad. My phone calls were monitored. I was followed. I felt unsafe.

'I wanted to come to the UK for a conference. In the end they gave me a passport, because they wanted to get rid of me as I am a troublemaker.

'I worked on reforming the Chinese alphabet using the Latin alphabet. I wanted to follow Western culture, its political and legal system. I dreamed of a single world language, like Zamenhof [who invented Esperanto]. I also wrote about the environment, the effects of pollution, before the authorities recognized any such problem.

'China does not want people to have freedom. The government worries that [they] would lose control.' He points out that economic growth and human rights do not run in parallel in China. Rapid industrialization brings social injustice and environmental disaster. Economic growth alone does not improve the lives of the people; even less does it further the wellbeing of humanity.

'Chinese leaders such as Hu Jintao (the Party's general secretary) and Wen Jiabao (prime minister) might want a little reform, but they are restricted by conservative influence from the Party and the military.'

THE JOURNEY TO SAFETY

Escape routes

This section tells how the threatened academics escaped. A few had a valid visa for admission to Britain, but a majority depended on the informal trajectories organized by those stigmatized as people-smugglers.

The theory and practice of asylum diverge sharply. The detained and tortured cannot go through official channels to request protection from democratic countries. The story of how they came to Britain opens a small window onto the clandestine movements of millions of people worldwide. People in despair ignore the formalities. They use any means to escape the fate of many of their colleagues and compatriots. This involves using ties of kinship, consanguinity, ethnic or religious affiliation, bribing corrupt officials, and people-smugglers.

Most academic refugees are not among the poorest in their country of origin, although since colonial independence, a significant number of the children of poor and rural families have reached university. These soon question structures of injustice in their country. Some refugees, associated with older colonial, monarchic or former privileged castes ejected from power often have savings to facilitate getting out of prison or crossing a border. Because most tyrannical regimes are corrupt, an exit can often be found from the labyrinths of state power by suborning officials, jailers and the police.

It is one thing to recommend rooting out corruption, but God forbid that the tyrannies from which people escape barely with their lives should be made more efficient in the dark arts of oppression. It is a mercy that pathways exist to evade the secret police and summary trial, trumped-up charges, arbitrary execution, the disappearance and the forced confession.

There is a distinction between human traffickers and people-smugglers: the former exploit the credulous and vulnerable, press them into bonded labour or prostitution; the second, although rarely animated by humanitarianism, often save lives. Many academics in this book owe their lives to people-smugglers. Trapped as a dissident in a Cameroon jail, tortured and abused, Joseph Ndalou was released with the complicity of a prison guard who shared the same tribal origin and language. Loyalty to the most repressive regimes is overridden by personal links; and undertaking the long journey into exile sometimes depends upon acts of personal kindness or solidarity.

'We were lucky. One of the prison guards knew us. He promised to make up a story that the prison had been broken into, so we could find a way out. And that's what happened. We were able to escape into the dark.

'We had to get as far away from the camp as possible. I was with another prisoner from a village close to mine. We walked avoiding all roads, and arrived home at four o'clock the following day. I couldn't stay with my family. I took refuge with a distant relative in a neighbouring village.

'In detention I heard of a guy who does trafficking. I had some money. Late at night I took a taxi to the city and contacted this man. It isn't hard to trace such people – everyone knows somebody who has gone that way. The whole plan took about a week.

'I had to empty my account to pay him. He did me a favour – I didn't have enough money to go to London, but he agreed to take me.'

Photographs were taken, passport and travel documents produced. Joseph never saw them: they were for recycling identities. 'We left Cameroon on 14 April 2004 and arrived in Paris at 6.30 a.m. from Douala. I just showed my documents to check in, but I bypassed both immigration and the police. My contact had squared the officials.

'I travelled with this man and two others to Paris. They checked the passport but waved me through. I was taken to a house. I had no idea where. The following day, the smuggler came with one other man in a car. It was a seven-seater, filled with groceries and bottles of wine, as though we had been in France for a day's shopping. We started at 8.30, drove onto the ferry. No questions were asked. The smuggler drove us to Victoria, and then released us with no papers. I was not scared. I had been through enough at home not to be frightened. He said, "Don't panic. Go to the nearest police station." I had the number of a school-friend in Leicester. He was shocked. I said I did not know where I was. He said, "Tell me what you see. Go inside, sit down and wait."

'After a few hours, he came. He didn't recognize me at first. I had lost weight and was looking stressed. We drove to Leicester. He was afraid, because I had no documents. He didn't know what to do with me.'

ℭ   ℘

Layla Almariya was in Benghazi prison for six months. She heard people crying and screaming, but saw no one. 'I was underground. When Amnesty International came to Libya, the security services showed them the well-known prisons, but not this one. They deny that any such place exists, and I doubt whether Amnesty knows of it.

'I didn't despair. They sentenced me to death with no trial, no court. Before my execution, I requested I might see my mother. The bodyguard was with us all the time. My mother hugged me, and I whispered to her, "I am going to be executed soon." They warned me I should say nothing to her about the death sentence. If I did [not], I might be released.

'I thought, "This is my last game with them." Within days my mother had paid a small fortune – $70,000. She was allowed to visit me again at the end of Ramadan. She whispered that she had found someone to help me get out of the country. I needed to find someone in the prison willing to assist.

'I had a friendly relationship with one guard, an elderly man. His daughter had died of cancer; he had been unable to take her to Tunisia for an operation. He depended on this job to provide his family with food. When my mother visited the second time, I pointed out this guard. She went to his home. She offered money. There were many guards, so no one would know who was involved. This man brought me food from his home. Sometimes he let me go to the toilet more than once, which was against the rules.

'The cell I was in was tiny. Sometimes the guard would let me walk outside for exercise. He told me about his daughter. He was tearful when he spoke of her. I told him who my father was, and he remembered his reputation. I benefited from that, long after my father was dead. People do not forget.

'He said, "Be ready on the second day of Eid and you'll go out with the visitors." He brought a plastic bag, with a *jellabiya*, so I could walk out like a visitor.[7] If I was caught at the main gate, I knew I'd be shot dead, but it was worth the risk. If I stayed I'd be executed anyway. The guard told me the number of the car and where it would pick me up. Later, in Britain, I was to do some training at the Foreign Office: I explained how people-traffickers saved lives. Some of them accepted it.

'I walked out unchallenged. I just got in the car and sat down beside someone I had never seen before. He took me to a small farm near the airport, where I met my mother and two sisters. They brought clothes for me. The trafficker gave me a wig to match the photo in the fake passport. He had paid money to people at the airport. I boarded the plane by the delivery door.

'It was a Libyan Airlines flight. There were 15 passengers going from Benghazi. He must have paid the pilot, because when he counted passengers, he missed me out. You can buy anything in Libya. Even freedom. I came from a wealthy family. If we had been poor, I'd have been executed.

'The flight was 3 hours 45 minutes. I felt wretched, because I might never see my family again. I thought, "I'm going nowhere." There were three flights that day – to France, Italy and England. The trafficker had tickets for each one.

'My mother said, "Don't argue, just follow."

'I asked, "Where are you taking me?"

'"London,"

'"Why?"

'"Do you want to go back to prison?" he said. I couldn't speak a word of English.'

Cʒ ℬ

Darius Zemani felt trapped in Tehran. Without work or livelihood, he was desperate to leave. 'In November 1998 or 1999, I met someone who could arrange my escape. I paid £5,000. I was taken from Iran through Turkey to Croatia. Then I walked for days. Finally a people-smuggler brought me to Slovenia. The police caught me, and I spent a few days in prison. Then on to Italy and Switzerland. I flew to Heathrow, and asked for asylum. A professor I had known in Tehran had been in Cambridge [and] said if I could prove my situation, and they believed me, they would help.'

Cʒ ℬ

When Immanuel Samere fled the scene of the accident in Eritrea, in which the truck taking him from the prison to work in the cotton fields collided with a bus, he and his companion walked to a village not far from the Sudanese border. 'My fellow-prisoner had an uncle there. We stayed one night, creeping into the village at 10 p.m. He promised to show us the way to Sudan. It was a two-day walk. There were guards on the border. We travelled over the mountains by night. If the Eritreans caught us, there would be serious consequences.

'We crossed successfully, and came to Kasala in Sudan, midway between Port Said and Khartoum. A truck driver agreed to take us. In Khartoum I had an uncle. The driver took us to where exiled Eritreans meet. Someone took me to my cousin's house. I stayed there some time. Even in Khartoum there is trouble. You cannot work or travel without official permission. If Eritrean Intelligence find you, they will kidnap you and take you back.

'When I was in Asmara, I had a friend who went to the USA to work as a nurse. I contacted her by e-mail. She told us she would help us leave Sudan. There are illegal ways if you have the money. She agreed to pay. I wanted to join her in the USA, but that was too difficult.

'I met an agent who could arrange a trip to the UK. He just said "Europe." I said, "OK, anywhere I can live in peace." The one condition was to ask no questions. My friend in America sent the $6,000 to pay the agent.

'They ask for your photo, but you don't see the passport. They just tell you your false name. You can't even ask where you are going. We went to the airport and took a flight, which landed in an Arab country. I don't know which one.

'My photo was inserted into a UK passport. The agent gives you the passport to hand to the immigration officer, then confiscates it as soon as you come through. We arrived in Manchester. I spent one night in a house – I have no idea where. Next day, the agent took me to the National Express coach station, and we went by bus to Liverpool. He showed me the Home Office building. "Go and ask for asylum." Sometimes they play a trick on you. The guy said, "I'll be back in a few minutes." I waited. One hour. Two hours. I realized I was on my own.

ભ   ୨

Abdul Lalzad went to Pakistan in December 1998. His family were staying in Peshawar, because after 1992 Afghanistan had become very unsafe and there was no schooling in Kabul.

'I couldn't stay in Afghanistan, because I knew they [the Taliban] would find me. They went to my house in Kabul and asked where I was. While I was with the ICRC [International Committee of the Red Cross], I had a certain immunity, but when they could no longer guarantee that I knew I had to go. In fact, if the Taliban had taken me from home, I'd have been killed, but because I was taken from an ICRC car, the outside world knew. The ICRC was running a big operation of relief in Afghanistan. We used to take NGO employees between the Massoud- and the Taliban-controlled areas.

'I had to use people-smugglers in Pakistan. They all operate travel agencies. Who are you, how much can you pay, where do you want to go? It is a bazaar. By direct flight it costs this much, indirect, that much. Netherlands, Germany, Russia, Dubai? They look after all the contacts – police, army, immigration officials. This system has now transferred itself to Kabul. They will almost itemize the cost of this corrupt official, that bureaucrat. If they trust you, they'll tell you exactly how it works.

'In Karachi they told me, "Tomorrow you'll fly with a Pakistani passport." They gave me an ID card which said that I was employed by the British Petroleum company. In Karachi airport, they spoke Urdu, which I don't understand. It was clear I wasn't a Pakistani, and I was going illegally. They took me to the Head of Police. Name? Abdul Lalzad. He looked down his list. My name was there. Take him. Obviously those who had paid their dues could go through.

'In transit at Dubai they have their own people. If they are in charge, no problem. If not, and something goes wrong, they'll deport you, but don't worry – we'll take you back. They had given me a different name on my photo. The passport had been falsely stamped to make it seem I had been in London several times. It was a British Airways flight. Someone from the agency came with me, a young man. He said, "Don't worry, be confident." As we are going through the passport check, the airline official, a British woman said, "Are you going to spend the New Year in London?" It was the end of December. I was told by the agent not to speak English. In fact, I shouldn't speak at all. On the flight he said he was going to the toilet, and after that he didn't come back.

'He had told me not to speak English at Heathrow. The official asked me where I came from. "Afghanistan, Afghanistan." I wanted asylum. He asked me to write my name, which I did. He said, "You think we are stupid? Where are you from?" I told him I was a professor from Afghanistan. "No, you are a Pakistani. If you don't tell us you are a Pakistani, we'll send you back." They thought no one from Afghanistan could be a professor or speak English.

'They searched my luggage, and found my ICRC card. That saved my life. They called the ICRC in Geneva, and they confirmed I was relief coordinator in Afghanistan. The police apologized. I had been following the instructions of the agents; and my failure to do so was my salvation.'

�☞   ☜

Matthew Douara, detained in Douala jail, believed he would never escape. He recognized an officer from his home area who befriended him. 'He gave me food daily, prepared by his wife.

'Eighteen of us were to be transferred to Yaoundé. My friend overheard jail officials making the arrangements. He said, "You will not survive if they take you there." He would make sure the guard on the gate was a friend. He gave me 5,000 francs. I escaped quite simply walking past a friendly guard.

'I walked three days, buying bananas in the bush. When I reached Edea, I asked for the local opposition representatives. They kept me nine days in hiding.

'They arranged for me to leave the country. I was dressed in a burka and given a woman's passport. This was June 2003. The flight was from Douala to Brussels, where I was detained for two days. They soon found out I was not a woman, but my passport did not say I was Cameroonian. I said I lived in France. They just let me go. I took a train to France, and from there to UK. I used a woman's passport, and was allowed into London without being stopped.'

�☞   ☜

Laurent Mpinde, after seven months in a Brazzaville jail, was woken early one morning. 'I was taken with other prisoners [in] a military truck to the southern region of Congo, where rebels had their headquarters. The intention was to shoot us, and then say rebels had killed us.

'Our life was saved by an officer. He said, "You are too young to die." He released us. He said we should run. Sometimes, he said, soldiers fire in the air, sometimes they miss deliberately. These regimes do not command the loyalty even of the people they privilege – police and army. They see the arbitrariness, the injustice of it, and do their bit to subvert the regime.

'We were free. We came to deserted villages emptied by government decree. The only people left were old and sick. It was not my home area. If anyone [rebels or government troops] had caught us, we would have been killed.

'I don't know why the officer saved us. As a teacher, many thousands of children pass through our hands. Our students often become soldiers. Maybe someone recognized us. What moves people to compassion? Later I met a former pupil of mine in Manchester. He lived in France, and was in Britain, visiting his family. You can meet [former] students anywhere – why not in the Congolese army?

'I took a pirogue across the Congo River, the boundary between the Democratic Republic of Congo and the Congo Republic. I understood some of the language of the *piroguiers* – the people who ply the canoes. They took me to the DRC. I started walking. I came to a village with a big church, a place of large-scale pilgrimage. I was sick. In prison I had been violated and beaten. I bled a lot. At the church, I met someone on a pilgrimage from Brazzaville. I asked her to contact my cousin-sister at home, who would help me.

'My cousin-sister contacted people-smugglers. I was taken to Kinshasa by truck. There, photographs and travel documents were prepared. I embarked with the smuggler and a woman on an Ethiopian Airlines flight from Kinshasa to Addis Ababa. He held my passport. We flew on to London, passing through customs and immigration without any problem.

'Once in London he left the woman with me, and gave me instructions [about] how to ask for asylum. I went to Lunar House. There was such a throng. "Come back tomorrow." I went back the next day and requested asylum.'

CƷ   ℬↄ

Asylum seekers have to endure many humiliations. They share lodgings with arbitrary companions, and have nothing in common – sometimes not even a language – other than flight from persecution. The highly qualified and the political dissident coexist with the peasant and the petty criminal. Some wish to study and prepare for a career in Britain, while others only drink and watch game shows. Overcrowding, shared beds, the distinctive male odour of cramped humanity, a pinched, undernourished existence. Yet as one man said, 'At least we are not dead – unlike friends tortured with electricity, raped with metal rods or made to line up in the grey dawn to be shot over the shallow grave they had been forced to dig in advance.'

Should people-smugglers, those venal rescuers, be punished for taking advantage of despair, or lauded for their humanitarian function? Clearly, both responses provide a quandary to those adhering to easy morality and clear distinctions between right and wrong.

Refugees are people who risk arrest, prison and death. With the stolen identities, aliases, forged papers and counterfeit documents that are their lifeline some people say they scarcely know any longer who they are. The expenditure of life-savings to save a life: who can blame either desperate people who have simply challenged a tyranny, or those making a risky but lucrative livelihood out of their plight? It may be deplored that mercy and rescue are dependent upon a very private enterprise of smugglers of people; but who can say which lives ought to be sacrificed to rid the world of their unsavoury practices?

The encounter with Britain – snapshots

Not all threatened academics reach Britain by these illegal routes; although many make clandestine payments. Some come assisted by other academics and university departments; others arrive for medical purposes, to meet relatives, as tourists or on business. But their relief at being in a secure place can easily be subverted by their first encounters with bureaucracy.

Most say they encounter suspicion from employees of the Border and Immigration Services. Those telling the truth find themselves greeted with scepticism, and the assumption that they are lying. To those falsely accused, beaten and imprisoned, this aggravates from the outset the sense of rejection, which can be reinforced by the often interminable wait for recognition that they are here as involuntary visitors, refugees, in need of the kind of solace and support that too often remain elusive.

Not until they have overcome these obstacles will they learn about another Britain of kindliness and fellow-feeling, an acceptance that doesn't question the memories of horror and loss, an enfolding assurance that they are indeed at last safe.

At Heathrow, the officials barely glanced at Layla's passport, which was French.

'We came by Piccadilly Line to Leicester Square. I was shocked to see people kissing in the street. I couldn't tell whether people were male or female. I went with the people-smuggler to Burger King for a meal. Then he took me to a night club to shelter from the cold and the rain. I was frightened by the drunkenness, the noise and lights. He gave me £20, directions to the Home Office and a ticket to Croydon from Victoria. I spent the night in a phone box.

'I arrived at Lunar House at 4.20 in the morning. There was a long queue. It was December, I was cold and hungry. I was seen at 4 p.m. I told the truth. They took the £20 from me. Why? Did they think I was lying? I was met with discrimination, contempt, disbelief. I was sick, but the interpreter said I was acting. I shouted, and she complained to the officer. I needed a doctor and asked her to translate. I had had no sleep for two days. It was a nightmare.

'At 1 a.m. a coach took me and other asylum-seekers to Dover. They gave me food. At a tribunal, I was twice refused asylum. The first time, the interpreter provided by the solicitor told a story that was not true.

'When I went to the Refugee Council, there was an endless queue. I met a Somali family from Kilburn, who took me home with them. I returned in the early hours of the morning. Still a long line. That happened three days in succession.

The security man hit me as I tried to enter the building. Someone said, "She's been here three days." He said, "I don't care if she's been here a year." I told him, "When I've learned the language I'll come back and talk to you."

'I was homeless for eight months. I slept rough, spent nights in churches and mosques. I was so tired I couldn't walk. The mosque in Willesden Green looked after me, as well as the Somali family. I was bleeding because I had a miscarriage. When I was raped in the jail in Libya I was a virgin, and didn't know I was pregnant. The National Asylum Support Service put me in contact with the Medical Foundation, where a doctor saw me. They were wonderful. They finally got me accommodation at last, in August 2003. I had been in the country since December 2002.'

༕ ༖

Matthew Douara from Cameroon found himself alone in London, abandoned by the people-smuggler. 'I was frightened. I spent two days just walking about. Then I saw a law firm advertised on an office building. I went in. They didn't specialize in Immigration Law, but they called a lawyer who did. He picked me up and paid for a hotel room for me. The next day I went to Croydon. I told them, "If you cannot keep me in this country, send me anywhere else, but not Cameroon."

'I was taken to a detention centre in Cambridge for ten days. I had a comfortable bed. Three days later I got a letter saying they found my claim for asylum unjustified. They would send me back to Cameroon.

'I asked the lawyer to appeal. I gave him the number of the British Council in Cameroon, because I had being doing consultancy work. The hearing was in Stoke on Trent. When I got there, I was surprised to see he [my lawyer] had a letter from the British Council testifying that I had indeed worked there. They acknowledged I had had trouble with the authorities. The lawyer had newspaper articles I had written, a letter from the chairman of the SDF (Social Democratic Front) and one from the Teachers' Trade Union. The lawyer said, "Do you know these names?" I gave the name of the director of the British Council. The lawyer also had video evidence from the SDF. He told me the solicitor had communicated with Cameroon, and everything I said had been confirmed.

'I went to Peterborough with other asylum seekers under the National Asylum Support System. Three months later, I got a letter saying I had indefinite leave to remain. Within 14 days, I went to the Job Centre for a Jobseeker's Allowance, and [was sharing] a flat in Peterborough. I learned that my brother died during that time. My parents had also been hassled by the police who wanted to know my whereabouts.

'My wife came with the children in 2004. Her passport did not show she was my wife. I couldn't work, because I did not have my certificates [professional qualifications]. I did some interpreting. It was irregular, but I hated benefit – getting money without working. I trained with the Public Services Interpreting Service. Then I went to a recruiting agency, who found me work in a food factory in Spalding.'

ɔ̃   ଡ

Hua Chan came to Britain for a conference in 1999 and asked for asylum. It was a long process. He was placed in accommodation in east London while the asylum application was considered. Like many in his position, he was shocked by the place in which he was expected to live. He found people noisy, inconsiderate and hostile. His period of waiting was marked by disputes with the local authority over noise. As a result of his insistence, he was taken to a psychiatric hospital, where it was said he had 'visual and audial hallucinations'. On appeal, he was released, but says he has had nothing but grief since coming to Britain. He was granted indefinite leave to remain and two years later became a British citizen.

Hua Chan is 'disillusioned' with the country of his exile. Communication is difficult, since his spoken English is not clear. People readily attribute stupidity or craziness to those they cannot understand, and this may have caused some of the persecution he says he has also suffered here. He finds it difficult to find work, particularly in an academic setting, where the ability to teach and express oneself clearly is a basic necessity. Hua Chan has taken a number of English language courses, but this has not really helped his linguistic competence. He was helped by CARA, and bought a computer with the grant he received.

He has initiated a long and extensive process of litigation without a solicitor with officials of authorities which, he feels, have infringed his human rights. He has lodged a number of cases with the European Court of Human Rights. He believes that although Europeans constantly advocate democracy, they do not know what it really is.

Hua Chan feels isolated and stranded – socially, culturally and emotionally. Yet he has no intention of going back to China. He studies each day, in pursuit of his objective of getting back into education.

The first time I met Hua Chan, his nephew from China was staying with him, a PhD student in Britain for three months to improve his English. I met him a number of times; both he and his uncle were grateful for my interest. The young man's English is very good.

The last time I met Hua Chan, his nephew had returned home, and he was missing him. He prepared a meal – carp and spring rolls – and we joked that he ought to set up a Chinese restaurant. His life is restricted – he has a small flat and apart from Housing Benefit, receives a little over £200 a month. This has not extinguished his hopes. He is planning to publish a book in Germany which, he is convinced, will earn him good money; and is still hoping to make a relationship, preferably with an English woman, that will also help him speak the language better. In spite of his experiences, his optimism and hopefulness are undiminished.

○3   &0

Darius Zemani spent five years awaiting the outcome of his asylum application. 'I spent 20 days in a hostel before going to Newcastle under a dispersal policy for asylum seekers. I was in a house in a poor part of the city with five other people. Some were Kurds, some Iranians. It was difficult because you are living with people you never chose and who never chose you. I tried to study every day, but it was very difficult. Some of them would bring teenage girls into the house. I said to one man, "You should not do that." He threatened me with a knife. I kept quiet.

'It is a terrible feeling to have no status. I telephoned my family. They said "Are you enjoying life?" What could I say? Five of what should have been the best years of my life spent in miserable conditions far from home, when I could have been a university lecturer. What was worse, my children blamed me. My daughter is now 18, my son 17. They understand now, but at the time, they just saw that I was not there.

'For five years, I saw myself as a useless person. I lost confidence in my power to do things which I knew I could do very well. On the other hand, it taught me to be brave.

'It was also difficult for my children. They arrived here with my wife two years ago. They have been clever enough to adapt. When they came, they didn't speak English. Both now have university entrance. The children tell me I did the right thing in speaking out, although while we were in Tehran, they wanted me to keep quiet.'

○3   &0

When Latefa Guémar arrived in Britain, she joined her husband in a Heathrow hotel.

'It was a horrible place. I was ill and pregnant. The doctor said, "This woman cannot stay here." Two weeks before I gave birth to my second daughter, we were moved to another hotel in Hounslow with two bedrooms. We were waiting for our asylum request to be processed. I asked them to disperse us before my older daughter started school. They sent us to Swansea.

'When we signed the dispersal agreement, they asked my preference. I had never been to Britain, so I had no idea. All I knew was that the weather is terrible, and Churchill won the war. I said I would be happy near the sea.

'My husband claimed asylum at his first interview at the airport. He was interviewed by someone very knowledgeable about Algeria. His second interview was in Liverpool. They said asylum will be granted within two or three weeks.

'It took 15 months. We were approached by BBC4, looking for families to follow over a two-year period for a film on integration. After some hesitation, we agreed. They filmed once a week over two years. It was a good piece of work.' The family suffered continuous low-level harassment – eggs thrown at the windows, car tyres slashed, insults. The police installed an emergency alarm connected to the police station.

'After the film was shown in January 2006, we received hostility from the neighbourhood and the British National Party. It was a problematic neighbourhood, but our friends were not living there. We only used it as a place to sleep and at weekends. A Plaid Cymru councillor helped us to move to the Gower, outside Swansea.'

ɔƷ   ଚଠ

Immanuel Samere from Eritrea was not believed when he told the Home Office his story and was placed in a hostel in Old Trafford. 'On my first day the guys there gave me £35 and sent me shopping at the Asda supermarket in Old Trafford. I had no idea what to do. I managed. You feel frightened of everybody. In the early days I often went days without speaking to one person.

'I was very unhappy the first three or four months. You cannot explain to anyone what has happened. If you look confused, people just turn away. It was December, very cold. It felt strange and hostile. One day I tried to speak to a stranger. A black guy. I thought he might be sympathetic. He must have been Jamaican. He told me to fuck off.

'A letter came, refusing asylum. I had a solicitor who found the reasons flawed. A court hearing was set. The solicitor sent a letter outlining our case against refusal. Even before the hearing, I heard from the Home Office giving me leave to remain indefinitely.'

ɔƷ   ଚଠ

Abdul Lalzad from Afghanistan was sent to a west London hostel. 'I met an Afghani there. They were going to disperse us. He told me, "If you know anyone in London, tell them and they'll let you stay in London."

'Then he said, "Tell me the name of Afghans you know, someone famous." He asked me the names of some engineers I knew. "Oh, I know him," he said [to one name]. He gave me his number and I called him.

'"This is Lalzad from Afghanistan."

'"What are you doing here?" He took me to his home – he was working as an interpreter for the asylum service.

'Then I was taken to the office to get Income Support. I was not allowed to work. I got permission to stay while my case was processed. I was given a room and £50 a week in a private house. With Income Support, I started my new life.

'I couldn't sit at home and lose all my experience and knowledge. I did an IT course for two months. Then I went to North London University to do an accredited course to validate [my] qualifications, because I had no certificates, no degrees – asylum seekers are often without documents. This way I could prepare a portfolio of my education – it proves proficiency in English and competence in one's field. I told them I had designed these systems and had taught at Kabul University, with which I'd been associated for over 20 years. I wanted to continue to study, even though I could not work officially.

'Of course I felt humiliated. I had so much skill and experience to offer. I couldn't understand why this society had no ability to distinguish between skilled and unskilled. There are so many engineers, doctors driving minicabs or washing up in kitchens. There is a language barrier for some, but that is easily resolved. What a waste.'

ᙂ   ᙆ

Laurent Mpinde from Congo was left by the people-smuggler who gave him instructions on asking for asylum. A woman took him to a flat, where he spent the night. 'It was a weekend. On the Monday, I went to Lunar House in Croydon. There were so many people, I had to go back the next day.

'I stayed in the flat three or four months. Little by little, you link up with people. I needed a lawyer and doctor because my health was bad. When I left the flat, the Home Office placed me in a hotel, and then sent me to Stoke on Trent.

'My efforts to obtain asylum have been degrading. At my first interview, the request was refused. I wonder if the people who run the place have any idea of the political situation in our country? Do they know what the army and police do to their opponents?

'At the appeal tribunal I complained of the superficiality of the first interview. I didn't know the system. I had an interpreter, and spoke only to him. I never even saw my lawyer. My English was poor. If you cannot speak the language, people think you are stupid. My lawyer abandoned me.

'I got a good lawyer from the Refugee Legal Centre, but Stoke on Trent was too far away, so I was advised to find another. Then my file was lost. I had to make copies of such papers as I had, but because I had not signed my first declaration when I asked for refugee status, it was invalid. I had to go before the appeal tribunal, although I did not understand what was said. My appeal was refused.

'I found a fourth lawyer, who urged me to make a fresh claim. I had nowhere to live, no support. I was taken in by some people out of kindness. My health deteriorated. I used to play football; and at the field, I met a man who said he could help me get work. I started in a warehouse, packing goods. At last I was doing something, I was earning some money. I could pay for my lodging. That went on for some months. I was still waiting for a reply to my new claim from the Home Office. One day, police and immigration authorities arrived and arrested me. "We have been looking for you."

'"Why?"

'"Your case is over."

'I had been studying English at Crewe. I went with my teacher to another lawyer. I would have to pay £135 an hour. I had saved some money. I was taken to a detention centre near Oxford. They said I was to be deported. I was ill on the bus. I couldn't walk. They took me to Harmondsworth. "Cooperate," they said, "and tell us everything." I told them I had made a new claim. They had no knowledge of it.

'Ten days later, a letter came, saying my claim had been refused. I was issued with a removal order. I was handcuffed and then taken back to detention. I contacted CARA, who had helped me with money for travel and studying and basic necessities. CARA found my sixth lawyer. At the next tribunal, Immigration said I had fought with their officers. They said the deportation would take place on a given date. I was to go via Paris. But there was no flight to Brazzaville that day.

'Immigration – or the company subcontracted to them – said the escort would have to be strengthened. I was taken onto the aircraft in handcuffs. They sat me in the plane. I made such a disturbance, the pilot said he would not fly. I was taken out, insulted and sworn at.'

Laurent later discovered that the Secretary of CARA, Professor John Akker, had contacted the Chief Removals Officer, and asked him whether his remit included sending people to their death, threatening to use his political contacts to publicize the case. Laurent was taken to Colnbrook Detention Centre. A fresh removal order was made. A lawyer CARA had engaged from the Refugee Legal Centre took out an injunction. A judicial review was ordered.

'It was November 2005. I went before a judge. Immigration lied. They said I had no right of appeal. They said I was violent. The judge told them, "You are immigration. You have no right to prevent an appeal." The judge saw no reason why I should be kept in detention.

'It was such a relief. I could not accept being detained again. I have never seen such a concentration of misery, sadness and hatred as I saw there. I was in Harmondsworth when the July bombings took place in London in 2005. When they heard the news, there was jubilation among some detainees. Although shocked – I can't see anything to rejoice over in such barbaric acts – I could

46. *Second Chance*, 1991.
47. Ibid.
48. Laurence Dopson, *The Independent*, 2 January 2002.
49. Vicky Rippiere and Ruth Williams, *Wounded Healers: Mental Health Workers' Experience of Depression*, Chichester, 1973.
50. Medawar and Pyke, 2000.
51. Ibid.
52. 28 September 1933.
53. David Zimmerman, 'The Society for the Protection of Science and Learning and the Politicization of British Science in the 1930s', *Minerva*, 2006.
54. SPSL Archive, Bodleian Library, cited *Second Chance*, 1991.
55. SPSL Archive, Bodleian Library.
56. Frisch, 1979.
57. Beveridge, 1959.
58. Paul K. Hoch, 'Emigrés in science and technology transfer , *Physics in Technology*, September 1986.
59. Snowman, 2002.
60. Lore Segal, *Other People's Houses*, New York, 1995.
61. London, 2000.
62. Peggy Fink was in Belsen after the British army liberated it in 1945. She worked with refugees from Nazi tyranny, and assisted the sad remnants of the camp in which a kind of social life was restored – schools were set up, religious ceremonies conducted by a rabbi who survived, a tent theatre put on plays in Yiddish. She recalls in particular '… a young woman who worked in my office, who was a survivor from the camp. I went away on leave, and when I returned I asked, "Where's Magda?" She had committed suicide. I thought how particularly dreadful it was to have survived that torment only to take your own life.'
63. Werner Pelz, *I Am Adolf Hitler*, London, 1969.
64. Personal communication to the author and extracts from an unpublished memoir, *From Auschwitz to Chartres*.
65. Segal, 1995.
66. Personal communication to the author.
67. Together with Sir Frank Macfarlane Burnet.
68. Leslie Brent, *A History of Transplantation Immunology*, San Diego and London, 1996.
69. Leslie Brent, *Sunday's Child: A Memoir*, New Romney, 2008.
70. London, 2000.
71. *Memories*, 2005 (unpublished) and personal communication to the author.
72. Paul Jacobsthal, *Early Celtic Art* (2 volumes), Oxford, 1944.
73. Literally: 'to this university no intruder, but ennoblement', probably meaning that Paul Jacobsthal was not thought of as an intruder, but that his contributions ennobled the university.
74. Ray Cooper, *Refugee Scholars*, Leeds, 1992.
75. Norman Bentwich, *The Rescue and Achievement of Refugeee Scholars*, The Hague, 1953.
76. Perutz, 1985.
77. The articles 'Remembering Internment' and 'Internment – the Sequel' appeared in the July and August issues respectively.
78. Peter Gillman and Leni Gillman, *Collar the lot!* London, 1980; Ronald Stent, *A Bespattered Page*, London, 1980.
79. Beveridge, 1959.
80. Ibid.

3   Until

1. *Lost Childhood and the Language of Exile*, ed. Judit Szekacs-Weisz and Ivan Ward, London, 2004.
2. SPSL Archive, Bodleian Library.
3. The World University Service had its origins in the 1920s, and grew out of the World Student Christian Fellowship. As European Student Relief, it helped people displaced by the First World War gain access to education. By 1939, then known as the International Student Service, it assisted those who had suffered under the Nazis, but soon expanded beyond Europe, as committees were established in Asia, Africa and later, Latin America. In 1950, it became known as World University Service. A scholarship programme for exiled students in the UK supported thousands from Chile, Argentina and South Africa. Always responsive to the changing circumstances of refugees, the Refugee Education Training and Advisory Service was established in the early 1990s. Now known as Education Action, it works within Western countries and globally, wherever refugees are forced to leave sites of conflict.
4. Luis Munoz, *Being Luis*, Exeter, 2006.
5. Ibid.
6. Munoz says the Chilean government was forced to close down the concentration camps in 1976, because the International Monetary Fund would not give a loan while they remained open; he was therefore indirectly indebted (not financially) to the IMF for his release.
7. Sulammith Wolff, *Children Under Stress*, London, 1969.
8. Munoz, 2006.
9. Albie Sachs, *The Jail Diary of Albie Sachs*, London, 1966; *Soft Vengeance of a Freedom Fighter*, London, 1990.
10. *Soft Vengeance of a Freedom Fighter*, 1990.
11. Ibid.
12. Maya Jaggi, 'Justice of the peace', *The Guardian*, 26 August 2006.
13. Albie Sachs, *Sexism and the Law: A Study of Male Beliefs and Judicial Bias in Britain and America*, Oxford, 1978.
14. E. Sylvia Pankhurst, *The Suffragette Movement: An Intimate Account of Persons and Ideals*, London, 1931.
15. Mbulelo Mzamane, *Children of Soweto*, Harlow, 1982
16. Jack Mapanje, *Of Chameleons and Gods*, London, 1981.
17. Jack Mapanje, *The Chattering of Wagtails of Mikuyu Prison*, Oxford, 1993.
18. Jack Mapanje, *Beasts of Nalunga*, Tarset, Northumberland, 2007. This book was shortlisted for the Forward Poetry Prize for best collection in the same year.
19. Jack Mapanje, *The Last of Sweet Bananas*, Tarset, Northumberland, 2004.
20. *The African Writers' Handbook*, ed. James Gibbs and Jack Mapanje, Oxford, 1999.
21. Imperialism's aftermath left African countries stranded between tradition and modernity, with social and welfare demands that treasuries could not satisfy. Postcolonial regimes too often became vehicles for personal advancement and corruption, and increasingly authoritarian. The reliance of many countries on primary products made them economically vulnerable, depressing prices and reducing government revenues. Later indebtedness led to conditions, such as privatization, liberalization, currency depreciation and significantly reduced welfare provision imposed on their economies by international institutions like the IMF and the World Bank.
22. Snowman, 2002.

4 Now

1. Albert Camus, *The Plague*, trans. by Stuart Gilbert, London, 1948.
2. A densely populated area between Baghdad and Tikrit, Saddam Hussein's birthplace, to the north.
3. Ryszard Kapuscinski and Neal Ascherson, *The Emperor: Downfall of an Autocrat*, London, 1983.
4. Mesfin Woldemariam, 'Whither Ethiopia', Ethiopian Economic Association: Vision 2020, November 2003.
5. The Dergue was the military junta headed by Mengistu.
6. A full length, loose outer garment with a hood.
7. The female version of the *djellaba*.
8. Dr Heaven Crawley is the Centre's Director.
9. Fred Halliday is Professor of International Relations at LSE.

Bibliography

The Bodleian Archive

The archive of the Academic Assistance Council and the Society for the Protection of Science and Learning, held in the Bodleian Library, Oxford, contains personal files; correspondence with other refugee organizations and funding sources; and negotiations with universities and government departments relating to the support of academics fleeing the Fascist and Communist regimes in Europe between 1933 and 1987. The archive post 1956 (Hungarian Revolution) is not catalogued, although the Council for Assisting Refugee Academics (CARA) has produced a useful box list which is available through the CARA office (details below).

The catalogue for 1933–56 is available through the following link: www.bodley.ox.ac.uk/dept/scwmss/wmss/online/online.htm or by contacting CARA. The archive from 1987 is held in CARA's office.

Council for Assisting Refugee Academics (CARA)
London South Bank University
Technopark
90 London Road
London SE1 6LN

tel: 020 7021 0880
fax: 0207 021 0881

e-mail: info.cara@lsbu.ac.uk
website: www.academic-refugees.org

Printed sources

(The) African Writers Handbook, edited by James Gibbs and Jack Mapanje (Oxford: African Books Collective, 1999).

Association of Jewish Refugees Journal, September 2007, letters to the editor. (See also below.)

Bentwich, Norman. *The Rescue and Achievement of Refugee Scholars* (The Hague: M. Nijhoff, 1953).

Bernal, J.D. *The Social Function of Science* (London: Routledge, 1939).

Beveridge, William. *A Defence of Free Learning* (London: Oxford University Press, 1959).

Brent, Leslie. *A History of Transplantation Immunology* (San Diego and London: Academic Press, 1996).

——. *Sunday's Child: A Memoir* (New Romney, Kent: Bank House Books, 2008).

Camus, Albert. *The Plague*, translated by Stuart Gilbert (London: Hamish Hamilton, 1948).

Carnegie, Rory and van der Gaag, Nikki. *How the World Came to Oxford* (Oxford: New Internationalist, 2007).

Clark, Ronald William. *The Life of Ernst Chain: Penicillin and Beyond* (Basingstoke: Palgrave Macmillan, 1986).

Cooper, Ray. *Refugee Scholars* (Leeds: Moorland Books, 1992).

——. *Retrospective Sympathetic Affection* (Leeds: Moorland Books, 1996).

Dopson, Laurence, *Professor Annie Altschul* (Obituary) (London: *The Independent*, 2 January 2002).

Ehrenburg, Eva. *Sehnsucht – mein geliebtes Kind* (Frankfurt am Main: Ner-Tamid Verlag, 1963).

Ferry, Georgina. *Max Perutz and the Secret of Life* (London: Chatto & Windus, 2007: p/back: Pimlico, 2008).

Fink, Peggy. 'Memories' (2005; unpublished).

Frisch, Otto. *What Little I Remember* (Cambridge: Cambridge University Press, 1979).

From Auschwitz to Chartres (unpublished memoir).

Gillman, Peter and Gillman, Leni. *'Collar the lot!' How Britain Interned & Expelled its Wartime Refugees* (London: Quartet Books, new ed., 1980).

Greville, Anthony. 'Remembering Internment' and 'Internment – the Sequel', *Association of Jewish Refugees Journal* (London: July and August 2007).

Hobsbawm, Eric. *Interesting Times* (London: Allen Lane, 2002).

Hoch, Paul K. 'Emigrés in science and technology transfer , *Physics in Technology* 17 No. 5 (September 1986).

Holmes, Frederic L. *Hans Krebs: The Foundation of a Scientific Life*, Vol. 1 (New York: Oxford University Press, 1991).

Jacobsthal, Paul. *Early Celtic Art* (2 volumes) (Oxford: Clarendon Press, 1944).

Jaggi, Maya. 'Justice of the peace' (London: *The Guardian*, 26 August 2006).

Lanouette, William. *Genius in the Shadows: a Biography of Leo Szilard – The Man behind the Bomb* (Chicago: University of Chicago Press, 1994).

London, Louise. *Whitehall and the Jews, 1933–1948* (Cambridge: Cambridge University Press, 2000).

Manchester Guardian, interview with AAC spokesman (Manchester: 28 September 1933).

Max Born – A Celebration. Published to commemorate the 50th anniversary of Max Born's award of the Nobel Prize (Berlin: the Max Born Institute, 2004).

Kapuscinski, Ryszard and Ascherson, Neal. *The Emperor: Downfall of an Autocrat* (London: Quartet Books, 1983).

Krebs, Hans. 'The Making of a Scientist', *Nature* 215, 30 September 1967, pp. 1441–5.

Lost Childhood and the Language of Exile, edited by Judit Szekacs-Weisz and Ivan Ward (London: Imago East West and the Freud Museum, 2004).

Lowe, Adolphe. *Economics and Sociology* (London: G. Allen & Unwin, 1935).

——. *The Price of Liberty: An Essay on Contemporary Britain* (Day to day pamphlets no. 36) (London: Hogarth Press, 1948).

Mandela, Nelson. *A Long Walk to Freedom: The Autobiography of Nelson Mandela* (London: Abacus Books, 1995).

Mapanje, Jack. *Of Chameleons and Gods* (London: Heinemann, 1981).

——. *The Chattering of Wagtails of Mikuyu Prison* (Oxford: Heinemann, 1993).

——. *The Last of Sweet Bananas* (Tarset, Northumberland: Bloodaxe Books in association with The Wordsworth Trust, 2004).

——. *Beasts of Nalunga* (Tarset, Northumberland: Bloodaxe Books, 2007).

Medawar, Jean and Pyke, Richard. *Hitler's Gift; Scientists who fled Nazi Germany*: (London: Richard Cohen Books in association with the European Jewish Publication Society, 2000).

Mikes, George. *How to Be an Alien* (London: Penguin Books, 1978 (first pub. 1954)).

Munoz, Luis. *Being Luis* (Exeter: Impress Books, University of Exeter, 2006).

Mzamane, Mbulelo. *Children of Soweto* (Harlow: Longman, 1982).

Oz, Amos. *A Tale of Love and Darkness* (London: Vintage Books, 2005).

Pankhurst, E. Sylvia. *The Suffragette Movement: an intimate account of persons and ideals* (London: Longmans, 1931).

Pelz, Werner. *I Am Adolf Hitler* (London: SCM Press, 1969).

Perutz, Max. 'Enemy Alien', *New Yorker*, 12 August 1985.

Pevsner on Art and Architecture, Introduction by Stephen Games (London: Methuen, 2002). See also Christopher Long's review in the Harvard Design Magazine no. 21, Fall 2004–Winter 2005.

Pevsner, Nikolaus. *Pioneers of the Modern Movement* (London: Faber and Faber, 1936). Republished as *Pioneers of Modern Design* (New York: Museum of Modern Art, 1949, and London: Penguin Books, 1960).

——. *The Buildings of England* (46 volumes) (London: Penguin Books, 1951–74).

Popper, Karl. *Logik der Forschung* (The Logic of Research), 7th edition (Tübingen: J.C.B. Mohr, 1982).

Rees, Laurence. *Auschwitz* (London: BBC Books, 2005).

Rippiere, Vicky and Williams, Ruth. *Wounded Healers: Mental Health Workers' Experience of Depression* (Chichester: John Wylie, 1973).

Sachs, Albie. *The Jail Diary of Albie Sachs* (London: Harvill Press, 1966).

——. *Sexism and the Law: A Study of Male Beliefs and Judicial Bias in Britain and America* (Oxford: Blackwell, 1978).

——. *Soft Vengeance of a Freedom Fighter* (London: Grafton Books, 1990).

Second Chance: Two Centuries of German-speaking Jews in the United Kingdom, coordinating editor Werner E. Mosse (Tübingen: J.C.B.Mohr, 1991).

Segal, Lore. *Other People's Houses* (London: Victor Gollancz, 1965; p/back: New York, The New Press, 1995).

Snowman, Daniel. *The Hitler Emigres: The Cultural Impact on Britain of Refugees from Nazism* (London: Chatto & Windus, 2002; p/back: Pimlico, 2003).

Wasserstein, Bernard. *Britain and the Jews of Europe, 1939–1945* (Oxford: Clarendon Press, 1979; 2nd ed., Leicester University Press, 1999).

Woldemariam, Mesfin. 'Whither Ethiopia', Ethiopian Economic Association: Vision 2020, November 2003.

Wolff, Sulammith. *Children Under Stress* (London: Allen Lane, the Penguin Press, 1969)

Zimmerman, David. 'The Society for the Protection of Science and Learning and the Politicization of British Science in the 1930s', *Minerva*, vol. 44, no. 1, March 2006.

Website

For Adolphe Lowe, see also: Matthew Forstater, University of Missouri – Kansas City, www.gsm.uci.edu/econsci/Forstater.html

Appendices

Academic Assistance Council letter, 22 May 1933

List of displaced teachers, 4 April to 15 May 1933

Academic Assistance Council letter, 16 June 1933

Letter of criticism from W. Brown & Son, 6 April 1936

English translation of Professor Einstein's speech

(Originals of the above documents are in the Special Collections and Western Mss section of the Bodleian Library.)

Nature 'Science and Learning in Distress', 17 December 1938
(Nature Publishing Group)

Appeal: The Society for the Protection of Science and Learning Limited, 1987

ACADEMIC ASSISTANCE COUNCIL

Rooms of The Royal Society

Burlington House

London W. 1

Telephone:
Regent 1468.

May 22, 1933.

Many eminent scholars and men of science and University teachers of all grades and in all faculties are being obliged to relinquish their posts in the Universities of Germany.

The Universities of our own and other countries will, we hope, take whatever action they can to offer employment to these men and women, as teachers and investigators. But the financial resources of Universities are limited and are subject to claims for their normal development which cannot be ignored. If the information before us is correct, effective help from outside for more than a small fraction of the teachers now likely to be condemned to want and idleness will depend on the existence of large funds specifically devoted to this purpose. It seems clear also that some organization will be needed to act as a centre of information and put the teachers concerned into touch with the institutions that can best help them.

We have formed ourselves accordingly into a provisional Council for these two purposes. We shall seek to raise a fund, to be used primarily, though not exclusively, in providing maintenance for displaced teachers and investigators, and finding them the chance of work in Universities and scientific institutions.

We shall place ourselves in communication both with Universities in this country and with organizations which are being formed for similar purposes in other countries, and we shall seek to provide a clearing house and centre of information for those who can take any kind of action directed to the same end. We welcome offers of co-operation from all quarters. We appeal for generous help from all who are concerned for academic freedom and the security of learning. We ask for means to prevent the waste of exceptional abilities exceptionally trained.

The issue raised at the moment is not a Jewish one alone; many who have suffered or are threatened have no Jewish connection. The issue, though raised acutely at the moment in Germany, is not confined to that country. We should like to regard any funds entrusted to us as available for University teachers and investigators of whatever country who, on grounds of religion, political opinion, or race are unable to carry on their work in their own country.

The Royal Society have placed office accommodation at the disposal of the Council. Sir William Beveridge and Professor C. S. Gibson, F.R.S., are acting as Hon. Secretaries of the Council, and communications should be sent to them at the Royal Society, Burlington House, W. 1. An Executive

Committee is being formed and the names of Trustees for the Fund will shortly be announced. In the meantime cheques can be sent to either of the Hon. Secretaries.

Our action implies no unfriendly feelings to the people of any country; it implies no judgment on forms of government or on any political issue between countries. Our only aims are the relief of suffering and the defence of learning and science.

LASCELLES ABERCROMBIE
S. ALEXANDER
W. H. BEVERIDGE
W. H. BRAGG
BUCKMASTER
CECIL
CRAWFORD AND BALCARRES
WINIFRED C. CULLIS
H. A. L. FISHER
MARGERY FRY
C. S. GIBSON
M. GREENWOOD
J. S. HALDANE
A. V. HILL
GEORGE F. HILL
W. S. HOLDSWORTH
F. GOWLAND HOPKINS
A. E. HOUSMAN
J. C. IRVINE
F. G. KENYON
J. M. KEYNES

A. D. LINDSAY
LYTTON
J. W. MACKAIL
ALLEN MAWER
GILBERT MURRAY
EUSTACE PERCY
W. J. POPE
ROBERT S. RAIT
RAYLEIGH
CHARLES GRANT ROBERTSON
ROBERT ROBINSON
RUTHERFORD
MICHAEL E. SADLER
ARTHUR SCHUSTER
C. S. SHERRINGTON
GEORGE ADAM SMITH
G. ELLIOT SMITH
J. C. STAMP
J. J. THOMSON
G. M. TREVELYAN

DISPLACED TEACHERS

The teachers in the list below have all been named in German newspapers as having been given leave of absence, or dismissed, or as having resigned in protest against other dismissals or action of students, between April 4th and May 15th, 1933. The list has been confined to institutions of a University character ; it includes full professors, extraordinary professors and *privat dozenten*, but not assistants engaged in research work. The great bulk of the persons named are actual professors. The list is known from other information to be incomplete, but it has appeared best to rely only on statements that have already become public in Germany, and so far as is known have not been contradicted.

BERLIN UNIVERSITY :

Name.	Subject or Position.
✓ Baade, Fritz - - -	Economics
✓ Birnbaum, Karl - -	Psychopathology
✓ Blumenthal, Franz - -	Dentistry
✓ Byk, Alfred - - -	Physics
✓ Cohn, Konrad - -	Dentistry
✓ Fischel, Oskar - - -	Art
✓ Friedenthal, Hans - -	Physiology
✓ Friedmann, Fried. Franz -	Tubercular Research
✓ Goldschmidt, - -	Penal Law
✓ Grossmann, Hermann -	Chemistry
✓ Haber, Fritz - - -	Chemistry
✓ Haentzschel, Kurt - -	Law
✓ Jollos, Victor - - -	Zoology
✓ Lederer, Emil - - -	Economics
✓ Lipmann, Otto - -	Applied Psychology
✓ Manes, Alfred - - -	Insurance
✓ Mittwoch, Eugen - -	Hebrew Philology
✓ Norden, Walter - -	Municipal Government
✓ Pokorny, Julius - -	Celtic Philology
✓ Pringsheim, Hans - -	Chemistry
✓ Richter, Julius - - -	Theology
✓ Rona, Peter - - -	Physiology
✓ Schur, Issai - - -	Mathematics
✓ Spranger, Eduard - -	Philosophy *over 60*
✓ Wolff-Eisner, Alfred -	Medicine

Resign with them (margin note)

BONN UNIVERSITY :

✓ Kantorowicz, Alfred -	Dentistry
✓ Loewenstein, Otto -	Psychopathology

BRESLAU UNIVERSITY :

✓ Cohn, Ernst - - -	Law
✓ Marck, S. - - -	Philosophy

FRANKFURT UNIVERSITY :

✓ Altschul, Eugen - -	Economics
✓ Braun, Hugo - -	Bacteriology
✓ Fraenkel, Walter - -	Metallurgy
✓ Heller, Hermann - -	Law
✓ Horkheimer, Max - -	Philosophy and Social Science
✓ Kahn, Ernst - - -	Economics
✓ Koch, Richard - -	Medical History
✓ Loewe, Adolf - - -	Economics
✓ Mannheim, Karl - -	Sociology
✓ Mayer, Fritz - - -	Chemistry
✓ Mennicke, Carl - -	Pedagogy
✓ Neumark, Fritz - -	Public Finance
✓ Plessner, Martin - -	Hebrew Philology
✓ Pribram, Karl - -	Economics
✓ Riezler, Kurt - - -	Classical Philology
✓ Salomon, Gottfried - -	Sociology

Name.	Subject or Position.
✓ Sinzheimer, Hugo - -	Law
✓ Sommerfeld, Martin -	German Philology
✓ Strupp, Karl - - -	International Law
✓ Tillich, Paul - - -	Philosophy and Sociology
✓ Weil, Gotthold - -	Oriental Philology
✓ Wertheimer, Ludwig -	Law
✓ Wertheimer, Max - -	Psychology

GIESSEN UNIVERSITY :

✓ Aster, Ernst von - -	Philosophy
✓ Lenz, Friedrich - -	Social Science
✓ Messer, August - -	Philosophy
✓ Mayer, Georg - -	Social Science

GOETTINGEN UNIVERSITY :

✓ Bernstein, Felix - -	Mathematics
✓ Born, Max - - -	Physics
✓ Courant, Richard - -	Mathematics
✓ Franck, James - -	Physics
✓ Honig, Richard - -	Law
✓ Noether, Emmy - -	Mathematics

GREIFSWALD UNIVERSITY :

✓ Klingmueller, Fritz -	Law
✓ Ziegler, Konrad - -	Classical Philology

HALLE UNIVERSITY :

✓ Aubin, Gustav - -	Economics
✓ Baer, Reinhold - -	Pure Mathematics
✓ Dehn, G. - - -	Theology
✓ Frankl, Paul - -	History of Art
✓ Hertz, Friedrich - -	Economics and Sociology
✓ Kisch, Guido - -	Law
✓ Kitzinger, Friedrich -	Law
✓ Utitz, Emil - -	Philosophy

HAMBURG UNIVERSITY :

✓ Berendsohn, Walter A. -	German Philology
✓ Cassirer, Ernst - -	Philosophy
✓ Heimann, Eduard - -	Economics
✓ Panofsky, Erwin - -	History of Art
✓ Plaut, Th. - - -	Economics
✓ Salomon, Richard - -	East European Hist.
✓ Stern, William - -	Psychology

HEIDELBERG UNIVERSITY :

✓ Anschuetz, Gerhard -	Law
✓ Eckardt, Hans von -	Economic History
✓ Radbruch, Gustav -	Penal Law
✓ Weber, Alfred - -	Economics

JENA UNIVERSITY:

Name.	Subject or Position.
✓ Brauner, Leo	Botany
✓ Josephy, Berthold	Economics
✓ Klein, Emil	Medicine
✓ Meyer-Steinegg, Theodor	Medicine
✓ Peters, Wilhelm	Psychology
✓ Schaxel, Julius	Zoology
✓ Simmel Hans	Medicine
✓ Vaerting, Mathilde	Philosophy

KIEL UNIVERSITY:

✓ Cohn, Gerhard	Economics
✓ Fraenkel, Adolf	Mathematics
✓ Husserl, Gerh.	Law
✓ Kantorowicz, Hermann	Penal Law
✓ Liepe, Wolfgang	Philology
✓ Neisser, Hans	Economics
✓ Opet, Otto	Law
✓ Stenzel, Julius	Philosophy

KOELN (COLOGNE) UNIVERSITY:

✓ Beyer, Richard	Economics
✓ Cohn-Vossen, Stefan	Mathematics
✓ Esch, Ernst	Economics
✓ Honigsheim, Paul	Philosophy and Sociology
✓ Kelsen, Hans	Law
✓ Lips, Julius	Sociology
✓ Schmalenbach, Eugen	Economics
✓ Schmittmann, Benedikt	Social Science

KOENIGSBERG UNIVERSITY:

✓ Hensel, Albert	Law
✓ Paneth, Fritz	Chemistry
✓ Reidemeister, Kurt	Mathematics

LEIPZIG UNIVERSITY:

✓ Apelt, Willibalt	Law
✓ Becker, Hans	Geology
✓ Everth, Erich	Journalism
✓ Goetz, Walter	History
✓ Hellmann, Siegm	Mediaeval History
✓ Witkowski, Georg	Literary History

MARBURG UNIVERSITY:

✓ Jacobsohn, Hermann	Sanskrit
✓ Roepke, Wilhelm	Economics

MUENSTER UNIVERSITY:

✓ Bruck, Werner, F.	Economics
Freund ✓ Freud	
✓ Hellborn	Botany
✓ Woldt, Richard	Social Science

TUEBINGEN UNIVERSITY:

✓ Hegler, August	Law (Chancellor)
✓ Weise, Georg	History of Art

BERLIN TECHNICAL HIGH SCHOOL:

✓ Chajes	Indust. Hygiene
✓ Frank, Fritz	Mineral Oil Techn.
✓ Holde	Chemistry
✓ Igel	Railway Engineering
✓ Kelen	Constructional Engineering

Name	Subject or Position.
✓ Korn, Aurthur	Phototelegraphy
✓ Kurrein, Max	Mechan. Engineering
✓ Lehmann, Erich	Photog. Chemistry
✓ Levy,	Economics
✓ Salinger,	Elect. Engineering
✓ Schlesinger	Mechan. Engineering
✓ Schwerin	Constructional Engineering
✓ Traube, [Wilhelm]	Chemistry

BERLIN COMMERCIAL HIGH SCHOOL:

✓ Bonn, M. J.	Economics

BERLIN HIGH SCHOOL OF POLITICAL SCIENCE:

✓ Jaeckh	President
✓ Simons [Hans O]	

BERLIN UNIVERSITY INSTITUTE FOR CANCER RESEARCH:

✓ Blumenthal, Ferd.	Medicine (Director)

BERLIN VETERINARY HIGH SCHOOL:

✓ Noeller, Wilhelm	Parasites and Tropical Diseases

BERLIN AGRICULTURAL HIGH SCHOOL:

✓ Brandt, Karl	

AACHEN TECHNICAL HIGH SCHOOL:

✓ Hopf, Ludwig	Mathematics
✓ Levy, Paul	Chemistry
✓ Mautner, Karl	Civil Engineering
✓ Meusel, Alfred	Sociology
✓ Strauss, Ludwig	Literature

BRAUNSCHWEIG TECHNICAL HIGH SCHOOL:

✓ Gassner, Gustav	Botany (Rector)

DRESDEN TECHNICAL HIGH SCHOOL:

✓ Holldack, Felix	Law

HANNOVER TECHNICAL HIGH SCHOOL:

✓ Lessing, Theodor	Philosophy

KOENIGSBERG COMMERCIAL HIGH SCHOOL:

✓ Feiler, Arthur	Economics
✓ Haensler	
✓ Kuerbs	
✓ Rogowsky	Economics

MANNHEIM COMMERCIAL HIGH SCHOOL:

✓ Bauer-Mengelberg, Kaethe	Economics
✓ Blaustein, Arthur	Economics
✓ Eppstein, Paul	Economics
✓ Gutkind, Curt Sigmar	Languages
✓ Koburger, J.	Insurance
✓ Mann, Ludwig	Medicine
✓ Moses, Julius	Philosophy
✓ Selz, Otto	Psychology (Rector)
✓ Strauss, Sigmund	Law

Telephone:
REGent 1468.

ACADEMIC ASSISTANCE COUNCIL,

Rooms of the ROYAL SOCIETY,

President:
The Lord Rutherford of Nelson,
O.M.,F.R.S.

Burlington House,

Hon. Secretaries:
Sir Wm. H. Beveridge, K.C.B.
Professor C.S. Gibson, F.R.S.

London, W.1.

16th June, 1933.

Dear Vice-Chancellor,

As you may already be aware, steps have been taken to form in this country an Academic Assistance Council to help University teachers, who on grounds of religion, political opinion, or race, are unable to carry on, at least for the time being, their work in their own country.   In case you have not already seen it we enclose a copy of the first statement as to the formation of this Council, which appeared in the papers on the 24th May.

The Council held its first meeting on June 1st and appointed an executive committee and, at the request of the committee, we now write to let you know about the work and plans of the Council, so far as they are formed.

It is contemplated that the main, though not the only, form of expenditure to be incurred by the Council should be in the provision of a part or the whole of the maintenance for displaced scholars and scientists for whom a chance of continuing their work is open in institutions of learning in this country.   With this in view we are forming as complete and detailed a register as possible of those who are likely to be displaced and in need of immediate assistance of this kind.

We should be glad to hear from you if your University is in a position to find openings for any of these recommended men or women (who will be finally selected by you) and if so, on what terms, i.e. whether you can contribute the whole or any part of the maintenance from funds already under your control or to be raised by you, or whether it will be necessary for the Academic Assistance Council to find the whole.   You will realise that, although the Council has funds in prospect, these are not likely to be adequate unless they can be augmented.

We are aware that some Universities and Colleges have already taken action, with the help of local support to raise special

-2-

funds or to find places for displaced teachers.   We cordially
welcome such independent action but hope that you will be good
enough to let us know of any such procedure in relation to your
University so that in due course we may have a complete record
of all that is done in this country.

We should add that, apart from the question of providing
facilities for the displaced scholars and scientists, we are
concerned in obtaining funds for their maintenance, among other
sources by appealing to individual members of the staffs of
Universities and Colleges.   Steps to organise such appeals by
groups of teachers have already been taken in certain University
institutions and we hope that this example may be followed.
Although this is probably not a matter in which you, as Vice-
Chancellor, can act officially, we should very much appreciate it
if you are able to indicate to us any active and prominent member
of the staff of your University who, in your view, might be
prepared to assist in this matter.

We shall be happy to give you any further information you
may desire about the work of the Council or to send you the
fullest particulars that we have of individuals who are already
displaced or threatened for the future.

Yours sincerely,

[Signed]   W. H. Beveridge.

C. S. Gibson.

Hon. Secretaries.

6 April 1936   W BROWN & SON, MET 6087
52. FORE STREET, LONDON, E.C.2

Dear My Lord.

You may not think it but it is really impudence to write asking donations from this part of the world. Opposite me and I have been here 20 years every one of the buildings has had a Jew fire, and there is one of Harris's friends there still.

Ones does not believe in physical illtreatment, but these pests deserve what they get. What country will tolerate them. Why. Firstly who wants their Abrahams who was willing to murder his own son. Their disgusting Samuels Noahs and so on.

These people are firstly and above all a Commercial race. Their answer is to be found in Stubbs gazette. In Womens wear last week of the twelve Bankrupts. ALL OF THEM WERE JEWS. Stalin a jew Litvinoff Jews and the same here. Who do they change their names.

Your Council may be clever people but they have had no commercial experience. Or they would not belong to such a thing.

The best way to deal with Jews is to have nothing to do with them and an Englishman can always beat a Jew by being honest which they cannot be for love or money.

The jew question will be a serious one here very shortly. Hitler is quite right in getting rid of them. They have lowered the business morality of the greatest city in the world namely The City of London. Why do not the Insurance Companies want them! Why do the Banks have to keep double eyes on the jew accounts!

A cold blooded heartless race. You come round Fore St if you want the jew question and we can show you the Bankrupts gents and those who will be going later on.

You talk of Universities. Get your Economists to work out how much the Jews have robbed England of and especially round this quarter. What about our own towns with 75% unemployed.

(W.D.S Brown)

Science and Civilization.

I am glad that you have given me the opportunity of expressing to you here my deep sense of gratitude as a man, as a good European, and as a Jew. Through your well-organised work of relief you have done a great service not only to innocent scholars who have been persecuted, but also to humanity and science. You have shown that you and the British people have remained faithful to the traditions of tolerance and justice which for centuries you have upheld with pride. It is in times of economic distress such as we experience everywhere to-day, one sees very clearly the strength of the moral forces that live in a people. Let us hope that a historian delivering judgment in some future period when Europe is politically and economically united, will be able to say that in our days the liberty and honour of this Continent was saved by its Western nations, which stood fast in hard times against the temptations of hatred and oppression ; and that Western Europe defended successfully the liberty of the individual which has brought us every advance of knowledge and invention—liberty without which life to a self-respecting man is not worth living.

It cannot be my task to-day to act as judge of the conduct of a nation which for many years has considered me as her own ; perhaps it is an idle task to judge in times when action counts.

To-day, the questions which concern us are : how can we save mankind and its spiritual acquisitions of which we are the heirs ? How can one save Europe from a new disaster ?

It cannot be doubted that the world crisis and the suffering and privations of the people resulting from the crisis are in some measure responsible for the dangerous upheavals of which we are the witness. In such periods discontent breeds hatred, and hatred leads to acts of violence and revolution, and often even to war. Thus distress and evil produce new distress and new evil. Again the leading statesmen are burdened with tremendous responsibilities just the same as twenty years ago. May they succeed through timely agreement to establish a condition of unity and clarity of international obligations in Europe so that for every State a war-like adventure must appear as utterly hopeless. But the work of statesmen can succeed only if they are backed by the serious and determined will of the people.

We are concerned not merely with the technical problem of securing and maintaining peace, but also with the important task of education and enlightenment. If we want to resist the powers which threaten to suppress intellectual and individual freedom we must keep clearly before us what is at stake, and what we owe to that freedom which our ancestors have won for us after hard struggles.

Without such freedom there would have been no Shakespeare, no Goethe, no Newton, no Faraday, no Pasteur and no Lister. There would be no comfortable houses for the mass of the people, no railway, no wireless, no protection against epidemics, no cheap books, no culture and no enjoyment of art for all. There would be no machines to relieve the people from the arduous labour needed for the production of the essential necessities of life. Most people would lead a dull life of slavery just as under the ancient despotisms of Asia. It is only men who are free, who create the inventions and intellectual works which to us moderns make life worth while.

Without doubt the present economic difficulties will eventually bring us to the point where the balance between supply of labour and demand of labour, between production and consumption, will be enforced by law. But even this problem we shall solve as free men and we shall not allow ourselves for its sake to be driven into a slavery, which ultimately would bring with it stagnation of every healthy development.

In this connection I should like to give expression to an idea which has occurred to me recently. I lived in solitude in the country and noticed how the monotony of a quiet life stimulates the creative mind. There are certain callings in our modern organisation which entail such an isolated life without making a great claim on bodily and intellectual effort. I think of such occupations as the service in lighthouses and lightships. Would it not be possible to fill such places with young people who wish to think out scientific problems, especially of a mathematical or philosophical nature? Very few of such people have the opportunity during the most productive period of their lives to devote themselves undisturbed for any length of time to scientific problems. Even if a young person is lucky enough to obtain a scholarship for a short period he must endeavour to arrive as quickly as possible at definite conclusions. That cannot be of advantage in the pursuit of pure science. The young scientist who carries on an ordinary practical profession which maintains him is in a much better position—assuming of course that this profession leaves him with sufficient spare time and energy. In this way perhaps a greater number of creative individuals could be given an opportunity for mental development than is possible at present. In these times of economic depression and political upheaval such considerations seem to be worth attention.

Shall we worry over the fact that we are living in a time of danger and want? I think not. Man like every other animal is by nature indolent. If nothing spurs him on, then he will hardly think, and will behave from habit like an automaton. I am no longer young and can, therefore, say, that as a child and as a young man I experienced that phase—when a young man thinks only about the trivialities of personal existence, and talks like his fellows and behaves like them. Only with difficulty can one see what is really behind such a conventional mask. For owing to habit and speech his real personality is, as it were, wrapped in cotton wool.

How different it is to-day! In the lightning flashes of our tempestuous times one sees human beings and things in their nakedness. Every action and every human being reveal clearly their aims, powers and weaknesses, and also their passions. Routine becomes of no avail under the swift change of conditions ; conventions fall away like dry husks.

Men in their distress begin to think about the failure of economic practice and about the necessity of political combinations which are supernational. Only through perils and upheavals can Nations be brought to further developments. May the present upheavals lead to a better world.

Above and beyond this valuation of our time we have this further duty, the care for what is eternal and highest amongst our possessions, that which gives to life its import and which we wish to hand on to our children purer and richer than we received it from our forebears. Towards these purposes you have affectionately contributed with your blessed services.

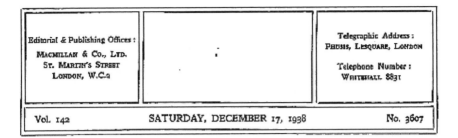

Editorial & Publishing Offices:
MACMILLAN & CO., LTD.
ST. MARTIN'S STREET
LONDON, W.C.2

Telegraphic Address:
PHUSIS, LESQUARE, LONDON

Telephone Number:
WHITEHALL 8831

Vol. 142   SATURDAY, DECEMBER 17, 1938   No. 3607

Science and Learning in Distress

IN the early summer of 1933, the Academic Assistance Council was founded, under the presidency of Lord Rutherford and with the active support of many distinguished men of science and other scholars, to find places in the fabric of world science and world scholarship for men and women driven from their countries and their work for racial, religious or political reasons. Such persecution was not new, even in the very recent past : it had happened again and again in Russia and was still happening : but the scale of its application in Germany and the distinction of its victims demanded immediate help. The Academic Assistance Council had no partisan, political or national bias. Indiscriminate relief was to be no part of its work. Its purpose was to act as a link between the scientific workers and other scholars displaced and the universities and research institutions of the world, so that their exceptional abilities exceptionally trained—to quote the noble declaration of the Council's founders—should not be lost.

It was hoped that the emergency would pass, but as the years went on, intolerance and persecution grew ; no end was in sight. The Academic Assistance Council took permanent shape therefore as the Society for the Protection of Science and Learning : its wider purpose was now to act as a clearing house of information and advice to exiled scholars, and to persons, institutions and departments desiring to help them ; its narrower purpose—within the limits of its resources—to offer temporary maintenance grants and other aids to re-establishment. The spread of 'racial' doctrine to Italy, the consequences in Austria and Czechoslovakia of the political events of 1938 and their reactions in neighbouring countries, the continuation of civil war in Spain, the extreme xenophobia of the U.S.S.R., and recent events in Germany, all these have added to the need, for information and advice on one hand, for direct assistance on the other. When a ship is in distress no sailor, and few landsmen, will not want to go to its help.

The Society has just issued its annual report, from which it appears that a widespread appeal is shortly to be issued : for funds on one hand ; for interest and sympathy, through membership, on the other. The problem has been complicated and enlarged by the events of 1938, but the Society has not turned aside from its original purpose and principles. It exists, not to advertise a particular point of view, but to do an honest job of work in seeing that ability and experience in science and scholarship are not wasted. It does not, it cannot, disregard human values ; but its charity is devoted to those who can contribute to the common stock of learning. It stands for the brotherhood of scientific endeavour, regardless of race and creed and politics : and it stands for it, not by passing pious resolutions or by putting out disguised political propaganda, but by trying to help colleagues in their need. Foreign scientific workers are found work which restores their self-respect and makes others realize their value in their common task ; so that, not seldom, they become self-supporting. From the start, however, the Society has done its best to avoid any unfair competition of exiled scientific workers and other scholars with those in the countries where they are seeking refuge, and has realized, and urged, that in the long run such competition is as little in

1052   NATURE   DEC. 17, 1938, Vol. 142

the interest of the exiles as in that of scientific workers as a whole.

The Society must maintain its authority and integrity in the face of its increasing task. In Germany alone, fourteen hundred university teachers and research workers have been displaced, many of them among the most distinguished in the world; not merely debarred from teaching and research, they are not allowed to make a living at all. More than four hundred Austrian men of science and other students have been displaced, and of these only about a hundred have been able to leave the country. The full effects of the 'racial' policy in Italy and of the partition of Czechoslovakia have yet to be felt; Spain, from which scholars of both parties have been helped, is still no place for tolerant, sensitive academic people; and the U.S.S.R. has disappointed our hopes by turning out those who originally found work and refuge there.

Caution in the circumstances must often seem intolerable to humane men, but the Society's stringent caution in accepting responsibility bears fruit. Work has been found permanently for about 550 scholars in thirty-eight different countries, from Australia to Venezuela; for about 330 temporarily in twenty-five countries. Turkey, which is building a new civilization, has welcomed numbers of the displaced university men.

In November 1937, the Society called an informal conference at Oxford of representatives of European universities, and the ideal of an international exchange for information and employment came nearer to realization. The Society's register of exiled scholars is now unique, authoritative and international. Any academic or research institution can have the benefit of its records of those "exceptional abilities exceptionally trained", lost to their own countries, but not, if the Society can prevent it, to the service of knowledge anywhere else in the world.

Funds and interest are, however, an imperative need; first, for the work of administration, information and advice; secondly, for direct help in human emergency. It is to be hoped that the wider educated public, particularly in the English-speaking countries, will respond generously to the appeal for support which the Society is making, and come to the help of science and learning in distress.

No. 3608, DEC. 24, 1938 NATURE 1109

News and Views

Society for the Protection of Science and Learning

PERHAPS there is no finer testimony to the work undertaken by the Society for the Protection of Science and Learning, the report for 1938 of which was referred to in NATURE of December 17 (p. 1061) than the extent to which it has received the active support during the whole of its five years existence of the university staffs in Great Britain. Not only have individuals and committees in the majority of academic centres lent ready assistance to their exiled colleagues from abroad in the way of advice and vigilance for new openings for them, but also they have contributed financially more than £10,000 towards the funds of the organization which seeks to aid academic refugees. The Society itself has arranged a week of meetings early next term to take place in the great majority of British academic centres, with the view of spreading information concerning the plight and prospects of academic refugees. Among those who have agreed to take part in these meetings are included : the Home Secretary, the Archbishop of York, Viscount Samuel, the Marquess of Reading, Sir William Bragg, Sir Henry Dale, Sir Richard Gregory, Sir John Hope Simpson, Sir Norman Angell, Sir Allen Mawer, Sir Bernard Pares, the Hon. Harold Nicolson, Mr. Philip Guedalla, Mr. Walter Adams, Prof. Gilbert Murray, Prof. Winifred Cullis, Prof. John Macmurray, Prof. P. M. S. Blackett, Prof. Lancelot Hogben, Prof. F. A. E. Crew, Miss Rebecca West and the Hon. V. Sackville-West. The Royal Society is giving a special reception to the academic exiles and those who have been working in their interests, in collaboration with the British Academy, on February 7 ; and on February 10 the evening discourse at the Royal Institution is to be given by Prof. Max Born, one of the most distinguished of the refugee men of science.

The Chemical Society

AT a meeting of the Chemical Society held at the Royal Institution on December 16, it was stated that Prof. Robert Robinson, Waynflete professor of chemistry in the University of Oxford, has accepted nomination to the office of president for the period 1939–41, which includes the centenary celebrations of the Society to be held in April 1941. The Long-staff Medal for 1939 has been awarded to Prof. I. M. Heilbron, for his outstanding contributions to the science of chemistry in the field of natural products, especially vitamin A and related natural pigments, the anti-rachitic vitamin D and its pro-cursors, and the constituents of the fish liver oils and of natural resins of the triterpene group. Prof. Heilbron was lecturer in organic chemistry in the Royal Technical College, Glasgow, from 1909 until 1914, and in 1919 became professor of organic chemistry there. In 1920, he proceeded to the University of Liverpool as professor of organic chemistry ; in 1933 he held the chair of organic chemistry in the University of Manchester. In 1938, he was appointed professor of organic chemistry at Imperial College, London.

AT the meeting of the Harrison Memorial Prize Selection Committee, consisting of the presidents of the Chemical Society, the Institute of Chemistry, the Society of Chemical Industry, and the Pharmaceutical Society, held on December 14, it was decided that the Harrison Memorial Prize for 1938 should be awarded to Mr. Alexander King. Mr. King received his chemical training at the Imperial College, South Kensington. From 1930 until 1931, he worked in the Physical Chemistry Institute of the University of Munich under Prof. K. Fajans, and from 1931 to the present date has held the post of assistant

APPEAL

The Society for the Protection of Science and Learning Limited

(formerly the Academic Assistance Council)

ORIGINS AND AIMS

The object of the Society is to help academic refugees.

The Academic Assistance Council, as the Society was originally named, was started in May 1933 in response to the dismissals of academic personnel which took place in Germany after Hitler came to power. The AAC assisted first those academics who were dismissed in Germany, and then, as fascist ideology spread, in Spain, Portugal, Italy, Czechoslovakia and Austria. After the outbreak of war many academic refugees who came to Britain from Allied countries occupied by the Germans sought help from the AAC, and by the end of the War assistance had been given to some 2,600 displaced university teachers, and advice and help to more than two thousand other scholars.

Many of the scholars so helped have become leading figures in the international academic community. Of the refugee scholars registered with the Society, 16 have received knighthoods; 16 have become Nobel Laureates; 71 Fellows or Foreign Members of the Royal Society; and 50, Fellows or Corresponding Fellows of the British Academy. These figures include offspring of early refugee scholars, now themselves distinguished academics.

In 1937 the AAC changed its name to the Society for the Protection of Science and Learning (SPSL). After the War, when other refugee organizations felt no need to continue their work, the SPSL foresaw the possibility of future threats to academic freedom. The McCarthy era in the United States did not create the large numbers of academic exiles that been feared, but the uprising in Hungary in 1956 did result in the expulsion of many university teachers, and with these the Society was closely concerned. Because of these events, the Council decided to put itself on a permanent basis, and in 1959 it became incorporated as a charitable organization.

Since the War we have helped displaced and persecuted scholars from many countries, including South Africa and the USSR, and more recently academics who have suffered as a result of political changes in Czechoslovakia, Greece, Poland, Brazil, Biafra, Bangladesh, Chile, Argentina, Zambia, the former Rhodesia, Uruguay, Ethiopia, Iran, Iraq and Turkey.

Many large groups of refugees have been brought to this country with government help (Ugandans, Chileans, Vietnamese). The numbers of displaced academics within these groups has varied considerably, but there have always been some. Most have come from Latin America, where military coups have been accompanied by savage military intervention in the universities. In Argentina, Chile, Uruguay and El Salvador, whole faculties and departments were closed down and hundreds of distinguished academics dismissed, imprisoned without charge, or sent into exile. The situation in Argentina and Uruguay has now changed for the better and exiles have been able to return. But unfortunately what the SPSL anticipated at the end of the War has certainly come about, and there are few signs that the general situation will be permanently improved in the foreseeable future.

PRESENT NEEDS

The Society's funds do not allow it to help more than a small number of displaced academics at any one time. These are the few who manage to arrive in this country, often with the help of British colleagues, or those who suddenly become refugees while working or studying here, as a result of changes at home. While there are today many other bodies concerned with human rights and refugees, with which the Society co-operates (Amnesty International, Writers and Scholars International, World University Service, and the British Refugee Council), the SPSL remains the only one concerned specifically with refugee scholars. In consequence cases are frequently referred to us by the other bodies. We cannot now meet the demand.

What the Society urgently requires are free funds which can meet the needs of refugee scholars from the moment they have been offered facilities at universities or research institutes here. When refugees arrive they need help immediately, not after months of waiting, nor at the start of the next academic year. Scholars who have suffered total disruption of their lives, as well as of their careers and academic pursuits, through dismissal, imprisonment, and in some cases torture, need help as quickly as possible to re-establish themselves. The SPSL is an organization which can act speedily, and this has always been its strength. Now we know of more people than we can help. More particularly cut-backs in higher education mean that we have to support people for longer periods than formerly while they look for permanent employment, which may have to be sought in some other country. In addition, fees for doctoral studies are now much higher than they were.

Covenant forms may be obtained from, or donations sent to the Secretary of the Society.

Index

Compiled by Douglas Matthews

Page numbers in *italic* indicate illustrations

The real joy in creating a puzzle was sharing it with someone. She wished she could send it to her best friend from home, Enna, who loved games just as much as she. The two girls had even made up a secret holo-alphabet they had both memorized so they could communicate privately. What looked like gibberish to their classmates back at Kaleidoscope Falls Elementary might be a complex message about after-school plans or the guest list for Enna's upcoming Bright Day party.

Sure, Vega belonged to Starling Academy's Puzzle Club, which met after school every Dododay and was filled with like-minded students. It was the first club she had joined since arriving at the school two years before. But the secret nature of the Star Darlings made this crossword something she could not share with anyone except them. So there were only eleven girls she could share it with, and unfortunately, none of them were particularly interested in brainteasers. In fact, they seemed to think Vega's obsession was a little weird. It had been just a starweek or two earlier that she and Leona had found themselves sitting across from each other at lunchtime in the Celestial Café. After they had ordered their meals from the hovering Bot-Bot waiter, Vega had turned to Leona excitedly and said, "Let's guess whose food will arrive first!" and Leona had just laughed.

CHAPTER
1

Vega sat on her neatly made bed, staring at the holo-crossword puzzle projected into the air above her Star-Zap. With two flicks of her wrist, she switched the position of two answers, then frowned and returned them to their original places. She nodded, finally satisfied. It was perfect. Vega loved creating puzzles almost as much as she enjoyed solving them. She appreciated crosswords, riddles, puzzles, brainteasers, mazes, and games—anything that challenged her and made her think in a fun and interesting way.

With another flick of her wrist, she erased all the answers, leaving the clues and a blank grid, ready to be filled in. She took a look at her handiwork and sighed.

ACROSS:

3. Student who went on second mission and identified the wrong wish at first.

5. 4-Down was replaced by another student, named _____.

7. Student who went on first mission and identified wrong Wisher at first.

9. Headmistress of Starling Academy. She came up with the secret plan to send twelve students to Wishworld to collect wish energy.

10. There were band tryouts, and a machine called the _____ chose the members. It also named the band the Star Darlings. That made 9-Across very upset, as it gave up our secret name.

DOWN:

1. This mean student wanted to be lead singer of the band, but she lost. I don't think we've heard the end of it.

2. The head of admissions. She stutters when nervous and trips a lot. Everyone feels a little sorry for her.

4. It was determined that this student's assignment as a Star Darling was a mistake, and she was replaced.

6. All the Star Darlings who have tasted this Wishworld drink love it.

8. Student who went on third mission. Her Wish Pendant was mysteriously ruined. She also did not collect any wish energy.

Answers: 3-A: Libby; 5-A: Ophelia; 7-A: Sage; 9-A: Lady Stella; 10-A: Ranker; 1-D: Vivica; 2-D: Lady Cordial; 4-D: Scarlet; 6-D: Lemonade; 8-D: Leona

Vega and the
Fashion Disaster

at all. They are immediately transported to a special containment center, as they are very dangerous and must not be granted.

3) IMPOSSIBLE WISH ORBS. These wishes are for things, like world peace and disease cures, that simply can't be granted by Starlings. These sparkle with an almost impossibly bright light and are taken to a special area of the Wish-House with tinted windows to contain the glare they produce. The hope is that one day they can be turned into good wishes the Starlings can help grant.

Starlings take their wish granting very seriously. There is a special school, called Starling Academy, that accepts only the best and brightest young Starling girls. They study hard for four years, and when they graduate, they are ready to start traveling to Wishworld to help grant wishes. For as long as anyone can remember, only graduates of wish-granting schools have ever been allowed to travel to Wishworld. But things have changed in a very big way.

Read on for the rest of the story. . . .

Because something quite unexpected happens next. Each and every wish that is made becomes a glowing Wish Orb, invisible to the human eye. This undetectable orb zips through the air and into the heavens, on a one-way trip to the brightest star in the sky—a magnificent place called Starland. Starland is inhabited by Starlings, who look a lot like you and me, except they have a sparkly glow to their skin, and glittery hair in unique colors. And they have one more thing: magical powers. The Starlings use these powers to make good wishes come true, for when good wishes are granted, the result is positive energy. And the Starlings of Starland need this energy to keep their world running.

In case you are wondering, there are three kinds of Wish Orbs:

1) GOOD WISH ORBS. These wishes are positive and helpful and come from the heart. They are pretty and sparkly and are nurtured in climate-controlled Wish-Houses. They bloom into fantastical glowing orbs. When the time is right, they are presented to the appropriate Starling for wish fulfillment.

2) BAD WISH ORBS. These are for selfish, mean-spirited, or negative things. They don't sparkle

Introduction

You take a deep breath, about to blow out the candles on your birthday cake. Clutching a coin in your fist, you get ready to toss it into the dancing waters of a fountain. You stare at your little brother as you each hold an end of a dried wishbone, about to pull. But what do you do first?

You make a wish, of course!

Ever wonder what happens right after you make that wish? *Not much*, you may be thinking.

Well, you'd be wrong.

Starling Academy

NAME: Libby
BRIGHT DAY: October 12
FAVORITE COLOR: Pink
INTERESTS: Helping others, interior design, art, dancing
WISH: To give everyone what they need—both on Starland and through wish granting on Wishworld
WHY CHOSEN: Libby is generous, articulate, gracious, diplomatic, and kind.
WATCH OUT FOR: Libby can be indecisive and may try too hard to please everyone.
SCHOOL YEAR: First
POWER CRYSTAL: Charmelite
WISH PENDANT: Necklace

NAME: Scarlet
BRIGHT DAY: November 3
FAVORITE COLOR: Black
INTERESTS: Crystal climbing (and other extreme sports), magic, thrill seeking
WISH: To live on Wishworld
WHY CHOSEN: Scarlet is confident, intense, passionate, magnetic, curious, and very brave.
WATCH OUT FOR: Scarlet is a loner and can alienate others by being secretive, arrogant, stubborn, and jealous.
SCHOOL YEAR: Third
POWER CRYSTAL: Ravenstone
WISH PENDANT: Boots

NAME: Sage
BRIGHT DAY: December 1
FAVORITE COLOR: Lavender
INTERESTS: Travel, adventure, telling stories, nature, and philosophy
WISH: To become the best Wish-Granter Starland has ever seen
WHY CHOSEN: Sage is honest, adventurous, curious, optimistic, friendly, and relaxed.
WATCH OUT FOR: Sage has a quick temper! She can also be restless, irresponsible, and too trusting of others' opinions. She may jump to conclusions.
SCHOOL YEAR: First
POWER CRYSTAL: Lavenderite
WISH PENDANT: Necklace

"Everything is a game to you, Vega, isn't it?" she said. Vega had blinked at her in surprise. It was—and why not? Games made life more interesting. She didn't get why the other girls didn't understand that. Not that she wasn't serious-minded—quite the contrary: she was as focused on her studies as a Starling could be. But she could make studying into a game, too.

As she recalled the conversation, Vega realized that was one of the last times she had heard Leona laugh. Leona's Wish Mission had been a terrible disappointment. (See 8-Down.) Although she had successfully granted her Wisher's wish, Leona's Wish Pendant had malfunctioned, and when she had returned to Starland, she had discovered it was blackened and burnt-looking. As a result, Leona hadn't collected a single drop of wish energy. The usually vivacious girl had been sad and withdrawn ever since. Lady Stella had done her best to convince her it wasn't her fault, but Leona was set on blaming herself.

Lady Stella told everyone to keep attending class (including their special Star Darlings–only class at the end of each school day), learning their lessons, and going on their Wish Missions as planned. The headmistress would be working with some leading wish energy scientists and some trusted faculty members to figure out what had gone wrong with Leona's Wish Pendant and how to fix it. Hopefully they would figure it out soon.

Vega's bass guitar was in its cerulean case, leaning in the corner of the exceptionally neat bedroom. She imagined that it was looking at her reproachfully, as the Star Darlings band hadn't had a rehearsal in a week because of their lead singer's absence during her Wish Mission. They had one scheduled for that day. Would Leona show up? Vega certainly hoped so. They were already down one member due to Scarlet's ouster from the Star Darlings (see 4-Down), and Vega feared that the additional loss of their lead singer could mean the end of the group.

Vega glanced down at her Star-Zap. It was nearly time for practice, and she realized she wanted to be on her way there before her roommate got back from Meditation Club. Vega's strong desire to vacate the premises surprised her. She stood up quickly and smoothed the blue coverlet, which was unnecessary, as its edges were pulled so tightly you could bounce a wharfle on it. She knew because she had tried. Vega's roommate, Piper, kept her side of the room just as neat as Vega's, and Vega counted her lucky stars every day for that. But that's where the similarity ended. Piper's side was dreamy and ethereal, with a gently undulating water bed covered with the softest of linens and more pillows than you could count, the largest embroidered with the word *dream*. Her star-painted dresser contained more nightgowns and pajamas than regular clothes; Vega was sure of it. She had not seen her roommate wear the same thing twice to bed.

Vega stole a quick glance at the mirror hanging on her closet door. Neatly bobbed blue hair, smooth and shiny. Electric blue jacket, sparkly tunic, leggings, and soft ankle boots. She was crisp, polished, and neat as a pin, as usual. She grabbed her bass and turned to head out of the room. The door slid open. Too late.

Piper stood in the doorway, blinking at Vega in her usual sleepy fashion. Her seafoam green hair rippled down her back, past her waist. Her long dress billowed around her feet. She was tall and slender, and whenever Vega looked at her, she couldn't help thinking of a graceful, flowing waterfall.

"Hey," said Vega.

"Hello there," said Piper languidly. She smiled slowly and sighed contentedly. "Meditation Club was starmendously relaxing today." She swiveled her head around and shrugged a couple of times. "I feel like a wet noddle-noodle, like I could just collapse in a heap."

"Maybe you need a nap," Vega suggested starcastically.

Piper's light green eyes lit up. "What a great idea!"

she said. She sauntered to her side of the room and reached for one of the week's worth of sleeping masks that hung from the wall on pretty pegs before kicking off her slippers, pulling on the mask, and curling up on her chaise lounge. She arranged a loosely knit pale green blanket over her. Within arm's reach of her lounge were a basket of holo-diaries for jotting down dreams and a large bouquet of glittery coral-colored flowers, which perfumed the room with an almost magical fragrance. Piper inhaled deeply. *"Mmmmmmm,"* she said sleepily.

Vega tried as hard as she could not to roll her eyes at her roommate. Not that Piper could see from under the sleeping mask anyway. Who needed to take an after-meditation nap? Wasn't that redundant? But then she immediately felt bad. From day one it had been quite obvious that ethereal Piper and practical Vega were complete opposites. Vega was direct and serious, and she liked rules. Piper was emotional, otherworldly, and unhurried. But they quickly learned that they had a common love of order and that they often saw situations from two very different angles, which gave them a multidimensional view on many issues.

Soon they developed a grudging admiration for each other. It was a struggle sometimes, but they had made it work. But then, as Vega recalled, things had changed dramatically. They had gone to bed planning a hike to the Crystal Mountains, debating what to bring for lunch, and had woken up the next morning scowling at each other. Piper had started relaying the previous night's dream, which apparently had featured Vega in a starring (and not very flattering) role, and Vega had just cut her off. Now relations between the two were chilly, though usually polite. She could tell it pained the sensitive Piper, and it wasn't pleasant for Vega, either. But there didn't seem to be anything they could do to fix it.

Piper raised her eye mask and looked at Vega. "Are you going to band rehearsal?" she asked.

"You're a regular detective," Vega heard herself say, an edge to her voice as she held up her guitar case. Piper gave a thin-lipped smile and pulled the mask back over her eyes.

Immediately feeling guilty for her rudeness, Vega quickly opened the sliding door, walked out, closed it, and stepped onto the dorm's Cosmic Transporter, a moving sidewalk that ran through it.

Unbeknownst to each other, once they were alone, the two girls gave simultaneous sighs of relief.

CHAPTER
2

"No, no, no, no, no," said Leona, stamping her foot so hard her golden earrings jangled. "You've got it all wrong. All wrong!" She dug her hands into her halo of golden curly hair in frustration.

Vega bit her lip, beginning to wish she had skipped rehearsal. From the looks on her fellow band members' faces, she suspected they felt the same way.

Leona turned to the band's lead guitarist. "Sage," she said. "You're playing too slow. This is rehearsal for a rock band, not an End of the Cycle of Life procession, for stars' sake."

Before the girl could respond, Leona turned to Libby. "And *you're* coming in too soon on the keytar," she scolded.

Libby sucked in her cheeks and stared down at the keys on her portable keyboard.

Vega held her breath, hoping she would be spared Leona's wrath. No such luck. Leona spun around and stared at her for a minute before she spoke.

"And, Vega, you were in the wrong key." She leaned her face close to Vega's. "Don't do that again," she concluded.

Vega felt her cheeks turn red. She generally appreciated Leona's big personality and even occasionally found her dramatic outbursts somewhat entertaining, but that day she felt the girl was just being a big bully.

She watched as Libby took a deep breath, closed her eyes, wiped the frown off her face, and opened her eyes. "Leona," Libby said kindly, "do you need a break?"

This only served to infuriate Leona further. "I don't need a break!" she screeched. "I need a new band."

Clover, who had reluctantly agreed to sub for Scarlet when she hadn't shown up for the last rehearsal, raised her drumsticks and hit the cymbal with a loud crash. She stood up. "That's it," she said. "Guess what, Leona? I don't need to take this. I'm just doing this as a favor. And now I'm out of here." She shoved her drumsticks into her back pocket and stormed off.

Leona spun around, throwing her hands into the air.

"Great, guys, just great," she said. "Now we're drummer-less again. And she wasn't even the problem. It's the three of you!"

Libby, Sage, and Vega glanced at each other. Nobody seemed to be in any rush to argue with the enraged diva. Finally, Libby spoke up. "Leona," she said, putting her hand on the girl's arm. "We understand that you're under a lot of stress right now. But you also have to see things from our point of view. We're learning new songs and we're trying hard and you need to be patient with us. Nobody is going to want to be in your band if you yell all the time. And I don't think you want us to quit, do you?"

Vega was impressed. Libby always could see both sides of a situation and lay them out clearly in a nonjudg-mental way. And Leona actually seemed to be listening to her.

"Yeah," Vega added. "You'd have to have tryouts all over again. What if Vivica comes back?"

Vivica was Leona's biggest rival and was still angry that Leona had beaten her to be lead singer of the group. Starting over would be completely unacceptable. Leona's shoulders sagged. "You're right," she said. "I'm just so upset about everything and I guess I'm taking it out on you guys. . . ." Her voice trailed off.

"Of course you're upset," Sage said in a calming

tone. "Listen, it's all going to be okay. We're a good group! Don't forget that we were the ones who were picked out of all the students who tried out. Maybe we should just hold off on practicing until you're feeling better about . . ." Vega noticed that Sage's eyes had lit on the empty spot on Leona's wrist where her Wish Pendant used to be. Once you noticed that, it was almost impossible to look anywhere else. Vega forced herself to stare at Leona's face. "Um, everything that happened," Sage concluded.

"Okay," said Leona softly. She gazed at the ground, unable to look anyone in the eye. "I'll let you know when I'm feeling more up to it." She smiled sadly. "I'm sorry."

The three girls watched as Leona headed toward the Big Dipper Dorm, the slightly bigger and fancier dorm where all the third and fourth years lived.

Vega turned to the two other girls. "Wow," she said. "Do you think she's ever going to get over what happened?"

"She had better," said Sage, "or she's going to lose all her friends. If she hasn't already." She shrugged. "Well, see you later. I have plans to meet some friends and listen to music at the Lightning Lounge." She turned and hurried off.

"What do you think?" Vega asked Libby. But the

pink-haired girl was holo-texting and held up a finger for Vega to hold her thought. Vega did.

"So what do you think about that?" Vega repeated when Libby was finished.

"What do I think? I think we'd better find Scarlet if we want to keep this band together," said Libby. "As much as she and Leona didn't get along, Leona usually behaved around her. And Clover was mad. I don't think she's coming back."

"So no one has seen Scarlet since . . . that day?" Vega asked.

"Well, Tessa told me that Scarlet stopped showing up for their Astronomics class," said Libby. "It's totally bizarre. Nobody's seen her. And nobody knows where her new dorm room is—or even if she has one." She shook her head. "It's a mystery."

Libby's Star-Zap pinged, telling her she had a holo-text. She read it, smiled, and put her guitar back in its pink case, then snapped the case closed. "Adora's at the Serenity Gardens," she reported, "so I'm going to paddle out there and hang out with her until dinnertime. Want to join me?" Vega declined, even though she enjoyed the gardens, a chain of star-shaped islands connected by footbridges that sat in the middle of Luminous Lake. Lush and beautiful, it was a wild place with towering trees, shady nooks, blossoming shrubs, creeping vines, and more varieties of flowers than you could count. The air smelled tantalizingly delicious. But there was a place she liked even better.

"See you at dinner, then," said Libby, walking off toward Luminous Lake. Vega knew she'd grab a hover-canoe at the boathouse on Shimmering Shores. Vega slung her own guitar case over her shoulder and headed to the hedge maze, her favorite spot in all of Starling Academy. The trickily curving paths, which led, eventually, to a lovely seating area in the middle, were surrounded on either side by tall green hedges, so you couldn't see over to the next turn. But this maze was special. Its paths were constantly shifting, so it had limitless possibilities. You never went the same way twice. It was quite challenging. This was delightful to Vega but entirely frustrating and confusing to most of the other students, so Vega knew she would have her privacy. An escape route had recently been added, after a first year had unwisely gone into the hedge maze without her Star-Zap and, unable to find her way out, had to sleep under a hedge overnight. Now a single red florafierce could be found blooming in each wall of the maze. All you had to do was pick it and the maze would immediately form a doorway out. But Vega would never consider using it. Finding her way in an ever-changing maze was too much fun.

Vega could feel all the frustrations of the day magically lift as she stepped between the leafy maze walls. She loved the way the thick hedges towered over her head and framed the blue sky above. She was convinced she did her best thinking as she wandered through its pathways.

She switched on her Star-Zap's holo-video and began recording. She liked to take holo-vids of her day and review them before she got into bed for the night. After she made the first turn, she had a choice of going left or right. Without hesitation, she took the left path. Turning, and turning, and turning some more, she meandered through until she found herself in the center of the maze, which that day featured a display of lallabelle flowers, formed into a star shape, of course. Nearby was a pretty little swing hung with creeping zeldablooms, fragrant and lush. She sat on it and swung back and forth, the slight breeze ruffling her short hair.

Vega opened her guitar case, lifted the blue embroidered strap over her neck, and began to strum, practicing her scales, starting with C major. Her fingers alternated over the frets as she picked out a sequence of notes. Practicing her scales soothed and calmed her, which was good, because Leona's outburst during band practice was still bothering her. It wasn't only that the girl had berated her fellow band members (Vega did not appreciate being yelled at for no good reason), but also that the usually confident Starling was feeling so downtrodden. Plus, she wondered, if they could even find Scarlet, could they convince her to return to the band? Not if Leona was acting like this; that was for sure. Vega thought there must be something she could do to help. Her fingers playing the notes, she swung back and forth, lost in thought. *That's it! I'll holo-text Cassie!* Cassie had struck up an unlikely but warm friendship with Leona. Unlikely because Cassie was as reserved and shy as Leona was loud and confident. But their opposite-personality friendship worked. Vega felt a twinge of remorse. It was just like how she and Piper used to balance each other out.

She reached into her pocket and pulled out her Star-Zap. I'M IN THE HEDGE MAZE. DO YOU HAVE A MINUTE TO TALK ABOUT LEONA? she holo-texted.

The response was immediate: I'LL BE THERE IN TEN STARMINS.

So Vega continued to play, lost in her thoughts about Leona, Scarlet, and Piper. Glancing at her Star-Zap, which sat nearby, she realized the ten starmins were almost up. She put her bass back in its case and began making her way toward the maze entrance. Then her Star-Zap beeped and flashed a small icon of her mother's face. It was in a red star, a reminder that she had not yet returned her mother's holo-call from two stardays earlier. Vega considered doing it right then and there, but she still wasn't ready. She knew her mom was going to ask her to come home for a visit (again), and Vega needed to come up with a reason that she couldn't (again). She had already used a fellow student's Bright Day celebration she couldn't miss, a Glowin' Glions game, and an extra-credit assignment. She was running out of excuses. Vega felt uneasy. She wasn't exactly sure when things between her and her mom had gotten so complicated, but she figured it must have been around the time the two had seemed to switch roles. Vega had reached the Age of Fulfillment and overnight, it seemed, had transformed from a carefree child to an über-responsible, grades-obsessed perfectionist. She was determined to get into Starling Academy at any cost and had focused all her energy on studying. (She took the entrance examination five times to get the rare perfect score, which she was sure would guarantee her acceptance. Luckily, she loved tests, seeing them as the ultimate game.) And perhaps because her mother, Virginia, realized she no longer needed to worry about her daughter, she changed from a constantly stressed-out single mom into a relaxed, fun-loving person. The two rarely saw eye to eye on anything these days, so Vega alternately missed her mom terribly and was relieved by the distance between them.

Vega turned a corner and spotted Cassie, who looked flustered. She had somehow gotten turned around and was headed the wrong way.

"Hey, Cassie," Vega called.

Cassie spun around, a frown on her pale, pretty face. She was wearing a white diaphanous baby-doll dress shot through with silver thread over a pair of calf-length white leggings and a white tank top. She had delicate silver sandals on her feet.

"Oh, there you are," Cassie said, sounding faintly put out. She blinked up at Vega through her star-shaped glasses, her silvery hair done up in her signature pigtail buns. Vega smiled at the girl.

"Stop it," Cassie snapped.

"Stop what?" Vega asked innocently.

"You're looking at me like I'm some precious little doll," Cassie replied. "You know how much I hate that."

"Sorry," said Vega with an embarrassed grin. She couldn't help it. It was true. Cassie was so tiny and cute, even when she was scowling.

"Well, thank goodness I found you," said Cassie. "You know how this maze drives me crazy."

Vega opened her mouth, about to mention that it was actually *she* who had found Cassie. But the irritated look on Cassie's face told her to keep that thought to herself.

"I'm glad you holo-texted me," Cassie said as the two girls made their way back to the hedge entrance.

They reached a place where they could turn either right or left. Cassie started to go to the right and Vega tapped her on the shoulder. "This way," Vega said, pointing in the opposite direction.

Cassie shrugged. "Whatever you say. You're the expert." She glanced at Vega. "So was Scarlet at practice today?"

Vega shook her head.

Cassie looked disappointed. "So weird," she said. "No one's seen her since that awful day. . . ." Her voice trailed off.

Vega winced, recalling the fear in the pit of her stomach when they all realized Lady Stella was going to tell one of them that she was about to be ousted from the Star Darlings. After all her hard work, it would have been such a blow to her. She had actually frozen with terror at the thought. But as she had looked around the room, she'd realized that each of the eleven other girls felt the same way.

Cassie looked at the ground. "I still feel guilty over how happy I was that it wasn't me," she said.

Vega nodded. "I think we all do."

A sly smile crossed Cassie's face. "Everyone except Leona," she said. "I think she was glad to see Scarlet go." The smile quickly left. "But now Leona's got her own troubles." She looked up at Vega. "Is that what you wanted to talk about?"

Vega took a deep breath. "It's just that Leona's not herself," she said. She filled Cassie in on that afternoon's outburst.

"Oh, that's bad," said Cassie, biting her lip. "She loves the band. That's such a shame."

Vega put her hands to her forehead. "We should be able to help her get through this. Get everything back to normal. But I have no idea how. That's where you come in. You two are such good friends." The thought of losing the band was very upsetting to Vega. She took everything seriously—her classes, her studies, the meals she ate (to give her energy), the time she went to bed (so she'd be well rested for the next day's classes). Even her beloved games—she was a stickler for following the rules. When she played her bass, it was the only time she ever really let loose and relaxed. She did not want to give that up.

Cassie grimaced. "We *used* to be good friends," she said. "But she's been keeping to herself lately. The only person she seems to want to spend time with these stardays is her new roommate, Ophelia." She thought for a moment, then nodded as if she had made up her mind. "I'm going to try to talk to Leona after dinner," she said. "Will you come with me?"

"Sure," said Vega, shrugging.

Cassie's mood brightened considerably. Vega thought that it was probably both because they had a plan and because they were approaching the end of the maze. Cassie breathed a sigh of relief as they walked out the leafy doorway. The Celestial Café came into sight, and Vega's stomach rumbled at the same time that the large star above the door began to blink, letting everyone know that it was dinnertime. Perfect. The two girls headed to the building. Inside the large, warmly lit room, soft music was playing. There was the soothing sound of students softly chattering and the clink of silverware against fine china. They headed to the table that had unofficially become the Star Darlings', with its stunning view of the Crystal Mountains. To the rest of the school, they were a group of girls—four first years, four second years, and four third years—who attended regular classes but required some extra help during last period. Only the Star Darlings; Lady Stella, the headmistress; Lady Cordial, the head of admissions; and a handful of professors knew who they really were. Vega found that some students treated her differently (a small number of those scornfully, though many were sympathetic), while most didn't seem to care that she was "different." Little did they know that Vega and her fellow Star Darlings were really special in the very best way. That didn't matter to Vega, who didn't really care what others thought of her. It was enough for her to be singled out as special by someone she had admired for a long time: Lady Stella. In the hopes that she would one day be chosen to attend Starling Academy, Vega had devoured every holo-article that had been written about the headmistress.

There were three empty seats at the table, and Cassie and Vega sat next to each other. They missed out on the seats facing the radiant Crystal Mountains, but the light of the setting sun hit the mountain peaks, refracting into stunning mini rainbows that bounced off the shining goblets and illuminated everyone's face.

"So how was Wish Theory class today, Adora?" Vega asked as she unfolded her soft cloth napkin and laid it on her lap. The Star Darlings always made certain to limit their conversations to non–Star Darlings business when they were in eye- and earshot of the rest of the student body. They had been warned countless times that the work they were doing was top secret. Even most of the faculty had no idea what was going on.

"A snore," said Adora with a rueful grin. Professor Illumia Wickes liked to let her students run the class discussions, which was oftentimes wonderful, unless you had an incessant talker in the class. "This girl named Moonaria would not stop talking. No one could get a word in edgewise."

Vega nodded in sympathy. She watched as Tessa entered the cafeteria and, seeing that the only free seat was next to her roommate, Adora, leaned over and whispered in her sister's ear. Gemma rolled her eyes and moved into that seat, leaving the seat next to Leona open for Tessa. Vega noticed that Cassie was openly staring at Leona, who kept leaning over to whisper in Ophelia's ear. Leona was being unusually quiet, and the rest of the girls stole glances at her, as well, used to being entertained by the girl at mealtimes. She would often lead the girls in a sing-along or start a game of holo-telephone. Once the message had started off as "Glow for it! You are starmendous!" But by the time it got to the end of the line, it had been completely mangled, and poor Cassie had squeaked out, "You've got it! Glowfurs are delicious!" and everyone roared with laughter. Cassie had seemed way more humiliated than she should have been about her mistake, in Vega's opinion. But she had not been able to figure out why.

Astra leaned over. "Why so quiet, Leona?"

Leona simply shook her head. Her expression clearly read *Leave me alone.* Astra looked like she was going to try again, but Cassie elbowed her in the ribs.

"Ouch," said Astra, rubbing her side. She and Leona both had very big personalities. The two usually enjoyed a friendly rivalry, which occasionally resulted in the butting of heads and angry words. But they rarely stayed mad at each other for long. Astra looked confused.

Finally, Cassie leaned over and whispered in Astra's ear. Vega wasn't sure what she had said, but she thought she could guess the gist of it: *Leave Leona alone; she's fragile.* Astra looked disappointed. Whether it was that she felt sorry for Leona or missed her sparring partner, Vega was not sure.

The look on Cassie's face as she watched Leona from across the table was also impossible to decipher—jealous, wistful, or maybe just curious. Next Vega studied Ophelia, who was smiling shyly, her orange-pigtailed head bent to the side to listen to Leona's whispered comments. She seemed like a very nice, quiet girl, and Vega found herself wishing that *she* was the Star Darling who had been assigned the new roommate instead of Leona. The fact that Piper would have to have been expelled from the Star Darlings for that to happen did not escape her, and she silently chided herself for her unkind thoughts.

Vega found her appetite was not diminished by the strange goings-on and polished off her garble-greens soufflé and moon cheese popovers. After the Bot-Bot waiters had cleared the table, she ordered a mug of piping hot Zing and a cocomoon pavlova. The food at Starling Academy was top-notch, and although she wasn't quite as into food as Tessa (who hadn't been able to decide between two desserts, so had ordered both), she appreciated eating well—especially after many nights of popping a premade Sparkle Meal into the oven when her mother was on the overnight shift at the hospital. As a nurse, her hours were long and she couldn't miss a day unless it was an absolute emergency. Vega had learned at a young age what constituted an emergency: not much. She sighed, remembering the many nights she had eaten alone at the kitchen table while doing her homework.

She looked around and smiled. Maybe that's why she felt so fierce about being a Star Darling and keeping everyone together and happy. It was nice to be part of a group, to literally have a place at the table among friends.

After polishing off the last bite of her dessert, Vega swigged the rest of her Zing and stood, pushing her chair back from the table. She was ready to march over to Leona, and she turned to ask Cassie to join her. Cassie grabbed her arm. "Let's wait a minute," she said softly, "and see where Ophelia goes. I'd like to talk to Leona alone." They discreetly followed the two Star Darlings out of the cafeteria. Sure enough, once outside, the two girls parted ways.

After a moment, Leona noticed their presence and gave them a wan smile. "Hello, girls," she said.

Cassie leaned forward for a closer look at Leona. "Did you take your sparkle shower today?" she asked in a concerned voice. Vega blinked, suddenly realizing that Leona's skin was not quite as glittery as usual. She once again wished she was as observant as Cassie, who never seemed to miss a detail. All Starlings had a shimmery glow, and they supplemented it with daily bathing in a shower of weightless sparkles. It was a great way to start the day, as it revitalized and invigorated you, improving

your mood and outlook and also refreshing your sparkle. Some Starlings took them twice a day, but Vega felt
that was a bit excessive and a daily shower was perfect.
It was funny: Leona, with her golden hair, coloring, and
clothing, always managed to look extra glittery. But not
that night.

"Of course," said Leona. Then she paused and
wrinkled her brow, thinking about it. "I mean, I think
so. Maybe," she concluded.

Cassie gave Vega a despairing look. Leona was usually vain about her appearance. This was so unlike her.

The Cosmic Transporter dropped them off between
the two dorms. The first and second years lived in the
Little Dipper Dorm, and the third and fourth years lived
in the Big Dipper Dorm. Cassie clearly wanted Leona to
invite them to her room, but the girl was not cooperat-
ing. She looked at them quizzically as they shifted their
feet. "Well, I'll see you la—" Leona started.

"Hey, mind if we drop by?" Cassie interrupted. "I
haven't been over in a while."

Leona shrugged halfheartedly. "Sure," she said.

They walked through the doors and stepped onto the
Cosmic Transporter that looped its way through the
large dormitory, dropping students off in front of their

doors. They headed to her room in a silence that seemed awkward to Vega. She and Cassie weren't used to having to carry a conversation when Leona was around. The transporter deposited the three in front of Leona's door, and she placed her hand on the scanner. The simple gesture seemed to take considerable effort. "Welcome, Leona," the soothing Bot-Bot voice said, and the scanner glowed bright blue as the door slid open. The girls stepped inside behind her.

"It's a little messy," Leona said awkwardly. "I've been kind of, um, busy lately."

A little! That was the understatement of the star-century. Vega was shocked by the state of the room. Offices, dorm rooms, public spaces, houses, classrooms, restaurants, stores—every space on Starland—were self-cleaning. Scrubbing, scouring, mopping, sweeping, vacuuming, and washing were unheard of on Starland, which was why Wishling tools such as mops, brooms, pails, cleansers, sponges, and, most of all, the frighteningly loud contraptions Wishlings called vacuums completely confused Starlings. But Starlings weren't entirely off the hook when it came to cleanliness: they still had to hang their clothes, place their holo-books on the shelves, and throw their garbage into the vanishing garbage cans. Leona had clearly not tidied up in a while. Vega shuddered with distaste as she took in the clothing draped over chairs, the burned-out lightbulb in Leona's three-sided vanity mirror, the pile of jujufruit peels on the floor. Her large round pedestal bed was unmade. Gliony, Leona's stuffed talking lion who never said the same affirmation twice, sat forlornly on the floor, on his head. Cassie picked him up and righted him. "Shine on, bright Starling," he said. Cassie placed him on Leona's shelf and patted his mane.

Vega looked around the room. Leona's stage, a golden star-shaped platform used for her daily performance, was littered with star-shaped stuffed creatures, pillows, and holo-magazines. The disco ball, which usually spun, filling the room with dancing stars of light, was turned off. The trunk she used to store her glamorous golden costumes was empty, its contents strewn about on the floor. The sheer messiness of Leona's side made the contrast with the other side of the room even more shocking. Leona's untidy half was giving Vega a headache, but she was shocked to see that Ophelia didn't seem to have anything *to* organize. Her side was just . . . sad. There was a plain solar-metal bed with a simple white moonfeather comforter. The tiny chest of drawers made it clear she didn't have a lot of clothing, either.

The lone spot of color on Ophelia's side of the room was a thin orange ribbon that trimmed her plain white bedding.

"Your roommate doesn't have a lot of belongings, does she?" Vega observed.

"No, she doesn't," said Leona with a hint of defensiveness. "She likes to keep things simple."

"Not a holo-book or a holo-photo?" Cassie pressed. "Not a single stuffed creature?" It was clear she was trying to keep her tone light, but Vega could see that Leona was starting to bristle at the questions. To Vega's surprise, the usually sensitive Cassie plowed on. She picked up a tiny crystal that sat on Ophelia's dresser and placed it in her palm. It was a miniature version of the beautiful crystal her own roommate, Sage, displayed in their dorm room, which she had received as a Bright Day gift.

"So tiny!" she marveled. "More like a chip than an actual crystal . . ."

"Put that down!" Leona snapped.

Cassie's eyes widened and she set it back on the dresser like it was burning her hand. She stared down at her silver slippers, looking like she might cry. Then she seemed to gather herself, taking a deep breath and sitting next to Leona on the rumpled bed. She launched into more questions.

"So what's your new roommate like?" Cassie asked. "Where did she come from? How did a first year get assigned to a third year, anyhow?"

Vega was staring at Cassie, willing her to slow down, but the girl was just getting started.

"You have to admit that it's a little weird that she doesn't have any belongings," Cassie added. "Where's her desk? Her bookcase? Her shelves?"

Leona stood up. "Did you come here to interrogate me about Ophelia?" she asked angrily. "Well, here's a star flash: I think she's great. She's sweet and the perfect roommate. Especially after that Scarlet," she spat out. "I'm so glad not to have to look at *her* weird stuff anymore."

"Leona, we were just—" Vega started.

"Ophelia's going to be back from the library soon, so why don't you just ask her yourself?" Leona interrupted. There was a grin on her face, but it looked angry and mocking. "Or better yet, why don't you just leave us both alone?"

"Sorry to have bothered you," Cassie muttered, jumping up from the bed. Vega followed her to the door, which Leona slid open with her wish energy manipulation skills. *She's good*, thought Vega. *Almost as good as I am*. Vega hurried into the hall, relieved to be out of the tense room. She felt lighter just standing in the hallway.

"Why are you bothering me, anyway?" Leona called after them. "You're just as annoying as Scarlet."

Cassie spun around so quickly that she knocked into Vega, who had to shoot out a hand and brace it against the wall to steady herself.

"Wait, you saw Scarlet?" they both cried.

But the door slid shut behind them with an angry bang.

CHAPTER
3

"**Well, that didn't go** very well," said Vega as the two girls, looking dejected, stood on the Cosmic Transporter on the way back to their dormitory.

After Leona kicked them out, they had stood there for a moment, wondering if they should knock and try to explain themselves. The door had slid open and they had smiled, eager to make amends. But Leona stuck her head out and said, "This isn't for you. Our scanner isn't working right and I have to leave it open for Ophelia in case I fall asleep before she gets back." She withdrew her head, then stuck it out again. "It's time for you to go."

Cassie had opened her mouth to reply, but Vega had stepped onto the Cosmic Transporter, pulling Cassie along with her. Enough was enough. Now Vega looked down at the smaller girl, who was frowning. "That must have been really hard for you," she told Cassie sympathetically. "You two were starting to become such good friends."

Cassie shrugged as if it didn't matter, but Vega was pretty sure she was still smarting. The girl's soft burgundy eyes flashed behind her large star-shaped glasses. "Well, at least now we know that Scarlet is still on campus!" she said. "I was afraid that she left the school."

Vega nodded. "We need to find her and see how she's doing." *And,* she added to herself, *convince her to rejoin the band.*

"Exactly!" said Cassie. "She needs to know that we're still her friends even if she isn't"—she lowered her voice—"officially one of us."

"I'll tell you one thing, though," Vega said thoughtfully, leaning on the railing. "Leona gets along really well with Ophelia, which is more than I can say for Piper and me these days, that's for sure." She turned to Cassie. "Hey, are you and Sage still bickering?"

Cassie opened her mouth to speak, then shut it.

"I said, are you and Sage still bickering?" Vega repeated.

Cassie's brow was furrowed. "I heard you the first time," she said. "And it just started me thinking. . . ." She looked down at her silver slippers, deep in thought, then lifted her head. "No," she said. "We've actually been getting along great. Ever since . . ."

"Ever since what?" Vega asked.

Cassie was nodding to herself. "That's so weird. I just realized the oddest thing. Sage and I have been getting along great ever since I got rid of that vase of flowers."

Vega made a face. "You mean those gorgeous coral flowers we all got? You got rid of them? Why would you do that? They're so pretty and they smell so good!"

Cassie tilted her head to the side. "They *were* pretty," she said. "And they did smell great." She paused for a moment to collect her thoughts. "And I can't really explain it, but I had this weird feeling about them. So one day I just threw them away. Sage was really mad at me at first and tried to get them back, but they had already vanished." Vega nodded. Once you put your refuse into a garbage can on Starland, it disappeared. Forever. "But she got over it amazingly quickly and we had a good laugh about it. And we've . . . we've gotten along ever since! How funny that I just put that together."

Vega barked out a laugh. "Oh, Cassie," she said. "Not to be rude or anything, but you have to admit that sometimes your hunches are totally wrong."

Cassie looked like she was about to argue, so Vega began to list examples. "Remember when you were convinced that the Bot-Bot waiter served you breakfast for dinner one night because it was mad at you, but it really just needed to be retuned?"

Cassie bit her lip. "Yeah," she said.

"Or when you thought that Lady Rancora stole your Star-Zap when it was obvious that she picked up the wrong one by accident?"

Cassie blushed. "Oh, you're right. I did act a little crazy then." Her determination returned. "But this time I'm pretty sure I'm on to something."

"I'm just saying that sometimes what seems like a hunch is just you being overly sensitive about things," Vega concluded. "And I just find it hard to believe that those gorgeous flowers we all got have some sort of power to make roommates argue with each other. Think about it. What would be the point? It's ridiculous!"

Cassie frowned. "I know it *sounds* strange," she said. "But I can't dismiss the fact that everything between us was better afterwards." She frowned. "But Leona and Ophelia are getting along great, right? I mean, she couldn't have stuck up for her any more than she did. And I know Leona had those flowers in her room. I saw them when they first got them. . . ." Her voice trailed off.

"That's true," said Vega. "So we're forgetting about that crazy idea?"

"Actually . . ." Cassie said with a frown, "I don't remember seeing any flowers in their room just now. Do you?"

Vega laughed. "I'm sure they had flowers, just like all of us." She thought for a moment. "In fact, I remember Scarlet complaining that they weren't black. Here, I'll prove it." She whipped out her Star-Zap and accessed the video album.

Cassie gave a low whistle. "Really, Vega? You holo-videoed the room? That's just weird."

Vega shrugged. "I holo-vid lots of things!" She turned it on and Cassie leaned over her shoulder to watch. She saw the strange room—half-messy, half-empty—come into view as the holo-camera scanned it and its contents (or lack thereof). Sure enough, the flowers were nowhere to be seen.

"See? No flowers," Cassie said triumphantly.

"I just can't believe that you think a vase of flowers could possibly make people not get along. It seems like a really big leap to take," said Vega.

Cassie stamped her foot. "I don't know why you can't see it! Sage and I and Leona and Ophelia are all getting along, and no one else is. It's so clear!"

Cassie certainly has a temper! thought Vega as they stepped off the Cosmic Transporter, pushed open the door to the dorm, and stepped outside. It was funny: the girl had been super shy at first, but when Cassie got to know someone, her true self certainly started to come out. They were greeted by the always soothing sound of the bloombugs' evening chorus. Cassie seemed to relax, for which Vega was grateful. Then came the sounds of students returning home for the evening; they chatted and laughed, their voices low and their bellies no doubt pleasantly full. The two girls paused for a moment between the dorm buildings, not quite ready to go inside the Little Dipper Dormitory. Vega squinted. "I think I see your roommate," she said. "Hey, what's that in the air following her?"

Cassie looked into the distance and grinned. "That's a Bot-Bot guide," she said. "MO-J4 to be precise. He has been following Sage everywhere, ever since she got back from her mission."

Vega guffawed. "I thought we weren't allowed to have pets on campus. That's grounds for automatic dismissal!"

Cassie' alabaster face grew even more pale, which seemed impossible to Vega. "It is?" she said worriedly.

"I was just joking," said Vega. "It is forbidden, of course, but the Student Handbook does not specifically mention automatic dismissal."

Cassie looked relieved.

Vega shook her head. "But Bot-Bots are like, neutral.

No emotions, you know? They certainly don't play favorites. They're supposed to help us all equally."

Cassie shrugged. "Well nobody told that to Mojo."

"Mojo?" said Vega. She gave Cassie a puzzled look.

"That's what he likes to be called," Cassie explained.

"*Likes* to be called?" Vega shook her head. This was highly irregular. "I don't get it," she said.

"Well, maybe it's because we're the Star Darlings," Cassie said with a shrug. "We're special."

But that didn't make sense to Vega. If MO-J4 was a special Star Darlings Bot-Bot, wouldn't he be following them all around? This was highly irregular and Vega didn't like it one bit. She shook her head as if to clear it and tipped it back to look at the stars which had just started to stud the darkening sky. Staring into the heavens always calmed her, and she brightened with an idea.

"Let's make a bet," she said to Cassie.

Cassie chuckled. "You and your games," she said, but her voice was kind. Perhaps the stars had settled her, as well.

"I just remembered that we have a botany lab on campus," said Vega.

"We do," agreed Cassie.

"So who better to tell us if there really is something odd about the flowers?" Vega asked.

Cassie nodded. "That's a great idea!"

Vega had a plan. "We can bring them in and leave them for observation," she suggested. "We won't say a word about them, just see what they can tell us. But here's the bet. If I'm right and they are simply ordinary flowers, you have to do a puzzle with me every starday for a double starweek."

Cassie sighed, but she was smiling. "Fine," she said. "But if *I'm* right and there's something wrong with the flowers, you have to help me with my Astral Accounting test. I'm just not absorbing the lessons the way I want to."

Vega would have helped Cassie with her Astral Accounting anyway (she adored numbers), but she simply said, "It's a deal." The two girls pressed their foreheads together, the traditional Starling way of sealing a deal.

Vega smiled. She knew that Cassie's imagination was getting away with her. The flowers would turn out to be normal, just as she thought, and she'd be able to share her rebuses and crossword puzzles with a friend for sixteen whole stardays. It was a win-win situation. They'd find Scarlet, and Leona would eventually return to her usual jovial self. Everything was going to be okay.

The two tore themselves away from the brilliant night sky and headed inside to the Cosmic Transporter, which would take them to their respective rooms.

"Good night," said Vega, who was dropped off first.

"Good night," said Cassie with a yawn. "I'll pick you—and the flowers—up in the morning before breakfast."

"See you tomorrow," said Vega. She placed her hand on the scanner and stepped inside. She checked the time on her Star-Zap. She'd be able to replay the day's lessons and listen to them twice before bed. Most students just listened to theirs at night as they slept. But Vega didn't like to take any chances. She wanted to graduate with top honors, and she'd do anything to make it happen. She put on her pajamas, sparkled her face, and brushed her teeth with her toothlight, then settled into bed with her earphones on. Piper, as usual, was already asleep.

Ding! Ding! Ding! Ding! Ding! Ding! Ding!

Cassie put her hand over the small bell that sat on the botany lab's front desk, to put an end to Vega's incessant ringing. The laboratory was located on the top floor of Halo Hall's science stellation, where the scientific departments and classrooms were located, and sunlight streamed through the glass roof, causing the two girls to squint at each other.

"That's enough, Vega!" Cassie said.

"Well, where are they?" Vega asked. She placed the

flowers on the desk. "We're going to miss breakfast. It's the most important meal of the day, you know." Although she was feeling quite impatient, she glanced around at the hydrongs of varieties of plants that filled the room. The botany lab boasted that it had a sample of every plant that grew on Starland, as well as several varieties that Starlings had brought back from trips to Wishworld, and it certainly appeared to be true. The air in the laboratory was moist and warm—pleasantly so, Vega thought—and the many blossoms perfumed the air with an intoxicating scent.

Vega spotted an interesting-looking specimen sitting on a shelf nearby. It was a short, squat, chubby plant and it looked tantalizingly fuzzy. *Go ahead, touch me*, it seemed to be saying. She reached out a finger toward the plant. . . .

"Careful!" someone said.

Vega jumped back and turned around. A woman in a white lab coat stood behind her, a blue holo–name tag pinned to her chest. Vega leaned forward and read it: GLADIOLUS ROSE, BOTANY LAB ASSISTANT.

"I'm Gladiolus Rose, botany lab assistant," she said unnecessarily. "Didn't mean to startle you," she added in an apologetic tone. "But I'd be careful if I were you. That's a cactus from Wishworld."

"What's a cactus?" asked Vega.

"Cactus plants are quite interesting, because they don't need much water. And they're very protective of themselves!" She laughed, waggling her bandaged fingers at Vega. "I learned the hard way. Those soft-looking hairs are really pointy little spikes that can get stuck in your skin!"

Vega backed away. "Thanks for the warning!" she said.

"Sorry for keeping you waiting," Gladiolus said. "I'm the only one on duty right now. Everyone else is attending a morning meeting, so I'm in charge of the lab at the moment. How can I help you?"

Vega lifted the vase of flowers off the desk. "We received these flowers as a gift. We don't recognize them and we were wondering if you could help us identify them," she said.

Gladiolus immediately looked intrigued. She reached for the vase and lifted it from Vega's hands. She studied the coral blossoms closely. "So interesting! They have the coloring of a roxylinda, but the flower is similar to a calliope," she said. She held up a single bloom. "But the leaves are more like those found on a violina. It's very intriguing! I don't think I've seen anything like this before. Perhaps it's some kind of new hybrid." She shook her head. "Of course," she added, "I'm still an assistant, so maybe one of the botanists will have a better idea of what these are. Can you leave them with us?"

"Yes," Vega and Cassie answered in unison.

Gladiolus leaned over and took a deep sniff. "I just can't stop smelling them. The scent is so similar to my favorite flower, the callistola, but they look nothing like them."

"Really?" said Cassie in disbelief. "I think they smell just like—"

Vega gave Cassie a gentle kick to stop her from talking. "I guess we'll be going now," she said. "We'll be in touch." She didn't want Cassie to give the assistant botanist any clues about the flowers.

Gladiolus smiled. "Startastic. This will be a fun challenge." She nodded, still staring at the flowers. "I'm . . . I'm almost compelled to keep sniffing them. It must be part of their makeup to attract insects to pollinate them. But how strange that it affects Starlings so strongly, as well! So interesting! Star salutations for bringing these in!"

The two girls said good-bye and left the lab. They broke into a jog when they realized how late it was, and raced each other to the Celestial Café. Most of their fellow Star Darlings had already finished their breakfast and set off for class. Only Clover remained, finishing a bowl of Sparkle-O's. The two girls placed a quick order with their hovering Bot-Bot waiter and soon received their astromuffins and glorange juice in to-go cups. They thanked the waiter.

"I wish you girls had time for a real meal," the Bot-Bot waiter said sadly, and they assured him they would make time for a proper breakfast the following morning. They munched their muffins on the way to class.

"So what class do you have now?" Vega asked before taking a long swig of juice.

"Wish Fulfillment," said Cassie with a smile. Professor Eugenia Bright was a captivating teacher and routinely won top honors as Starling Academy's favorite professor.

"Lucky," said Vega. "I have Wish Identification."

"With Professor Lucretia Delphinus?" asked Cassie. "Then you have my sympathies."

Tiny and tough, Professor Lucretia Delphinus was an inspiring teacher, but her temper could be mercurial. When she was in a happy mood, her class was a dream and Vega didn't want it to end. But if she was feeling cranky, everyone needed to watch out. On those days, Vega would sit through the whole class willing time to fly and trying hard not to steal glances at her Star-Zap to check on its progress. Once, Professor Lucretia Delphinus caught a student surreptitiously checking her Star-Zap, and she grabbed it from the girl and read the offending holo-text out loud. Most unfortunately, it had said DO YOU HAVE GOOD PLD OR BAD PLD FOR CLASS TODAY?

The girl had tried to explain that *PLD* stood for *Positive Light Definition*, but PLD herself would have none of it. There had been detention as a result—for everyone.

"I can't wait to find out what's going on with the flowers!" said Cassie excitedly, changing the subject. "The wait is going to kill me."

"Me too," said Vega teasingly. "I can't wait to discover that they're just ordinary flowers and that you'll be playing games with me all double starweek!"

Cassie shook her head. "Didn't you hear what she said? She'd never seen anything like them before!"

"Only because she's still an assistant," said Vega. "As soon as one of the real botanists takes a look, they'll identify them in no time."

Cassie shrugged. "I guess time will tell," she said. "How long do you think it will take? I wonder if we'll hear from them tomorrow. Do you th . . ." Her voice trailed off. "Vega? Vega, are you even listening to me?"

But Vega had just spotted a flash of pink and black ahead and wasn't listening at all. She grabbed Cassie's arm, dropping her half-eaten muffin. It fell to the floor unnoticed and was promptly squashed by a foot clad in a shiny bright-yellow shoe.

"Scarlet!" she managed to say. "I think I see Scarlet!"

Cassie's eyes lit up. "Where?" she asked eagerly.

"Up ahead!" Vega grabbed Cassie's hand, marveling briefly at how cold it was, and dragged her through the crowd, elbowing students out of her way in her excitement.

"Watch it!" said a fourth year with purple braids, turning around with a scowl.

"What's your hurry?" asked another as Vega accidentally knocked into her. "So rude!"

Cassie ducked under another girl's elbow as Vega spotted her target—a girl in a black miniskirt, pink-and-black-striped leggings, and a matching hoodie pulled over her head. Vega reached out and grabbed the girl's arm before she could disappear.

The girl spun around and smiled pleasantly at the two. "Hey, can I help you?" she asked, pulling down the hood and exposing her pale pink curls.

Vega felt the sinking feeling of disappointment in her stomach. "Starscuse me," she mumbled. "I thought you were someone else."

The girl nodded and turned away.

Cassie gave a strangled laugh. "She was much friendlier than Scarlet, anyway."

Vega grinned despite herself. "You're right."

The two girls stared at each other for a moment. Vega shrugged. "Oh, well," she said. "Here I am." She was standing right in front of her Wish Identification classroom. "See you last period," she told Cassie, and turned to go into the classroom.

"See you last period," said Cassie. Vega saw her own look of disappointment mirrored in the girl's expression.

★

"Vega! Starland to Vega!" someone said with exasperation.

Vega sat up straight with a start. She suddenly realized that every Starling in class was staring at her. The formidable professor was standing right in front of her, snapping her fingers in her face. *Oh, starf.*

"I'm sorry," she told the teacher, who was looking at her expectantly. "Can you repeat the question?"

Professor Lucretia Delphinus looked disappointed. "My most ardent student not paying attention," she said with a sigh. "And here I was, thinking that my lesson was particularly interesting today!"

Vega was deeply embarrassed and felt her cheeks flush hot and sparkly. She hated disappointing her teacher and being called out in front of the other students. She could imagine what they'd say: *See, she's one of those remedial class girls who don't belong. I knew she wasn't so smart after all!* But she had been mulling over the events of the past two days and had zoned out.

"I asked, 'Are you paying attention?'" Professor Lucretia Delphinus said with a smirk. "I guess I know what my answer is."

Half the class tittered, relieved that they weren't the ones caught in the starlight. The other half winced in sympathy.

"Sorry," said Vega.

"Not as sorry as I am," said Professor Lucretia Delphinus, which, as intended, made Vega feel even worse.

★

Vega was relieved to head to "remedial class" at the end of the day. She always felt much more relaxed when she was surrounded by her fellow Star Darlings. She settled herself in her chair, set her Star-Zap just so in the corner of her desk, and switched it on to begin recording so she wouldn't miss a word the teacher had to say when she arrived. Vega recorded everything, including the teacher's greeting and farewell, and appended her own thoughts to the recording. If a fellow student ever missed class, she always went to Vega, because Vega took the best and most thorough notes in the school.

The door slid open and the teacher stepped inside. Vega's heart sank. Was this a joke? That day's visiting lecturer was none other than Professor Lucretia Delphinus herself!

"Greetings, students," she said as she walked into the classroom briskly. The Star Darlings sat up straight and silenced themselves immediately. She smiled when she saw Vega giving her a sheepish look. "Vega! All has been forgiven," she said. "We start anew right now." Vega smiled back tentatively.

The professor sauntered down the aisle and paused at Vega's desk. "I'm only hard on you Star Darlings because I expect great things from you," she explained.

Vega nodded, relieved.

"Today we are going to concentrate on wish identification," she said. "This is the most difficult part of the wish-granting process." She looked around the room. "Why is that?" she asked.

Vega's hand shot up. She was eager to impress.

"Yes, Vega?"

"Because we don't receive a firm indication of when a wish is identified, the way we do when the Wisher is first identified. It can be different for everyone. Starlings have to rely on their gut feeling because they have no indication they are on the right track at all."

The professor nodded. Then someone caught her eye. "Ah, a new student," the teacher said. "What is your name?"

"Ophelia," the Starling answered, her cheeks flushed and sparkled.

"We'll start off with an easy question for you, Ophelia. How do you know when you have identified the correct Wisher?"

Ophelia looked panicked. "I . . . um . . . uh . . ." Shamefaced, she stared down at her desk. "I . . . uh . . . can't remember."

"Tsk, tsk, tsk," said the tiny teacher. "This is the difference between a successful mission and coming back from Wishworld with an empty Wish Pendant."

With a strangled sound, Leona stood up and ran out of the room.

Professor Lucretia Delphinus looked surprised. "Was it something I said?" she asked. She shrugged. "Vega, can you help Ophelia out?"

Vega could and did. She sat back in her seat, happy

to have redeemed herself. After class, she got an approving nod from the professor, and she left the room with a bounce in her step. Cassie caught up with her, her cheeks pink from exertion. After surreptitiously glancing around to make sure that Ophelia was not in earshot, she spoke.

"Excuse me?" asked Vega. She bent down closer to Cassie to hear better.

"Did you see that?" Cassie asked in a hushed voice. "It's so obvious that Ophelia shouldn't be here. I wish we could find Scarlet and tell her that!"

Vega shook her head. "Just because she's slow to catch on doesn't necessarily mean she's not Star Darlings material," she said. "But it would be great to find Scarlet and see if she knows why she was kicked out. I'm sure there's a perfectly rational explanation."

"If you say so," said Cassie. But to Vega, she did not look convinced one bit.

It was pretty clear that Cassie was not a morning person. Vega, on the other hand, was. She almost burst into laughter when she knocked softly on Cassie's door (so as not to disturb the still-sleeping Sage) bright and early the next morning and the girl emerged from her room.

Vega looked as crisp and neat as usual, wearing a blue tunic and footless tights, her usual serenely sophisticated style. Cassie, who tended to prefer dainty comfort in her outfits, walked out of the room with a scowl on her face, her pigtail buns askew, her dress tucked into her leggings, and two different silvery shoes on her feet. Vega untucked the girl's dress for her and pointed to her feet. Cassie glanced down, groaned, and returned to the room to find a matching pair of shoes.

But Cassie's grumpy expression began to relax as soon as they stepped outside into the early-morning starshine. They were headed to the botany lab to check on the flowers.

"Don't you think it's weird that we haven't heard from them yet?" Cassie asked as they boarded the Cosmic Transporter. Vega shortened her step a bit to match Cassie's stride.

"Maybe they're busy," suggested Vega. "Our flowers probably aren't too high on their priority list."

"Well, they should be," said Cassie grumpily. They exited the Cosmic Transporter in front of Halo Hall and walked up the white marble stairs.

When they reached the warm, moist lab, Cassie lunged forward and gave the bell a single polite ding before Vega could get her hands on it. A vase of crimsonalias sat on the desk nearby. Cassie gave Vega a look. *Don't even think about ringing that bell,* her expression seemed to say.

Gladiolus Rose strolled through a doorway, wiping her hands on her white lab coat. "Hello," she said. "How can I help you?"

Cassie gave Vega a glance. Didn't the assistant recognize them? It was almost as if she was meeting them for the first time.

"We, um, were just checking up on the flowers we dropped off the other day," Vega explained.

The woman looked behind her and lowered her voice. "I haven't shown them to anyone yet," she said. "The person I wanted to show them to, Professor Peony, has been in a terrible mood lately, so I didn't dare approach her."

"Gladiolus!" someone called out in a peevish tone.

Gladiolus rolled her eyes and began rearranging the bright red crimsonalias. "That's her," she said. "Looks like today isn't going to be any better." She leaned forward. "Listen, I'll try to show the flowers to her later today if I can. I promise!"

"Gladiolus!" Professor Peony called again, a rising note of annoyance in her voice.

"Coming!" Gladiolus called back loudly. She looked

down at her hands and realized she had snapped one of the crimsonalia branches in two. "My stars," she said. "Look, I've got to go. Why don't you come back in a couple of stardays, and I'll hopefully have an answer for you by then."

The two girls sighed. "Fine," said Cassie. As soon as Gladiolus left the room, Cassie whirled around to face Vega. "Did you hear that? They're arguing!"

Vega shook her head. "All I heard was one impatient professor. Hold your galliopes."

"Fine," said Cassie with a shrug. "We'll find out soon enough." She rubbed her hands together. "I can't wait till I'm proven right."

"Time will tell," said Vega. "You might just be joining me for sixteen straight stardays of puzzles."

"Oh, boy," said Cassie, feigning excitement.

"That's the spirit," said Vega with a grin.

They walked to the Celestial Café. The light wasn't flashing yet, so they settled themselves on the steps, which were cool, still holding a bit of the chill from the previous evening. Just then, Leona and Ophelia walked by, arm in arm. Cassie stiffened. Then she sighed. "I just miss my friend," she said. "And I'm worried about Scarlet. I wish things could go back to the way they used to be."

Vega laid a hand on Cassie's arm. "Everything is going to be okay," she said. She just hoped she was right.

The Star Darlings were quieter than usual that morning at breakfast. They all seemed to have a lot on their minds. But the air of melancholy didn't do anything to affect Vega's appetite. She quickly polished off her order of starcakes and was wiping her chin with her napkin, about to starscuse herself from the table, when there was a muted buzzing noise, like a swarm of happy glitterbees discovering a bluebeezel garden.

Twenty-four eyes widened and twelve hands reached out to grab their Star-Zaps in unison.

S.D. WISH ORB IDENTIFIED. PROCEED TO LADY STELLA'S OFFICE IMMEDIATELY.

From the other side of the table, there was an excited yelp, which was quickly hushed. Adrenaline coursed through Vega's veins, and it took all her will to keep herself from jumping out of her seat and running as fast as her legs would carry her to Lady Stella's office. That wasn't allowed. She breathed in and out deeply several times to maintain her focus. The other Star Darlings were also admirably composed. Either alone or in pairs, the girls pushed out their chairs, stood, and strolled out of the cafeteria casually—chatting to one other, grabbing an extra astromuffin, looking like it was just another day. Vega glanced around at everyone, fully aware that behind their calm exteriors, they were all just as tense and excited as she was. *We should join the acting club when this is all over,* thought Vega. *We're naturals!*

Vega arrived in Lady Stella's office right after Leona and Ophelia and just before Clover. They filed in and took their usual seats. As Vega drummed her fingers impatiently on the table, Libby twirled a piece of her pink hair around her finger, Leona scowled, Ophelia looked positively terrified, and Adora hummed tunelessly. "Stop it," snapped Tessa, and the two started to argue.

Then Lady Stella appeared in the doorway and everyone immediately hushed. Tall and regally beautiful, she wore a silver turban, and her lips were painted a brilliant shade of red. She spread her arms, her full sleeves ballooning out at her sides. She looked down at them with a tender smile.

"I realize you're all very excited and tense," she said. "But Star Darlings must always be respectful of each other. I just want to remind you that you were chosen not for your singularities but because of the way the twelve of you fit together, like the pieces of a puzzle. You must support each other at all times, not tear each other down."

Vega looked around the table. Everyone was rapt. She marveled at how even when they were being scolded by Lady Stella, everyone still looked grateful to have her attention.

"We're sorry, Lady Stella," said Tessa. Everyone murmured agreement.

Lady Stella clasped her hands. "As you know, a Star Darlings' Wish-Watcher has spotted a Wish Orb that has begun to glow," she told them. "This means that a Wisher's wish is ready to be granted, and one of you is the perfect Starling to fulfill that wish. One of you"— she paused—"will shortly be on your way to Wishworld to begin a journey that, if all goes well, will be beneficial to both you and your Wisher. And Starland itself, of course," she added. "Now we will head to the Star Caves once more for the Wish Orb presentation."

Lady Stella realized that one student was looking quite confused. She smiled at her kindly. "This is all new to you, Ophelia," she said to the new Star Darling. "You see, underneath the school are secret caves known only to me, the Star Darlings, and a special few of my trusted advisors. That is where we have our own secret Wish-House, where special Wish Orbs are planted. When a Wish Orb begins to glow, we hold a secret ceremony to determine which of you is best suited for the mission based on your talents and the nature of the wish."

Ophelia nodded mutely, her face drawn. She made Cassie, who (as usual) looked slightly ill at the possibility of going down to Wishworld, look starmendously excited in comparison.

Lady Stella walked to her desk, pulled open the top drawer, and reached inside. A hidden door in the back wall slid open and Ophelia gasped. A faint musty chill snuck into the room. Silently, the Star Darlings stood and made their way to the door in a calm and orderly fashion. There was no pushing or shoving or arguing as each girl patiently waited her turn to pass through the doorway and carefully made her way down the circular staircase, gripping the cold banister. Vega heard someone say, "After you, of course," and someone else said, "No, you first," and she grinned, knowing that the girls were going out of their way to show Lady Stella just how civilized and supportive they could be. The hard soles of Vega's blue clogs made sharp ringing sounds on the metal stairs. She felt light-headed, and the hand not clutching the banister was all fluttery, like it was trying to escape from the end of her arm. *I've never felt quite this nervous before*, she thought, surprised by her reaction. Just before every other Wish Orb presentation, she had been as matter-of-fact as usual. She wasn't sure what was going on with her this time.

At the bottom of the steps, she jumped when Cassie put a cold hand around hers and gave it a squeeze. She smiled at her friend's thoughtfulness, especially since she knew how nervous Cassie must be.

"I'm sorry Scarlet isn't here," said Cassie in a low voice. "She loves these caves."

Leona turned around and scowled at them both. Vega ignored her and looked around the gloomy space, not certain what Scarlet found so appealing about the caves. They were dank and drippy, and they smelled old and musty. Strange creatures inhabited the dark corners, and you never knew when one might dart out and run across your foot, its claws scrabbling over your instep. She shivered at the thought, then had a sudden realization: that was exactly why the dark and mysterious Scarlet liked the caves, actually!

They walked through the gloom single file as Lady Stella led them down several twisty hallways, then came to a stop in front of a nondescript door. Vega blinked. She was fairly certain they had come an entirely different way the time before. The headmistress pushed open the door and grinned as glorious sunshine poured into the dark hallway. Ophelia gasped. And just like that, the flutterfocuses that had been dancing around in Vega's stomach vanished. That was exactly what was supposed to happen; she could feel it. She was suddenly, strangely, gloriously calm. She had this. She just knew it.

CHAPTER
4

And as she would soon find out, she was right. She watched as Ophelia gaped at the room. They were standing in a special Wish-House that had been built just for them. Although they were deep underneath Halo Hall, they could still look up through the glass roof and see blue sky and puffy white clouds drifting by.

"But . . . but . . . but it's impossible!" Ophelia said.

Leona shrugged. "Impossible . . . yet here we are," she replied.

Lady Stella led them to the center of the room, and they all grouped around the raised platform, where the Wish Orb would appear.

Lady Stella cleared her throat and Vega turned her attention to the headmistress. "As you know, or don't yet," she said, indicating Ophelia, "the Wish Orb will choose which of you is the best match for its wish." She clapped her hands and the room darkened. A beam of light shot down from above and illuminated the middle of the platform. It opened and a single Wish Orb appeared. There was a sharp intake of breath. Although they all (except Ophelia, of course) had seen this three times now, it was still a magical sight. The Wish Orb was round and looked like a beautiful iridescent bubble made of the finest spun glass. It glowed with remarkable intensity. There was a slight breeze, warm and refreshing at the same time, and the orb began to move around the platform, pausing for a moment in front of each girl. Adora held out her hand as if to touch it, and the look of sadness on her face when it moved away was heartbreaking. Leona looked away as it passed, as if it pained her too much to see the orb. Cassie let out a large sigh as it went by (of relief, Vega was sure of it). The orb paused in front of Vega, and she held her breath, steeling herself for the disappointment she would feel if it moved on to the next Star Darling. But that moment never came. Vega looked at Lady Stella questioningly. The headmistress beamed, leaned over, and took the orb carefully in her hands. It lit up her beautiful face, and she turned to Vega. Her eyes sparkled with pleasure as she said, "The orb has chosen. It's yours, Vega."

★

Vega set three separate alarms on her Star-Zap that night, but she didn't need any of them, for Piper woke her up at the crack of dawn, talking in her sleep. Or to be more specific, yelling.

It was mostly gibberish and made no sense to Vega, but a couple of the words were clear: *help*, *stop*, and was that *thief*? Rubbing sleep from her eyes, Vega swung her legs out of bed, crossed the room, and shook Piper's shoulder, perhaps a bit more roughly than she intended. "Wake up!" Vega said. "You're dreaming!"

The sparkle of the morning stars was just starting to peek over the horizon, and the room was still deep in shadows. Vega switched on a light. She saw that Piper's eyes were open, but she was staring at Vega confusedly, like she didn't recognize her. Her cheeks were flushed and she had a terrified look on her face, her eyes darting around the room. "She stole my Wish Pendant! Where is my Wish Pendant?" she cried, looking around wildly. Vega still wasn't sure Piper knew where she was or even who Vega was. It was a little scary.

Vega's arm shot out and she began frantically rummaging around on Piper's nightstand, knocking over a glass of water. (It instantly dried, as spills always did on Starland.) Where was her Wish Pendant? Finally, her fingers closed on the cool metal of the bracelet. She held it aloft. "Here it is," she said soothingly. "Piper, it was only a dream." She slipped it onto Piper's wrist, which seemed to calm her immediately.

An expression of great relief flooded Piper's face. But then she looked up at Vega reproachfully. "Only a dream? Really? You know how important dreams are!" she said coldly. "Especially to me!"

Vega shrugged. "Sorry," she said. "I . . . I wasn't thinking."

Piper sat up in bed, her fingers tightly wrapped around her Wish Pendant, as if the dream villain was going to reappear and try to wrest it away from her.

"Hand me my dream diary!" Piper demanded. This was very unlike her, and Vega stared for a moment. Piper corrected herself immediately. "Um, would you mind getting me my dream diary?" she asked sheepishly.

"Sure," said Vega. She hurried across the room and grabbed the top holo-diary in the basket. She handed it to Piper, who grasped it in her hands and closed her eyes, clearly trying hard to recall the dream. She finally tossed down the diary in frustration. "I can't remember!" she said sadly. "It's slipping away. All I can recall is that someone was chasing me, trying to take my Wish Pendant. I stopped to rest and they grabbed it." She thought hard. "I can't remember the face. Or even if it was a man or a woman. But it seemed so real. . . ." Her voice trailed off.

Vega shivered. Piper was usually all relaxation and sleeping masks but at times could get quite creepy without warning. This was one of those times.

Vega looked at Piper for a moment, trying to return her to reality. "Well, I guess it's time to get ready for my Wish Mission," she said. No reaction. "My Wish Mission to Wishworld," she said loudly. Piper still sat up in bed, staring into space. *All this drama over a silly dream!* Vega thought. *She* was the one who should be anxious this morning, not Piper!

But it didn't register with Piper. She slowly stood up and walked to the sparkle shower room. "I'll take a sparkle shower now," she said. "Maybe that will help calm me down."

Vega shook her head. She had assumed it would go without saying that she would get to take the first sparkle shower of the day. She laughed. It wasn't like she had big plans or anything. She was just going to hitch herself to a blazing shooting star and hurtle down to a distant world. No big deal.

While she waited her turn, she neatened the already spotless room, returning Piper's holo-diary to the basket and making both of their beds. Piper's soft seafoam green sheets were so tangled up Vega wondered if she had actually been running in her sleep. She accessed the Wishworld Outfit Selector but, after flipping through various options, decided she was happy with the choice she had made the previous night.

Vega stood over her bedside table, staring down at her Star-Zap. Her mother's face surrounded by a red star still sat in the corner of the screen, indicating the unreturned holo-call. She briefly considered calling her back, as it would be comforting to see her mom's face before her mission, despite the questions she would have to answer about scheduling a visit and the half-truths she would have to tell about her schooling. But then the sparkle shower room door slid open and Piper stepped out, a fresh glow on her skin.

"I feel much better," she told Vega.

"Great," Vega replied.

Vega abandoned her phone, grabbed her soft blue bathrobe, and stepped into the sparkle shower room. She glanced at the mirror. Her shiny blue hair was slightly mussed, and she smoothed it. Her bright blue eyes, the color of cloud-free skies, stared back at her. She was surprised to realize she still felt calm and relaxed. She took a long sparkle shower, even though she knew she would shortly be transforming her skin from sparkly to dull. It still was invigorating and good for the spirits. She slipped on a loose blue dress with a turquoise starburst on the front and a pair of pretty sandals. When Piper was ready, the two girls headed to the Celestial Café. The Star Darlings had all been instructed the day before to have a quick but nutritious breakfast and head straight to the private balcony of the Wishworld Surveillance Deck to see Vega off before classes began. As Vega approached the table, she was surprised to notice that the other Star Darlings looked more nervous than she felt. Leona appeared particularly out of sorts, staring down at her glass of glorange juice and not engaging in conversation with anyone—not even Ophelia, who looked more lost and lonely than usual. Maybe Leona was jealous of Vega's mission? Resentful that Vega was likely to collect wish energy? Or just feeling sad that her mission had not gone well and she most likely would not get a chance at redemption? Vega wasn't sure and she certainly wasn't going to ask.

There was a tray of baked goods in the middle of the table, and Vega grabbed a fruit bun and sank her teeth into it, then licked her hand as a blob of ozziefruit jam leaked out. *Yum.* Glancing down at her Star-Zap, Vega realized it was already time to go to the deck. She stood, her chair making a loud scraping sound on the floor. Cassie nodded at her across the table. Vega left the room, knowing that the other eleven would soon be following her, drifting out casually in groups of two and three so as not to arouse any suspicion from their fellow students.

She walked a little more quickly than usual and hopped into an empty Flash Vertical Mover car and pressed the button. The doors slid shut and she took a deep breath, enjoying the solitude. The Wishworld Surveillance Deck towered ridiculously high above the campus, but the Flash Vertical Mover zoomed her up in mere starsecs. She swallowed hard to keep her ears from popping. Soon she was stepping out onto the deck. She had it all to herself, and she stood there for a moment, marveling at the view. It never ceased to amaze her that far below on Wishworld, Wishlings were living their lives, going to school, and making the wishes that kept life on Starland proceeding as usual. And soon she would be a crucial part of one Wishling's life, if only for a short time. She took a deep breath and monitored how she felt again. Fine—no flutterfocuses in the stomach, trembling hands, or racing thoughts. She was ready and confident in her ability to take on any challenge she was given.

The door opened and Tessa and Gemma joined her on the private balcony. Gemma opened her mouth to begin her usual chattering, but her older sister shushed her. Vega gave Tessa a grateful glance. She was quickly realizing that the time just before you took off on a Wish Mission was sacred and special, meant to be savored.

Lady Stella appeared, almost out of thin air. "Hello, Vega," she said. Her eyes were kind and warm. She squeezed Vega's shoulder and leaned down to speak to her privately. "You have the skills, you have the brains, and you certainly have the drive, my dear," she said. "Just make sure to see the forest for the trees. Don't get too caught up in the details, and try to see the bigger picture. This mission is tailor-made for you."

Vega felt warm pride rush through her. "Thank you for your confidence," she said.

The door opened and the rest of the Star Darlings spilled onto the balcony and clustered around Vega, giving her effusive hugs and showering her with good wishes. It was a little disorganized, and just as Vega began to feel overwhelmed by all the attention, Cassie noticed and stepped in, lining everyone up to say their farewells in an orderly fashion. Vega smiled at her friend in thanks.

Piper approached Vega, a slightly sleepy look still in her eyes. She grasped both of Vega's hands in her own. "I was so worked up this morning I totally forgot about your mission," she said, looking ashamed. "Good luck, Vega."

Adora gave her a quick firm squeeze. "You'll be a superstar," she said. "There's no doubt about that."

Leona was next. "I hope you are able to collect wish energy," she said sadly. "Keep your eye on your Wish Pendant."

"I will," Vega promised her.

Libby said, "Take it from me: make sure to double-check that you have the right wish!"

"And the right Wisher," added Sage, poking her head over Libby's pink shoulder.

"Star salutations to you both," Vega said. She was touched that the girls were so willing to point out their mistakes to help her.

Gemma and Tessa stepped up to Vega together. "You're going to be startastic," Gemma told her. "Out of this world. The Wisher who gets you as their

Wish-Granter is going to be absolutely starstruck! As a matter of fact—"

Tessa interrupted. "As a matter of fact, good luck from both of us," she said, dragging her sister away. She called back, "Don't forget to bring back some of that chocolate Sage talked so much about if you can!"

Cassie simply gave Vega a kiss on the cheek.

Ophelia was the last to approach Vega. "You don't look scared at all," she said shyly. Her large ochre eyes were wide with wonder. "Now how do you get down to Wishworld again?"

Before Vega could answer, Lady Cordial appeared and handed Vega her backpack. It was a pretty blue with a glittery star on it.

"Star salutations," said Vega.

Lady Cordial, who was perhaps nervous she would start stuttering, as she often did when she was around large groups of Starlings, simply nodded.

"Vega! We need you!" Lady Stella called from the edge of the roof. "The Star Wranglers have spotted a shooting star!" The crowd parted as Lady Stella held out her hand. It was almost as if things were happening in slow motion for Vega. She stepped forward to join Lady Stella and watched in silence as the wranglers tossed out the lasso and just missed catching the star. It hurtled through the heavens and disappeared. "Awww!" everyone said. Luckily, the wranglers spotted another one almost immediately. They tossed out their lasso again and caught it. Sparks shot out as it strained against its restraints. Burning bright and beautiful, the star hovered in the air before them as the wranglers struggled to keep it steady.

Once Vega was safely attached, she paused to take one last look at everyone, their faces hopeful and concerned. "Good-bye!" she called. "I'll do everyone pr—" Then her words were lost in a loud *whoosh* as she was released into the heavens, the wranglers no longer able to keep their grip on the star, which was desperate to continue its fiery arc.

Vega zoomed through the sky as whirling multicolored lights, intense fiery flares, and twinkling stars flashed by. But despite the distractions, she was somehow able to remain studiously focused on her Star-Zap. (She had made this journey once before, when she had helped Leona.) As soon as the screen began to flash COMMENCE APPEARANCE CHANGE, she was ready. She concentrated hard and could see from an errant wisp near the corner of her eye that her hair had changed from cerulean to a very dark brown—almost black. She pressed a button on her Star-Zap and was instantly wearing the outfit she had carefully picked out the night before—a skirt made out of a rough material the Wishlings called denim, a simple blue-and-white-striped long-sleeved T-shirt, and a matching denim vest. On her feet she wore pretty blue woven shoes called espadrilles. She put her hand on her Wish Pendant, which was the sparkling buckle of her belt, and began to say the words that would begin the last step of her physical transformation: "Star light, star bright, first star I see tonight: I wish I may, I wish I might, have the wish I wish tonight." The Wish Pendant began to glow, and she gasped as the glitter was swept off her skin in a sudden rush of warm air.

PREPARE FOR LANDING, the Star-Zap read. Before she knew it, the surface of Wishworld was rushing up to meet her. She held her breath and landed gently in a grassy park. She blinked for a moment, taking in her surroundings, and let out her breath in one big whoosh. She hadn't realized she was still holding it. It appeared that she had landed in a park at the bottom of a large landmass surrounded by water. The park was empty save a mother sitting on a bench next to a baby stroller, her back to Vega. The child, who had apparently witnessed Vega's arrival, pointed at her and said, "Star."

"That's right," said the mother in a loud sunny voice,

pointing to a nearby yellow vehicle driving by on the street. "Car!"

Following the instructions she had been given, Vega waited until the star had sputtered out, then picked it up and began to fold it. When it was the size of a wallet and could not fold any more, she placed it in the front zippered portion of her backpack. She looked at her Star-Zap for further instructions. PROCEED DIRECTLY TO THE GEORGE ROBERT INTERNATIONAL SCHOOL FOR GIRLS, it said. Detailed directions followed, along with an estimated walking time of thirty starmins. Vega looked at her pretty shoes and immediately accessed her Wishworld Outfit Selector. She switched to a pair of blue sneakers and was off!

The farther uptown Vega walked, the bigger the buildings became and the more crowded the streets got. She stared openly at people and no one seemed to care or notice. She passed stores, gaping doorways that led to deep stairwells labeled SUBWAY, small parks filled with what looked like the youngest and oldest Wishlings and their respective caretakers, and lots of vehicles of all shapes and sizes, none self-driving. This part of Wishworld was noisier, dirtier, and stinkier than the first Wishworld place she had visited during Leona's mission. It was also much busier and more vibrant, she had to give it that.

Finally, she arrived at the school. The large, impressive white stone building stood in the middle of the city block. She admired the tall steps, the supporting columns. It reminded her a bit of Halo Hall. The street in front of the school was packed with idling cars, waiting to pick up students, she assumed.

She stole a glance at her Star-Zap and noted the time: 3:01 P.M. Just then, the doors burst open and students began to trickle out. Within moments the trickle became a flood.

Vega, who had just begun to climb the stairs, was pushing against the tide. A girl, her eyes glued to her phone, came straight toward her, and Vega stepped neatly out of the way, bumping right into someone else. "Starscu . . . I mean, excuse me," Vega said, but the girl didn't seem to hear. Forcing her way through the onslaught of students, she squeezed inside the door and found herself in the crowded school vestibule. She blinked, trying to get her bearings. A sign on the wall caught her eye. AFTER-SCHOOL CLUBS, it said, with an arrow pointing up. She looked down at her Wish Pendant, which was beginning to glow very faintly.

After-school clubs, here I come, she thought, taking the stairs marked *up,* which were empty, two at a time. (The stairs marked *down* were bustling with students.) She reached the second floor and pushed open the heavy door. There she found a woman in a navy jacket sitting behind a table, a clipboard in front of her. She was speaking to a boy holding a potted plant. "The Venus Flytrap Club is in room 222," she told him. She turned to Vega. "Welcome!" she said, looking over her glasses at her. "How can I help you?"

"I am Vega. I am a new student."

The woman nodded. "You are Vega. You are a new student," she said automatically.

"Which club are you headed to?" the woman asked. That question stumped Vega. What kinds of clubs did Wishlings have? Was there a star ball club? A wish energy manipulation club? Probably not.

"Oh," Vega said, smiling. She made a guess. "Puzzle Club?"

The woman's brow furrowed and she scanned her list. She looked up. "No, no Puzzle Club. Though that does sound like fun," she said. "Are you sure that's the right club?"

Vega thought again. "Ahhh, ahhhh . . ."

"Acrobatics Club?" the woman suggested helpfully.

It was as good as any. "That's it!" said Vega.

"Room 212," the woman said. "Right down the hallway." As Vega turned away, she heard the woman say, "Mmmmm, I smell pound cake!" *So it's true,* Vega thought. To Wishling adults, Starlings smelled like their favorite baked good from childhood. *Maybe to put them at ease or something,* Vega thought. It was odd but kind of nice when you thought about it. Her very presence brought back pleasant childhood memories.

Vega glanced down at her belt buckle Wish Pendant and noticed that the glow was a bit brighter than before. She paused in front of room 212. What were the chances that her Wisher would be in this club? She shrugged and opened the door. At least it was a start.

The floor of room 212 was covered with thick padded mats. Girls wearing tightly fitting shirt-underwear combinations were sitting on the mats, doing splits and stretching. Vega found their costumes to be very odd and was a little taken aback that no one was wearing pants.

A girl in a red, white, and blue underwear suit turned to her. "Hey," she said. "You must be new. Welcome!" She looked Vega up and down. "Where's your leotard?"

"My what?" asked Vega. *Mission 4, Wishworld*

Observation #1: Some Wishlings wear a legless article of clothing called a leotard. Function: unclear at this point.

The girl laughed, apparently assuming Vega was kidding with her. "No worries," she said.

"Oh, I wasn't worried," Vega assured her.

The girl laughed again. "We usually start with some headstands," she informed Vega. "Then we move on to forward rolls, bridges, handstands, back flips, and then we end with a pyramid!"

Vega raised her eyebrows. "Oh," she said. It sounded very busy. She watched as the girl dropped to the ground, placed her head on the floor, and balanced her knees on her elbows before extending her legs straight up into the air. Once she was certain of her balance, she began bending her legs in different poses. The other girls followed suit.

Vega was game. After several attempts, she was able to shakily stand on her head. She felt very proud of herself in the split second before she spilled onto the floor. She put her head back down and was face-to-face with her middle, about to balance her knees on her elbows, when she realized that her belt, mere inches from her face, was no longer glowing. *It's been fun, Acrobatics Club,* she thought as she got to her feet. *But I have to move on.*

With an apologetic grin, she headed toward the door. The girl who had first welcomed her looked at Vega as if she had betrayed her. "We were going to put you on top of the human pyramid!" she said.

"Maybe next time," said Vega. She shuddered at the thought, relieved to be dodging that experience.

Once she was back in the hallway, her Wish Pendant began to glow faintly again. Her Wisher was near. There was no question about it. She just needed to be patient.

Vega decided to try the classroom next door. She opened the door, and the teacher and two students looked up eagerly from the bucket they were inspecting. Vega stared. What could possibly be going on there?

"Welcome to Composting Club!" the teacher said.

"Is everyone here?" Vega asked.

"Um, yes," the teacher said. She laughed sheepishly. "We're a small club."

Vega looked down at her pendant. No glow at all.

"Sorry!" she said, starting to close the door. The students looked disappointed for a moment but immediately returned to examining the bucket. Vega never found out exactly what was inside. *Mission 4, Wishworld Observation #2: Composting Club does not seem very popular. Look into this.*

She watched with interest as several students parried in the Fencing Club, their faces obscured by strange masks. Her eyes widened as students pantomimed being trapped in invisible boxes, pulled ropes she couldn't see, and walked into a nonexistent gust of wind in Mime Club. And the smells coming from Cooking Club were tantalizing. But she was on a mission. Until the light glowed on her pendant, she had to keep looking. *Just how many clubs does this school have, anyway?* she wondered.

"Forty-seven," someone said.

Vega spun around. She hadn't realized she had said the words out loud. A girl stood in front of her, her orangey hair cascading down her back in rippling curls. Her eyes were bright blue and her pretty face was covered in freckles that reminded Vega of constellations.

"How many clubs did you say?" Vega asked.

"Forty-seven," the girl repeated.

"That's a lot of clubs," Vega said shakily.

The girl grinned. "There's something for everyone," she said. "And then some." She cocked her head at Vega. "So let me guess. You're new and haven't found the right club yet?"

"That's right. I'm Vega, by the way."

The girl stuck out her hand. "Katie."

Vega recalled immediately that she was supposed to

grasp and pump the hand, otherwise known as "shaking." Libby had certainly made a mess of that on her Wish Mission! While Vega made contact, she took a quick glance at her Wish Pendant, which told her that this girl was not her Wisher. Too bad. She seemed nice.

Katie smiled at Vega. "You want to join a really fun club? Come with me," she said. She set off down the hallway. Not knowing what else to do, Vega followed her.

CHAPTER
5

Katie pushed open the door to room 261. "Come right in," she said. About ten students sat in a circle. Vega stared at them. They had large balls of thick string in their laps and long sticks in their hands. They moved the sticks back and forth. It was very strange.

"What club is this?" Vega asked.

Katie laughed. "You're so funny! What else could it be? It's Knitting Club, of course!"

Vega knew that the only reason she was making everyone laugh was that she didn't understand Wishling ways, but she still enjoyed it, basking in the warm glow of her classmates' grins. Back home she was the serious one; on Wishworld she already had a reputation as a joker. It felt good to be thought of as funny.

"Welcome," said the teacher, a tall thin woman with curly brown hair and thick glasses. "I assume you know how to cast on?" She handed Vega her own ball of string and two of the pointy sticks. "You can borrow these for today. Next week you should bring your own yarn and needles."

Vega knew that no matter what happened, good or bad, the Countdown Clock would have run out of time before next week's class. Still, she nodded in agreement. She was afraid to ask what "casting on" was, in case it was a special Wishling skill that everyone was born with. So she stared at the needles and the ball of yarn, willing herself to figure out how to do it. As you might imagine, that didn't work. Not about to waste any of her precious wish energy in the attempt to acquire knowledge, she decided she'd fake it. But she had no idea what to do. She was tempted to leave the room and consult her Star-Zap for possible directions, but then she glanced down at her lap and saw her Wish Pendant. It was glowing! Her Wisher was near. Startastic!

She looked around the room eagerly. Who could it be? The girl with the long dark hair and nervous laugh who was knitting so quickly her needles flashed? The girl with the short blond hair who was creating what looked like the world's longest (and lumpiest) scarf? Or maybe it was the girl who was sitting next to her, scowling as she ripped out a row of stitches?

Keep cool, Vega, she said to herself. *You'll figure it out.* She remembered what she had learned in Wishers 101 class: FIGGO—Fitting In Guarantees Good Outcome. She picked up the needles and began to wrap the yarn around them. *Maybe this is how you start*, she thought in desperation.

She looked at Katie for help. But she was talking a mile a minute to another girl and gesturing with one of her needles. The other girl was half-listening, a nervous eye trained on the moving needle in Katie's hand.

Vega stared down at her own needles helplessly.

"Hey, do you need help?" someone asked.

She looked up hopefully. A girl was smiling down, peering at her from behind funny-shaped eyeglasses without any lenses in them, her curly black hair cut with uneven bangs and one side longer than the other. Always-precise Vega was surprised to find that rather than looking strange, the haircut gave the girl an endearingly off-kilter look. Her simple black sweater had a bright pink fuzzy neckline. She wore a slim black skirt and bright pink tights, and her chunky black boots looked artfully beat-up. They were embellished with bright paint splatters. Vega looked at her admiringly.

Vega was more of a dress-for-comfort kind of girl, but even she could tell the girl had style.

"I just finished my project, a shrug," she said, holding up an adorable abbreviated sweater that had only arms and shoulders. It was made out of glittery maroon wool. "I don't have anything to do, so I'm all yours!" She sat down in the chair next to Vega's. "Give me your hand," she said. Vega obeyed, and the girl laid the end of the yarn on Vega's palm, looped over itself. "Now watch," she said, sticking her fingers through the loop and pulling the yarn through. "See? A slipknot. That's how you start."

She took Vega's knitting needle and poked it through the hole. Then she showed her how to cast on, making an X with the needles, looping the yarn around the back needle, pulling it underneath, and then slipping the other needle through to steal it back.

"Now you try," she said.

Vega stuck out her tongue in concentration. After a couple of false starts, she began to get the hang of it. She smiled. It was an odd Wishling pastime, but she could see its appeal. *Mission 4, Wishworld Observation #3: Knitting seems complicated, but it's not as hard as it looks. It's actually quite relaxing!*

"Hey, you're a good teacher," she said. "What's your name? I'm Vega."

"Hello, Vega," the girl said. "I'm Ella. So, are you ready to knit?"

Vega nodded. It was the same process, except after you pulled the stitch underneath, you slipped it off one of the needles and onto the other.

"I'm knitting!" Vega cried.

"Amazing," said the girl. "You're a quick learner. Once you do a couple of rows, I'll teach you how to purl." She looked down at Vega's waist. "Hey," she said. "What a cool belt buckle! How does it glow? Does it have a battery or is it solar powered?"

Vega nearly dropped her knitting as she looked down at her belt. It was definitely glowing. Still, better safe than sorry. Her eyes on the belt, she walked away from Ella and stood next to another girl, who looked up at her in confusion. The belt buckle dimmed. She sidled up to Ella, who had started knitting again. It glowed once more. Ella smiled and shook her head. "You're so funny!" she said.

There it was again! Vega grinned. She was having the best time on Wishworld. She had learned to knit, found her Wisher, and made several Wishlings laugh.

Her mission was off to a startastic start!

When Knitting Club was over, Vega returned the needles and yarn to the teacher and promised (falsely) that she would bring her own supplies the next week. Then she turned around to look for Ella. But Ella was gone.

Vega ran to the top of the stairs. She spotted Ella's pink collar and multicolored boots just as they disappeared through the door.

"Ella! Wait!" she called. Vega ran down the steps, but when she pushed open the door, her Wisher was nowhere to be found. There was a line of cars waiting to pick up students. *Ella must be in one of them,* she thought. She stepped off the curb and tried peering through the windows of one. But all she could see was her own curious face and dark brown hair, which she still hadn't gotten used to. It was impossible to see inside the car.

The window rolled down. It was Katie. "Hey, Vega, are you looking for your driver?" the girl asked.

"Um . . . no," said Vega. "Just looking for Ella."

"Don't know what to tell you. She disappeared," said Katie with a shrug. "She's good at that."

"Okay, thanks," said Vega. She turned to walk away.

"Hey, do you need a ride somewhere?" Katie asked, leaning her head out the window.

Vega looked down the street one last time. But Ella was definitely gone. "Um, sure. As long as your dad doesn't mind," she said, indicating the man who sat behind the wheel.

Katie laughed. "You crack me up. You know that's my driver!"

Katie opened the door and slid over. As Vega settled into the soft black seat, Katie handed her a black buckle on a strap.

"Thanks," said Vega, taking it from her and holding on to it.

Katie looked at her funny.

"What?" said Vega.

Katie burst into laughter. "Oh, Vega!" she said fondly. She reached across her and snapped it into the latch. The strap felt snug against Vega's torso.

"Oh, it's a restraining device!" she said. Self-driving Starland cars never, ever got into accidents, so Starlings were free to move about in their vehicles at all times. Vega felt oddly constrained but didn't say anything.

Katie smiled. "So how did you like Knitting Club?" she asked. "I was right, pretty fun, huh?"

"Yeah," said Vega. "I liked it." Then she added, "So, um, what's Ella like?"

"Oh, she's really nice. She's in my class," Katie said.

Vega sat up straight. "Oh, really?" she said. "Uh . . . me too!"

"You are?" said Katie. She shrugged. "That's cool. She's new this year. She has all these great outfits, because her mom is a famous fashion designer." She looked embarrassed. "I actually tried to Google her mom once, but I couldn't find anything. She must be, like, totally exclusive."

Google? Vega tried to look wise. She nodded. "Totally. Well, that makes sense, about her mom being a fashion designer, that is. She did have on a startas—I mean, a fantastic outfit."

"It was pretty sick," said Katie.

Vega stared at her. Perhaps Katie had misunderstood her. "Oh, no, I meant that I enjoyed it," Vega explained.

Katie grinned and gave Vega a friendly punch on her arm. "There you go again."

Mission 4, Wishworld Observation #4, thought Vega. *Sometimes Wishlings use words the opposite way. For example,* sick.

"Oh, you'll see," said Katie. "She wears a cool outfit every day." She thought for a minute. "I guess I don't really know all that much about her. She kind of keeps to herself. She never invites anyone over. It could be because her mom designs her clothes at home and everything needs to be top secret," she mused. "Or maybe it's because her mom has to travel a lot."

"Oh," said Vega. She started thinking. Maybe Ella's wish was to spend more time with her mother. She wondered how she would make that happen. Maybe she could suggest they take up a hobby together. . . .

Katie was looking at her intently. "I said, where should we drop you off, Vega?"

Vega snapped back to reality. *Uh-oh.* She had no idea what to tell her. Then she had a sudden brainstorm. "Your house?" she suggested. "My mom's at work, so I have some time to kill."

The other girl's face lit up in a smile. "Excellent," she said. "Maybe you could stay for dinner!"

"I'd love to," said Vega.

After a couple more blocks, the car stopped and the driver got out and opened the door for them. They stepped onto the sidewalk under an awning.

"Thank you, Michael," said Katie. "See you tomorrow!"

"Thank you," echoed Vega.

A smiling man in a fancy uniform held the door of the building open for them. "Good evening, Katie," he said.

"Good evening, Henry," she replied.

They walked through the lobby, past a large marble table, on which rested the largest vase of flowers Vega had ever seen. She literally could have taken a dip in it. They stepped into the elevator, where another uniformed man was waiting.

"Hello, Ernest," Katie said, and he nodded, taking the girls straight to the right floor. "Going up!" he said.

Vega followed Katie down a polished hallway to a door. Katie rang the doorbell, which chimed melodiously. A woman, clad in a gray dress with a white apron over it, answered the door.

"Welcome home, Katie," she said.

Katie gave her a quick hug. "Marta, this is my friend Vega. She's going to stay for dinner tonight."

"Very good," Marta said. She nodded and disappeared.

"Is that your mom?" asked Vega curiously.

Katie snorted. "No, my mom doesn't wear a uniform, silly. And I don't call her by her first name, either. That's our housekeeper." She playfully punched Vega in the arm again. "You're so funny!"

My *mom wears a uniform*, thought Vega. She realized she had to start keeping her observations to herself. She wasn't really blending in. In fact, she was starting to stick out like a sore thumb. How soon before her funny comments caught some unwanted attention?

"Want a tour?" asked Katie.

"Sure," said Vega.

The tour took half an hour. They started in the sun-filled living room, which was bigger than the apartment Vega grew up in. They saw the dining room, with a table big enough for fourteen; the huge gleaming kitchen; and at least four bedrooms. Vega lost count. "My mom and dad's room is that way," said Katie, pointing to an unexplored wing of the house. Off a library, filled from floor to ceiling with real paper books, was a balcony that overlooked a huge green rectangle. "That's the park," Katie explained.

Vega nodded. Which park? She wanted to ask, but she knew enough by then not to.

The tour continued: The windowless media room with a huge screen, plush red theater seats, and a popcorn machine. The maid's room. The laundry room. They ended the tour in Katie's enormous bedroom—complete with huge canopy bed, private bathroom, a crafts table, and a gigantic walk-in closet.

Vega's eyes were huge. "My stars," she said.

A bell jangled.

"Dinnertime!" said Katie. The two girls washed their hands and headed back to the dining room. Luckily, Katie waited for Vega, or she would probably have gotten lost trying to find it.

The enormous dining room table was set for two. Vega didn't think twice about that. She had often eaten alone when her mother worked late. She sat at the table, unfolded her napkin, and placed it across her lap.

Just then a lovely woman in a long black dress swept into the room. Her shining blond hair was twisted into a sleek updo. Vega admired the sparkling white crystals she wore around her wrist and neck.

"This is my mother, Mrs. O'Toole," Katie said. "Mom, this is my new friend Vega."

"You look beautiful!" Vega exclaimed.

"She's dressed like this because she's off to a benefit tonight," Katie explained.

"Vega. What a pretty name," said Mrs. O'Toole. "I'm pleased to meet you."

"Pleased to meet you," Vega repeated. What a lovely Wishling expression!

"And what a pretty haircut," Katie's mother said. She took a closer look at Vega's hair. "Look at that! There's a hidden layer of blue underneath in the back!"

"There is?" said Vega, reaching back to touch her hair.

Mrs. O'Toole and Katie laughed the same tinkling laugh. "Your new friend is funny," Mrs. O'Toole said to Katie.

"Tell me about it," said Katie.

Mrs. O'Toole turned to her daughter. "Daddy and I will be out late tonight, so you must listen to Marta. And go to bed when she tells you." She sniffed the air. "Did Marta make lemon meringue pie?" she asked.

Katie gave her mom a strange look. "I don't think so," she said. Then her eyes lit up. "Hey, can Vega sleep over tonight?"

"I'm sure her mother is expecting her," Mrs. O'Toole said worriedly. "And it is a school night. And we've never met, so I can't imagine that her mother would allow—"

"Why don't I stay over tonight?" interrupted Vega. "My mother won't mind."

Katie's mother got a funny look on her face. "Why don't you stay over tonight?" she said. "Your mother won't mind."

Katie looked puzzled, but delight won out over confusion, and she hugged Vega, then her mother. "That's totally dope, Mom!" she said.

"Glad to be so dope," said her mother. "Word."

"Now you're embarrassing me," said Katie.

A man in a white shirt, a black suit, and a black bow tie strode into the room. "Who's embarrassing you?" he asked. "Is it me in my penguin suit?"

He looked dashing, so Vega knew he was kidding. He

introduced himself to Vega, then said to Katie, "I'm getting dragged to another of your mother's charity events. I'd much rather stay home and watch baseball with you!"

Katie grinned. "Tomorrow night, Daddy. The whales need you."

He rumpled her hair. "Tomorrow night it is." He stood up and smiled. "You girls are in for a treat. It smells like Marta made chocolate layer cake!"

★

After dinner Vega watched as Katie did her homework. Sitting silently as Katie struggled with math was particularly painful for Vega, so she stood, walked to the window, and looked up, searching the night sky. But to her dismay she couldn't see a single star.

There was a scratching sound at the door and Vega whirled around. To her surprise, two enormous furry creatures bounded into the room. Vega took one look and screamed.

Katie looked up and laughed. "Don't be scared. That's just Felix and Oscar. My mother raises Afghan hounds," she explained.

Vega stared at the tall, slender, long-haired creatures. "They're dogs?" she guessed.

Katie laughed. "Well, they're not hamsters," she said.

"They're not?" said Vega.

Katie grinned. "Vega, you are too much. They're my mother's show dogs."

They put on shows? Vega wondered. *What is their talent?* But she wisely kept her thoughts to herself this time.

"They compete in dog shows all over the country," explained Katie. "They are the most spoiled dogs in the city, I swear. They have their own water fountain in the kitchen, their own special shower room, and they eat meals prepared by a doggy chef. You can't make this stuff up."

Vega tentatively held out her hand and one of the dogs licked it. It was kind of gross and kind of cool at the same time. She patted its head and then, emboldened, began to stroke its silky fur. The other dog poked her with its long nose, looking for attention, too.

Katie grinned. "You'll never get rid of them now."

"Katie?" asked Vega.

"Yeah?"

"Does everyone at school live in as big a place as this?"

Katie thought for a moment. "Most of them, I guess," she said. She frowned. "Actually, not everyone. There are some FA kids who live outside the city, in smaller apartments."

"FA kids?" asked Vega.

"Financial aid," Katie explained. "You know. The kids that get scholarships to be able to go to school."

"All schools aren't free?" asked Vega. That was strange. They were on Starland.

"Definitely not," Katie said. "Especially ours!"

That night Vega lay in an impeccably decorated guest room under crisp white sheets and a blanket the color of the early-morning sky and as soft as a baby's skin. She ran over the day's events and her next steps, making a mental list.

1) Make secondary contact with Ella.
2) Get invited over to her house.
3) Determine wish.
4) Make wish come true.

And then she couldn't help adding:

5) Help Leona become happy again.
6) Find Scarlet (and convince her to rejoin band).
7) Check on flowers in botany lab (and hopefully collect on bet!).

8) Try to get along better with Piper.

9) Call Mom back.

★

As Vega thought of her mom, she pictured her curling up in bed with a good holo-book and some jellyjoobles, her mom's favorite thing to do after a long shift at the hospital. Then Vega got a weird lump in her throat and she had to get up and drink a glass of water. But it didn't help. So to feel better, she closed her eyes and repeated her mantra over and over again:

You are the missing piece of the puzzle.

You are the missing piece of the puzzle.

You are the missing piece of the puzzle.

You are the missing piece of the puzzle.

You are the missing piece of the puzzle.

You are the missing piece of the puzzle.

Until she fell finally fell asleep, a peaceful smile on her face.

CHAPTER
6

"Shouldn't we wait for your parents?" asked Vega
as she slathered jam on a delicious-smelling crossed-sant,
or at least that's what she thought it was called. Surely
this gigantic spread was not for just her and Katie. She
popped a fat red berry with little yellow seeds all over
it into her mouth and poured herself a glass of freshly
squeezed glorange juice.

Or-ange, she corrected herself.

"Oh, no, I'm sure they were up really late last night,"
explained Katie.

Vega felt another lump rise in her throat as she
recalled how her mother had greeted her with a tasty
breakfast every morning before she went to school,

regardless of how late her mom had worked the night before.

It was pleasant to ride to school in the luxurious car and have the door opened for them, like they were famous or something. The girls walked up the stone steps and Vega followed Katie into her classroom. She walked right up to the teacher and introduced herself as she had been instructed. "Hello, I am Vega, the new student in your class," she told her teacher, Ms. McKenney, a woman with green eyes, auburn hair, and an easy grin.

It worked like a charm. And it made her happy when Ms. McKenney said that the room smelled like coconut layer cake.

Vega got settled at her new desk and waited patiently for her Wisher to appear. She was starting to get anxious when Ms. McKenney shut the door and started the morning's attendance and Ella still hadn't arrived. Finally, to Vega's relief, there was a knock on the door. Ms. McKenney opened it. "Thanks for joining us!" she said to the red-faced girl. She said it kindly, but Ella looked miserable as she slunk to her seat behind Katie.

"Your driver got stuck in traffic?" Katie asked sympathetically.

Ella raised her eyebrows. "Yeah, something like that," she muttered.

Vega was not a fashionista; she was the furthest thing from it, actually, as she preferred function over form at all times. But once again she had to admire Ella's outfit choice: a black cape with a hood over a pair of jeans with artfully arranged multicolored patches and a pair of distressed ankle boots. She could see Scarlet (poor Scarlet) wearing that exact same cape. The arms, she decided as she watched, looked very much like bat wings. Yes, Scarlet would be all over that cape in an instant. Ella removed the cape and hung it over the back of her seat, revealing the sparkly maroon shrug she had completed in Knitting Club the day before.

As the morning progressed, Vega was disappointed to discover that there were no clues to be had about Ella's wish. The girl seemed to have it all—smarts (she finished a math problem everyone else but Vega, of course, was struggling with), admirers (three girls told her they were going to join the Knitting Club, too, so they could learn how to knit a shrug just like hers), and style. What could Ella want that she didn't have? Vega wondered. The only possible lead she had at the moment was Ella's busy designer mom. She'd have to look into that, and soon.

The bell rang for lunch and the students stood at their desks, putting books and papers and writing utensils into their backpacks. "Class! Class!" shouted Ms.

McKenney. "Don't forget that Bring Your Parent to School Day is coming up on Friday. There are still some parents we haven't heard from, so please have them fill out the slip and return it to me as soon as you are able. We would like all our parents to participate if possible!"

She indicated a list pinned to the bulletin board. Vega stole a glance at the list on her way out the door. Ella's name was not on it. She got a shiver of excitement and wondered: *Could this be my first clue?*

She could be on to something. She watched with interest as Katie turned and spoke briefly with Ella.

Ella disappeared into the surge of students in the hallway, and Vega hurried to catch up with Katie. "What did you say to Ella?" she asked.

"Oh, I just told her how excited I am to meet her mom," she said.

"And what did Ella say?" Vega asked.

"She said she doesn't think it's going to happen. Her mom is in Paris and she doesn't think she'll be back in time," Katie said, frowning. She crossed her fingers. "Fingers crossed she can make it!"

Vega headed to the cafeteria in search of Ella. She couldn't find her anywhere, and finally her hunger got the better of her and she got into the lunch line behind some other students. The line was long, and she used the opportunity to try to discover her special talent. She ran down a mental list. It wasn't levitation or making time stand still (or speed up). She turned to the girl behind her and tried out mind reading (nothing). She stared at a cookie, willing it to disappear. Nothing. Finally, it was her turn to order her lunch. She glanced up at all the unfamiliar menu items. Pizza. Hamburgers. Chicken tenders. Tomato soup. Grilled cheese. Suddenly, she had an idea. She surreptitiously tapped her elbows together three times for luck. "I'll have a slice of pizza please," she told the woman pleasantly. Then she thought, *Give me a grilled cheese. Give me a grilled cheese. Give me a grilled cheese.*

The woman reached for the pizza, then stopped, a puzzled look on her face. Before Vega's delighted eyes, she shook her head, picked up a toasted sandwich, and handed it to Vega uncertainly.

"Thank you so much!" Vega said effusively. Now she was certain! Her star talent was mind control! This was a tough one because she knew that she couldn't use this talent directly on her Wisher. So she wasn't sure exactly how she was going to use it, but she was certainly glad to have the knowledge in her back pocket.

She grabbed some napkins (paper, which was odd to her) and then stood uncertainly, balancing her tray as she scanned the room, looking for a familiar face. She smiled when she spotted Katie. Even better, there was an empty seat at her table. Vega headed over.

"Vega!" said Katie. "Sit down. You remember Luna, Callie, and Lila from class?"

The girls smiled at her and Vega nodded back, although she had been so focused on Ella, she hadn't noticed any of the other students.

Vega sat and took a bite of her grilled cheese sandwich. She was pleasantly surprised by how tasty it was. She chewed and swallowed. "So what happens on Bring Your Parents to School Day?" she asked.

"Oh, parents come in and talk to the students about their jobs," Katie explained.

"Are your parents coming in?" Vega asked.

"My dad is supposed to come in and talk about derivatives," she said. "I love my dad to death but . . ." She gave a dramatic jaw-cracking yawn. "Will either of your parents be able to come?"

Vega's eyes widened. "Oh, I don't think so," she said. "They're, um, away." That certainly wasn't a lie. They were both away from her at the moment; that was for sure. Vega's dad even more so, ever since she was three staryears old. He visited her sporadically and sent her a Bright Day gift every staryear, but he had a new family now in Light City, and every Bright Day she got a staryear older, but his gifts did not. It was like she was five staryears old permanently, in his mind. Vega couldn't throw the gifts away, as inappropriate as they were, and she kept them in the bottom drawer of her dresser. She rarely opened the drawer; it made her very sad to look at them.

The rest of the girls at the table started talking excitedly about who would be the most interesting parent. One girl's mother was a famous actress. Another girl's father had written a best-selling book. Another girl's mother was something called a plastic surgeon, which seemed like it could be quite interesting, as some Wishlings apparently liked to alter their looks. That thought was quite foreign to Vega, because every Starling was innately proud of his or her unique appearance.

Katie grinned. "I hope Ella's mom comes in. I want to ask her where she gets her inspiration from."

"That's right," said another girl. "I mean, her designs are to die for. Ella always looks so good!"

Vega had a free period after lunch, so she headed to the library to wander through the stacks of those paper books Sage and Libby had told her about. She smiled when she stepped inside. The room had floor-to-ceiling windows and a balcony, and everywhere she looked were books, books, and more books, in all colors of the rainbow and all shapes and sizes. Some had hard covers and some had soft covers. Some had the sharp smell of a just-printed page and others had crumbly pages and the odor of history and decay. She wandered through the stacks, pulling out titles and leafing through them. She reached for an extra-large book, called *Guinness World Records*, and was staring with fascination at the picture on the cover—a photo of a man with hundreds of smoking sticks shoved into his mouth—when she looked up and realized that the empty space allowed her to see through the stack to the other side. And there stood Ella!

The girl was stock-still, her fingers crossed and her eyes screwed tightly shut. Could she be . . . could she be wishing? Vega's heart began to race. She whipped out her Star-Zap and pressed the holo-vid button. An actual Wisher in the act of wishing! Everyone would want to see this! "I'm going to try again," she heard Ella whisper. She screwed her eyes shut and crossed her fingers. "I wish this lie of mine would just go away!"

A sudden electric jolt ran through Vega and she dropped her Star-Zap with a clatter. "*Starf!*" she cried.

When Vega straightened up, her Star-Zap in hand, Ella was standing right next to her, glowering. "Were you *spying* on me?" she demanded.

Vega held out her hands to Ella. "Don't be mad at me," she implored. "I can help you! Just tell me—what do you wish you hadn't lied about?"

Ella stared at Vega, furious. "You want to know what I really wish?" she whispered harshly. "I wish that you would leave me alone. Do you think you can help me with that?"

CHAPTER
7

The entire rest of the day, Vega got the silent treatment from Ella. And everybody noticed.

Katie went up to Vega as they made their way to gym class. "What did you say to Ella?" she asked. "Whoa, you are totally getting frozen out."

That was a good way to describe it, Vega thought. There was a definite chill in the air anytime Ella was around. Vega didn't know what to do. Her Countdown Clock told her she had twenty-one starhours to grant the wish. She felt like a failure. She was definitely the first Star Darling whose Wisher wouldn't acknowledge her existence.

In the locker room, Vega was handed a uniform that was tight in the places it should have been baggy and baggy in the places it should have been tight.

"Oh, boy," Katie said when Vega walked into the gym. "That's unfortunate."

Vega shrugged. She had way bigger problems than an ill-fitting gym uniform. "Do you think we'll play lodgeball?" she asked Katie, remembering the game that Sage had told her about witnessing her Wisher play during her mission. "Maybe Ella and I will be on the same team."

Katie chortled. "Oh, Vega, you're so funny," she said. "And it's not just that ridiculous uniform. Lodgeball!" The gym teacher stood in front of the room, a whistle around her neck. "Today we start our lessons in square dancing," she announced.

Up went a chorus of groans, which the gym teacher ignored. "Square dancing is a type of folk dance," she went on. "Please break up into groups of eight and form a square, two partners on each side."

Katie grabbed Vega's hand and together they formed one side of a square. Vega noticed with disappointment that Ella positioned herself as far away from Vega as she could while still remaining in the gymnasium. She shook her head. How was she going to fix this?

Vega turned to Katie. "What's so bad about square dancing?" she asked.

"You'll see," replied Katie grimly.

But Vega didn't see. It turned out she absolutely loved square dancing. It might have been the orderly way everyone moved. It might have been the sheer novelty of it. Or it might have been the opportunity she had to promenade, do-si-do, and swing with seven different people. Because every time she promenaded, do-si-doed, swung her partner, or allemanded, she got to chat with someone else.

"So tell me about Ella," she said under her breath as she promenaded with a curly-headed girl named Grace.

"Oh, she's nice," Grace said. "She's got great style."

When Vega bowed to her side, she asked a blond girl, "Have you ever been to Ella's house?"

"Never," was the answer. "She never invites anyone over." She lowered her voice. "I think it must be because her mom has some secret designs lying around the house or something. The fashion industry can be cutthroat!"

"Now everybody swing," called the teacher, and Vega found out about every trend Ella had started as she linked arms and swung around with each dancer. Arm warmers. Cat-eye glasses. Two different-colored socks. Mismatched earrings. Paint-speckled shoes. "This," said a girl, holding up a necklace with a brightly painted key on it. "We all wear them now, just like Ella," she explained.

Just then a shiver went down Vega's spine and her skin began to tingle. It was subtle, but it had to be a sign, didn't it? She turned to grin at Ella, across the gym, who glowered back at her. Did she know Vega was talking about her? Vega was pretty sure she had figured out what Ella's lie was. Now she just had to talk to Ella and convince the other girl to let her help fix it. This was going to be a piece of pie. She smiled smugly, mentally congratulating herself for remembering the Wishling phrase that Sage had shared with everyone.

Back in the classroom, Vega received an unexpected opportunity from Ms. McKenney. "Class," the teacher announced, "I want you to pair up to do your writing homework tonight. Your assignment is to interview a classmate with these questions." She held up a sheaf of papers and began handing them out.

"Katie, you're paired with Ivy," she said. "Jill and Maya, please take turns interviewing each other."

Vega saw her chance. She closed her eyes and concentrated. This was going to take an awful lot of her wish energy reserve, so she hoped it would work.

"Ella, you are paired with . . . Lu . . . Lu . . . Lu . . ." She clearly wanted to say a particular name, but it wouldn't come out. "Vega," she finally said.

It had worked! The grin on Vega's face was as intense as Ella's grimace. Maybe even more so.

★

Vega leaned her back against the locker next to Ella's. Ella was aggressively shoving books into her backpack and trying to ignore Vega. But the Starling was fully determined to use this opportunity to her advantage.

"So shall we head to your house?" Vega suggested hopefully.

Ella looked up suddenly, and Vega saw a flash of something in her eyes—anger, or could it be panic? But the girl smoothly said, "Oh, they're polishing our marble entryway today. Let's go to your house instead."

Vega actually did panic. "I . . . um . . . my . . . can't," was all she managed to say.

Ella had the good grace not to laugh at Vega's awkwardness. "Okay then, let's go to the Munch Box," she said, narrowing her eyes at Vega. "Let's get this over with."

The two girls left the school in silence and headed down the steps together. Ella led Vega down the block to a friendly little coffee shop with cozy booths and a counter with funny round seats that appeared to be bolted to the floor. The two girls settled into a booth. Ella started rummaging through her bag. She pulled out a mirror, a wallet, and a small paperback book before she found what she was looking for—a notebook and a purple pen.

Vega stared at the book. "Is that a book of crosswords?" she asked excitedly.

"It is," said Ella. "I do them on the subway." Then she got a horrified look on her face and barked out a laugh. "That was a joke! As if I ever take the subway! I do it in the car when my driver takes me to school."

"What's the subway?" asked Vega. *Starf!* she thought. *Maybe she'll realize I'm not a Wishling!*

But Ella grinned and reached over to give her a friendly punch in the arm. "Right? Nobody who goes to George Robert Prep actually takes the subway!"

Ella picked up a menu and began flipping through it. "I'm getting a hot fudge sundae with chocolate ice cream," she said decidedly.

The menu was so thick and jam-packed with unfamiliar food choices that Vega didn't know where to begin. Chops! Specials! Breakfast served all day! What in the world was a jelly omelet? Or a gyro? Vega was totally overwhelmed, so she simply said, "Me too." She hoped she would like it.

Shortly afterward she discovered that she most certainly did. The sundae, a tantalizing mountain of round scoops of brown, slathered with a thick dark brown sauce, was placed in front of her. A fluffy crown of white and a bright red fruit with a stem sat on top. It looked amazing. Vega licked her lips in anticipation.

"Let's dig in," said Ella, brandishing a long spoon.

The sundae was simply perfection in a chilly metal cup—a lip-smackingly delicious combination of creamy, sweet coldness and warm goodness in every bite. The white fluffy cream was sweet and as light as air. Vega was in heaven. She made a mental note: *Bring a hot fudge sundae home for Tessa.*

While they ate, Vega pulled the list of questions out of her backpack. She gave the stuffed blue star keychain a squeeze for luck. "Do you mind if I go first?" she asked Ella.

"Shoot," said Ella.

"What?" asked Vega, totally confused.

Ella laughed. "Go ahead."

"What is your greatest joy?" Vega asked her.

Ella bit her lip and stared into space. "I guess it's

being creative," she said slowly. "Like I'll show up for school in paint-splattered shoes or two different-colored socks, and the day after, one girl is doing it, and then the next week it's five girls, and soon it's a trend in the entire school. Even the older girls are copying my style."

Vega wrote that all down. It was fun to write in a paper notebook with a writing utensil—very old-fashioned and extremely satisfying.

"What is your biggest dream for the future?" was the next question.

Vega looked up. Ella's cheeks were flushed and she looked excited. It was the first time Vega had seen her look relaxed and unguarded.

"I'm going to be a fashion designer," she said. "I'm going to create new fashions that no one has ever seen before. I'm going to come up with something people will be talking about forever, like the jumpsuit or the maxi dress."

"Just like your mom," said Vega.

Ella looked away. "Yeah, just like my mom."

"And last but not least, what is your biggest fear?"

Ella stared into the distance. She opened her mouth, then closed it. "Um, my biggest fear is that everyone . . ."

Vega leaned forward. "Yes?"

"That everyone . . ." she thought for a moment and frowned. "That everyone . . . um, won't like my fashions," she concluded.

"That's it?" asked Vega.

"That's it," Ella said firmly. "Now your turn."

Vega, with some creative thinking and some serious self-editing, was able to answer the questions. She spoke about her dream of being a top student and her love of puzzles of all kinds. And all of a sudden she found herself explaining that her biggest fear was not making her mother proud of her, after she had worked so hard to provide for Vega. She had never put those thoughts into words, and she grew teary as she said them. When she looked up, she saw that Ella looked a bit tearful, too.

The two girls smiled at each other. "That was great," said Ella. "I really learned a lot about you today."

"Me too," said Vega. "You're a really interesting person."

Ella checked her watch. "All right, well, I guess I had better go," she said reluctantly.

"Oh, is your driver waiting?" Vega asked.

Ella got a funny look on her face, then nodded. "Yes, my driver is waiting. That's right." She grabbed the key pendant that hung around her neck, as if she was checking that it was there.

It's now or never, Vega thought. "I know what your lie is," she blurted out.

Ella bit her lip. "You do?" She didn't look angry anymore, just sad and embarrassed.

"Your mom isn't really in Paris," Vega said.

Ella nodded. She looked ashamed but almost relieved.

"You don't want her to come in for Bring Your Parents to School Day because you don't want the other girls to pester her into making them fashions. You want to keep her creations all to yourself!" Vega concluded.

Ella stared at Vega, who sat back in the booth, feeling triumphant.

Then Ella stood up. "You couldn't have it any more wrong if you tried," she said. She threw some money on the table and stormed out of the coffee shop, the bell over the door tinkling cheerfully and adding a merry note to a decidedly unpleasant parting.

Vega watched her go, her heart sinking. She suddenly felt tired and cranky. She decided she would head to the school roof, where she would pitch her invisible tent. She glanced at her Star-Zap and accessed the Countdown Clock. Nineteen starhours and counting. *Starf!* She was running out of time. If she didn't have Ella's wish granted by the next day at noon, Leona wasn't going to be the only Star Darling who didn't collect any wish energy!

CHAPTER
8

"What are you doing here?" Vega asked.

When she had opened the flaps of her tent the next morning, she was shocked to see Clover standing at the edge of the roof, admiring the view.

Clover turned around, raised her eyebrow, and smirked at Vega. Her look said, *You know why I'm here.*

"I guess I already know," said Vega with a sigh. "My mission is dangerously close to failing?"

"Your mission is dangerously close to failing," confirmed Clover. She walked over to the tent, her arms folded tightly across her chest. "Spill it."

So Vega did.

"There's only one thing to do," said Clover. "You've got to find her, figure out what she actually *did* lie about, and fix it, all in"—she checked Vega's Countdown Clock—"four starhours."

"I think I can do it," said Vega. "I just need to get her alone. We started to have a connection yesterday. . . ."

"Well, let's find her right away," said Clover. "You just have to keep thinking. Is there a detail that you missed . . . a small clue that will help us figure it all out?"

The two girls left the roof and headed downstairs. They walked down the hallway to Ms. McKenney's classroom. When they got there, it was crowded with students and their parents, all of them buzzing with excitement. A doctor in a white lab coat was wheeling a human skeleton into the room. A book editor arrived with a stack of books to hand out. "Signed by the author!" bragged Luna.

"Hi, Vega," said Katie's dad. He took the stack of charts from under his arm and placed it on Katie's desk.

"This is going to be deadly," whispered Katie. "I can't watch!"

Vega grabbed her arm. "Where's Ella?" she asked.

"I overheard Ms. McKenney saying she wasn't coming in today," answered Katie. "I guess her mom didn't come back from Paris after all. What a disappointment."

Vega just stared at her. That was way more than a disappointment. That was a disaster!

Just then Callie and her mother rushed into the classroom. Callie's mom, who ran a modeling agency, was carrying a big shiny box filled with head shots. Callie looked repulsed. "You'll never believe it," she said. "We couldn't get a cab, so we had to take the *subway*."

"Ewwwww," said Lila. "My mother never lets me take the subway."

The subway . . . the subway . . . Why did that seem so familiar? All of a sudden Vega remembered her and Ella's words. "Is that a book of crosswords?" Vega had asked. And Ella had said, "It is. I do them on the subway."

And Ella's mom had not gone to Paris. . . . And the key she wore around her neck . . . It wasn't the latest trend in necklaces—it was her house key! Her distressed boots? Well, it was quite possible they were just old.

"Oh, my stars," said Vega. "I had it all wrong. It's so simple. I'm such an idiot."

Clover grinned and opened her mouth as if she was about to say something.

"Don't you dare agree with me!" said Vega.

Clover just smiled.

"I'll explain it all on the way to Ella's house," said Vega. "But first I've got to find out where she lives!"

All she had to say was "You forgot to tell me what Ella's address is," to the school secretary, who handed it right over, no questions asked. Oh . . . there was *one*. It was "Are they serving German chocolate cake in the cafeteria today?"

Clover laughed. "So it's true! We do smell like dessert!"

Vega looked down. Her wish energy was depleted. She stared at the address in her hand. There was no way around it. They were going to have to take the dreaded subway to get there.

★

"I don't know what everyone is freaking out about," said Clover as they sat in the subway car. The train rocked and shimmied as it sped through the underground tunnels.

"It gets you where you want to go pretty fast, it doesn't cost a lot, and it provides free entertainment," said Vega, listing the subway pros on her fingers. She pointed to a young man who had just finished playing his guitar and was walking through the car, offering people money from his hat.

"Thank you," she said, removing one Wishling dollar. That was certainly generous of him!

He had a funny look on his face, but then he laughed. "Um, you're welcome," he said.

"So spill the stars," said Clover, crossing her arms.

"I put it all together," said Vega. "She takes the subway. She lives outside the city. She said her mother was not in Paris. Katie told me that some students at George Robert aren't as wealthy as the others. Some kids get financial aid because the school costs so much. I'm pretty sure Ella's lie was that she told everyone that her mother is a successful fashion designer. I think maybe business isn't going very well and she doesn't want everyone to find out about it, because it would embarrass her mom."

The train emerged from the tunnel onto an elevated track.

Clover frowned. "You really think that's it? So what's her wish then?"

Vega thought hard for a moment. "She wishes that . . . she never said that about her mom?" Her brow furrowed. "But that's an impossible wish." She sighed. "This is all very confusing. I'm not sure how to fix this and time is running out." She looked down at her Star-Zap. "And this is our stop."

They exited the train car and found themselves on an open-air platform with a pretty mosaic sign. They headed downstairs, crossed a large boulevard, and headed straight down the block. There were fewer trees in that neighborhood and not as many flowers. Not as many people, either. Little Wishlings ran down the street and rode their tricycles while their caretakers watched, smiling.

Finally, they reached Ella's building—a solid brick fortress at the end of the block. Vega could see the tall skyscrapers of the city in the distance. Against the bright blue sky and soft fluffy clouds drifting by, it looked magical, like a fairy-tale city.

Vega used the last grains of her wish energy to push open the locked door. She and Clover rode the elevator in silence. They rang the buzzer for 6F.

No answer.

"I can't believe it!" said Vega. "Where is she? What are we going to do?"

The door swung open. Ella stood there, looking furious. "What are you doing here?" She looked at Clover. "And who is this?" she asked.

"This is my friend Clover," said Vega.

"Pleased to meet you," said Ella. "Nice boots."

"Thanks," said Clover, glancing down at her soft-brown fringed footwear.

Ella turned back to Vega, her mouth set in a thin, hard line. "Now get out of here," she said. "My mother is home. I don't want her to know what happened. She might think I'm embarrassed of her and that would kill me."

"I think I can help you," said Vega.

"No one can help me," retorted Ella. "I've gotten myself into this stupid mess and I don't know how to get out."

"You have to trust me," Vega said. "I'm here to help you." She smiled at Ella. "Sometimes when I'm feeling lost I say a special phrase to myself. I call it my mantra. And it helps me, it gives me strength. Do you want to say it with me?"

Ella rolled her eyes. But she gave a small smile and shrugged. "Sure," she said. "I've got nothing to lose."

Vega grasped Ella's hands in hers and recited her mantra: "You are the missing piece of the puzzle."

Ella gasped and stepped back. "How did you know?"

"I . . . um. . . ." Vega stammered. How did she know what?

Ella grabbed Vega's hand and pulled her inside the apartment. Clover was right behind her. The apartment was spotless, very cozy, and welcoming.

The small foyer had a tiny hand-painted table and a

mosaic-framed mirror. In the living room was a massive red-and-gold-striped couch, a festive rug, and an antique chandelier hanging from the ceiling. The hallway that led to the kitchen and bedrooms had a dining room table and a china cabinet filled with vintage china in many different patterns. The sunny kitchen had fun antique signs advertising SARSAPARILLA: 5 CENTS A GLASS and FRESH EGGS. Ella took the girls into her neat bedroom, which had a stunning view of the city skyline.

"What a lovely place," said Vega.

"Thanks," said Ella. "On weekends my mom and I go to flea markets and thrift stores. We love to decorate."

Then her face hardened. "I got myself into a real mess," she said. "When I first got the scholarship to the school I was excited, but a little nervous that I wouldn't fit in. But I decided I was going to just tell the truth. Then I met Katie and I really liked her. She asked what my parents did and I told her that my mother was a housekeeper for a famous fashion designer, and I guess Katie only heard the 'famous fashion designer' part. She told everyone, and I don't know, I guess I liked the way it sounded. People were suddenly really nice to me. And then instead of correcting them, I let it go."

Vega was confused. "Wait, so then who makes all your great clothes?"

Ella smiled and shrugged. And there in the corner was the answer—a sewing machine and a dress form with a half-made skirt on it.

"You really are the missing piece of the puzzle!" said Vega.

"Now you know," said Ella. "I take old castaway clothes that my mother's employer gives her and stuff I find at vintage stores and I redesign them into clothes for me." She shook her head. "The girls at school are going to be angry when they realize that the clothes they were gushing over aren't couture—just stuff I sewed together in my bedroom." She looked at the ground. "Now I'll be the laughingstock of the school."

"You've got it all wrong, Ella," said Vega. "The girls in school are going to be lining up to take lessons from you. It's going to make your lie go away."

"Really?" said Ella.

"Really," said Vega. "You just have to trust me."

CHAPTER
9

Vega had to convince the principal that George Robert Prep needed a forty-eighth club—Sewing and Fashion. She didn't want to do it the forceful way; she really wanted to convince the woman that it was a good idea, for Ella's sake. She told the principal the whole story, trying hard not to check her watch as she did it. There were mere starmins left.

"So all we need to do is borrow the PA system," said Vega. "Make a quick announcement. Two starm—I mean minutes, tops."

"This is highly irregular," said the principal. She sighed. "But I'll allow it." She headed back to her office. And as the door closed, Vega heard the principal ask her secretary, "Just who is that girl again?"

★

Ella cleared her throat. Her hand shook as she read the announcement that the three girls had cobbled together on the ride back to the city. "Hello, everyone. Ella Silverstone here. I have an exciting announcement to make. I know you all thought that my mother was the designer behind all my fashions, but it really was me!" She made a face like she was going to be sick, then soldiered on. "And guess what? I'm starting a new after-school club called Designing with Ella. We'll learn how to take old articles of clothing and transform them into fashions that are completely unique and one of a kind. I have room for twenty students and it is first come, first served. See you this afternoon in room 228."

She shut off the intercom. "First come, first served," she said with a shudder. "Why did I say that?"

The end-of-the-day bell rang and the three girls could hear the students running down the hallways, anxious to get outside. "Do you think anyone is going to show up?" Ella asked.

"I do," said Vega. *I hope*, she thought.

They stood, and Vega and Clover each picked up a box filled with old clothing and fabric scraps Ella had brought. Ella hoisted her sewing machine and they headed up the stairs.

The woman with the clipboard sat behind the table. She looked at them expectantly.

"We're going to Designing with Ella," said Vega.

"Never heard of it," said the woman.

"It's in room 228," said Ella. "It's a new club."

The woman waved them through.

Standing in front of the door, Ella took a deep breath. Then she opened the door.

"Oh," she said softly.

Vega peeked over her shoulder. The room was full of girls all eager to join Ella's club.

"Pick me, pick me!" a girl said. "I love fashion."

"Ella!" said another. "I loaned you my history notes last week, you owe me one!"

Ella looked around the room, a grin spreading across her face.

"Ella!" Luna shouted. "Is your mom coming today?"

Ella took a deep breath. "No," she said. "She isn't coming. I have to tell you the truth. My mom actually isn't a fashion designer. I made all the clothes myself."

Katie pushed to the front of the room. "Who cares?" she said. "That doesn't matter. All we want is to make clothes just like you."

"That's right!" said Luna. "So, am I in?"

Vega gasped as an incredible shower of multicolored sparkles rose from Ella and bounced around the room. She turned and caught Clover's shocked expression. "It's so beautiful!" she breathed. Ella's wish—for her lie to go away—had come true.

Ella turned to Vega and Clover. She looked stunned, tearful, and very happy, all at the same time. "Thank you," she said. "I can't believe it. My wish has come true."

"Believe it," said Vega.

Epilogue

Vega stood in front of Lady Stella's office door, collecting herself. She tried to make her face look serious, but she was so proud and so excited that it was impossible to stop smiling. Mindful of Leona's feelings, she managed to dim the wattage of her grin, at least a little bit. Nope, there it was again.

Her mission had not been easy. She had misinterpreted it and had a difficult time figuring it out. She had almost completely alienated her Wisher. She was especially grateful to Clover. She knew she wouldn't have collected the wish energy without her help.

Just as she raised her hand to knock on the door, she reached into her pocket and stole a glance at her

Star-Zap. The red star around the image of her mother's face was still there, a visible reminder of what a terrible daughter she had been. She resolved to call her mother on the way back to the dorm that evening. She'd make a plan for a visit home for certain.

Vega placed the Star-Zap back in her pocket, adjusted her collar, and knocked on the door. It slid open. The moment she stepped into the room, everyone jumped to their feet and started cheering. She stood there, grinning and feeling proud, slightly embarrassed, and totally wonderful. She'd had no idea that a standing ovation could feel quite so good. Even Leona was cheering.

When the excitement died down, Lady Stella called Vega forward and handed her the orb. It felt warm and substantial in her hand, and she liked the weight of it. It started to glow so brightly Vega wished she had on her safety starglasses. Then, before her eyes, it began to transform into a flower: first a stem sprouted; then the orb itself was surrounded with petals—deep blue giving way to icy blue. "It's a bluebubble," Vega breathed. "My favorite flower of all." Glowing points of light orbited the blossom. "The petals open and close so regularly you can use it to tell time," she told the others proudly.

Vega was even more delighted when her Power Crystal, a gorgeous queezle, emerged. It was stunning!

Sparkling crystalline blue nuggets were held together by their own internal magnetic force. Vega held it up and took a closer look. "Is it . . . is it Eleanor's Equation?" she asked Lady Stella in disbelief.

The headmistress nodded in affirmation. "Yes," she said. She turned to the others. "The nuggets may seem to be arranged chaotically," she explained. "But they actually represent a precise mathematical equation."

Lady Stella took the flower, which was beginning to transform into a Silver Blossom, and placed it on her desk.

Clover shook her head. "I was only there to help," she said. But Vega could tell that she was pleased.

To her chagrin, Vega noticed that Leona looked away and Ophelia gave her a quick, supportive hug. This couldn't be easy on her.

Just then Vega remembered something. She had made a quick stop at the diner just before she left for home. "Tessa, don't think I wasn't listening," she said. "I brought you back something chocolate—a hot fudge sundae!"

Tessa clapped her hands. "Startastic!" she said.

Vega reached into her backpack, pulled out the paper bag, and handed it to Tessa. Everyone oohed as it made a rustling sound. Licking her lips in anticipation, Tessa reached in and pulled out the container and a pink plastic spoon. Libby grabbed for it, admiring the color.

Tessa lifted the lid. "Ta-da!" she said.

Everyone stared at the sloppy brown mess inside.

"You brought me soup?" Tessa asked.

"Now you know," Lady Stella said with a tinkling laugh. "Wishling food . . . often requires refrigeration!"

Vega laughed. "Here's my last Wishworld observation—ice cream melts!"

Vega pressed the END HOLO-CALL button on her Star-Zap. Why wasn't her mother answering? Was she mad at Vega for taking so long to call back? That seemed very unlike her. But Vega still felt a tiny bit worried. Her mission had opened her eyes to a lot of things, including the importance of being proud of where you came from. She wanted to call her mom and hear her voice and tell her she loved her and was grateful for all the sacrifices she had made. Ella had helped Vega see all that, and she felt that the mission had been eye-opening for them both.

She yawned. She was so sleepy! Traveling to Wishworld and granting a Wisher's wish had certainly taken a lot of energy out of her! She didn't feel like moving her feet, so she willed the Cosmic Transporter to pick up the pace. The sooner she was under the covers, the better. It didn't work, of course.

It seemed like the slowest journey to her dorm room ever. Finally, she stood in front of her door and placed her hand on the scanner. "Welcome home, Vega," said the Bot-Bot voice. "And congratulations on a job well done!"

"Star salutations," Vega said automatically. She stepped inside the dark room and stopped in her tracks. She had been away only a couple of stardays, but she suddenly realized how homesick she had been. She placed her hand on her pride and joy—a large, beautiful secretary desk that had belonged to her great-grandmother on her mother's side. It had a curved top that rolled up and down like a dream (despite its age) and dozens of perfectly labeled drawers and nooks inside. Vega's mother told her that her great-grandmother had been just as organized and precise as she.

She placed her Star-Zap on top of the desk.

"You remind me so much of her sometimes," said someone with a familiar voice. Vega spun around. The room seemed empty. Was she hearing things?

She gasped as a figure stepped out of the shadows. Vega recognized who it was immediately and raced across the room, then fell into outstretched arms. She inhaled the comforting and oh-so-familiar smell of gossamer perfume, boingtree needles, and hospital disinfectant.

"Oh, Mama," she said. "I'm so happy to see you. But how . . ."

"Piper called me and suggested I come for a visit," she said. "And I'm so glad she did. I've missed you so much, starshine."

Tears filled Vega's eyes as she heard her childhood nickname. She concentrated her wish manipulation energy and the light switched on. She looked up and saw the tiny crinkles around her mother's violet eyes, the curve of her chin, her striking cheekbones. Her mother's thin, graceful hands, equally capable of holding a child's hand and lifting a heavy patient, stroked her blue hair. That was what Vega had been missing. The empty space she had been feeling was filled.

★

Vega lay in bed, content. Her mission had been a resounding success, both for her and for her Wisher. She and her mom had parted with big hugs and a plan to spend the upcoming holiday relaxing and playing games together. She sighed with happiness.

Just then her Star-Zap buzzed. She was so sleepy she

considered ignoring it, but her curiosity got the better of her and she reached out for it.

Sure it had been strange to have to say "Not much" when her mother had asked her what she had been up to lately. Only the most incredible adventure of her entire life, that's all! And it had been so tempting to brag (a little) about how she had saved her Wish Mission, just in the nick of time. To say nothing about the Wish Blossom and Power Crystal she had just received. It had been hard to dim the wattage of her huge smile when that happened, but she managed to tone it down a bit, for Leona's sake. Vega would have liked nothing better than to have been able to pull the Power Crystal out of her bag and show it to her mother. She sighed. Maybe someday . . . She pressed a button and a holo-text appeared in front of her.

She read it, read it again, and then gasped. Piper murmured in her sleep but didn't wake up. Vega read the holo-text again to make sure she wasn't mistaken. But there it was, clear as day: MEET ME IN THE HEDGE MAZE TOMORROW. WE NEED TO TALK. SCARLET.

Scarlet Discovers True Strength

Prologue

"So you're saying Vega heard from her?"

"Cross my stars. A holo-text. She got it last night."

"Well, what did it say? Where has she been this whole time? Is she in Starland City? Did she run away?"

Scarlet recognized the Star Darlings' voices outside her window immediately. She didn't have to peer down, but she did. She could also tell right away that they were talking about her. *How dare they?* was all she could think.

Scarlet was perched up in the loft of her dorm room—her *new* dorm room—a place that, these stardays, she seldom left. It had all happened so fast it still felt like yesterday: Lady Stella's informing her that her being assigned to the Star Darlings was all a "starmendous and most unfortunate" mistake, and that, as a result, she would need to be reassigned to a new dorm room so her replacement—some meek-looking orange-haired first-year student—could move into hers. At first, Scarlet had looked at that, at least, as the silver lining, since she and her roommate, Leona, had been bickering. But it didn't take long for her to realize that there would never, in a moonium staryears, be any silver linings to the cloud she had found herself in.

"It didn't say where Scarlet's been, unfortunately." That tinkly voice belonged to Cassie. Scarlet gazed down at the top of the first-year student's silver-white pigtailed head. She and her roommate, Sage, were walking along the path between their Little Dipper Dorm building and the Big Dipper Dorm, where third and fourth years, like Scarlet, lived. Scarlet couldn't help smiling as she thought how clueless they were; she was right there, just two floors above them, and they had no idea. "All the holo-text said," Cassie went on, "was for Vega to meet her in the hedge maze . . . which makes me wonder if Scarlet's still here at school. . . ."

Sage tossed her long lavender hair dramatically from one shoulder to the other, a habit that had always made Scarlet roll her eyes. "I don't know," Sage said. "If Scarlet was at school, don't you think she'd go to classes? I mean, she's already been kicked out of the Star Darlings. Does she want to get kicked out of school, too?"

Kicked out! She nearly leaned out to yell, "I was not *kicked out*!"

"She wasn't kicked out . . ." said Cassie.

Thank you! thought Scarlet. Cassie always had seemed a little smarter than the rest.

". . . exactly. I mean, she didn't do anything wrong."

"Mistakes happen, I guess," Sage said. She shrugged and re-tossed her hair.

Mistakes . . . thought Scarlet. *Mistakes?* Accidently using your roommate's toothlight was a *mistake*. Being told that you, in fact, weren't Star Darlings material? That wasn't a *mistake*. It was just plain wrong!

"I don't know. . . ." Below, Cassie slowed to a stop, pulling Sage with her. Their arms were linked, as Starling arms usually were when they walked together.

"What?" said Sage.

"It's just . . . so many strange things are going on. There's poor Leona . . . ruining her Wish Pendant and not getting a Power Crystal when her mission was otherwise such a success."

"Well, wasn't that her fault? She never used her special powers."

"I know . . . but to ruin your Wish Pendant?" Cassie shook her head.

Above, Scarlet nodded sympathetically. Leona's ruined Wish Pendant didn't come close, of course, to Scarlet's losing her place as a Star Darling, but it had to hurt.

"And then, of course, there are those flowers," Cassie went on. "Have you noticed, by the way, that we aren't fighting anymore?"

"Oh, Cassie!" A laugh bubbled out of Sage as she started to pull Cassie forward. "You and your conspiracy theories. You are too cute! Really, you are."

CHAPTER

1

"Hellooooo?"

Scarlet turned from the window at the sound of a reedy, shrill voice calling from below. She slid from the window seat and peered down the stairs. "Who's there?" she said cautiously, not sure she wanted to know.

As she started down the curving ladder, a Starling came into view. It was a woman—an old woman, Scarlet could tell immediately—grinning and bent over a crystal-tipped cane.

"Hello?" Scarlet said. Her eyes swept the room uneasily for a glimpse of her roommate, Mira. "Er, excuse me," she said, not finding her, "but how did you get in?" Usually, Scarlet was the one sneaking up on people, not the other way around. Plus, as far as she knew, the only way to open the door was by using the palm scanner outside. Then it had to approve you. So how did the woman get in? "Er . . . can I help you?"

The little old Starling craned her neck to peer up at Scarlet. "Why, hello, and star salutations, dearie," she said sweetly. Her voice cracked with age. Wire-rimmed star-shaped glasses rested halfway down her nose, and silvery lilac curls framed her pinched but pleasant face. "As a matter of fact, you can. I'm looking for my granddaughter, Mira. The Bot-Bot guard at the front told me this was her room?"

"Oh . . ." That made a little more sense. Scarlet guessed family members' hands must work on the palm scanners, too. Not that she would know. After two and a half staryears at Starling Academy, her own family had still never visited her, not once. The only time Scarlet saw her parents was when she met them on tour. They were classical musicians and composers, famous throughout Starland for their otherworldly sounds and scores. Scarlet's mother played the halo-harp, her father the violin, and they traveled staryear-round throughout Starland, recording holo-albums and selling out the most prestigious concert halls. Even when they played in

Starland City, Starland's capital and the home of Starling Academy, rehearsals and interviews kept them so busy that Scarlet always had to go to them. Their schedules were simply too full to fit in a visit to the school.

Growing up, Scarlet had toured Starland with her parents, living out of suitcases, staying in five-star hotels. In between shows, her mother or father—depending on whose turn it was—would tutor her backstage as they tuned their precious instruments. By the time she had reached the Age of Fulfillment, Scarlet had met every dignitary on Starland—but not many other kids.

Scarlet's parents were naturally proud and not surprised when she showed an interest in music. They were astonished, however, when she chose to play the *drums* and began to wear a lot of black. At first, she'd just wanted to shock and annoy them and rebel against their stodgy ways. And she succeeded—particularly when she started adding black streaks to her hot-pink hair. Soon, though, she found herself loving the drums and her adopted color, too. Both made her feel strong. Both let her show her feelings without having to say a single word.

Still, Scarlet needed more. She needed a life that was truly her own, which was why she had applied to Starling Academy. She was stunned when she got in and sure she would struggle in her classes, but she found they were easy for her. The only things that were hard were fitting in and making friends.

"What's the matter, dearie?" The elder Starling chuckled. "Glowfur got your tongue?"

"Oh . . . star apologies," Scarlet said quickly. She was suddenly aware that she probably seemed rude. "Uh, yes. Yes, this is Mira's room. But, well . . ." She looked around and shrugged. "She's not here."

"Oh, what a pity!" The woman's face folded into a pained expression, like one of those comedy/tragedy masks that hung over Mira's bed. She sighed and shook her head slowly. "Well. I suppose I'll just wait for her, then. I should have told her I was coming. Hopefully she won't be long." She shuffled across the room, smiling sweetly and looking ever so slightly confused. "Please do forgive me for surprising you. I didn't realize she had a roommate, you see. I could have sworn the last time she wrote to me she said she lived alone."

"She did," said Scarlet. "I just moved in." She tried to sound less bitter than she felt.

"Ah, good!" said the old woman. "Glad to know I wasn't wrong." She tapped her head just above her ear. "Two thousand and three and still sharp as a prism. So what's your name, my dear?"

"It's, um, Scarlet."

"Scarlet! How lovely! We had a glowsow on the farm with that name when I was a girl. So!" She crossed the star-trimmed corners of her shawl. "Just moved in, you say. Does that mean you're new?"

"No, ma'am . . ." Scarlet shook her head and turned back to her loft, longing to climb back up. She was usually so glad her new roommate, Mira, was always at "play rehearsal," or whatever that drama stuff she loved so much was. For once, though, Scarlet wished she would hurry back to their room so her grandmother would have someone else to talk to.

The old woman, meanwhile, settled onto the bench in front of Mira's dressing table with a frail yet eager sigh. She took a moment to catch her breath and take in Scarlet's side of the wide, softly lit room. Her eyes lingered on the hot-pink drum set perched on a raised platform across from Scarlet's black-and-fuschia-covered bed. Scarlet's things had been moved for her the same starday Lady Stella had broken the news. When her Star-Zap finally led her to her newly assigned room on the other side of the Big Dipper Dorm, it wasn't clear who was more put out: Mira, who'd been quite content having a single, or Scarlet herself.

"Are those drums?" asked the old woman, pointing.

Scarlet nodded. What else would they be?

"Ooh! What fun! Can I try them?" She was already out of her seat. She hobbled over to the platform, raised her cane, and gave the cymbal a powerful smack.

CRASHHH!

"Don't! *Stop!*" Scarlet cried, hurrying over. "I mean, I'd rather you didn't, um, please." Scarlet didn't want to be rude, but nobody—not even a little old Starling—was touching her precious drums. "Maybe you'd be more comfortable waiting for Mira in the Illumination Library. I'm sure a Bot-Bot guide could show you the way."

"Oh, starry nights, no." The old woman grinned and set her cane back on the polished star-studded floor. "I'm just as comfortable as can be. Where is my lovely granddaughter, though, do you know? I'm just as eager to see her as I can be."

Scarlet didn't know, though she wanted to be helpful. If Mira had ever said anything to her about where she was going, Scarlet was too focused on her Star Darlings problem to care. Besides, Scarlet preferred for other Starlings to keep their noses out of her business, so she tried to set an example by keeping her nose to herself, too.

"I'm not sure . . . maybe play rehearsal?"

"Oh, yes, you're right, I'm sure!" crowed the old woman. "That Mira is quite an actor! Destined for stardom! Don't you think?"

"Is she? I don't know," Scarlet confessed. "I've never seen her act." Since leaving her parents to attend Starling Academy, she'd tried to steer clear of theaters and auditoriums. Quite frankly, she also had yet to see the appeal in running around, dressed up like a fool, pretending to be somebody else.

"Moon and stars!" Mira's grandmother gasped. "Never? What a shame. Oh, but surely you've seen her act *sometime*. . . ."

Scarlet shook her head. "Star apologies. No."

"Never?" The old woman leaned forward, twisting slightly. The corners of her mouth twitched, one at a time. A bluish star-shaped freckle on her cheek began to sparkle. Scarlet watched it closely, the familiarity clicking at last. How hadn't she noticed it before?

"All right, I'll admit it." Scarlet sighed to hold back a groan. "I saw her once."

"Really? You did see her? When?"

"The Time of Shadows production. Our first year at school."

"Oh, that was a good one!"

Scarlet stifled a smile as she clicked her tongue and slowly shook her head.

"It wasn't?" The woman's blue eyes grew round. "You really don't think so? Why not?"

"Well, some parts were good . . . like the scenery. . . . And the props could have been worse."

"What about the acting?" croaked the old woman.

Scarlet looked down and smiled.

"*Well?*" Mira's "grandmother" waited, tapping her cane against the floor, sending sparks into the air. "Wasn't it good? Of course it was! We got a standing ovation at the end!"

"*We?*" Scarlet glanced back up, raising one eyebrow in a sharp arch.

The old woman threw back her head. "*Starf!* You knew it was me!" she groaned. Then she laughed and tossed off her shawl so it dangled behind her. "Tell me I had you going there for a while, though," Mira said as she pulled off her wig. Her long indigo hair spilled down her back in shimmering waves. Beneath a thick layer of stage makeup, a whole galaxy of bright blue freckles flashed like sunlight on a lake.

"For a starmin," muttered Scarlet. She did have to live with her, after all.

"Really? Is that all?" Mira sighed. "Sunspots. I guess that's why you're not in that remedial group any-more." She grinned at Scarlet—then blanched in the heat of Scarlet's simmering glare. "No offense!" she said quickly. Like everyone at Starling Academy, it seemed, Mira assumed the special class the Star Darlings went to last period was for extra help so they didn't fail out of school. "Star apologies. I just thought . . . you know . . . since it was a mistake and all . . ."

"It was a mistake, all right," hissed Scarlet.

"Are you mad?"

Am I mad? thought Scarlet. Did a glowfur eat Green Globules? She was mad, all right. Madder than Leona when she'd had to try out for her own band!

Suddenly, Scarlet's Star-Zap beeped. A holo-text was coming in.

She read it: IN THE HEDGE MAZE. R U STILL COMING?

It was Vega, waiting to meet.

"Forget about it. I'll be fine," Scarlet snapped as she climbed off her bed.

She'd be perfectly *startacular* . . . just as soon as she set everything straight again.

CHAPTER
2

Scarlet burst out of the Big Dipper Dorm and hopped onto the Cosmic transporter. She passed the dancing fountain as she headed to the hedge maze, ignoring the water's friendly wave. She knew all too well that once encouraged, the fountain would only work harder to try to keep a Starling there.

The campus was quiet, as it often was after dinner, when most students flocked to the Lightning Lounge. That was a place, though, that Scarlet usually avoided. Everyone was far too sociable and eager to hang out and chat. One couldn't even lie back and gaze at the stars from underneath the retractable roof without some shiny Starling leaning over and saying, "Ooh! Aren't they pretty?" or "Do you think they look the same from Wishworld?" Scarlet's jaw ached from holding back rude responses, like "*No*, they look like globerbeems from Wishworld. What a startacularly silly question! Of course they look the same!"

Scarlet didn't care much for the hedge maze, either—for a different reason. The hedge maze drove her crazy, the way its pattern constantly changed. No sooner would she think she'd found a way out than a path would turn, a wall would shift, or a leafy new hedge would suddenly appear. Where the fun in *that* was, Scarlet had no idea. She thanked her stars for the single red blossom in every hedge wall that would open a door when plucked. She plucked one every time. Vega, on the other hand, would never have dreamed of doing such a thing. She loved the maze and spent more time there than all the other Star Darlings combined, so it was the best place Scarlet could think of to get a few words with her—alone.

Even before she spotted Vega, Scarlet saw her sapphire aura. The constantly changing maze, however, made actually reaching her hard.

"Vega!" Scarlet finally shouted through the glittery hedge wall. "I'm over here! Come! Hurry up!"

Vega was beside her in a starsec, only slightly out of breath.

"How did you get here so fast?" asked Scarlet as a new wall of hedge popped up behind Vega.

"Easy," Vega said. "I waited for the hedge to shift left, then ran south ten degrees, then doubled back through the—"

Scarlet held up her hands. "That's all right. Never mind. I don't care." At the same time, though, it was exactly this love of puzzle solving that gave Scarlet hope that Vega could help.

"So what did you want to talk about—*finally*? It's good to see you, by the way. Where in the universe have you *been*? We've been worried about you for star-days. So . . . did you want to hear about my mission?" Vega smiled proudly, ignoring Scarlet's immediate sneer. "You'll be happy to know that—unlike Leona's . . ." Vega sighed. "Poor thing. Anyway, unlike Leona's mission, mine was a *great* success. Another Power Crystal collected! Not that I didn't have a little issue—but everyone does, it seems. I found my Wisher fairly easily. It's the wish *identifying* that's so tricky. I know they always tell us that, but you don't really know until you try. Luckily, Clover came down and helped me figure it out in plenty of time. It was actually quite an interesting wish. . . ." She paused, finally noticing Scarlet's pained expression.

"Really, Vega? Do you truly think I wanted to meet to hear all about a Star Darlings mission when I can't go on one anymore?" Scarlet shook her head and her black hair swung back and forth across her eyes. "I thought you were smarter than that. That's about the *last* thing I want to talk about."

"Of course!" said Vega. "What was I thinking? Star apologies." She reached out to pat Scarlet's shoulder, but Scarlet shrank away. "So then . . . what is it? Oh!" Vega nodded. "It's the *band*! You want to come back. That's startastic!" She clapped. "We need you! We really do! Clover was filling in, but she couldn't take Leona anymore. Not that *you* should worry about her. Yes, she's mad that you dropped out, but she also knows what a starmendous drummer you are."

"Freakin' fireballs," Scarlet groaned. "The band is the *second*-to-last thing on my mind!" Sure, she missed the band—well, she missed playing the drums—but she definitely wasn't ready to go back to it, and she wasn't sure she ever would be. Of course Vega, who played the bass, was fine. And Sage and Libby were okay, too. Sage wasn't the best guitarist, but she had good instincts and worked to improve. Libby tried way too hard to make everyone happy, in Scarlet's opinion, but she was

startastic on the keytar. It was Leona who drove everyone crazy by bossing them around. Frankly, Scarlet was
surprised she didn't try to play every instrument herself.

"Then *what*?" said Vega. Under her bangs her forehead wrinkled. For Vega, the only feeling worse than
having the incorrect answer was not having an answer
at all.

"Something's wrong. Very wrong," said Scarlet.

"Ah." Vega nodded. "I see. I know. You're right. It's
so unfair. It really is. And I'd feel exactly the same if I
were you, I'm sure."

"What? *No!*" Scarlet scooted out from under Vega's
hand again. "I mean, yes. It's unfair. Of course. But
it's unfair because it's a huge mistake. That new girl—
Ophelia, or whatever her name is—should never have
been picked to take my place!"

"You don't think so?"

"I do not!"

Vega sighed and crossed her arms. "Truth be told,
you could be right. I've been wondering about her
myself."

"You have?"

Vega nodded. "She's so far behind in Star Darlings
class—which made sense in the beginning. No one

expected her to know anything yet. But she's just not catching up. Do you know she still can't manipulate a watt of energy? Not a single watt! Ooh!" She suddenly jumped as a branch reached out to tickle her ribs. "Come on, we should keep moving," she told Scarlet. "The maze doesn't like it when you stop."

Vega moved to link her arm with Scarlet's. But Scarlet had never been the touchy-feely, arm-linking, hand-holding type. Instead, she put her hands behind her back as they moved along the ever-twisting starlit path.

"You know," said Vega, sensing Scarlet's impatience with their route, "if you just focus and look for a pattern, you have a much better chance of making it out. It's when you try to fight it that you end up feeling trapped."

"Whatever," said Scarlet. "Just get me out of here."

So Vega linked arms with Scarlet (despite her protests) and they quickly made their way out of the maze.

"Star apologies," said Scarlet, "but I just can't play peekaboo with a bush and think at the same time. You're good at solving puzzles, Vega. I've never had patience for them. So think: why would someone so new and totally unprepared to grant wishes be picked to take my place when my wish-granting potential's so starmendously high?"

"You're right. I do like puzzles . . ." said Vega. "At the same time, though, this was Lady Stella's decision, and we have to trust her, don't you think? Still . . ." She paused. "It is strange." Scarlet could sense that an idea was being born in Vega's mind. "And if you talked to Cassie, she'd tell you that's not the only strange thing going on."

"I know," said Scarlet.

"You do?"

Scarlet shrugged and scowled. "I might have . . . overheard her . . . talking about me, and Leona's Wish Pendant."

"And the whole flower thing?" Vega's bright blue eyebrows shot up.

"She did say something about flowers . . . but I didn't actually get that part. What flowers was she talking about?"

"The bouquets," said Vega. "You know. The ones we all—all the Star Darlings, I mean—had delivered to our rooms?"

"Oh, those." Scarlet nodded. She did remember, though she hadn't thought it strange at the time. "So you still don't know who they're from?"

"No," Vega said, "but that's not even it. Cassie has this crazy idea that they were making us fight with each other over the littlest things. In fact, she's so sure, she took my bouquet to the botany lab to be evaluated. She'd already thrown hers and Sage's away."

"What do *you* think?" Scarlet asked. "Do you think Cassie might be right?"

Vega smoothed her hair back. "No, I don't. In fact, we made a bet. If I was right, she would do a puzzle with me every day for a double starweek."

"And if she was right?"

"I'd help her study for her Astral Accounting test."

Scarlet frowned.

Vega winked. "I know. Win-win. But I'm not too concerned about helping her study. Piper's still annoying me as much as ever. She makes these sounds when she's meditating. . . ." Vega closed her eyes and cringed. "Ugh! I can hear them all the way from upstairs in her part of the room. It sounds like a Bot-Bot on the fritz. Like this high, whiny *ohmmmm*." She winced. "How about you and Leona?" she asked Scarlet. "How were you getting along? Before you switched rooms, I mean."

"Oh, I don't know. Leona and I had our testy moments. . . ." Scarlet shrugged. "But I'm sure we would have anyway. So what did the botany lab say?"

"Nothing . . . *yet*. But we should probably hear soon."

"Promise to tell me when you do."

Vega drew an X over her heart. "Cross my stars—and moons. But . . . how? I mean, when will I see you again? Where have you been all this time?"

"I've been . . . around," said Scarlet vaguely. "They gave me a new roommate. Her name's Mira."

"I don't know her," said Vega.

"Neither did I."

"Is she nice?"

"She's fine," said Scarlet. "We don't really know each other yet. She isn't around that much, and I pretty much stay in my loft all the time, so maybe we never will. . . ."

"Have you been to any classes since . . ."

"No," said Scarlet bitterly.

"Don't you think you should?" Vega gently asked. "I mean, I can understand dropping out of Leona's band. No one—well, except Leona maybe—blames you for that. But even if you're not in the Star Darlings anymore, you're still a student at the school, and you can still go to Wishworld and grant wishes one day . . . but only if you graduate, of course."

Scarlet looked over her shoulder, past the hedge maze, toward the majestic Crystal Mountains, which glimmered across Luminous Lake. Vega was right, she guessed. Not that Scarlet was worried about falling behind in any subjects. Her classes seemed to get easier for her every year. But hiding from everyone and everything, while it made life simpler right then, wasn't helping her solve her problem, either.

"You can't hide forever," Vega went on, almost as if she'd peeked into Scarlet's mind. "How about I make you a deal like I made with Cassie?"

"I don't make deals," muttered Scarlet. "But what?"

"You start going to your classes, and I'll do whatever I can to help you get to the bottom of what went wrong."

CHAPTER
3

The next day, Scarlet went through the motions of going to morning assembly, classes, meals . . . all the things she was *supposed* to do. But the more she tried to act like everything was normal, the surer she was that everything was wrong.

She didn't even try to move all the desks in Wishful Thinking class, and yet with a single eyebrow raise she did exactly that. She was just as surprised as everyone else when it happened but was determined as always not to let her emotions show.

Even Professor Dolores Raye's mouth fell open. "Who did that?" she gasped.

In the far corner of the room, Scarlet slowly raised her hand.

"Oh, my stars!" said Professor Raye. "I didn't even see you back there, Scarlet. Welcome back to class, by the way. I must say, I've never seen such control in a third year. Those are very special powers. Er . . . now, if you don't mind, would you be so kind as to move the desks back to where they were?"

This only confirmed something Scarlet had already begun to sense: somehow, instead of feeling less special since leaving the Star Darlings, she felt as if her wish energy powers were stronger than ever before.

At lunch, Scarlet managed to sit by herself: no small feat in the Celestial Café. The tables were large and round and designed to encourage Starlings to linger and talk for starhours. Scarlet sequestered herself at an empty corner table, where she promptly spilled her mug of Zing. "Forget it," she told the Bot-Bot waiter who appeared instantly with another as the puddle disappeared. Instead, she ordered a steaming bowl of stewed garble greens—the smell of which was guaranteed to keep other Starlings far away.

Rather than eating, though—she *hated* garble greens— Scarlet observed the Star Darlings from afar. They sat together, as they had since they'd been summoned, at the middle table near the window overlooking Luminous Lake. Astra was dressed in her neon-trimmed fiery-red star ball uniform. It could have been a game day or not. With her, you never knew. Cassie was nose-deep in a holo-book, and Gemma was giggling and prattling away. Listening to Gemma was one thing Scarlet did not miss in the least.

Vega noticed her and waved so that the others couldn't see. She flashed Scarlet a sparkly smile of friendly encouragement, which Scarlet accepted reluctantly.

As she watched them all, Scarlet couldn't help remembering what Vega had told her in the maze about roommates bickering. And, indeed, they were. If they weren't barking at or arguing with each other, they were sitting far enough apart that they didn't have to talk. Cassie and Sage were the only roommates who appeared to be enjoying each other's company—and Leona and Ophelia, who were sharing a glimmerberry shake.

What a dud, thought Scarlet as she studied Ophelia. There was nothing at all best or brightest or star-charmed about her—at least from what Scarlet could see. While the Starlings around her radiated confidence, brilliance, and power, Ophelia gave off an awkward, muddled aura of confusion and fear.

So why was she there instead of Scarlet? Instead of *anyone*, really . . . but especially Scarlet.

Scarlet remembered the explanation Lady Stella had given when the headmistress had delivered the shocking news.

"I'm truly sorry, Scarlet. Star apologies don't begin to express how I feel. But accidents happen, even on Starland, and I'm afraid one has occurred here. As you know, I chose the twelve Star Darlings myself, using an intricate algorithm comprising numerous factors, including grades and test scores and energy records."

"Yes?" Scarlet had said. She could tell something grave was coming, but she had no idea what on Starland it could be.

"Naturally, great care was taken with the data, and yet . . . somehow, somewhere, a glitch occurred along the way . . . and your name, most unfortunately, was given to me in error."

"I don't understand . . ." Scarlet had whispered with what little breath she could find in her chest.

"I must say, I don't, either. And yet the holo-records Lady Cordial has shown me are as clear as the night sky. Your scores and those of another Starling, Ophelia, were mixed up in the holo-files. Therefore, *she* is the right-ful twelfth Star Darling—something you, Scarlet, were never truly meant to be."

Naturally, Scarlet had argued—vehemently. But the energy had been spent in vain. She left Lady Stella's office stinging, as if a hive of angry glitterbees had attacked her, and the feeling still hadn't gone away. The black hole Scarlet had felt in her stomach at that moment was still there, just as deep. In fact, sitting in the Celestial Café, watching Ophelia in her place among the other Star Darlings, only made the feeling worse. Scarlet knew her grades and scores were strong, so the whole thing already made no sense. But in what crazy parallel universe could a starling such as Ophelia have one score higher than Scarlet's, let alone a whole file's worth?

Scarlet blinked and slid her now cold bowl of garble greens across the table before standing up and leaving the café. She had Lighterature next period, but she didn't care. The thought of sitting in a class full of happy, care-free Starlings made her want to zap something. Besides, they were reading a tragedy by Shakestar that she had read hydrongs of times—*Romea and Jupiter.* The whole star-crossed romance thing made her want to hurl. So when she left the Celestial Café, she turned away from Halo Hall and headed across the Star Quad, straight back to the Big Dipper Dorm.

The building was empty except for the Bot-Bot guard inside the front door. "Star greetings, Scarlet," it welcomed her.

"Star greetings," she muttered back.

Scarlet stepped onto the Cosmic Transporter as it rolled through the halls.

Outside her door, Scarlet placed her hand on the palm scanner. The door opened with a gentle *whoosh*. As she walked in, the door slid smoothly closed. Scarlet scrunched her eyes to dim the lights and gazed around the room. Her eyes fell on her drum kit on its platform. *Yes!* That was just what she needed to do! Bang out a few dark and angry riffs . . . or maybe a few hydrong.

Scarlet hadn't played the drums much at all since she'd left the Star Darlings. Before that, she'd played hours every day—either with Leona's band or in their old room while Leona sang. They found it was the one thing they could do together without getting on each other's nerves. As soon as Lady Stella told her she was out of the Star Darlings, however, Scarlet stopped going to band practice, too. Every other member was still a Star Darling, and the last thing she needed was to hear them talk about their missions—or deal with their pity or, worse, their phony good cheer. The only place she could play was her room, but lately the inspiration just hadn't been there.

That day, she felt different, though. The drums seemed to be calling to her. She grabbed her sticks and climbed the platform and sat down. She waited a moogle for the stool to adjust itself beneath her, then gave her bass drum pedal three fierce stomps: *BAM! BAM! BAM!* The energy in the room flickered and rolled away from the star-shaped drum pad in powerful glittery waves. Scarlet smiled and whacked the cymbals—*CRASH! BANG!*—one at a time. She did it again . . . and again . . . and again . . . and again. *CRASH! BANG! CRASH! BANG-A-DEE-BANG! CRASH! BANG! CRASH! BANG-A-DEE! BANG-A-DEE! BOOM!*

With her eyes closed, she let her arms fly in a series of rolls and riffs, wherever they wanted to go. If her eyes had been open, she would have seen the energy aura surrounding her glow brighter and brighter pink. But the light grew so blinding she would have soon had to close them again.

Scarlet had never played her drums so hard before or felt so energized. All her frustration, her bitterness, her confusion dissolved with every beat. Finally, after what felt like a moogle but could have been a staryear, Scarlet had to stop. Exhausted, she let go of her drumsticks and let them twirl in the air above the tom-tom while her head fell back. As her eyes opened, she let out a gasp at the dazzling sight of pure sparkling energy pulsing throughout the room.

Did I do that? Scarlet wondered. There was no other source she could see.

Gradually, the energy faded, but Scarlet's clarity did not. From the beginning, she had suspected there was something not right about Ophelia's replacing her. Now she was sure. And if *she* didn't get to the bottom of it, who else on Starland would? Maybe Vega could help her. But maybe not. Who knew? *And why wait to see,* Scarlet thought as her eyes fell on her roommate's jam-packed costume closet, *when I have all I need to do it on my own?*

CHAPTER
4

The door to Scarlet's dorm room slid open and a small, distinguished-looking man stepped into the hall. He wore a long silver topcoat with a wide forest-green collar and half-moon-shaped buttons as big as ears. His own ears were covered by a burnt-orange fedora tilted so far forward it concealed his face. The only feature not hidden, in fact, was the very tip of his emerald beard. Pausing, he stroked the bright green whiskers as his head swiveled right and left. Satisfied that the hall was empty, he raised a star-studded shiny black combat boot and boarded the Cosmic Transporter as it rolled past him.

Scarlet hoped her disguise (courtesy of her room-mate's closet) was convincing. The first test was the Bot-Bot guard at the front door.

She brushed past it, keeping her head down and her velvet collar up.

"Star greetings, Scarlet," the Bot-Bot guard said cheerfully.

Scarlet sighed. "Star greetings," she mumbled without turning. Bot-Bot guards were a useless gauge, she guessed. They could read an aura a floozel away. Hopefully, the Starling adults where she was going would be easier to trick.

Once outside, Scarlet headed directly for the enormous star-shaped building between the hedge maze and the Celestial Café. Although it wasn't geographically at the center of campus, it was the hub in every other way. Halo Hall, as it was called, housed all the Starling Academy classrooms, as well as the Astral Auditorium, where assemblies and performances were held. In the hall, too, were various offices, including that of Lady Stella, the headmistress. Its most spectacular feature was the gleaming lone white tower attached to the Wish-House. At the very top sat the Wishworld Surveillance Deck, the platform where Starlings could observe

Wishworld and its Wishlings through telescopes and where they waited to catch a shooting star when their day for a Wish Mission came at last.

Normally, a Starling walked up the white starmarble stairs and entered through the front doors. Since this starday was far from normal, however, Scarlet hurried around the Bot-Bot guard at the front and made her way into Halo Hall through the back. After all, she wasn't going to some old class in Stellation four or five. She was on a mission to right what was wrong.

If only she knew exactly where she needed to go.

As far as offices went, Scarlet was familiar with only two: that of the perky guidance counselor, Lady Solara, who had made it her mission to "light Scarlet up," and Lady Stella's. Both were offices Scarlet hoped to stay well clear of, since she didn't want to see either administrator just then. Fortunately, they were clustered with other faculty offices in Stellation one and she was fairly certain that the office she was looking for was in Stellation two . . . or maybe three.

She decided to try the second wing first, since it was closest. Like every hall, its walls and floor were made of gleaming rainbow-hued starmarble. In that wing, they gave off a pink-tinged glow. Up near the ceiling ran a series of windows, letting light from outside shine in.

Scarlet hurried down the hall, passing door after door. As she did, she lifted her hat brim ever so slightly to read the holo-signs outside of each.

SUPPLY ROOM, read one star-shaped plaque. STAR-ZAP REPAIR AND MAINTENANCE, announced the next, followed by TECHNOLOGY, SWIFT-TRANSPORTATION SERVICES, and WISH ENERGY MANAGEMENT. Then Scarlet read the holo-sign by the door at the end: BOT-BOT SECURITY.

Freakin' fireballs, she thought. *Security! Time to turn around!*

Heart thumping, she scurried back down the hall and rounded the corner into the safety, she hoped, of Stellation three. *Please let me find what I'm looking for here*, she wished.

That hall looked basically the same, except the glow given off by the marble walls was a bit aquamarine. These doors, too, had holo-signs, and Scarlet read the first one on her right: ADMISSIONS. Lady Cordial's office. Of course. Scarlet remembered it now from her own Time of Applying, when she had first visited the school. She'd come alone, since her parents had been on tour and unable to take the time off. Lady Cordial, the head of admissions, had been pleasant in their interview but not as welcoming as one might have hoped—especially one with test scores such as Scarlet's, which were practically off the charts.

But that was Lady Cordial, Scarlet now realized: stiff and skittish and often at a loss for words. Scarlet had eventually learned, like every Starling Academy student, not to take things too personally with her.

On the other hand, Scarlet's next interview with Lady Stella had been one of the best starhours of her whole life. There was something about the headmistress that made every Starling feel as if she'd known her for staryears. Scarlet had already *thought* she wanted to go to Starling Academy, but meeting Lady Stella had sealed the deal. The headmistress didn't care if Scarlet didn't like rainbows as much as rain clouds or loved the most unloved of Starling colors—black. She seemed to know, too, that Scarlet wasn't half as interested in learning to grant wishes as she was in living on her own. And yet she welcomed Scarlet into Starling Academy with warm and open arms. Lady Stella had always seen Scarlet for who she was and admired her for being herself, which only made Scarlet feel worse about having to leave the Star Darlings—and more determined to get back in.

With that in mind, she moved on, shifting her hat to continue reading each star-shaped sign.

ATTENDANCE, ACCOUNTING, ALUMNI RELATIONS, STUDENT LIFE, FACULTY LOUNGE . . .

"'Faculty lounge'?" *Hmmm.* Scarlet paused. So *this*

was where their professors hung out when they weren't teaching the finer points of Wishful Thinking or giving a pop quiz on wish identification. She could only imagine what they did in there. Compare lesson plans? Share grading tips? Complain about students, such as Scarlet, who liked to bark out answers instead of politely raising their hands? She pictured them gathered around a table, sharing sighs and cups of Zing.

"Are you going in?"

Scarlet froze.

The person behind her spoke again. "Star apologies. I don't mean to rush you." A hand reached over Scarlet's shoulder to cover the scanner in the middle of the door. "It's just, well, my class ran a few moogles over and I'm late for my massage."

The scanner glowed bright blue. "Welcome, Professor Nicola Cecelia," a Bot-Bot voice greeted the teacher—her Astral Accounting teacher, Scarlet realized—as the door to the faculty lounge opened wide.

Starf! thought Scarlet as her eyes took in the scene. She was careful to keep her hat low, but she could still make out much of the room—everything from the frozen cocomoon yogurt bar to the manicure/pedicure stations to the hot tub *and* swimming pool! Most classes were still in session, so the lounge was far from full.

Nevertheless, there were plenty of teachers already enjoying themselves. Professor Elara Ursa, the Wishers 101 teacher, was having her hair done by a Bot-Bot stylist as she read a holo-magazine. Professor Eugenia Bright, meanwhile, was playing a rather intense spark-filled game of star-pong with Professor Dolores Raye. Giggles spilled out of a holo–photo booth, but Scarlet couldn't see who was inside. She sniffed. Was that zoomberry trifle she smelled? She sniffed again. *Mmm* . . . yes, it was . . . and glorange meringue pie, as well. Scarlet's mouth was already watering by the time her eyes found the buffet.

"Come on in!" By now, Professor Nicola Cecelia had slipped around Scarlet and stood inside. Reaching up, she pulled a silver-star-topped comb out of each side of her tight plum-colored bun. With a shake, she let her hair tumble down loose over her shoulders, and it stopped well below her waist. "Don't be shy. Substitutes are welcome. More than welcome, in fact!" She flashed a smile far sunnier than Scarlet had ever seen on her normally dour face. "You could probably use a break the most. These students are bright, but give them half a chance and they'll wear your glow away. Whose class did you have, by the way? I didn't realize anyone was out. I hope you didn't wear that hat and coat all day. You know, there are Bot-Bot valets to see to things like that."

For a moogle, Scarlet was actually tempted to play along and follow her teacher inside. Before, she had thought that the students' Lightning Lounge had everything a Starling could ever desire. But its cozy fireplaces, pillows, and walls of holo-screens were nothing compared with the faculty's giant lounge. The only problem was Scarlet knew that as soon as she took her hat off, she would give herself away. Frankly, she was surprised—*star*tled, even—that Professor Nicola Cecelia hadn't raised a single violet eyebrow at her beard, which was steadily shifting sideways.

"*Ahem.*" Scarlet cleared her throat as deeply as she could. "Star salutations," she said gruffly. She gave the brim of her hat a dapper tap, the way she'd seen her father do. "But, *ahem*, I'm looking for another, *ahem*, room. *Ahem.*"

"Oh." The teacher's grin faded. "I see. And what room is that?"

"*Ahem.* Er, holo-records."

"You mean the holo-records room right there?" Professor Nicola Cecelia pointed a delicate sparkly purple-polished fingernail at the next door down the hall.

Scarlet turned and squinted to read the sign. STUDENT HOLO-RECORDS. There it was!

"Star salutations!" Scarlet said—too quickly, she

feared. But then Professor Nicola Cecelia's head suddenly snapped around. Her Bot-Bot masseuse was summoning her, rather impatiently by then.

"*Starf!* Got to go. So there it is. Glad I could help. Oh! And so you know, Lunadays we always play astro-poker in the lounge. I almost always win, but still, keep it in mind."

Scarlet let out a long sigh as the door slid shut between them. She hadn't even realized she'd been holding her breath. She checked to make sure no other teachers were coming. They weren't. She sighed again.

It took just a starmin to reach the door of the holo-records room. Then the only question left was, how was she going to get inside?

CHAPTER
5

Scarlet knew better than to try the hand scanner. That would only give her away. There were other ways to get into a room, though, especially now that Professor Nicola Cecelia had confirmed the strength of her disguise.

Scarlet checked her reflection in the mirrorlike surface of the polished marble wall. She slid her beard back to the center and gave it a fluff. She tugged her hat down even farther and propped her collar higher. Satisfied, she raised her fist and rapped on the door . . . once . . . twice . . . three times.

While she waited for the door to open, she went over the story she'd already rehearsed a hydrong times in her mind:

"Hello, my name is Sir Copernicus, and I am here on behalf of Sir Andromedus and Lady Melodia, the famous musicians, as I'm sure you're well aware. Apparently, they've sent numerous holo-requests for their daughter's records, none of which has received a reply. You can imagine what an eclipse they're having. One would think a school like this would have all its stars in a straighter row. But since they're clearly not, the family has sent me to retrieve Scarlet's records, as they're on an extended tour across the Star-Belt region and so could not do it themselves. It's crystal clear, of course, that you're very busy, so I wouldn't dream of taking up your valuable time. Rather, if you'll just point me in the direction of the third-year holo-files . . . Star salutations for understanding. I'll take it from here, if you don't mind."

Scarlet would be free to compare all her scores to Ophelia's—and anyone else's she chose. Leona's, for one . . . Gemma's maybe, too . . . Then she would at least understand why *they* were all Star Darlings and she suddenly was not.

It had to work. It just had to. Otherwise, Scarlet didn't know how she was going to go on. She couldn't keep avoiding everyone and everything forever. Her grades would suffer, and so would she. But until she had some real answers, she would never, in a hydrong star-years, be able to relax.

The only problem was the door wasn't opening. So Scarlet took another breath and knocked again. She tapped the toe of her thick-soled boot. Sparks bounced up from the floor. Did she have to *keep* knocking? She raised her fist. She guessed she did. That was when she noticed, for the first time, the hand scanner—or not the scanner, but what it said.

Scarlet groaned.

She should have looked at it sooner, but she'd been too focused on the door. Instead of displaying a hand outline along with the unnecessary PALM HERE message, the scanner scrolled a series of words: OFFICE HOURS: SUNRISE TO APEX. PLEASE COME BACK. STATUS: CLOSED.

★

On the way back to the dorm Scarlet shed her disguise behind a lumilac bush about halfway to the building. Classes had ended and Starlings were wandering about, and if one more student had pleasantly waved and called, "Star greetings! Welcome to Starling Academy!" Scarlet would have exploded into a moonium bitter, red-hot stars right there in front of them. When she wasn't in disguise, the other students knew better than to try to talk to her or even share a smile. After Scarlet's more than two staryears at Starling Academy, her reliably antisocial reputation preceded her.

Thankfully, Scarlet made it back to her room before Mira, so she had time to put everything away. The floppy orange hat went back on the hat rack, and the coat went into Mira's costume closet, along with the itchy beard. Scarlet had just sat down at her drums and picked up her drumsticks when the door slid open and Mira breezed in.

"There you are!" Mira pointed one long glittery finger at Scarlet. The other hand perched on her hip. She was dressed as a regular Starling student for a change, even if she had a cobalt blue scarf the size of a bedsheet around her neck. "*Starf!*" she exclaimed. "*So* many Starlings have been asking me about you! Especially all those remedial Starlings, like Leona and Adora—and Ophelia now. 'Where's Scarlet?' 'Have you seen her?' 'Could you please give her a holo-message for me?' I'm like, 'Send her your own holo-message.' And they're like, 'We do, but she won't reply.'" Mira cocked her head and frowned. "Did you lose your Star-Zap or something? We could literally find it in a moogle with my Zap-locate app, you know."

"I didn't lose it," mumbled Scarlet. "I've just been busy."

"Oh." Mira's eyes skimmed Scarlet's drum kit. "Right. Okay. I see. Well, don't let me stop you." She shrugged and tossed a long triangle of scarf over her shoulder. It took three tries before it stayed. "I'm zipping right back out again, anyway. I just popped in to get my holo-script before rehearsal. Now . . . where did I leave it do you think . . . ?"

"Why don't you just memorize your lines overnight?" asked Scarlet. Wasn't that what sleep and headphones were for, after all? So Starlings could play back and absorb class lectures and textbooks and anything else they needed to learn?

Mira sighed. "You don't know anything about acting, do you?" She tossed her head to show that *she* did.

Scarlet lowered her own head to hide the smile she couldn't keep from springing up. Oh, after her day, she knew about acting. . . . Too bad Mira hadn't seen her. She would have been impressed.

"A script," Mira went on, "is just the beginning. Like a supernova!" She held her fists out and flashed open her fingers. "It's merely the raw matter from which superstars are born. In rehearsal, we're taking notes constantly and making changes. It's not just memorizing a hydrong lines," she said, scoffing. "It's a *process. A journey*. You know?"

Scarlet nodded, hoping to satisfy Mira, though she'd stopped listening at "beginning."

"Is that your script?" Scarlet pointed to a holo-book near the edge of Mira's makeup-crowded table, behind a long sparkly teal wig on a tall silver stand.

"Is it?" Mira picked up the holo-book and brought it close enough to read. "Star salutations! It is! Okay, I'm off. Again." She paused then, leaning toward Scarlet. "Are you sure you're okay? You know, you look a little green. . . ."

"I do?"

"Mmm-hmm. Around here." Mira stroked her cheeks and chin.

The beard! Scarlet realized. Quickly, she rubbed her face to brush off whatever green glitter was stuck to it. "I'm fine," she said. "Don't worry about me. Just go do your script journey . . . process . . . whatever you call it."

Scarlet had lowered the window shades and blinked off the lights by the time Mira returned. The room had a soft, dreamy violet glow. Dinner was over, as was star-gazing hour, though lights-down had yet to come. Except for the secret Star Caves, of course, no place ever got truly dark on Starland, the way places on Wishworld did. In fact, it actually got brighter as the sun went down and all the wish energy stored in every atom on Starland approached its maximum glow potential.

Scarlet "acted" again, this time as if she was sleeping, in case Mira had more questions to ask her or, worse, offered unwanted advice. She lay as quiet and still as a moonbeam and waited for Mira to take her nightly sparkle shower and slip into bed herself. Actually falling asleep, however, was impossible. The thoughts whizzing through Scarlet's mind simply would not let her rest.

At last, Scarlet had no choice but to get out of bed. She couldn't lie there for a moogle more. Mira was fast asleep, though restlessly muttering something like "Wait! Where's my mark? Somebody moved it from stage left!"

Scarlet slid out from her silky black sheets and scooped her combat boots off the floor. As light as a flutterfocus, she tiptoed past Mira, blinked open the door, and, still wearing her pink-and-black polka-starred pajamas, slipped out into the hall.

To save energy, the hallway Cosmic Transporter ceased flowing after lights-down, but Scarlet was happy to walk. She left her feet bare on the off chance that some other wakeful Starling might hear the *clomp-clomp* of her boots through their chamber doors. Starlings slept exceptionally soundly . . . still, "better safe than lost in space," as Scarlet's father sometimes said.

It wasn't Scarlet's first venture out after lights-down. She'd been taking walks on restless nights since the beginning of the year, when she'd literally stumbled upon the entrance to the mysterious Star Caves. That was before Lady Stella had taken the Star Darlings there, via a secret door in her office, to show them the Wish Cavern she'd had built in the deepest chamber for them and them alone. It was there that the headmistress kept their Wish Orbs. Scarlet knew she had looked as awed and surprised by the caves as everyone else at the time. That was yet another example of her acting talents, she supposed, since she had already discovered the caves herself more than a starweek earlier.

She had arrived at school, as usual, stardays before everyone else. She'd had quite enough of her parents and living out of a suitcase for one Time of Lumiere break. She had checked out her room and was aimlessly riding the Cosmic Transporter around the dorm when she noticed the neon sign on the door in front of her. STARLING ACADEMY STAFF ONLY, it temptingly flashed.

Naturally, she got off and opened it (after peeking over each of her shoulders to make sure she was alone). But it was just a plain old supply closet full of baskets of star-pong balls, sparkle-shower gel, and stuff like that. Because nothing on Starland ever got truly dirty, there were no cleaning supplies, of course. There were, however, a few dust mops and feather dusters for adding an extra layer of stardust to anything that might need shining up. Scarlet had never actually used one, since Bot-Bot maids were always there to shine her hotel rooms. Curious, she took a step into the closet to pull a duster down and see exactly how it worked. "Freakin' fireballs!" she exclaimed as the toe of her boot caught on something and sent her stumbling into a wall of shelves. The next thing she knew, glo-pong balls were raining down on her head like the Perseid meteor shower.

Scarlet looked down as the balls bounced and flashed around her, and that was when she saw the trapdoor. A rogue glo-pong paddle had kept it from closing completely, and that was what had tripped her up. Without thinking twice, she raised the panel and waited as a bunch of glo-pong balls spilled through the hole. She listened to them bounce down a long winding set of metal stairs for several moogles, until they hit a distant floor . . . then, flipping her Star-Zap to flashlight mode, she climbed in to see for herself exactly what was down there.

Since then, not counting her trips with the Star Darlings, Scarlet had been down to explore the Star

Caves more than a dozen times. She'd covered only a tiny fraction, she knew, but on each visit she tried to delve a little deeper than before. This night, without really thinking, she headed due north, down a wide winding tunnel, roughly in the direction of Halo Hall.

As ever, the cave air was cool, like at the top of the Crystal Mountains, but also damp and slightly musty, like her boots before they dried out after a day in Starland snow. The air clung to Scarlet as she moved. Without a doubt, the energy was different down there. What Scarlet liked best of all about the caves was the light that came from glowing rocks set in the walls. It gave her the feeling of being in outer space, where the only light came from distant twinkling stars. Every now and then, as Scarlet walked, a big cold drop of water would splash somewhere on her hair or face. One time, she'd caught one on her tongue. She couldn't say it had much taste.

Suddenly, she heard a high *squeak*, followed by the rustling of wings, and sensed a bitbat swooping down. Scarlet lifted her arm and held out her hand. A starsec later, a silvery-white creature the size of a glowfur settled onto her finger and dangled upside down.

"Star greetings," said Scarlet.

The bitbat blinked its wide fluorescent green eyes

and squeaked twice more, as if in reply. Why bitbats made the other Star Darlings nervous, Scarlet would never know. They were as gentle as any flutterfocus, she thought, just not as hyperactive and ostentatious. Unlike every creature that lived on the surface of Starland, Star Cave creatures did not show off.

The creatures were her second favorite thing about the caves. She envied their solitude, their privacy, their freedom to be themselves and to be alone.

As quickly as it had appeared, the bitbat took off again. Scarlet watched it fly deeper into the cave.

"What's down there?" she called out, following it.

She tried to keep up, but the bitbat was too fast. By the time she rounded a tight corner, Scarlet had lost it in the darkness.

But she had found something else. . . .

CHAPTER
6

Scarlet was dressed and out of her room the next morning before Mira was even awake. Scarlet hadn't slept a wink. She'd spent most of the night in the room at the top of the stairs she'd discovered in the Star Caves, after losing sight of the bitbat. Was it luck that those stairs had led to a trapdoor into the Office of Student Holo-Records? Or was it somehow fate?

Halo Hall would not open officially for another hour but she couldn't see waiting around. She raced across campus to the entrance and begged the Bot-Bot guard to let her in.

"I have to see Lady Stella!" she said. "It's urgent! It can't wait!"

"Star apologies, Scarlet," the Bot-Bot guard replied

mechanically. "Halo Hall is not open, nor is Lady Stella in. Would you like to make an appointment? I can help you with that, if you wish. Lady Stella's office hours are eleven to thirteen starhours. She has another meeting scheduled from twelve to twelve-eighty. What time do you request?"

Scarlet's energy sizzled. That was exactly the problem with thickheaded Bot-Bots. They didn't *understand*. She didn't need an *appointment*. She needed to see the headmistress right *then*!

"Sc-sc-scarlet! Er, st-st-star greetings."

Scarlet turned to see the head of admissions, Lady Cordial, walking briskly toward the door with a stack of files and a mug of Zing.

"Star greetings, Lady Cordial," said Scarlet, bowing.

"You're up early. Feeling better?" She stood before Scarlet, smiling in an awkward but sweet way. Scarlet realized she hadn't seen the head of admissions since learning that her being a Star Darling was a mistake.

"I know what *happened* . . ." Lady Cordial paused and cut her eyes to the Bot-Bot guard, who, like everyone else, knew nothing about the top secret group. "If you don't mind, I'm going to turn off your hearing for a star-sec," she told it.

"Yes, Lady Cordial. As you wish."

Lady Cordial fixed her eyes on its head and narrowed them. "Can you hear me now?" she asked.

She waited.

"Very good. So, er, I was s-saying . . ." She turned back to Scarlet. "I know this mix-up with Ophelia was, well, quite a . . . quite a blow, I'm s-s-sure. Of course, I take full responsibility for everything." She lowered her head and shook it. "How it happened, I'll never know."

"But that's why I'm here! I don't think it *did* happen!"

Lady Cordial's head rose slowly, as Starland's sun was doing just then. "St-st-star excuse me? You don't think *what* happened?"

"I don't think there's been a mix-up!" blurted Scarlet. "I mean, yes, there's been a mix-up—but it's the mix-up that's a mistake! I looked at my holo-records and there's no way in the Milky Way that the scores recorded in them are mine! On the other hand, Ophelia, whose records I also checked, has exactly the scores that I should have. And that's why I'm here—to tell Lady Stella that our scores were switched somehow!"

"*What?*" Lady Cordial gasped. Her cup of Zing slipped out of her hand. Scarlet jumped back and used her energy to catch the cup in midair, but not without hot liquid splashing over her tights and boots.

Of course, it all disappeared in a starsec, as spills on Starland always did.

"St-st-star apologies," said Lady Cordial. She blinked her cup back into her hand and clutched both it and her folders to her chest. "Clearly, you've taken me by star-prise here. Moon and st-st-stars . . ." She took a breath. "If this is true, why . . . er . . . we have more problems than we thought. . . . I must look into this immediately. And inform Lady St-st-stella, of course."

"I'll go with you!" Scarlet told her.

"No, no. St-st-star s-s-salutations, but you've done your part—and more." Lady Cordial's smile slowly returned. "Please, Sc-sc-scarlet, let me take this from here. It's, er, the least I can do."

★

Scarlet was so excited she couldn't eat breakfast. And no way could she go to class. How could she sit through another lecture on energy manipulation when her whole life was about to change? About to get back on track, at last!

She had to find some way to pass the time, though, while she waited for Lady Cordial to set everything straight. She flipped open her Star-Zap, tapped Vega's icon, and dictated a holo-text.

MYSTERY SOLVED! MEET ME IN THE ORCHARD.

Within a starmin another message came through: NO WAY! *MENDOUS NEWS!

When Vega arrived, she was not alone to Scarlet's surprise. Cassie, with her pinkish white pigtail buns and her star-shaped glasses, was arm in arm with her.

Scarlet knew Cassie, of course, from the Star Darlings class but not very well beyond that. The first-year Starling had become particularly close to Scarlet's old roommate, Leona—something Scarlet could never understand, since Leona was, without a doubt, the most self-centered, self-absorbed Starling Scarlet had ever met.

Still, besides that, Scarlet had to admit that what she did know of Cassie, she admired. Cassie was never too loud or bubbly or bossy, and it was clear that behind her glasses, a very intelligent mind was hard at work.

"You don't mind that I brought Cassie, do you?" said Vega. Something about Scarlet's expression must have prompted her to ask. "I promised her I'd tell her the next time we met. I told her about your . . . theories, and of course—"

"I think you're right!" Cassie cut in. She leaned forward and pushed up her glasses. Her normally soft pink glow flashed bright, almost blindingly white. "I don't care what Leona says. There is no way in the galaxy that Ophelia could grant a wish. Tell us everything!" she said. "What have you found out?"

So Scarlet told them everything. . . .

"Moon and stars!" Cassie gasped at the end. "So when will you hear back from Lady Cordial?"

"Soon," Scarlet said. "I'm sure."

"Oh, I hope it's all a mistake, the way you say!"

"Does that mean you'll come back to the band?" Vega asked. "You know, there was just an announcement this morning—did you hear?—that this year for Starshine Day there's going to be a battle of the bands. We could win with you playing, Scarlet. I really think we could. In fact . . . maybe you should come back, no matter what, even if it turns out no mistake was made."

"First of all"—Scarlet's eyes narrowed—"there *was* a mistake. A starmendous one. That's just a fact. Second, as I've said a hydrong times now, the band is about the last thing on my mind."

Vega and Cassie lowered their eyes and traded glances.

"Star apologies," said Vega. "Of course. We can talk about the band later. One thing at a time. So . . . if there was a mistake . . . how in the stars did it happen? How did your and Ophelia's scores get switched?"

Scarlet shook her head. "That's what I don't know." Her eyes flashed and flickered between Vega and Cassie. "You're the puzzle solvers. Any thoughts?"

"These things happen, I suppose," said Vega.

Cassie frowned. "Not here. Not at Starling Academy. All these 'mistakes,' 'coincidences,' 'mysteries'—they don't just *happen* here."

Vega nodded reluctantly. "Agreed."

"So do you think somebody switched our records?" said Scarlet. "On purpose? But those things don't happen here, either . . . do they?"

The three Starlings traded worried looks. They were all thinking the same thing, but no one was quite ready to put such a dark thought into words. Then, suddenly, Cassie's lacy silver sweater pocket beeped. She pulled out her Star-Zap and read the holo-text. Behind her glasses her eyes grew big and round.

"It's the botany lab!" she exclaimed. "They've finished testing the flowers and have the results!"

"Well? What did they find?" asked Vega.

"They don't say. They just say to come."

"That's one connection I still don't see," Vega told her. "And it's not just because I want to win our bet. I was hoping Piper and I would get along better when the flowers were out of our room. . . ."

"And did you?"

"No. Nothing changed. In fact, you should have heard how she went on about my letting you take them to the lab to be studied. You would have thought I'd stolen her bed."

"Really . . ." Cassie's nearly translucent eyebrows slid together as she frowned.

"But then suddenly yesterday," Vega went on, "she gave me this sweet holo-poem she'd written . . . and this morning we meditated together." She smiled at Cassie's and Scarlet's dumbfounded expressions. "Cross my stars! I know!"

"There might still be a connection . . ." said Cassie.

Vega shrugged. "There's only one way to find out." She slipped one arm through Cassie's, then the other through Scarlet's.

"You want me to come, too?" Scarlet eyed Vega's elbow and gingerly unhooked her arm.

"Of course," said Vega. "Right, Cassie?" She tried not to look too hurt by Scarlet's initial response.

"Moon and stars, yes," said Cassie, smiling warmly. "We're in this together now."

CHAPTER
7

The botany lab was in Halo Hall in the science stellation, where the Starlings' Wishology and Astrophysics classes—among dozens of others—were held. Those labs, though, were on the lower floors. The botany lab took up most of the top floor and had a ceiling made of glass so the hydrongs of plants and flowers growing there had all the sunlight or starlight or moonlight they could want.

Naturally, there were specimens from all over Starland: featherjabbers, mellomallows, even nomadic druderwomps—shrublike knots of glittery branches that were constantly uprooting themselves and lazily rolling around the lab until they got bored and decided to stop and spread their roots, inevitably tripping someone up.

The lab was best known, though, for its extensive collection of flora samples from Wishworld. It was the largest collection on Starland, in fact. Generations of Wish-Granters had brought back everything from Spanish moss to buttercups to fragrant evergreen trees. Scientists were still working to get those to bloom ornaments the way they did on Wishworld . . . but so far, they'd had no luck. Scarlet's personal favorites were the dandelions, which were like two flowers in one, the second better than the first: a starburst of yellow petals followed by tickly cloud-white fluff. And best of all Wishers used them to make wishes! Plus they didn't overwhelm you with that cloying flower smell, which was always such overkill, Scarlet thought.

The three Starlings—Scarlet, Vega, and Cassie—entered and were met by a pair of turquoise-haired technicians in sturdy star-covered overalls under long shimmery white lab coats.

"Ah! Star greetings, Cassie," said one, a short woman with a blue holo–name tag reading GLADIOLUS ROSE. "Oh, my stars, you got here quickly! You must have ridden a laser beam!"

She clasped her hands and bowed, as was Starland custom. Her partner did the same. He was taller by a moonstone and wore a hard-to-miss star-shaped bandage on his nose.

Cassie bowed in return, as did Vega and Scarlet.

"We couldn't wait to hear the results of your tests!" Cassie told the lab technicians. She nodded to the man. "What happened to you, by the way?"

"What? Oh, this?" The man patted his bandaged nose, then turned to his flickering silver-tinged partner, who guiltily sucked in her cheeks. "Flying flowerpot . . . Funny story . . ." He sighed. "Or at least it will be, I hope, one starday."

"Why don't we show them those flowers?" said his partner.

He nodded. "Good idea."

"After you. Please." She waved him past.

"Star salutations, but please, no, after you."

They went on like that, back and forth, until Scarlet couldn't take one more exchange.

"Why don't you show us *together*?"

"Great idea!" they said in unison. "To the back of the lab. This way."

The Starlings followed them down a winding aisle between empty workstations.

"Where is everyone?" Vega asked.

Gladiolus Rose picked up an uprooted kaleidoscope

tree sapling and set it on a counter between a broken beaker and an upside-down microscope. "Most of the botanists decided to go home early yesterday. We stayed to finish this job. The energy in the air was rather . . . *tense*, you might say. Lots of name-calling, flowerpot flinging, energy sapping, I'm afraid."

"Not much work getting done," said her partner. "Not safely, anyway."

Scarlet gazed around at the mess and couldn't help cracking a smile. She could only imagine the scene that must have made it.

"That sounds like Piper and me," said Vega. "Until yesterday afternoon." Suddenly, her expression began to change. "When exactly did your fighting stop?"

"Almost as soon as we put them behind glass," Gladiolus Rose answered. "When was that?" She turned to her partner. "In the afternoon?"

"Indeed, it was."

Cassie's eyes grew round, and so did Vega's. Scarlet's jaw dropped slightly, too.

"Are you saying you think the flowers made you bicker and fight?" asked Vega.

"I'm afraid so," the techs said together. "Star apologies!" They bowed and laughed.

"As you can see," said Gladiolus Rose, "arguing is

not in our nature. So as soon as it started, we knew that something was starmendously wrong."

"The moment we put them behind glass, however," the man said, "the fiery tempers cooled."

He pointed to a glass case at the end of the lab. Inside, the Starlings could see Vega and Piper's lavish coral-colored bouquet.

Scarlet instantly remembered the flowers, though she'd given them little thought when they showed up in her room. Not surprisingly, Leona had claimed them for her half of the room almost immediately, so Scarlet paid even less attention to them after that.

"You were absolutely correct in suspecting those flowers of negative energy," Gladiolus Rose told Cassie as they moved toward the case. "The things are full of it, in fact. The measurements we recorded were frankly *floozels* off the charts. It's as if each and every flower was grown in negative-energy-infused soil."

Scarlet scowled and spoke up. "But isn't that impossible? Every Bad Wish Orb is destroyed immediately. That's one of the first things we learn when we get to this school."

"Moon and stars! We didn't think negative energy even *existed* on Starland," said Cassie with a gulp.

Scarlet hadn't thought Cassie could look any paler—and yet, somehow, she did.

Gladiolus Rose shook her head. "It doesn't. Technically," she said.

"What do you mean?" Vega asked.

The two lab technicians exchanged grim glances.

The tall one cleared his throat. "There have been leaks in the past . . . from the Bad Wish Containment Center."

"*But* that was *hydrongs* of staryears ago," his partner assured the Starlings. "There have been mix-ups, too . . . bad wishes mistaken for good ones at first. . . . But such a thing is exceedingly rare, and by the time the mistake is corrected, almost all the potential negative energy has yet to be released."

"'Almost'?" Vega said.

"Almost." The woman nodded. "So, yes, it's not beyond the spectrum of possibility for there to be a microjoule in the air. But nowhere near enough to account for the concentrations we're seeing here. It's unprecedented, frankly." She turned to peer into the case. "Never before, at least in this lab, have we seen negative plant life half as powerful—or *negative*—as this."

"So . . . what you're saying, then," said Scarlet, "is

that this mystery still isn't solved. You don't know where the flowers came from."

"Not yet. No. But our tests aren't finished. There are a few more we can do. Hopefully, we can identify the exact source of the negative energy and even pinpoint where the flowers were grown."

"How long will it take, do you think?" asked Vega.

"I'd say a starday . . . maybe two . . . three at most." Gladiolus Rose shrugged. "It's difficult to say until the rest of the staff returns to work."

Her partner gazed around the overturned lab. "We were also hoping to straighten things up a little first. That's one thing about this Wishworld dirt . . . it doesn't seem to clean itself up. It just sits there when it's spilled."

"Well, we can help you with *that*," said Vega matter-of-factly. She looked down at the loose Wishworld dirt scattered across the floor. Her eyes narrowed as she focused her energy on gathering the dirt into a pile. As soon as she collected it all, Vega flicked her wrist and lifted it in a steady stream, using her finger to steer it into the nearest flowerpot.

Scarlet looked over to see Cassie starting to use her energy, as well. One by one, on the counter in front of Cassie, overturned plants were popping upright.

"Star salutations!" said the lab technicians.

Vega beamed. "It's the least we can do! Scarlet . . . ? What are you waiting for over there? The faster we clean up this lab, the faster they can run more tests."

"Why don't we just zap up some Bot-Bot maids?" said Scarlet, looking bleakly around the room. She would rather have linked arms with Leona than do that job, even with the help of her energy manipulation.

"And where would be the fun in that?" asked Vega brightly, adjusting a trayful of laser-bean seedlings just so.

Suddenly, she jumped, and so did Cassie. Both Starlings pulled out their Star-Zaps.

"Moon and stars!" gasped Cassie. She looked at Vega, who was just closing her device and slipping it back into her fitted coat.

"What is it?" asked Scarlet.

Cassie hurried over to Scarlet and whispered so the lab technicians wouldn't hear: "Another Wish Orb's been identified." Only a few faculty besides Lady Stella and Lady Cordial knew of the existence of the Star Darlings, and it was imperative it stay that way. "We have to go to Lady Stella's office. Immediately. To find out whose wish this will be."

"I'm coming, too!" Scarlet moved toward the lab door.

"Did your Star-Zap go off?" Cassie asked.

Scarlet stopped and put her hand on the pocket of her hooded vest. She hadn't felt any vibration. She looked, but she knew the answer was no before she saw the screen. "I'm going anyway."

"I don't know. . . ." Cassie shook her head. "Lady Stella knows best, and if she didn't summon you, I don't think that you *can* go."

"But I'm a Star Darling!"

"*Shhh!*" Cassie quickly glanced over her shoulder. Luckily, the lab technicians were in the far corner, straightening some crooked holo-screens.

"But I *am* a Star Darling!" Scarlet hissed. "If there's a wish assignment, I should be there!"

Vega had come over, too. Both she and Cassie took Scarlet's hands. "Patience, Scarlet. If you truly are a Star Darling—and I certainly don't doubt it—then the stars will realign for you, all in due time," Vega said.

Scarlet yanked her hands away and squeezed her lips together tightly. She was close to saying something she just might regret.

"We'll let you know what happens," Cassie assured her.

"Whatever." Scarlet raised her chin and looked away.

She would have liked to see how much patience Vega or Cassie or any other Star Darling would have were she to trade places with one of them.

High above, over the ceiling skylight, a pink cloud the shape of a galliope's head slowly drifted past. She closed her eyes and thought of Wishworld, somewhere beyond it, orbiting through space full of wishes.

"Keep your stars up," said Vega. She reached out and gave Scarlet's arm a squeeze. "If we see Lady Cordial, we'll ask her about your reports. . . . I'm sure we'll have some good news for you by the time you're done helping here!"

★

"*Well?*"

"*Starf!*"

"*Scarlet!* Moon and *stars!*"

"You scared the light out of us!" Vega gasped.

"Star apologies." Scarlet stepped all the way around the column she'd been standing behind and pulled her hood back from her face. They were in the hall outside Lady Stella's office, where Scarlet had been lurking for a starhour, or quite possibly longer. She could have waited for Vega and Cassie to holo-call or text her, but waiting had never been Scarlet's style.

"Why were you hiding?" asked Cassie.

"I wasn't *hiding*. I was just trying to stay out of sight . . ." Scarlet explained.

Cassie and Vega wrinkled their glittery foreheads.

"Anyway," Scarlet went on. "What happened? Who got the mission? And what did Lady Stella have to say about *me*? I didn't see Ophelia come out. Have they already told her about the mistake?"

Vega's cheeks flashed ever so faintly. Cassie's lip slid beneath her teeth. Scarlet couldn't tell if they looked more like they'd eaten too much zoomberry cake or like someone had stolen cake from them.

"What's wrong?"

Vega's and Cassie's eyes met and something passed between them. Scarlet felt her glow dim as it did.

"Tell me."

Vega took a deep breath. "The Wish Orb was Ophelia's."

"The Wish Orb . . . the Wish Orb was *what*?"

"The Wish Orb was Ophelia's," Vega said again, letting her breath out as she did.

"Wait . . . so what are you saying?"

"The Wish Orb was Ophelia's," Cassie patiently repeated.

Scarlet's glow returned in a flash, this time hot pink. "I get that," she muttered. "But are you saying . . . Are you saying a *Star Darling* Wish Orb chose Ophelia? Are you saying the next Star Darling mission is *hers*? Are you saying . . ." Scarlet closed her eyes and opened them slowly. "Are you saying Ophelia is going to go to Wishworld to grant a wish instead of *me*?"

Vega nodded.

"Or at least almost there," Cassie said.

"Star apologies, Scarlet. For what it's worth, we believed you . . . but you were wrong, I guess." Vega reached out to touch Scarlet's shoulder, but Scarlet stepped away.

"I wasn't *wrong*," she snapped. "There was nothing to be wrong about. Scores are scores. I saw what I saw. Tell me . . . Lady Cordial . . . what did she have to say?"

Vega and Cassie responded with shrugs.

"Not much," said Vega, "as usual. She just wished Ophelia lucky stars."

"That's all? She didn't mention the holo-records? Did she at least look starprised?"

"*Everyone* looked starprised," said Vega.

"Especially Ophelia," Cassie agreed.

"Actually, Lady Cordial probably looked the least

starprised," added Vega. "Maybe she'd already looked into your theory, Scarlet, and all the holo-records, and didn't see what you think you saw."

"No one's saying you're lying, Scarlet—or that we were happy to see you go. . . . And we're definitely not saying there aren't weird things going on. . . ."

"But I don't think your leaving the Star Darlings is one," added Vega.

"You can still help us get to the bottom of the flower mystery!" said Cassie brightly.

"*Flowers?* Are you shooting my stars? I don't give a crater about your flower mystery," Scarlet fired back. "I hope whoever sent them sends you a hydrong more, in fact!"

CHAPTER
8

The rest of the day passed in a haze of bitter disappointment for Scarlet. She skipped lunch in the Celestial Café and filled her stomach with cocomoons and gloranges from the Starling Academy orchard instead. Since Starland fruit grew back, full and ripe, as soon as it was picked, Scarlet didn't have to worry about taking too much—or getting in trouble for it.

Skipping class was another story. That wasn't as easy to do. So Scarlet sat through hers, hood pulled down, in the farthest back corner of each room. She barely listened to the lessons, though, since what did they matter to her now? Did she even want to go to Wishworld to grant wishes? The more she thought about it . . . who *cared*?

So as Professor Andromedus Galapas droned on about the Enlightenment and the lighterature of the day, Scarlet drafted a holo-message to her parents, begging them to take her . . . *somewhere*, since they didn't exactly have a home.

Dear Mom and Dad,

Wherever you are, please come and get me. As soon as you possibly can. Or if you're too busy, feel free to send a Starcar and I will come to you. It's taken me almost three staryears, but I finally see that I was wrong and you were right. I was lucky to be able to travel all around Starland with you, having tutors instead of teachers who think they're so shiny and bright at some silly snooty school full of Starlings who act like they're the center of the whole universe. I made a starmendous mistake applying to Starling Academy. I wasn't meant to grant Wishling wishes. Never mind what I said about hating the idea of a family trio. I was wrong. Take me back, please, so I can play the drums with you.

Love and stars,
Scarlet

She read it over . . . raised her finger . . .
She sighed and hit DELETE.

"You'd like to go, Scarlet?"

"Huh?" Scarlet heard her name and looked up.

Professor Galapas was staring at her. So was the rest of the class. Open holo-books hovered in front of everyone but Scarlet, their text projected into the air.

"You raised your hand? You'd like to read aloud next?"

"What? No, sir. I mean, I didn't mean to." Scarlet looked at her finger, which was still in the air, then back at the teacher in the front of the room.

His bald head gleamed like the ice-covered summit of the Crystal Mountains. His face was as round as a star ball and just as bright. When he wore dark robes, as he usually did, it was almost as if the moon was up there teaching the class.

"'*Mean* to.' A mere technicality. Some things are written in the stars. Please, Scarlet, *enlighten* us. Just pick up where Leona concluded, if you don't mind."

Scarlet panicked slightly, and her eyes cut to her old roommate, whose seat was always front and center in every room, like she was a curly-haired sun for the world to orbit.

"Um . . ." She opened her holo-book and projected a page. She had no idea if it was the *right* one. Before she could read, though, and know for certain, the image in front of her blinked. The page changed, and Scarlet sensed Leona looking at her with a half smile on her bright gold-flecked face.

★

"You owe me."

Scarlet had barely escaped from Constellation Classroom 315 when a voice behind her made her stop.

"What?" She knew the voice before she turned. Still, she hadn't expected Leona's expression, which was somewhere between "Please, don't leave me" and "Gotcha!"

"You owe me," Leona repeated.

"Uh . . . star salutations . . . ?" Scarlet said. Leona had been unexpectedly generous in giving Scarlet the correct page number, she supposed. She bowed and reluctantly worked to soften her permanent frown.

But Leona shook her head. "I don't want your salutations."

"Then what do you want?"

Leona crossed her tawny, sparkling arms over her gold mesh tunic. "I want you to come back to the band."

"Oh." Scarlet jammed her hands in the pockets of her hoodie. "Star apologies. No can do. Besides, have you

happened to notice you have a new roommate? *Ophelia?*"
She could feel her cheeks glowing hotter and hotter. "I'm
not a Star Darling anymore."

Leona shrugged. "Who said you had to be one?"

"Uh, you did, I'm pretty sure."

"Did I?" Leona squeezed one eye shut, trying to
remember. "Well, if I did, then I changed my mind."

"Great. Then find one of the other hydrongs of
students here to be your drummer, because I'm not
interested," Scarlet said.

"Oh, come *on*," Leona groaned. "Stop *pouting* already
and just come *back*. At least until Starshine Day, so we
can win the battle of the bands."

Scarlet laughed. "You're hystarical, you know that,
Leona?" She shook her head in disbelief. "Do you
honestly think I care one proton about some Starling
Academy battle of the bands? Or if the Star Darlings
win? *Especially* after the way you wrote me off the
moogle you found out I wasn't a Star Darling anymore?
How about I put this in your own words, the ones you
said when I came to you then: 'I don't give a star.' How's
that? Hmmm? Now you know how it feels."

Leona stood there, her glow visibly faded. She clearly
didn't know what to say. Scarlet would have been happy

with a simple "star apologies," but that was a lot to ask, she guessed.

Or was it?

Leona's golden lips slowly opened and a word began to form.

Beep!

She jumped at the sudden sound of her Star-Zap and quickly pulled it out. Whatever the holo-text said, it made her eyes pop, and whatever word she'd had primed disappeared.

"Gotta fly!"

"What happened?" asked Scarlet.

Leona paused. "It's Ophelia . . ." she began. Then she checked herself and turned away.

"What about her?" Scarlet went on.

But by then, Leona was gone.

★

If Leona had any idea Scarlet was following her, she didn't let on. When it was clear that she was heading to Lady Stella's office, Scarlet hung back a little more. She hugged the cool marble wall at the end of the corridor and watched Leona and the other Star Darlings file over the threshold. . . . Then, just as the door started closing, Scarlet silently slipped through.

The Star Darlings were all so excited no one took notice of the pink-tinged shadow making its way to the back of the room. Scarlet slid into the corner, behind a potted boingtree. The branches were far enough apart for Scarlet to peek through but full enough of bright color-changing leaves to serve as an excellent screen.

She looked for Lady Stella but couldn't see her. The Star Darlings seemed starprised by her absence, as well, and stood chattering anxiously instead of taking seats around the large full moon–shaped table in the center of the room, as they'd normally do.

When Lady Stella finally entered through the hidden door in the back of her office, which led to the Star Darlings' secret Star Caves, her face wore uncharacteristic lines. She paused to consider every Star Darling, gazing deeply into each pair of eyes.

"What's up?" Gemma blurted.

"*Gemma!*" Her sister, Tessa, elbowed her in the ribs.

"I'm afraid," Lady Stella began, "that something quite troublesome is up. There are problems with this latest mission."

"What kind of problems?" Sage asked with a flash. "The same kind of problems we've had before?"

"I'm afraid not," said Lady Stella. "These are far graver. . . . Ophelia's Wish Orb has gone black."

A unified gasp whooshed through the room, as if every air molecule was sucked out. From the shadows, Scarlet watched the stunned Star Darlings grab and squeeze one another's hands. A black Wish Orb meant not only a failing mission but the potential loss of a Starling, as well.

"So . . . what do we *do*?" said Leona. "Someone has to *help* her!"

"Yes, someone does," Lady Stella agreed.

"I'll go!" said Leona. "I'm ready right now. I can do it this time! Send me!" She moved toward Lady Stella, but the headmistress motioned her back.

"Star salutations, Leona, for your generous offer, but—"

"But what? I can't go because I failed my mission? But I thought you said that wasn't my fault!"

"No, it's not that, Leona," Lady Stella assured her. Calmly she waved away the sparks that were sputtering out of Leona's ears. "I'm afraid only a Wish Orb can pick who goes, as on every other mission when help is required. This situation, of course, is far more dire. But the same procedure is required." Then Lady Stella reached into the folds of the long silver robe she wore. In her hand sat Ophelia's Wish Orb. Each time before, when Lady Stella had gathered them to see who the Wish Orb would choose to help grant the wish, the orb had lost some of its glow. But this orb smoldered dully like a lump of crater coal. It was the ugliest thing Scarlet, or any other Starling, had ever seen in her life.

Lady Stella spread her fingers and let the orb rise and hover between her and the Star Darlings. After a moogle, it began to move . . . slowly drifting past each glittery, worried face in search of the one it would choose.

"Where is it going?" asked Vega as it floated up to her last, then swerved. "It's not choosing any of us? It's flying away. It's trying to get out of the room."

"No . . . it's not," said Cassie, pointing. "Look. It's heading into the corner over there, toward that kaleido-scope tree."

Sure enough, it was. Scarlet watched it approach, just as confused as everyone else. As it reached the tree and stopped, however, she understood at once.

"It chose me!"

Scarlet stepped out from behind the tree, beaming. It was the first smile she'd worn in stardays. She'd almost forgotten how smiling felt. In her palm rested the Wish Orb, which had firmly settled there as soon as she had held her hand out.

"*What the stars?*" exclaimed Gemma.

Tessa was too shocked to respond to her sister with her usual reproach.

"That's impossible!" said Leona. "She's not a Star Darling anymore!"

"And yet . . ." Lady Stella glided toward Scarlet, wearing an expression of not unhappy starprise. "Scarlet, I do not know how you got here, but Ophelia's Wish Orb has indeed chosen you. And it is you who must go help Ophelia—and hopefully make the wish come true."

CHAPTER
9

By the time Scarlet's shooting star delivered her to Wishworld, she had fully transformed from a Starling into as convincing a Wishling as a Starling could be. Her skin was flat and freckled, without a hint of sparkle or a tinge of pink. Her eyes were brown instead of rose-colored. She had even toned down her hair so it was black with a single streak of bright pink.

Scarlet was pretty sure, too, that the outfit she'd ultimately chosen would convince any Wishling she might encounter that she'd lived there all her life. First she'd picked those pants Wishlings adored—according to Professor Margaret Dumarre, who knew the ways of Wishlings inside and out. Dungarees, she called them, though most Starlings who'd been to Wishworld seemed to refer to them as jeans. Scarlet also wore a deep burgundy hoodie made of a dense, rather stiff Wishling fabric, with a puffy black vest over that. Finally, on her feet were brand-new boots from Lady Stella, which would be her Wish Pendant from then on. One day, on her own mission, the rows of star-shaped energy-absorbing jewel buckles would light up when she met her Wisher and absorb all the wish energy produced when that Wisher's wish came true. For now, however, Scarlet was careful to pull her jeans down to cover as many of the jewels as she could.

Scarlet stood where she'd landed, in a Wishworld meadow filled with green grass and yellow flowers, canopied by a bright blue sky. In the distance, she could see a sharp steeple and the starkly angled rooftops of what looked like a small town.

So strange . . . she thought as she looked around. *And so . . . uncomfortable, as well.*

She sensed it first on her back . . . then on the top of her head, under her hood: a deep, inescapable feeling unlike any other she'd ever had. It didn't take away from the excitement of being on Wishworld at last . . . it just distracted her a bit.

Scarlet pulled down her hood and that helped a little, especially when a light breeze swept through her hair.

But the uncomfortable feeling soon returned, stronger than before. Scarlet slipped off her vest and began to fan herself. That made a big difference, she discovered with relief.

Curious, she checked her Star-Zap to see what the temperature was. *Solar flare!* she thought as she realized how much warmer it was there than on Starland. Quickly, she reactivated her Wishworld Outfit Selector and dialed up a tank top.

Ah, much better, she thought.

She wasn't there to worry about her comfort, though, Scarlet reminded herself. She was there to do a job—and, even more important, to prove what she could do! She needed to fix whatever mess Ophelia had made and get a wish granted and wish energy collected as soon as Starlingly possible. Ophelia had already squandered half the time the Wish Orb gave her, so there wasn't a moogle left to waste.

Quickly, she folded up her star and slipped it into her pocket. Then she switched her Star-Zap to locator mode.

"Take me to Ophelia!" she told it, and directions appeared instantly.

To Scarlet's starprise, the directions led her away from the town and into a vast field. It appeared to be full of some kind of crop, from what Scarlet had learned of Wishling ways of growing food. The plants stood in straight rows and were tall—much taller than she—with long, pointy, floppy green leaves. Near each stalk bloomed tight tubelike flowers nearly the size of Scarlet's arm, each with dark silky threads spilling from its top.

They gave off a distinct sweetish scent, too, which made Scarlet's nose begin to twitch. . . .

She stepped forward and bumped right into something. "*Starf!*" she said, stepping back. She stepped forward again. Same thing. As she reached out into the air in front of her, Scarlet's hand encountered a smooth surface. Aha! A smile spread across her face. It was the smooth surface of an invisible tent!

"Ophelia?"

Scarlet knelt down and cautiously parted the flaps of the glitter-covered tent—Ophelia's glitter-covered invisibility-cloaked tent, to be exact. As she did, a glittery, wide-eyed, freckled face peered out with a tiny panicked squeal.

"*Eeh!* Oh! *Oh,* thank *stars* you're here!" Ophelia gasped, bursting out of the tent and into Scarlet's arms.

Scarlet fell backward onto the star-studded back pockets of her jeans.

"Star apologies!" said Ophelia, clambering off her.

"It's just so good to see a friendly—oh . . . um . . . to see a familiar face, at least."

Indeed, Scarlet's face was far from friendly then. She could feel the irritation hot beneath her sneer. "What in the stars are you doing in your tent, Ophelia? And please tell me you've changed your appearance and you don't still look like *that* to everyone here. . . ." Scarlet knew Starlings always looked glittery to each other, no matter where they were or what form they assumed. Something, though, about the way Ophelia was flashing and hiding made Scarlet think she just might look glittery to Wishlings, too.

Ophelia looked down at her shimmering skin and wrung her hands, which only amplified their glow. "Those answers go together, I guess." She looked up miserably and gulped.

"You were supposed to change your appearance and find your Wisher!" Scarlet said, disgusted. "Did you try to do *either* of those things?"

Ophelia nodded meekly. "I tried. But I don't know . . . nothing seemed to work. . . ." She pulled out her Star-Zap and showed it to Scarlet. "This was supposed to help me change my appearance, right?"

Scarlet nodded.

"Well, nothing happened. . . ."

"What do you mean 'nothing'? It's so easy. . . . No Wishworld Outfit Selector, either?"

Ophelia shook her head. "And when I asked it to take me to my Wisher . . ."

"What? What did it say?"

"It said, 'Reply hazy. Ask again.'"

"So did you?"

"Only a hydrong times," Ophelia groaned. "Finally, I just tried to go and find her in that little town on my own."

"Like *that*?" Scarlet asked, looking Ophelia up and down.

"Well . . . what else could I do?" she said meekly. "But I didn't try for very long. Everyone was staring and asking me questions like 'Is there a circus in town?' and 'Are you a clown?' What's a circus and what's a clown, anyway?"

"Um, they're like royalty," Scarlet guessed, since she didn't know.

"Oh." Ophelia nodded. "So, anyway, I gave up because of that. And because of this thing, too." She held her hand out toward Scarlet. On her wrist was a thick yellow bracelet studded with star-shaped jewels.

"Is that your Wish Pendant?"

Ophelia nodded. "Pretty, isn't it?" She sighed.

"Did it ever glow?"

Ophelia shook her head. "Not even a little," she replied. "I thought it was because I couldn't find my Wisher, but now I'm not so sure that it's not broken, too. . . . But anyway, that's why I'm here." She gazed at the field around her tent. "I didn't know where else to go, and at least my Star-Zap could do this. I really wanted to make this mission succeed. Truly, Scarlet, I did." She sniffed. "I didn't mean to fail." Her glittery orange eyelashes fluttered as glittery orange tears welled in her eyes. "I'm just so happy to see you, Scarlet! Truly, I am! How in the stars did you know to come?" She paused as another question suddenly popped into her head. "But why . . . how is it *you*, Scarlet? I thought . . ." She stopped and bit her thumb.

"It's okay. Go ahead and say it," said Scarlet. "You thought I'd been kicked out of the group for good? You're right. I was. But I never should have been. It was all a big mistake."

"So you're back in?" exclaimed Ophelia. She wiped her tears and began to grin. "That's starmendous! I'm so happy for you! And so relieved . . ." She sighed. "So. Shall I wait here while you go find the Wisher and grant her wish so we can go home?"

"I wish," Scarlet muttered.

Ophelia looked confused.

"It's still your wish," Scarlet told her. She shrugged as Ophelia's smile of relief collapsed. "Hey, don't blame me. I don't make the rules. According to Lady Stella, I'm here to help. That's all."

Ophelia gestured toward her Starling garments, then to her fluorescent-orange pigtails.

"Here." Scarlet dialed up APPEARANCE TRANSFORMATION on her Star-Zap and placed it in Ophelia's hand. "Try mine and see what happens."

Ophelia clutched it tightly, holding her breath.

"Recite the mantra!" Scarlet reminded her. "And put one hand on your bracelet!"

"Oh, right . . . Star light, star bright, first star I . . ."

"See tonight."

"See tonight. I wish I may, I wish I might, have this wish I . . ."

"Wish!"

"Wish . . . tonight."

Scarlet watched with more irritation than relief as the sparkle finally drained from Ophelia's skin and hair like sand through an hourglass.

She noticed a bit of loose glitter clinging to her arms and the frizzy ends of her dull orange pigtails.

"Shake," Scarlet told Ophelia.

She did.

"How do I look?" Ophelia asked, rubbing her newly green eyes and inspecting her pale pink fingernails.

"Dull," Scarlet replied approvingly. "Now dial up the Wishworld Outfit Selector and let's get out of here. See that?" She pointed to the steadily counting-down timer in the Star-Zap's upper left corner. "That's how much time we have left to grant this wish. One moogle longer and the mission fails."

Ophelia gasped. "But . . . isn't that less than a Wishworld week?"

Scarlet shook her head. "More like less than a Wishworld day."

"Oh, I hope we can grant it," said Ophelia. "It will be so hard to go back if we don't. . . ."

Scarlet laughed. She couldn't help it. Ophelia had so much still to learn.

"What's so funny?"

"Don't be silly," said Scarlet. "You'll just use your star." Scarlet sighed. This was way worse than she had imagined.

"My star?" Before, Ophelia had looked anxious. Now she simply looked confused.

"Your star," said Scarlet. "The one that you came on.

The one you have folded up in your backpack . . . Wait. What? No! Don't tell me you don't!"

Ophelia shook her head slowly—once in each direction. Her mouth trembled, but no sound came out.

"Well, where is it? What did you do with it?" asked Scarlet. She groaned. "Oh, don't tell me you let it fizzle out!"

"I didn't mean to . . ." said Ophelia, sniffling back tears. "Nobody told me about folding it up. . . ."

CHAPTER
18

No working Star-Zap . . . No shooting star . . .
Was it even possible for Ophelia to get back to Starland,
Scarlet wondered, even if they found Ophelia's Wisher
and somehow she granted her wish in time? They could
use Scarlet's Star-Zap to lead them in the right direction,
at least, which Scarlet quickly had them do. But how, if
every other Star Darling so far had collected less energy
than she'd hoped to on her mission, could an incompetent Starling like Ophelia ever collect enough to enable
Scarlet's star and Star-Zap to take them both home?

The answer, Scarlet realized, was that it wasn't her
problem! And she couldn't help smiling as she thought
about it more. Sure, it would be too bad if a wish didn't
get granted. Scarlet valued the energy wishes produced

as much as anyone else. And yet . . . if it meant Ophelia was stuck on Wishworld and out of the cosmos at least for a little while, that would also mean Scarlet's Star Darling status would return and her reputation would undoubtedly be redeemed. And Scarlet would just make up for the energy loss on her own mission, when the next Wish Orb chose her!

The thought burned so brightly in Scarlet's mind she couldn't think about anything else, including the quaint, quiet Wishworld town she and Ophelia soon found themselves in.

"Moon and stars . . ." Ophelia murmured as she hung close by Scarlet's side. She'd tried to link arms with Scarlet but had instantly sensed her mistake. "Wishworld is so much different than Starland City. Somehow, I thought they'd be more alike."

"This *town* is different," Scarlet agreed as she, too, took in the scene. Unlike the gleaming high-rise-filled Starland capital that went on for floozels—not including the suburbs, which stretched beyond that for floozels more—the Wishworld town appeared to be built around a single two-way street lined with tidy little stores. Scarlet read some of the signs in the windows and above the rectangular glass doors: LEE'S HARDWARE, GRANNY'S TOYS AND GAMES, MARVIN'S LUNCHEONETTE, ANNIE'S FUDGE

AND ICE CREAM SHOPPE. She wasn't sure what every word meant, but she felt like she got the idea.

A few dull yet cheerful adult Wishlings strolled along the sidewalks, greeting one another as they passed. "Hey, there," a man said warmly to Scarlet and Ophelia. He was pushing a cart full of folded papers and rectangular packages. Those were covered with paper, too. He stopped at the corner by a large blue boxy container with a slightly dented rounded lid. The Starlings watched him reach into the pocket of his short blue pants and pull out a key on a cord. He used it to open a door in the side of the box, where he found *more* paper.

"He's one of the Wishlings who asked me about the circus," whispered Ophelia. But he didn't seem too curious about her anymore. If he or any of the Wishlings in the town thought Ophelia or Scarlet looked out of place, they were not letting on.

"This seems like a small town," Scarlet told Ophelia. "I don't think all cities on Wishworld are this size. Just like on Starland, there are all different kinds. Have you ever been to Solar Springs?"

"Solar Springs?"

"You know, where Gemma and Tessa are from?"

Ophelia shook her head.

Scarlet shrugged. "You're not missing much. It's a lot

like this place. So where *have* you been?" she asked.

Ophelia tapped her fingers together. "Nowhere," she replied. "I've never been outside of Starland City before. I mean, until now."

"Not even Old Prism?" Old Prism was the original Starland settlement and the most popular tourist destination on Starland. Nearly every family took at least one vacation there.

But not Ophelia's family, evidently. She looked down and shook her head in reply.

"I didn't mean to make you feel bad," Scarlet assured her. "Star apologies. I'm just starprised. You know, you're lucky you don't have parents like mine who dragged you all over Starland with them."

"Do you really think? I think you're lucky to *have* parents," said Ophelia. She added, "I never actually got to know mine."

Scarlet caught a breath and swallowed it. Those were not words she'd expected to hear. She instantly wished she could take her own words back. But it was too late. *Now what?* she thought. How was she supposed to respond to something like that? *So you're an orphan? You need parents? Feel free to take mine!* Scarlet had never been good at finding the right thing to say. That kind of stuff was hard.

Luckily, she didn't have to say anything, because Ophelia said something first.

"Stars! Look! Palm scanners!" Ophelia pointed across the street at a square yellow box set on top of a pole. Inside, a big red hand flashed on and off. There was another one, they noticed, on their own corner, high above their heads. And they did resemble palm scanners—in some ways, Scarlet thought—but something about them wasn't quite right. First of all, yes, they were much, much too high for a Wishling palm to reach. Plus, there were no doors to be opened that Scarlet could see.

"I wonder how you reach them," said Ophelia. She stood on her toes and stretched her hand as far up to the one on their corner as it would go. Still, there was more than an arm's length between her hand and the red one, even when she jumped.

"Let's figure that out later," said Scarlet, "when we have to."

"Right," said Ophelia. "Of course."

Just then, a large yellow Wishling vehicle rolled past them on those round black things that Wishlings called . . . whorls? Wools? Whirls?

"That's a school bus!" said Scarlet. "And look! Here come some more."

"What's a school bus?" asked Ophelia.

"Are you serious?" said Scarlet.

She was.

"They're like starbuses, but they roll along on the ground instead of hovering above it. They take Wishling students to school when they don't already live there."

"Oh! So we're getting close to a school?"

"Very close," said Scarlet. She looked down the street at a large tan building with a tall gray pole planted in front of it.

"Look, Scarlet! Stars!" said Ophelia, pointing to the flag up at the top.

There wasn't enough breeze to keep the tricolored banner flying, but now and then it caught a gust. Scarlet saw the stars and instantly counted half a hydrong.

"So is that a school?" Ophelia asked as they watched the first yellow bus and several more exactly like it turn in and pull to a stop in front of the building.

Scarlet nodded and checked her Star-Zap. It was precisely where their directions led.

"It's so quiet. Where are all the Wishlings?" said Ophelia.

That was when they heard the bell. It came from inside the school, but even from that far away the ringing hurt their ears.

"What was that?" Ophelia asked Scarlet just as the doors to the school burst open and a flood of young Wishlings came pouring out.

Scarlet and Ophelia stood and watched lines form beside each school bus while other Wishlings simply walked away. . . .

"Oh, stars! Did we miss the school day?" Ophelia said with a gasp. "Is everyone going home? What are we going to do? I'll never find my Wishling now!"

"Not if you stand here like that, you won't," muttered Scarlet, grabbing her by the arm. She dragged Ophelia toward the school and pointed to her bracelet. "Keep an eye on your Wish Pendant!" she reminded her, sure that she'd forget. "We'll know we've found your Wishling as soon as it starts to glow."

Scarlet eyed Ophelia's bracelet, too, as they hurried past each bus. The lines outside the vehicles had all but disappeared. Engines were revving and drivers were calling, "All right! Find a seat and sit in it back there!"

"Superstar! There it goes!" said Scarlet as the bracelet blinked. "Your Wisher must be on this bus!" A moogle later she sighed. "Oh . . . no . . . The sun just caught a facet. It isn't glowing. Never mind."

She turned as a group of girls brushed past them, then paused by the closest bus. One girl was quite tall by Wishling standards, with laser-straight rows of tight black braids. The others were of average Wishling height. One had straight fair hair that hung smoothly down her back. The other's hair was dark and thick and curly and seemed to defy the basic rules of Wishworld gravity that Scarlet had learned in school.

"So you're sure you can't come home with us?" that girl was saying.

"Sorry. I really am," the tall girl said. "I have . . . all these chores to do today."

The fair-haired girl sighed heavily.

"You know this project is due on Friday," the first girl said. "And we're *all* supposed to contribute. This is a big part of our grade."

"Yeah. A *big* part." The other girl flipped her pale hair back with a toss of her head. "And we're doing *all* the work. I mean, I wish you'd said something about all these doctors' appointments and your piano recital—and today's chores—when we started on this."

"I . . . I . . ."

"If it's just chores, can't you do them later?" said the curly-haired girl. "Won't your mom understand if you just explain?"

The tall girl chewed on either side of her bottom lip.

"Well, you see . . . it's my *step*mom . . . and, well, she's, like, *soooo* mean."

"Oh . . ."

"Sorry . . ."

The two girls nodded sympathetically.

The tall girl heaved a heavy sigh, as if that was the story of her life.

"So what about *tomorrow*?" The girl with the fair hair asked more gently. "Can you at least come home with us then? If the chrysalises start hatching today, like I think they will, we'll have our butterflies and that'll be it."

"Oh, I hope they hatch today!" said the curly-haired girl.

"I know, right? I can't *wait*!" Her blond friend clapped quickly, as if beating a snare drum. "*Ooh!* You know what we should do? We should have a big butterfly party and celebrate!"

"Yes!"

The two traded *aha* grins while the third girl looked down at her shoes.

"Your stepmom would let you do that, wouldn't she?" the blond girl asked.

The tall girl shrugged. "I don't know. . . . She's so mean, like I said. . . ."

"All aboard!" the bus driver called down through the door just then. Both girls looked up and waved.

"Coming." The curly-haired girl turned back to the tall girl. "See you tomorrow, I guess, Arden."

"See you tomorrow, Chloe. Bye, Sydney."

"If the butterflies hatch, we'll text you."

"Great. Yes, definitely do."

"Um . . . sorry . . . about your stepmom and all. . . ."

"Thanks . . ." the girl murmured. "It's kind of hard."

"It's her!" Scarlet leaned over and hissed to Ophelia, more into her pigtail than her ear.

"Do you really think so? How do you know?" Ophelia turned to her. "Are you sure?"

Scarlet twisted her mouth in irritation. "Check your Wish Pendant and you'll see. I'll bet my stars it's that *stepmother.*" Her eyes narrowed at the thought. "It's a classic Wishworld wish! She's probably been wishing to get rid of her . . . once and for all. But that's an impossible wish. *Well?*" She nodded toward Ophelia's wrist. "What are you waiting for? Check your bracelet!" Why she was so eager for Ophelia to find her Wisher, Scarlet didn't know. Just a few moogles earlier, she had wanted desperately for Ophelia to fail—but now, oddly, not so much.

She was as sure as a sundial the bracelet would be glowing like a fiery flare. But no . . . the star-shaped jewels on the bracelet were as lifeless as they had been before.

"I thought we'd found her. Didn't you?" Scarlet looked over her shoulder at the tall girl, still so close to them, watching her friends' bus pull away.

"Maybe she is my Wisher," said Ophelia. "Maybe, just like my Star-Zap, my Wish Pendant is powerless, too. . . ." She looked down at her wrist in frustration. Then, suddenly, her head bent farther down. "Did you bring a glowworm here with you from Starland?" she asked, pointing toward the ground.

"What?"

"You're glowing. There, on your ankle. Under your . . . what do you call those again?"

"Jeans," said Scarlet, distracted, as she followed Ophelia's eyes. Her ankle *was* glowing . . . even through the heavy pants!

She yanked up her cuff to discover the hot-pink starbuckles on her own Wish Pendant boots shining like quasars on her feet.

She looked up at Ophelia. "It's not a glowworm, it's my Wish Pendant."

Ophelia's eyes were as round as moons. "Why is *your* Wish Pendant glowing?"

"Don't ask *me*! *How should I know?*"

CHAPTER
11

The next thing Scarlet knew, her Wish Pendant faded from twinkling star to flat pink stone.

"What happened?" gasped Ophelia.

"I don't know. . . ." Could it have been some sort of false alarm? Then she looked up to see the tall girl had moved and was walking down the street. The Wisher just wasn't close. That was how Wish Pendants behaved.

"Come on. You've got to catch her!" Scarlet snapped at Ophelia as she hurried to follow the girl.

"Star greetings, Wishling."

The tall girl stopped midstride on the chalky gray sidewalk. "Excuse me?" she said, slowly turning, with a stiff note of dread in her voice.

Ophelia, who'd offered the greeting, covered her mouth with one hand. "Sorry! Forgot!" she whispered to Scarlet.

"*Hi.*" Scarlet looked back up and smiled at the Wishling. "Sorry." She pointed her thumb toward Ophelia. "My friend here thinks she's so funny when she says weird things like that."

The girl's eyes skipped back and forth between Scarlet and Ophelia. "Sorry, but do I know you? Do you go to this school?"

"No," said Ophelia innocently before Scarlet could stop her.

Scarlet smiled as she gritted her teeth. Had they been on Starland, sparks would have been shooting straight out of her ears.

"What she means is no, this isn't our regular school," Scarlet explained hurriedly. "But *temporarily*, yes, we go here." She checked to make sure Ophelia was listening carefully. "We're *exchange* students, you see."

"Really? That's so cool. Where are you from?" the girl asked.

"Where are we from?" *Good question*, thought Scarlet as her mind suddenly went blank. She tried to remember some of the names of places she'd learned in Wishworld Relations, names she'd imagined using on missions just like this hydrongs and hydrong of times. . . .

"Orion!" Ophelia blurted, lifting her chin and looking proud.

"Orion? Where is that?" asked the girl.

"It's just up there in the—"

Scarlet pulled Ophelia's arm down from above her head and put her other hand over Ophelia's startled mouth. "Did you think she said *Orion*? She said *Ohio*!" Scarlet laughed.

"Oh." The girl nodded, then grinned with a friendly shrug. "Well, welcome to Florida, I guess. I'm Arden. Nice to meet you."

"Hi. I'm Scarlet, and this is Ophelia. Nice to meet you, too," Scarlet replied before Ophelia could speak. She wasn't quite sure how Ophelia would have answered that introduction. She only knew somehow it would have been wrong.

"If you like, I could show you around," Arden offered.

"Really? That would be startastic!" exclaimed Ophelia.

Scarlet swallowed a groan and closed her eyes.

"Would you excuse us for just a minute?" Scarlet asked the girl, who shrugged.

Scarlet dragged Ophelia away from Arden by her backpack. "Ophelia!" she muttered. "You have to stop saying things like 'startastic' and 'star greetings.' Those are Starland phrases. Wishlings say things like 'awesome' and 'sick.' It's one of the first things we learned. Remember? Back in Wishers 101. What have you been learning at Starling Academy, anyway?"

"Star apologies . . ." mumbled Ophelia. "I guess I just forgot."

"Well, start remembering!" hissed Scarlet. "Or better yet, don't say anything else. Just let me do the talking. Okay? You worry about focusing all your energy on granting Arden's wish." She quickly checked her Star-Zap. "This clock is counting down very fast!"

"Yes. Okay." Ophelia nodded, and Scarlet hoped she understood. Scarlet wasn't sure how she'd gone from thinking it might be all right if Ophelia failed to being determined to see her succeed. It was almost as if she had no choice but to make the mission work.

"Is everything okay?" Arden asked when Scarlet and Ophelia returned.

"Everything is great."

"So, what do you think? Do you want to hang out? Do you want me to show you around? What haven't you seen yet?" asked Arden. "I know it's a pretty small town, but we have a really nice park. It's kind of famous for its butterfly attraction . . . er, um . . . but we can skip that part. It's not really all that great."

"Thanks," said Scarlet. "That sounds really nice. Really, it does. But . . ."

"But what?" Arden asked.

Scarlet tried to assume the expression she'd seen the other girls give Arden before—the one that seemed to say, "I feel so sorry for you, poor girl."

"You probably have to go straight home," said Scarlet.

"No," said Arden. "Not really." She smiled and shook her head. "I mean, I have to go home eventually, but later on—by dinnertime—not, like, right away."

Scarlet was confused and could tell that her face showed it. "Are you *sure*? I'd hate for you to get in trouble with your stepmother."

"How did you know I have a stepmother?"

"Er . . . I guessed, I guess?"

"Wow. Good guess," said Arden, who looked surprised but not upset.

"You probably wish you didn't have one," Scarlet went on, nodding. "Or at least that she wasn't so mean." She snuck a wink at Ophelia, then watched as Arden's expression slowly changed.

"No, my stepmother's great. She's not at all mean. In

fact—don't tell my mom this—but she's nicer than her sometimes."

Now it was Scarlet's turn to flip expressions. "But doesn't she make you stay home? And do all the chores? You know, and work all day and night?"

Arden's nose wrinkled and she started to giggle. "What are you talking about?" She looked down at her red ruffled skirt and sleeveless yellow tee. "Do I look like Cinderella? The only chores my stepmom makes me do are the dishes, sometimes, and make my bed . . . not that I ever do."

"But . . ."

Arden waited for Scarlet to finish, but Scarlet wasn't sure how to go on. Why had this Wishling told those others that she had a mean stepmother if she didn't? And most important, what was her wish, then? To have a *mean* stepmother? No, of course not. Why would any Wishling want that?

So then what could it be? Scarlet tried to think. She glanced at Ophelia, who was blank-faced, clearly trying to catch up. She wasn't going to be much help in figuring this out; Scarlet could tell from her frown. Then something else that Scarlet had heard before suddenly popped into her head—something about doctors' appointments. . . .

Of course! That had to be it!

There were no doctors on Starland, of course. There simply was no need. All the positive wish energy on Starland kept Starlings healthy throughout their Cycle of Life, until they began their afterglow. But Scarlet had learned in school about Wishworld doctors and all they did for Wishlings whenever they got sick. She'd also learned about the kinds of wishes that Wishlings often made when doctors couldn't help. Of course, those were impossible wishes, and maybe that was why Ophelia was having so much trouble. But Scarlet was sure they could help her make a more appropriate one.

"You're not well, are you?"

"Excuse me?"

"You're sick. Well, don't worry. We'll find a way . . ."

"But I'm *not* sick. I'm fine. Really. Why?" the girl asked, touching her cheeks. "Do I look bad or something?"

"No, no. You look good. It's not that," Scarlet said. What could she say now? If the Wisher wasn't sick and her stepmother wasn't mean, what wishes were left? Had she also said something about a piano recital?

Or . . . could it be that she wasn't their Wisher at all?

What a starmendous waste of time!

Scarlet looked down to check her Wish Pendant. It

was still glowing . . . which was odd. But it wasn't like this was *her* mission, so maybe it didn't mean anything.

"Omigosh," the girl said suddenly, as if a holo-text had just come through. "I get it." She turned to Ophelia. "You must have heard me talking to Chloe and Sydney."

Ophelia's cheeks filled like balloons as she worked to keep the words in.

"Yeah," Arden went on, not needing a reply. "Some of those things I said back there . . . they weren't exactly true."

"But *why*?" Ophelia blurted. "It sounded like they needed your help."

That was actually a good question, Scarlet thought, so that time she let it go.

"Oh . . . it's complicated," said Arden. She sighed and looked away.

"They're mean girls," said Scarlet knowingly. It was a common basis for wishes, unfortunately, but those weren't too hard to grant.

"No," said Arden. "They're fine. They're really nice and fun. And I want to be their friend. That's why I *wanted* to be in their lab group for this science project."

"Oh," Scarlet said, confused. Was this something Wishlings often did, she wondered—fail to make any sense?

"I didn't know they'd want to study butterflies. . . ." As she said that, Arden winced.

"What's wrong with butterflies?" said Scarlet.

"Are you afraid of them?" Ophelia asked.

Scarlet turned to Ophelia and did all she could not to roll her eyes. "Of course she's not afraid of *butterflies*!" she muttered. Could a Starling be more dim?

"I know," said Arden. "It's ridiculous, isn't it? But I can't help it. Do you know, I can't even look at pictures of butterflies without wanting to throw up? I tried to suggest other topics, but they were so into the idea. And they'd already ordered the caterpillar kit and everything. There was nothing I could say or do. Their minds were totally set."

"Did you tell them you were scared?" asked Scarlet. That seemed easy enough to do.

Arden nodded. "I tried to. But they thought it was a joke. They just laughed and said stuff like 'Can you imagine? Afraid of butterflies!'"

"So . . . they *are* mean," said Scarlet.

"No, they weren't being mean at all. They thought I was being funny. They thought it had to be a joke." Arden kicked a rock and sent it bouncing off the curb and into the street. "I guess I could have told them I was serious . . . except then, instead of laughing at the idea, they would have laughed at me."

"So what are you going to do?" Scarlet asked. She reached for Ophelia and pulled her near. She could sense a wish a breath away and wanted to make sure Ophelia heard it.

"What I've been doing, I guess: making up excuses to stay away. So I'll get an F on the project and Chloe and Sydney will never talk to me again. But what else *can* I do? I *wish* I wasn't afraid of butterflies . . . but we all know wishing doesn't help." She took a few steps away to kick another rock while Scarlet hung back and pumped her fist.

Yes! she thought as a sharp but not unpleasant jolt ran up and down her spine.

Scarlet turned to wink at Ophelia, but Ophelia's eyes were on the ground.

"Ophelia!" Scarlet nudged her with an elbow. "Your Wisher just voiced her wish! She doesn't want to be afraid of butterflies!" she hissed.

"Really? Oh! Sorry," Ophelia said. She glanced over her shoulder at Arden. "What do I do now? Oh . . . and what are butterflies? Are they, like, wings or something you can put on toasted Wishling bread?"

CHAPTER
12

After a quick explanation of what butterflies were ("They're basically like flutterfocuses, only they don't change color or light up."), Scarlet told Ophelia her plan.

"It's easy. We learned about these kinds of fear wishes in Wish Fulfillment, remember? No? Right. Of course you don't. Never mind. Basically, we have to get her to talk more about her fear and where it comes from. Then we have to reassure her that butterflies mean her no harm. Then we need to introduce her to butterflies. It's supposed to be little by little . . . but of course we don't have a lot of time. Luckily, there's that butterfly attraction she talked about—which is perfect! We just take her there! *Zap!* Done!"

"Talk, reassure, introduce," said Ophelia. She nodded

so her pigtails bounced like springs. "Star salutations, Scarlet. I'll try. I really will." Ophelia's chin was trembling, but she managed a smile. And somehow, before Scarlet could help herself, she was returning a grin.

Scarlet could feel it inside her. . . . *Ew!* Something was warming up and softening, like stars melting into thick molten glass. Scarlet tried to will it all back into sharp jagged crystals, but no—it was too late.

It was easy to be mad at Ophelia for taking her place, and even easier to scold her for making so many mistakes. And yet this whole situation wasn't Ophelia's fault any more than it was Scarlet's. The most important thing, whether Scarlet liked it or not, was to help Ophelia as much as she could to make Arden's wish come true.

"No," Scarlet told Ophelia sternly. "You're a Star Darling. You need to do more than try. You need to grant this wish. So go!" She pointed to Arden, who was walking away. "What are you waiting for?"

They caught up to Arden at the corner. She grinned at them warily. "So now you know my secret. You probably think I'm super weird."

"What are you talking about?" said Scarlet. "Everyone's scared of something. Take Ophelia here." She shot a quick nod at her partner.

"Me? Oh, yes! *Me!* I'm afraid of everything!" Ophelia

said. "Black holes . . . asteroids . . . gamma radiation . . . and even those energy bunnies that collect under the bed."

Scarlet and Arden both stared at her, speechless.

"Anyway," Scarlet said. "Being scared is nothing to be ashamed of. But it is something you can try to change."

"How?"

"Why don't we go to that park you were talking about," said Scarlet, "and talk about it there?"

★

The park was a short walk from the school, away from downtown. A dark metal arch marked the entrance at a corner where two roads crossed.

"Wait!" Arden grabbed Scarlet's and Ophelia's arms as they reached the corner across from it, just before they stepped off the curb. She pointed to the palm scanner across the street and the big bright red hand that was flashing at them.

"Right. The palm scanners," said Ophelia. "But I couldn't reach it. Can you?"

She started to jump as she'd done before in town, to reach the box above them. Scarlet almost joined her. But then she saw Arden laughing—not meanly, just as if they were all in on a joke. Clearly, Ophelia was way off. That wasn't a palm scanner at all. But if Ophelia was helping lift Arden's mood, why not play along?

"*Very* funny," said Scarlet. She chuckled and grabbed for Ophelia's arm. Just then, the hand stopped blinking and began to glow a steady red. As it did, a car whizzed past them, followed by another and more after that.

Scarlet watched Arden press a button on the side of the post on their corner, then read the small sign next to it: PUSH BUTTON TO WALK. A moogle later, the hand disappeared and was replaced by a white symbol of a walking man.

"Are you coming?" said Arden as she stepped off the sidewalk and into the street. "The light's going to change back if we don't hurry up."

"So . . . it's not a palm scanner?" Ophelia whispered to Scarlet as they followed. "I'm sorry. I messed up again."

"Hey, she's smiling," said Scarlet, nodding ahead. "I think you might actually have done something right."

"So this is our park," Arden said as they walked through the arch. She lifted her arms and stretched them out to her sides, turning slightly left and right. "It's small, but it's pretty nice."

It *was* nice, Scarlet had to agree, in an overly green Wishworld way. It was strange, and almost refreshing, to see grass so singular in color—and such straight paths that refused to move. It was actually nice to get away from all the glitter and sparkle of Starland and appreciate not just how colorful and brilliant things were but other qualities, as well. Like how the little brown creature on the branch high above them sounded, whistling its curious tune.

And the way the grass smelled. Scarlet took a deep whiff, which Arden noticed. She nodded as if she understood.

"They must have just mowed."

Ah, thought Scarlet. So that was what that sharp tangy scent was. Scarlet didn't even know how the grass on Starland smelled, she realized, or if it smelled at all. Starland grass always stayed the perfect length, so it never had to be cut.

Ophelia, meanwhile, was pointing at a large dull but colorful, oddly shaped structure behind a green metal fence. At the center was an elevated platform sheltered by a yellow roof. Along with a ladder, there appeared to be several other means by which to reach the platform: a winding blue ramp; a slick yellow pole; a thick knotted rope; and, last but not least, a long sloping red tube, out of which a small Wishling boy abruptly popped.

"What's that?" Ophelia asked.

"What's what?" Arden replied. Her eyes darted from

pole to ramp to tube, not quite sure what Ophelia could mean.

Scarlet pulled Ophelia close. "It's a playground. A *Wishling* playground," she clarified. She had seen them before from the Wishworld Surveillance Deck, but Ophelia obviously had not. If she had, she would have known that Wishling playgrounds were nothing like those on Starland, with their gyro-seesaws and anti-gravity slides and energy trampolines. There was one apparatus Starland and Wishworld shared, however, and Scarlet pointed it out to Ophelia. "See?"

Ophelia's eyes followed Scarlet's away from the platform, along a track of evenly spaced metal bars to a triangular frame from which hung three rubber slings on chunky black chains.

"Lucky stars! *Swings!*" Ophelia exclaimed. "Can we?" She turned to Arden first, then Scarlet. "I love swings so much!"

"*Now?*" Scarlet said. "*Really?* We came here to *talk*, Ophelia, remember? *Not* play."

"Star a—So sorry. Yes. Of course."

"We could do both," Arden said, shrugging. "I mean, why not? I haven't been on a swing in years." She grinned, suddenly looking happier than she had since they had met. "No one else is using them. It'll be fun.

C'mon! Let's go!" She left Ophelia and Scarlet to follow as she headed toward the playground gate.

"Star apologies. Truly," Ophelia murmured to Scarlet. She scrunched her freckled nose. "I didn't mean to delay the mission further. Don't worry. I won't do it again."

Ophelia dropped her backpack next to Arden's just inside the fence.

"Oh, no . . ." said Scarlet, eyeing it.

"What now?" Ophelia moaned. "What did I do?"

"You lost your key chain. I don't know what it's for. But I'm sure we'll find out now." Each Star Darling had received a glittery stuffed star attached to her backpack. Wishers called them "key chains."

"What key chain?" said Ophelia. "I don't know what you mean."

"Didn't you get one right before takeoff?"

"Nooo . . ." Ophelia said slowly. "No," she repeated, more surely.

"Oh . . ." said Scarlet. "Good," she declared. One less thing to worry about, at least.

They turned to watch Arden skip up to the middle swing and fall into the hard rubber seat with a smile.

"Well," Scarlet whispered to Ophelia with the barest of smiles, "what are you waiting for? Let's go."

By the time they joined Arden, the Wishling was flying back and forth, her feet nearly extending past the bar overhead.

Excited, Ophelia took the swing on Arden's right, gripping the chains extra tight in each hand. "*Wheeee!*" she cried as she leaned her head back and eagerly kicked out her feet. After a moogle, however, she sat back up. "Aw . . . mine's broken," she said.

"Mine, too," said Scarlet. It hadn't moved a shortsnip since she'd sat down. She raised her feet once more, just to be extra sure . . . but no, it did not want to move.

Between them, Arden slowed until her own swing was barely swaying. "What do you mean they're broken?" She gave Scarlet's chain a little tug, then peered behind her at the seat. "It looks okay to me."

"Oh, that part's fine, yes. It's the swinger," explained Scarlet. "It's not working." She lifted her feet again. "See? It doesn't fly like yours. It just sits here. Whatever." She shrugged. "It's no big . . . what do they say . . . deal?"

"You know, you have to *pump* to swing," said Arden. "You know . . . like this. . . ."

Scarlet watched Arden lean back and kick her legs out, exactly as Ophelia had done. But unlike Ophelia, Arden didn't stop there. That was only the first step, it seemed. Arden next swung her body forward and sharply bent her knees. Scarlet watched the swing respond by gliding backward, at which point Arden leaned back again. As she kept going like that, whipping herself back and forth, she made her swing fly higher . . . and higher . . . and higher still!

Who would have ever thought that Wishlings had to power their own swings? thought Scarlet.

Fortunately, this "pumping" wasn't half as difficult as it looked. Even Ophelia was successful almost immediately, much to her delight. Scarlet could have used a push to start, but after a few rough kicks and bends, she quickly began to catch up.

They all stopped at just about the same time but for different reasons: Ophelia because her Star-Zap fell out of her pocket when she practically flew upside down; Arden because she saw it fall and wanted to stop and help; Scarlet because as soon as she saw Arden reach for the Star-Zap, she knew she had to grab it—fast!

"Cool phone!" said Arden, who was already out of her swing and running her finger along the Star-Zap. Instantly, the top flipped up.

Scarlet's heart nearly stopped as she stared at it, terrified that a holo-something would suddenly appear. Only after a moogle did she remember that it had no energy. *Lucky stars!* she thought with a sigh of relief.

"It's actually a Star-Z—" Ophelia started to correct her.

"A Star-Zee?" Scarlet cut in, laughing. "Honestly, Ophelia. You make up the funniest names." She took the Star-Zap from Arden and handed it to Ophelia with a tight, open-eyed smile. "Here you go. Maybe put that in your backpack, why don't you. And keep it there. You'd hate for your *phone* here to break."

"Right . . ." said Ophelia. "Right! My *phone*!" She ran over to her backpack and dropped it in. She returned to the swing set, out of breath. "Better?" she asked with a grin.

Scarlet nodded. "Much better. Now." She sighed. "I think it's time we *talked*, don't you?" She turned to Arden and put her hands on her shoulders. "Here," she said. "Have a seat." Gently, she guided her back into her swing, then sank into her own. She didn't have to look at the Countdown Clock on her Star-Zap to know that there wasn't much time left in their mission. She could see the sun drifting steadily down toward the treetops. That meant there wasn't a moogle to waste.

"We're going to help you get over this fear of yours," she told Arden. "But first you need to talk."

"Talk about what?"

"Your fear," said Scarlet. "When it started. Where it

came from. All that good stuff. So go ahead. Fire away."

Arden's face, which had been so warm and open, seemed all of a sudden to hang a CLOSED sign. "My fear of butterflies . . . oh, no . . . I don't want to. It's too hard to talk about. I just can't."

"But . . ." Scarlet paused to check the sun again. "But you *have* to talk about it," she blurted.

Scarlet could feel her own face getting hot and probably red—especially when Ophelia spoke up from the next swing: "That's okay. We understand."

"Thanks." Arden twisted her swing toward Ophelia.

"I know what it's like not to want to talk about something," Ophelia continued. "You probably do, too, Scarlet. Right?"

"No." Scarlet frowned impatiently. "Well . . . okay . . . yes, maybe. Sometimes."

"It's just so embarrassing," said Arden.

Ophelia nodded. "You don't want to be reminded of it. I know."

"It was literally the worst day of my life," said Arden.

"I can only imagine," said Ophelia gently as she rocked her swing from side to side.

Scarlet's eyes, meanwhile, flashed from Ophelia to Arden, as she observed their exchange of trusting smiles.

Arden was actually about to talk, Scarlet realized—thanks to Ophelia, no less!

"I was at my grandparents' house—they live on a big farm. And I was little. I'd only just turned five. It was before dinner. I was playing hide-and-seek with my older cousins out in the fields around the barn. We used to do that all the time. So I see this big tree out at the edge of the meadow, and I decide to go hide behind that. The trunk was literally *this* thick." Arden held her arms out wide. "I mean *huge*. Big enough to hide three or four kids . . . I don't know, maybe more. And so tall that when you stood under it and looked up, you couldn't see the top at all. My grandmother says it was a big tree even when she was a kid, so you can imagine how old it must be now.

"Anyway, I ran up and stood there, hiding behind it—all by myself—while my cousin Jason ran around with no idea, busy finding everyone else. And then . . . I started hearing this kind of *rustling* sound all around me . . . kind of like a cat purring, only *really* loud. And the next thing I knew I was covered, I mean literally *covered*, in all these"—Arden shuddered—"all these *butterflies*! Evidently, they were roosting there—thousands of them—on their way to Mexico for the winter. My grandmother says they migrate through her farm every year. Which is why I refuse to go back there, by the way."

"But the butterflies aren't there all the time, are they?" asked Scarlet.

"No. Just the fall, when they're flying south. But just the thought of being there . . ." She winced and shivered again. "I love my grandparents . . . but it's just too hard. I get nauseous just thinking about it."

"So what did you do when the flutterfo—I mean butterflies landed on you?" asked Ophelia.

"I screamed. Like crazy," Arden said. "I mean, I was five and all alone. Sure, I realized pretty quickly that they were butterflies, but I still thought they were going to eat me alive. I couldn't get them off. It was like they were stuck to me with pins. They wouldn't let go with their little"—she cringed—"*feet*. I tried to brush them and shake them and knock them off, but they were in my hair, my clothes, everything, refusing to let go. Then, finally, I tried to run. But of course I couldn't see. So I tripped . . . and fell . . . and landed on the ground, on, like, a hundred of them." She paused to take a breath. "Basically killing them all. So there I am, lying on all these dead butterflies, covered with hundreds more. All by myself. Screaming. Crying. Oh—and I wet my pants, I was so scared. Did I happen to mention that?"

"*Aw . . .*" Ophelia patted her shoulder.

Scarlet leaned forward. "So what happened next?"

"Finally—after what literally felt like forever—my cousins and my grandma found me. By then, the butterflies had gone back up in the tree—except for the ones I murdered, of course. When they found out what happened, my cousins laughed and called me 'butterfly bait' for the rest of the weekend. In fact, they still call me that today. It's become a little family joke, that nickname."

"That's terrible!" said Scarlet.

Arden nodded. "Yeah, it is."

"I hope you call them something back!" Scarlet said. "I know some good names, by the way, if you need any suggestions."

"Oh, but I'm sure they don't mean to be mean," said Ophelia. "They probably just don't understand."

Arden hung her head, shaking it slowly. "They sure don't. Nobody does."

"We do," Ophelia said softly. "We know exactly how you feel." She glanced over Arden's shoulder at Scarlet. *What should I do next?* she mouthed.

Scarlet tried to think. . . .

Just keep going! she told Ophelia—not with words but by rolling her arm.

"You know what I think?" said Ophelia.

Arden waited to hear.

"I think . . . I think anybody would be scared of butterflies after that happened to them."

"Thanks," said Arden. She smiled a little. "And thanks for this. . . ."

"For what?"

"For letting me talk about it. To be honest, it feels kind of good. Do you know, I don't think I've ever told anyone that story before? Never, in all these years. And in a way, I think the story I actually remember was a little better than the one I was trying to forget."

"What do you mean?"

"Well, I mean, the butterflies were scary—for sure. But for some reason I'd remembered them biting me, like they had little teeth. Now, though, I realize that they didn't do much more than tickle me."

"Hey! It's our turn!"

Scarlet turned, along with the others, to find a long line of young Wishling children standing behind them, looking as if *they* might bite.

"You can't hog the swings!" said the first one.

"Yeah! No hogging!" chirped another. "Besides, you're too old. My mom said."

"Swings are for kids!" they started chanting. "Swings are for kids! Swings are for kids!"

Ophelia shuffled her swing toward Arden's. "Um, can we get out of here? They scare me."

Arden laughed. "Yeah, sure. Let's go."

CHAPTER
13

"**I can't believe** I'm doing this," said Arden.

Behind her back, Scarlet and Ophelia leaned in to share a smile of so-close-they-could-taste-it success. They were standing on the path that led to the butterfly exhibit, in front of a sign that read BUTTERFLIES! 200 FEET AHEAD.

"My stars," Ophelia whispered to Scarlet. "Did you know butterflies had two hundred legs?"

Scarlet studied the sign. "I didn't," she whispered back. "It's kind of starmazing that they can fly. . . ."

The wooden sign also had a carving of a butterfly, which Arden was regarding with an anxious expression.

"Don't worry," said Ophelia. "Like we said, if you don't want to go in, you don't have to."

"No, of course not. . . . But let's keep going," Scarlet said.

The path turned, and as it did, the exhibit itself came into view.

"Ooh! It's such a pretty structure!" said Ophelia.

Scarlet had to agree. The side they could see had multiple rising and falling arches, almost like the curves of a cloud. The walls appeared to be made of some kind of netting and were decorated with large colorful pictures of butterflies. No two were the same. Through the net, it was easy to see a veritable jungle of trees, vines, and blooming bushes growing inside. What they couldn't yet see—from such a distance, Scarlet figured—was any butterflies.

"Just imagine if that place glittered!" said Ophelia. "How stunning it would be!"

"I think they might light it up at night on the weekends," said Arden.

"*Really?*" Ophelia's face brightened at the thought (as much as a face on Wishworld could).

"Yeah, but I'm not sure. I've never actually seen it. It's just something I've heard."

"Ooh! I'd love to stay and see it. Scarlet, do you think we can?"

"Why couldn't you?" asked Arden.

"Let's just keep going," said Scarlet. "Shall we? I mean, if that's okay?"

Arden nodded. She took a deep breath and moved forward, ever so slowly. Her feet seemed to fight her for every step. Scarlet could hear Arden telling herself, "I can do this. I can . . ." between rapid shallow breaths.

Yes, Scarlet thought. She *was* going to do this. She was going to overcome her fear. Scarlet looked at Ophelia and pointed to her bracelet. *Be ready!* she mouthed. What was crazier, Scarlet wondered: that Ophelia's mission just might be successful or that Scarlet just might be happy for her?

As they got closer to the exhibit, they found themselves walking among dense vibrant flower gardens dotted with butterfly-shaped signs bearing various facts.

One showed the process a caterpillar went through to become a butterfly.

"'Metamorphosis,'" read Arden. "That's what our project is about."

"Wait? Is that really how butterflies are made? They start out as *those*?" Ophelia pointed to a caterpillar, then to a butterfly. "You'd think something that delicate and pretty would be made of flower petals and stardust."

"You're funny," Arden said. She suddenly looked more relaxed.

Scarlet could see how Ophelia had taken Arden's mind off her fear—without even meaning to—so she decided to try it herself. After all, she *was* there to help.

"This is interesting," she said. "Did you know butterflies don't eat? They can only drink. And they taste with their feet. That's uncommon, right?"

Arden laughed again.

It worked! Scarlet could practically feel the wish energy ready to come out of this Wisher, and she could tell that Ophelia was sensing it, too.

"Oh," Ophelia went on, not really getting the humor in anything but still happy to play along. "And look here. This says that they have four wings, two on each side, and only *six* legs. Not two hundred?" She paused to frown, seriously confused.

"Two *hundred*! You're so funny!" Arden giggled. "Both of you." She stopped in front of another sign. "Ooh," she said. "Check this out. According to this, butterflies can see ultraviolet colors. It helps them know which flowers have the nectar they want. *Hmmm.* What's so special about seeing ultraviolet colors?" She grinned. "I mean, can't everyone?"

"I don't get it," Ophelia whispered to Scarlet.

"You don't have to," Scarlet murmured back. "Just so it works. How about this one?" she said more loudly, pointing to another sign. "This is also about what butterflies see. It says butterflies are attracted to bright colors, especially yellow and red. *Hee-hee!*"

She waited for Arden to laugh . . . or chuckle . . . or at least smile. Instead, though, she looked over to see Arden staring down at her bright yellow T-shirt. She touched the hem of her ruby red skirt.

"Er, what's wrong?" Scarlet asked.

"I can't do this."

"But you have to—I mean . . . yes, you *can*."

"Maybe. But not today. Not dressed like this. What if they land on me? Uh, I thought I was ready. I did. But I'm not. I'm really not." She held out her hands. "Look." They were trembling like leaves in a solar storm.

Scarlet looked over at Ophelia. Did she have an idea? Any idea at all? Scarlet had done everything she could think of to help grant this wish in time, but it just wasn't enough in the end.

With the tiniest nod, Ophelia lowered her eyes back to Arden's hands and gently picked one up. "You know, you're not alone. We're here for you. Whatever you need. Would it help at all if Scarlet and I stayed right by your side and maybe held your hands?" She looked back at Scarlet warmly, clearly expecting her to reach out and take Arden's other hand. "Scarlet?"

"Well . . . I don't know. Here's the thing. *Would* it help?" Scarlet was skeptical at best. She'd never bought into that whole Starland hand-holding-all-the-time thing. What was the point? She didn't know. To other Starlings, linking arms and holding hands came as naturally as glowing, but to Scarlet it always felt forced. In fact, getting that close to others just made her feel more alone.

But Ophelia wasn't letting go, and neither was Arden.

Oh, why not? Scarlet finally thought.

She reached out and put her hand lightly on Arden's, surprised at how warm and soft it felt. Arden squeezed, and Scarlet nearly jumped. Instead, though, without even thinking about it, she flashed Arden a smile and squeezed back.

"You know . . . it's so weird how I met you today," Arden said with a small but grateful smile. "It's almost like a fairy godmother sent you or something."

"Well, *that* sure didn't happen," Scarlet said.

"Close, though." Ophelia grinned, then caught Scarlet's "*Really?*" face. "What? Oh. That's a *joke*."

"So, shall we try this again?" Scarlet said. "Together?"

"Okay." Arden took a deep breath. "Just . . . don't let go."

Hand in hand, they walked down the last bit of path toward the butterfly building and up to the wide glass door. Inside, they could see the stars of the exhibit: hydrongs and hydrongs of butterflies. Some were tiny, no bigger than a pinky. Others were almost as big as a hand. Some were yellow and black, some were orange, and some were all white. And some were the exact same blue as Vega's hair!

"Now, just so we're clear, if I start to scream or faint or anything like that, we're coming right back out."

"Of course," said Ophelia.

"We've got you," said Scarlet. She placed her other hand on Arden's, as well.

"Okay." Arden took a long and slow breath in, held it, then let it out quickly. "I think I'm ready."

"Wait . . . what? Oh, no . . ." groaned Scarlet.

"What's wrong?"

"We have a problem, I'm afraid." Scarlet nodded toward the door—to the sign hanging in the middle, right over the handle, where it was impossible to miss. In the most unsparkly black block letters, it read very simply CLOSED.

"What? What does that mean?" said Ophelia as she read it. "Does that mean we can't go in?"

"That's totally what it means," said Arden. "Look." She pointed to another sign to the side of the door that listed the operating hours. "They're closed every

Thursday. Oh, well. I guess this fear just wasn't meant to be conquered all in a day. But at least I got a little closer to facing it, right?"

"Right," Scarlet sighed.

A little closer. Great, she thought. If only energy could be captured from that.

But no. They needed a wish to be fully granted. And they needed it granted soon. Not the next day or that weekend, when Arden suggested they return.

"We're going in today. Right now," said Scarlet as she worked to unlock the entrance with her mind. She clasped Arden's hand more tightly and pulled her toward the door. "We've come this far. We can't stop now. C'mon, Ophelia. You too."

"What? How? But we can't. It's closed!" said Arden, confused but stubbornly holding her ground.

"Um, Scarlet. Scarlet." On the other side of Arden, Ophelia tried to get Scarlet's attention by waving wildly with her hand. "*Scarlet!*"

"What? It's no big deal. We'll go in and come right back out."

"But that's just it. I don't think we have to," said Ophelia, pointing.

Scarlet followed her finger to Arden's shoulder. . . .

"Freakin' fireballs!" she gasped.

Ophelia grinned. "I know! Right?"

"What? What is it?" Arden asked. She started to turn her head.

"No, no. Don't move," Scarlet calmly warned her.

Arden froze. "What is it? Tell me, please."

"Okay . . . there's a . . . there's a *butterfly* on your shoulder," Scarlet said as gently as she knew how.

"What?"

"It's very small."

"How small?" asked Arden.

Scarlet held up her first finger and thumb two inches apart. "It's kind of light gold," she said, "with black outlines. . . . There's even some orange and a little blue."

"It sounds kind of pretty," said Arden.

"Oh, it is!" said Ophelia.

"I think . . . I don't know. . . . Should I look?"

"Yes!" said Scarlet and Ophelia together.

"But slowly," said Scarlet. "Don't scare it away."

Slowly, very slowly, Arden swiveled her head to the right, until she could just barely see the butterfly out of the corner of her eye. Her heart must have been racing, Scarlet thought, if her own fluttering heart was any gauge. And Ophelia . . . Scarlet glanced at her and saw she was smiling at Arden. How excited she must be. . . .

"How do you feel?" asked Ophelia gently.

"I feel okay. . . ." Arden's eyes left her shoulder for just an instant to flit from Ophelia to Scarlet. "And you know what's even better? What I don't feel is afraid!"

Scarlet was ready for the wish energy to flow out of Arden, but she wasn't prepared for such an intense and powerful stream. It burst forth with such force that Scarlet staggered back, and Ophelia did, as well. Arden just stood there, oblivious, as Wishlings always were. She could only assume it was the butterfly they were reacting to, so she smiled and said, "Don't worry. It won't hurt you."

Of course, that was the last thing Scarlet was worried about. The first thing was making sure every drop of energy made it into Ophelia's Wish Pendant, which Ophelia seemed to have forgotten all about. Scarlet held her own hand out and pointed to her wrist to try to remind her, but Ophelia replied by shaking her head. That was when Scarlet realized the wish energy was already flowing into a Wish Pendant.

Not Ophelia's at all—but Scarlet's.

Epilogue

Scarlet was so happy about all the wish energy she had collected that she didn't even mind giving Ophelia a ride back home on her star. Scarlet hadn't planned on holding Ophelia's hand the whole time, but somehow it turned out that way, and they were still holding hands when Lady Stella's door opened to welcome the returning Starlings in.

Maybe that was why every jaw in the room seemed to drop. Or maybe it was Scarlet's smile, which she couldn't hold back and for once didn't even try to.

"Scarlet . . ." Lady Stella walked forward, her stardust-flecked silver robe flowing behind her in a shimmering diaphanous cloud. "I owe you star salutations and, more importantly, star apologies." She stood before Scarlet and humbly bowed. "Clearly, you always were—and always will be—meant to be a Star Darling. If there was any doubt whatsoever left, this resolves it once and for all."

With that, the headmistress extended her arm. In her upturned palm was the Wish Orb, which she handed to Scarlet. It felt heavy and warm and then began to transform into a flower. "It's a punkypow," said Scarlet with a smile. The burgundy star-shaped petals were aglow.

And then her Power Crystal, the ravenstone, emerged. It was so beautiful and made Scarlet feel very special, indeed. "Take it, and hold it dear," said Lady Stella.

"Oh, I will. I will," said Scarlet. Her own heart seemed to stop as she received the gem and felt the pulse of its energy through her hands.

Meanwhile, Lady Stella, still smiling, but more sadly, turned to Ophelia. As she spoke, she shook her head. "To you, Ophelia, I must also offer star apologies. It is clear you are not a Star Darling, as we had believed."

Scarlet looked down. She remembered how those words had crushed her, and she could only imagine they'd wound Ophelia the same way. When Scarlet finally made herself look at the Starling, however, the words seemed instead to have lifted a great weight off Ophelia. Her whole aura had changed. Not only was she brighter and more sparkly, she looked almost happy—content and relieved. Her eyes skipped from Lady Stella to Scarlet, then around to each of the dumbstruck Star Darlings, who hadn't moved since the two Starlings had glided in.

"*What the stars?* Who's next?" Gemma suddenly blurted. "*Starf!* Hey!" she cried as Tessa elbowed her ribs.

Lady Stella clasped her now empty hands tightly in front of her, as if in prayer. "I know this is quite a lot for you to take in, particularly on such an . . . intensely emotional day. We've all been through quite a lot—especially, of course, Scarlet and Ophelia—which is why I think it's best to retire for now. Rest assured that Lady Cordial and I will work diligently to ensure that nothing like this happens again." She turned her head respectfully toward the admissions director, who'd stood off to the side in semi-shadow throughout the whole Wish Blossom presentation.

Lady Cordial took a step forward and bowed to the headmistress. Her deep purple bun looked especially tight. "We most c-c-certainly will," she said, her eyes still on the floor. "No mis-s-stakes like this. Ever again."

As fast as Scarlet had fled from the other Star Darlings when she'd learned she'd been dismissed from the group, she fled even faster now that she was back in. She could see everyone waiting to congratulate her and *embrace* her (*ugh!*) outside Lady Stella's office, and suddenly, it all seemed too much for her to bear. She would deal with them all later—be sociable—Scarlet thought as she rushed past them, but right then, more than anything, she needed to be by herself. She'd already hugged and held hands more in one day than she had in the whole rest of her time at Starling Academy. She was overwhelmed. She needed to breathe.

The holo-text came as she was descending the spiral staircase into the Star Caves.

WHERE DID YOU GO? it flashed as Vega's picture appeared in the upper corner of the screen.

Scarlet almost didn't answer, but then another line came through . . . and another after that:

WE HAVE TO TALK!

YOU WERE RIGHT!

AND SO WAS CASSIE!

THE LAB RESULTS CAME IN WHILE YOU WERE GONE!

And . . . ? Scarlet waited. *Well?* she thought. What had they found out?

Finally, she texted back:

WHAT DID THEY SAY?!

She realized she was holding her breath as she stared at her Star-Zap, waiting for Vega's reply. At last, the screen flashed again, this time with both Cassie's and Vega's faces, one in each corner. Cassie's picture coyly winked.

HERE'S A HINT: ISLE OF MISERA.

FOR MORE, MEET US IN THE HEDGE MAZE.

ASAP!

So as fast as possible, Scarlet spun and ran back up the stairs.

The Isle of Misera? That sad, barren, negative-energy dumping ground? Could it be that the Star Darlings' flowers had come from there?

Cassie Comes
Through

Prologue

 You there, Vega?

 I'm here, Cassie. In the maze with Scarlet waiting for you!

 ???

 Didn't you get my holo-text?

 That's so weird. I didn't get it. You know I hate that maze, anyway. Can we just talk now?

Sure. I'll add Scarlet.

 Hey, Cassie.

 Hey, Scarlet! Starkudos on your Wish Mission!

 Star salutations! It wasn't easy, that's for sure.

 So I just told Scarlet we found out that the flowers that were delivered to the Star Darlings are from the Isle of Misera!

 Crazy! No wonder everyone was fighting so much. But I thought that place was off-limits. Who do you think sent them? And why?

 That's a very good question. And as a matter of fact, that's not the only strange thing going on at Starling Academy . . .

 You mean the way I was kicked out of the group and replaced by Ophelia? And then had to go down to Wishworld to save her stars?

 Yes, plus I just finished Vega's crossword puzzle . . .

 Star salutations! I'm impressed! So, what did you think?

It's pretty starmazing!

 I had to make some changes and move some answers around to get it to line up so perfectly. I'm glad you enjoyed it!

 Um, yeah, it was a startastic layout . . .

 but I was talking about the actual content.

 I mean, when I saw all those the clues together, it was eye-opening!

 Spit it out, Cassie!

 Think about it! Look at 3-Across, 7-Across, and sorry, your mission, too, Vega—everyone has had a problem identifying either her Wisher or the wish. And 10-Across: Leona's private band tryout invite got holo-blasted to the entire school and our top-secret name was revealed. Or how about 8-Down: Leona's Wish Pendant got ruined and she didn't collect any wish energy.

 Plus me, Ophelia, the flowers . . .

1) I l♥ve, l♥ve, l♥ve that my puzzle got you thinking, Cassie! 2) Wow. I was only looking at them as puzzle clues. But when you actually read them one after another, it's pretty crazy!

 Starzactly.

 There is a lot of weird stuff going on, that's for sure. And what about my and Ophelia's deliberately switched grades?

 Was that ever proven?

 Well, not yet, but · · ·

 Listen, we need to stay calm. Do you think it could just be a coincidence?

 No way!

 Well · · · we've been brought together to do something so controversial it has to be kept secret from everyone else at Starling Academy—to collect wish energy on Wishworld before we graduate. I'm afraid that maybe we're being sanitized.

 ???

Okay, now I'm really confused!

 Darn you, starcorrect! I meant sabotaged!

 That's terrible! But . . . by who?

 Okay, I don't know how to say this. I know you think I can be paranoid. . . .

 Um, well, maybe because just yesterday you were convinced that someone stole your starglasses, and they were sitting on top of your head!

  Okay, so maybe you have a point. But . . .

 Yes?

 Well, um, what if someone really is out to get us? What better way to do it . . .

 Waiting . . .

 . . . than from within? What if it is someone here at Starling Academy? Or even worse . . .

 What could be worse?

Well—

 What if it's one of us . . . a Star Darling???

 I hope you're wrong . . .

And if I'm not?

 Then there's only one thing to say: Oh, starf.

 You said it, Starling.

CHAPTER
1

"Well, there you are, Itty!" Cassie cooed as her pet glowfur landed on her shoulder and nuzzled her pale cheek. Itty's soft pink fur tickled Cassie's face and made the tiny girl giggle. Cassie smiled at the little creature in the mirror as she finished twisting her long, glimmering pinkish-white hair into a second pigtail bun, fastened it in place with a starpin, and reached up to give the creature a quick tickle. Itty chirped delightedly and the stars on her golden antennae twinkled. The glowfur rewarded Cassie with the "Song of Contentment." Cassie, who had heard it many times before, hummed along.

"That's really pretty," someone said. Cassie turned around to find her roommate smiling at her. Sage, freshly gleaming from her sparkle shower, was wrapped in a soft lavender towel that matched her hair and eyes.

Cassie nodded in agreement. "Can you believe that glowfurs have twenty-six distinct songs?" she asked. "And that each glowfur has her own version of each tune? This is one of my favorites. After the 'Song of Joy' and 'Song of Enchantment,' of course."

"Yes, I can believe it," said Sage. "Only because you've told me a moonium times!"

Although Cassie's first impulse was to scowl at Sage, she just rolled her eyes and laughed instead. That was the key to having a pleasant relationship with her roommate. Cassie was beginning to realize that Sage didn't mean to offend; she just liked to say whatever was on her mind.

Sage opened her closet door with her wish energy manipulation skills and quickly got dressed behind it. When she emerged, she was wearing a loosely woven shimmery sweater over a long sleeveless dress that flickered and changed color as she moved—exhibiting more shades of purple than Cassie knew existed. Cassie preferred to wear more delicate outfits, mostly in white and pale shades of silver and pink, but she appreciated the bold color of Sage's flowing, comfortable clothes. Sage shook her head in mock seriousness. "Actually, what I really can't believe is you still haven't gotten caught," she said with a laugh.

"That's because Itty and I are very careful," said Cassie, smoothing her silvery tunic with the ruffled hem. Itty took off from Cassie's shoulder and circled the room, still singing her song. Cassie smiled at Sage. "And because I have a very discreet roommate."

Sage nodded from the floor, where she crouched, buckling her sparkly sandals. "I *am* discreet, aren't I?"

"You are," said Cassie. She poured Itty's daily allotment of Green Globules into a crystal bowl and Itty zoomed over, her bright blue gossamer wings fluttering madly as they struggled to hold up the weight of her plump little body. She knocked over a pile of holo-books in her rush to enjoy her breakfast. Cassie had read the Starling Academy Student Manual from cover to cover and knew quite well that pets were expressly forbidden to live in the student dormitories. She told herself that she had taken Itty to school with her because the creature would have been lonely back at her uncle Andreas's mansion. He was away on book tours more often than he was at home. But the truth was that Cassie simply couldn't part with her pet, who had once belonged to Cassie's late mother. When Itty sang her evening song,

Cassie was reminded that her mother had fallen asleep to the very same tune many staryears ago. It wasn't much, in the grand scheme of things, but it brought her great comfort. So Cassie had packed up Itty and her various glowfur paraphernalia and successfully smuggled her past the Bot-Bot guards on the first day of school.

But keeping Itty a secret from her roommate had not been easy. There had been that unpleasant moment when, to avoid suspicion, she had to eat a Green Globule after Sage's nosy little brothers had found a bag of them under her bed. Her face wrinkled up at the distasteful memory. And there had been the time when Sage woke to Itty's singing and tried to convince Cassie that she and her "stellar voice" needed to join the starchoir. (Cassie's voice was actually quite mediocre, so she had feigned a sore throat, missing tryouts.) But it turned out that Sage had already guessed Cassie's secret and accepted her small and furry extra roommate. Cassie had had another stressful period during the time when she and Sage hadn't been getting along and she had grown nervous that her roommate might turn her in. But Sage had proved to be a loyal roommate, even when the two were bickering.

It was those flowers! thought Cassie, staring at the spot where the vase had sat, its coral blooms fragrant, enticing, and perpetually fresh and dewy. But Cassie had had a feeling that something was not quite right with them, and her hunches were often correct. There was suddenly a lot of tension in the room, and Cassie had realized that she could just not get along with her roommate. In a moment of impulse, she had grabbed the flowers and tossed them into the vanishing garbage can, and things had returned to normal between them. And then she had convinced Vega that they should bring *her* flowers to the botany lab. They had discovered that the flowers came from the Isle of Misera, a place off-limits to Starlings. But who had sent them? And why? That was still a mystery. Cassie made it her mission to destroy the rest of the flowers, but it wasn't easy. She had tried to explain to the rest of the Star Darlings that the flowers were having a bad effect on them, but everyone had just laughed. She had a theory that the longer someone kept the flowers, the more attached to them that person became, so she'd had to get creative. On her fingers, she ticked off the roommate pairs who no longer had flowers in their rooms. Vega and Piper's flowers were still sealed in the botany lab, awaiting more testing. She had tossed Gemma and Libby's when they were in the middle of a heated argument over who had forgotten to turn off the sparkle shower. She had only been able to convince Tessa to get rid of the flowers once she told her that their strong odor interfered with the delicious smells of her baking. And Leona and Ophelia's had simply disappeared. (She still hadn't figured that one out, but at least they were gone.) That left one roommate pair who still had the flowers in their room—Clover and Astra. Cassie needed to get right on that as soon as starpossible.

Sage finished buckling her sandals and walked to the door, her lavender braids gleaming.

"Ready to go to the Celestial Café?" she asked Cassie.

"Ready!" said Cassie. Itty zoomed in for a kiss on her furry head and began her good-bye song.

Cassie hurried to the door. "Oh, let me," she begged, so Sage stepped aside. Cassie concentrated on opening the door with her wish energy manipulation skills and the door began to tremble, almost imperceptibly, as if it was trying to decide whether it wanted to be opened or stay closed. A starmin or two later, after Cassie's pale face flushed silver from the effort, the door slid open fluidly.

Cassie grinned and turned to Sage. "You're like my good-luck charm, Sage," she said. "I wish I was as good in Wish Energy Manipulation class as I am in our room." She shrugged. "I guess I get stage fright or something."

Sage nodded and for a starsec Cassie thought she caught a small flicker of a smile on her roommate's face.

But it disappeared as they stepped into the hallway and onto the Cosmic Transporter.

Cassie's stomach grumbled. "I wonder what to order for break—" she started.

"Stop right there!" a voice barked.

Cassie sighed. They were moving along on the Cosmic Transporter and couldn't stop even if they wanted to, for stars' sake. But Sage laughed merrily. "Hurry up, MO-Jay!" she cried.

The Bot-Bot guide zoomed after them eagerly. His official name was MO-J4, but Sage thought that was a little too formal and had settled on the nickname, which he had embraced wholeheartedly. MO-Jay had taken an instant starshine to Sage during her orientation tour and had been delighted by anything Sage did or said ever since. Most Bot-Bots acted by the holo-book with a preset vocabulary and a limited range of programmed reactions. But MO-Jay was special. He had a personality that was silly and fun, and he often greeted Sage with special jokes and an occasional gift left on her doorstep.

Cassie couldn't help feeling a little envious as MO-Jay excitedly told Sage about the morning's sunrise and showed her a holo-vid he had taken of it just for her. Sometimes Cassie wished that she and Itty could talk, like Sage and MO-Jay did. Though she wasn't quite sure what Itty would say. Most likely "More Green Globules, please." Or maybe "Rub my glowbelly for another star-hour if you don't mind." The only present Itty had ever given her (besides the gift of music) was a half-eaten Green Globule, left in the toe of a silver slipper. And by the time Cassie had found it, it was as hard as a meteorite. Cassie had tossed it into the vanishing garbage can. She knew exactly what Green Globules tasted like, even at the peak of freshness: horrible.

Still, she wouldn't trade Itty for all the wish energy in Starland. She half listened to Sage and Mojo chat away. She smiled, remembering that Sage had initially confided to her that she found MO-J4's slavish devotion a bit annoying. But then the silvery Bot-Bot had started to grow on her. Sage told Cassie she was used to small annoying creatures, referring to her younger twin brothers, who could be quite a handful. As an only child, and an orphaned one at that, Cassie had nodded in apparent sympathy. But Cassie would actually have liked nothing more than an annoying sibling (or two or even three) to liven things up around her uncle's quiet home. That was why she liked Starling Academy so much, she realized. It was lively and there was always something going on to keep her entertained. Like that time when Astra had bet everyone that she could do a triple flip off the starbounce while eating a half-moon pie. It looked like she was going to win the wager when Leona had jumped up and—

Just then she realized that Sage was trying to get her attention. "Cassie!" she was saying, snapping her fingers in Cassie's face. Cassie blinked. "We haven't even discussed the new Scarlet situation yet!" she said. "I mean, that was so unexpected. So what do you think about her reinsta—"

Cassie held up her hand. She turned to MO-J4. "I'm going to remind you that everything you hear is strictly confidential," she told the Bot-Bot. Even though he was extremely devoted to Sage, the Star Darlings couldn't risk anyone's—or anybot's—leaking information about their secret mission.

MO-J4's eyes flashed as if he was annoyed, or perhaps disappointed, by the request, but he politely nodded. "Certainly, Cassie," he said smoothly.

Sage nodded solemnly. "So what do you think about Scarlet's reinstatement?" she asked. "It's just so strange."

Cassie frowned and bit her lip. She adored her roommate and completely trusted her, but still . . . She and Scarlet had promised Vega that until they had some more evidence they would keep to themselves their fears about what they thought was going on. No need to throw everyone else into a tizzy if there was a reasonable explanation for everything, Vega had argued. Cassie and Scarlet had reluctantly agreed.

"Well, it was certainly a sur—" she finally started.

"I think it's simply wonderful!" MO-J4 exclaimed. "Now the group can get back together and you can win the Battle of the Bands on Starshine Day. Beat that Vivica, just like she deserves!"

"All right, see you later, MO-Jay," she said. They had reached the Celestial Café. The light was shining above the door. Breakfast was ready to be served and another day was about to unfold.

Sage smiled at Cassie. "And our starday begins," she said. "Hope it's a good one."

Cassie tapped her elbows together three times for luck. She herself was hoping for a day filled with more clues. Something strange was going on at Starling Academy; she was almost sure of it. She just needed some tangible proof.

CHAPTER
2

"**How many times** do I have to tell you?" Clover scolded her roommate. "No star balls at the breakfast table!" She rolled her eyes, turning to the rest of the Star Darlings sitting around the table as if she was an exasperated teacher and Astra a naughty Wee Constellation School student. "She throws that thing around all day long. It never stops. It's driving me crazy! I wake up in the middle of the night and there she is, tossing that ball!"

"I told you, Coach Geeta said we have to practice as much as we can to prepare for the big game," retorted Astra, her flaming red hair pulled into two braids. Two matching glittery spots appeared on her cheeks. Cassie knew Astra well enough to know that meant she was getting angry.

"I'm sure she didn't mean in the Celestial Café!" Clover practically shouted. The rest of the Star Darlings looked at each other uncomfortably. The usually fun-loving Clover was being very rigid, and Astra was being way more stubborn than usual. It wasn't enjoyable to watch the two butt heads so forcefully. Cassie held her breath as Astra grinned wickedly and tossed the shining orb into the air again, her hands poised to catch it. She made the ball hover in the air over the table for a moment, showing off the skills that made her Starling Academy's most talented star ball player. Just then a Bot-Bot waiter zoomed in with a breakfast tray.

"Yum!" said Astra, distracted for a moment. "Am I hungry! I had quite a workout this morning!" And Cassie watched in shock as the shining orb crashed down, faster than she thought possible. "Oh, my stars!" said the Bot-Bot in dismay as it hit his tray with a loud smack, sending stacks of steaming starcakes and glasses of glorange juice flying onto the table.

The girls stared at the scattered starcakes and the puddles of glowing glorange juice on the fancy table-cloth. Tessa, who hated to see any food go to waste, quickly snatched up a starcake and took a bite out of one of its perfect five points. Clover looked furious. The rest of the girls exchanged glances. They knew Clover was overreacting, since the mess immediately disappeared, as messes always did on Starland. "Pardon me," said the Bot-Bot apologetically as he neatly stacked the plates and zoomed back to the kitchen for a replacement breakfast tray. Cassie nudged Vega's leg under the table. But the girl didn't react. Cassie did it again.

"Did you just kick me?" Astra scowled across the table at Clover.

Oops, thought Cassie.

"No, I didn't!" Clover retorted. "But maybe I should!"

The two girls glared at each other. Cassie noticed that although both their mouths were set in grim lines, there were matching looks of confusion in their eyes. It was as if they couldn't understand why they were so angry at each other, and they weren't very happy about it, either.

That's it, thought Cassie. If there had been any question in her mind about the negative effect of the vases of flowers, it had just been answered. Everyone else was getting along well (with the exception of Leona and Scarlet, who would probably never get along under any circumstances, but that was another story). She, Vega, and Scarlet had to come up with a plan to dispose of the flowers—that starday.

The rest of breakfast went by without incident, and

Cassie leapt up from the table as soon as she took her last bite of astromuffin. She hurried out of the cafeteria, excited to get to her first class of the day—Intro to Wish Identification. Never slowing her pace, she hopped onto the Cosmic Transporter that looped through campus, and she jumped off at Halo Hall. She bounded up the steps and through the large imposing doors, which dwarfed her tiny figure. Although Cassie's secret Star Darlings lessons had placed her far beyond the rest of the first-year class, and she often found boring the introductory lessons she had to attend to keep up her cover, she was really looking forward to that day's class. They were going to attempt wish identification on a Starlandian creature. Cassie tapped her elbows together three times for luck, hoping they'd be studying a glion or a galliope, or maybe even a twinkelope. She would love to hear its trumpeting call in person. Being up close with any one of those majestic creatures would really be a thrill, as would trying to figure out what its wish could possibly be. She quickened her pace down the starmarble hallway, toward the wish stellation. She didn't want to be late.

"Cassie, wait up!"

Now what? thought Cassie as she abruptly stopped, the soles of her silvery ankle boots squeaking on the floor. She turned around impatiently. But her scowl disappeared. To her starprise, it was Leona pushing through the crowd of students to get to her side. *Imagine that.*

"I need to catch my breath!" Leona gasped, putting her sparkly golden hand to her sparkly golden throat. "You practically ran right out of the Celestial Café. I've been chasing you ever since!"

"You look really glowful," said Cassie appreciatively, taking in the girl's aura. Leona had been looking decidedly unglimmery ever since her failed mission. That had concerned all the Star Darlings, since Leona was naturally extra golden to begin with.

"Star salutations," said Leona, holding out a sparkly arm and admiring it. "I'm starting to feel a bit better."

"I'm glad," said Cassie, and she really meant it. It felt good to be talking to Leona. Sure, they had been in Star Darlings class together and seated at the Star Darlings' table at the dining hall, but this was the first time they were talking one-on-one since their argument about Ophelia.

That she and Leona, so different at first glance—very nearly opposites, in fact—had become such fast friends had starprised her. Cassie had initially felt intimidated by the bold, brash third year, never in a moonium staryears dreaming that the two would have anything in common—or that she would actually enjoy spending time with a girl who seemed always on the lookout for an admiring audience. Cassie had assumed that Leona would be exhausting to be around, but the truth was that Leona's zest for life energized and inspired her. And she learned that Leona had a kind and generous side that was easy to overlook at first glance.

Their unlikely friendship had begun one evening on the way back from dinner shortly after school had started. The Star Darlings were on the Cosmic Transporter heading back to their dormitories. Cassie recalled that Leona was singing a song about the beauty of lightfall, her arms thrown out and her eyes closed. Cassie thought that the girl looked more luminous than anyone else, her golden hair a brilliant halo around her radiant face. She was shocked when Leona had impulsively grabbed her hand at the end of the song. "We're going to the roof," Leona had announced, and before Cassie could argue, she had whisked her into the upperclassman dormitory and up onto the roof deck. Cassie, who had thought she preferred always being in the background, was surprised to discover she enjoyed being in the golden spotlight of Leona's attention. The two girls had lain on lounge chairs well into the night, staring at the magnificently star-studded sky, squealing when they spotted a shooting star. They pointed out constellations to each other, and when they ran out of names, they made some up. Leona told Cassie all about her family, about how she loved them fiercely but sometimes felt held back by their limited view of the world. And Leona had been the first person at Starling Academy who Cassie had told about her parents, tentatively pointing out their stars, which winked at her as they always did. Leona had known that no words were required at that moment, just a warm hand to hold as they sat in silence and stared into the heavens. The two didn't realize how late it was until they saw how the stars had completely shifted across the sky. Cassie had had to sneak back into her dorm long after lights-out. In fact, she had felt a little thrill of naughtiness when she'd placed her hand on her room's palm scanner and the Bot-Bot voice had said, "Good evening, Cassie," in what she was certain was a disapproving tone.

But her friendship with Leona had practically ground to a halt after the Starling's disastrous mission. While Cassie understood how disappointed Leona was when it was discovered that she had not collected any wish energy, she was surprised when Leona had completely shut down and frozen her out. Instead Leona had chosen to spend time with her new roommate, and Scarlet's replacement as a Star Darling, Ophelia. And once Cassie had started asking questions about Ophelia—who, everyone agreed, didn't seem to be Star Darlings material at all—Leona had taken great offense. They had pretty much avoided being alone together ever since.

Sure, Cassie felt a slight glimmer of resentment that Leona had dropped her friendship so abruptly, but her delight in seeing her friend looking so much better won out. Leona gave her a blinding megawatt smile and Cassie grinned right back. All right, maybe Leona's smile wasn't *quite* as intense as it had been before all her mission troubles, but it was still pretty dazzling.

Leona slipped her arm through Cassie's. She leaned down as if to tell Cassie a secret. "So can you believe it?" she whispered, her breath tickling Cassie's ear. "You know they moved Ophelia into the Little Dipper Dormitory. Not only did I lose the sweetest roommate ever, but I'm sharing a room with weird old Scarlet again."

"Poor you," said Cassie, feeling a stab of guilt. She was fond of Scarlet—or as fond as anyone could be of the secretive and somewhat strange girl. But her pleasure at being back in Leona's good graces outweighed her loyalty to Scarlet.

"All that black!" Leona groaned. "And the constant skateboarding messing up my beauty sleep. And remember, she plays the *drums* and she always forgets to turn on the muting switch. And her weird stuff lying around. Globerbeem cases and old meepletile skins. Ugh." She shuddered with distaste. "Imagine what new oddities she's collected since I've seen her last." She sighed and made a sad face. "And what's going to happen to Ophelia? She may not be a Star Darling, but she's such a sweet Starling." She gave Cassie a sidelong glance and her eyes widened. "You know something? She's an orphan, too! But she has no one at all, not like you with your famous uncle to take care of you. As a matter of fact, she grew up in an orphanage in Starland City. She hadn't made any friends in Starling Academy until she met me. And now she's all alone again."

"Oh," said Cassie. She hadn't known that about Ophelia. She had been so focused on the wrongness of Ophelia's being a Star Darling that it hadn't occurred to her to think about the girl's feelings. Now all Cassie felt was sympathy for her. No one but a fellow orphan could understand the unspeakable pain of losing both of your parents at a young age. Of feeling so achingly alone, like you belonged to no one, adrift in a world that was suddenly empty and terribly frightening. And the devastating realization that life would never, ever be the same. For a girl who was searching for a place to fit in, being offered the chance to be a part of a secret group and then having it suddenly taken away must have been devastating.

Cassie swallowed hard. "I . . . I . . . I'll keep an eye out for her," she heard herself say.

"And you'll talk to her, see how she's doing?" Leona pressed.

Cassie nodded. "I will. Cross my stars and hope to shine."

"Star salutations," said Leona. "I'm worried about her. I really am."

Cassie nodded. "Well, here's my classroom," she said. She unlinked her arm from Leona's and impulsively gave her a quick hug. She tried to step back, but Leona held on for a moment longer than Cassie was expecting.

Leona had missed her. And that was a pretty nice thing to realize.

CHAPTER
3

When Cassie stepped inside, she saw that her classmates were clustered together in the front of the room. *Professor Lucretia Delphinus is either teaching the class how to shoot holo-dice or the Starlandian creature's already here,* she thought with a grin. But she had no one to share her little joke with. Cassie had a well-deserved reputation as a quiet girl who liked her privacy and never spoke out of turn, and her classmates respected this and tended to leave her alone.

She was okay with that. *Still,* she thought as she stood uncertainly at the front of the class, *it would be nice if someone would turn around and say hello or move over to make room for me in the circle.* But she wasn't surprised that no one did. What was disappointing to her was that she knew her fellow classmates (and sometimes professors, as well) often took her reserved nature for aloofness or, worse yet, thought she had nothing to contribute. She did have a lot to offer; it was just that she liked to get all her thoughts in order before she opened her mouth. She didn't like idle chitchat, throwaway comments, or speaking for the sole purpose of hearing herself talk. She couldn't fathom being like Gemma, who could make small talk with anyone—teachers, students, parents, staff, strangers. Gemma was quite well liked because of it. But Cassie found the girl's constant chatter simply exhausting.

The one place Cassie truly felt at ease was among her fellow Star Darlings. They seemed to appreciate her thoughtful, deliberate responses and had learned never to rush her to speak her mind before she was ready. She felt as if she had found her place. That's why all the strange things that were going on were making her feel extra nervous. How she hoped it wasn't a fellow Star Darling who was responsible. *That is,* if *anything is going on*, she reminded herself, hearing Vega's voice of reason in her head. There could be a logical explanation for everything, couldn't there?

The crowd of students hadn't shifted an inch. Cassie stood on her toes to try to peer over them, but as she expected, it was useless. She overheard snippets of conversation: "How startastic!" and "I can't wait to guess what the wish is!" She bit her lip in anticipation.

"Okay, class, time to get started," Professor Lucretia Delphinus called out. "Everyone to your seats."

The girls reluctantly scattered and Cassie headed to her desk. She plopped down into the chair, which immediately adjusted to her height, build, and preferred seating position, the ultimate in classroom comfort. Vega had told her that the seats in Wishworld classrooms were hard and rigid. That didn't make sense to Cassie at all. She couldn't imagine how you could pay attention to your lessons when you were uncomfortable.

Now that the students were all seated, Cassie was frustrated when she realized that she still couldn't see the creature. Her professor, a tiny woman in a voluminous swirly purple-and-blue skirt that looked like a moonstorm, was somehow positioned in a way that precisely blocked her view. She craned her neck, but she was unable to see behind the woman.

"Star greetings, students," said Professor Lucretia Delphinus. "Welcome to your first wish identification workshop. Today we will be granting the wishes of our special guest, Mica." She stepped to the side and Cassie finally caught a glimpse. The creature was sitting in the middle of the teacher's desk, staring into space. Cassie felt her spirits drop. It wasn't a majestic glion who could be wishing to climb to the top of the Crystal Mountains and graze on the rainbow lichen that grew there or a galliope who might want to take a lucky student for a ride on his broad back, her fingers laced through his glittering mane. She would not be hearing the bellowing call of the many-antlered twinkelope anytime soon. No, that day they would be guessing the wishes of a much smaller and decidedly less glamorous creature—a creature Cassie knew almost as well as she knew herself: a glowfur.

Cassie shook her head and laughed to herself. This wasn't going to be challenging at all. She sighed and waited for the class to begin.

The professor continued. "We'll be honing our wish identification skills as we try to determine exactly what Mica is wishing for this morning." She clasped her hands together and smiled at the students. "I'll start with an easy question. Who can tell me what type of creature Mica is?"

Hands shot into the air. Cassie kept hers down. Too easy.

"Gloryah?" said the professor, pointing to a student with a pinkish-orange glow. Cassie liked her; she had a sweet disposition and was exceedingly polite, a trait Cassie admired greatly.

"A moonbug!" said Gloryah. But her brow wrinkled as the words came out of her mouth. "No, that's not right. I mean a—"

"It's a glowfur," interjected a student named Aerabelle disdainfully. She snorted. "Even my baby sister knows the difference between a glowfur and a moonbug!"

"I knew that!" Gloryah said. She looked around the room, appealing to her classmates. "I really did!"

Cassie gave Gloryah an understanding smile (though, really, who could mix those two up?) and turned to bestow a frown on Aerabelle, who had dusky purple curls and a deceptively sweet round face. You were not supposed to react negatively to your classmates; that was one of Starling Academy's basic rules. Being kind and supportive—no matter how silly you thought a comment or question was—helped create an atmosphere of civility and support, which encouraged sharing and open dialogue, per the Student Manual. Aerabelle had apparently skipped that chapter.

"Be kind, Aerabelle," the professor said in a warning voice. She might have been tiny, but her toughness was legendary. Her eyes flashed with annoyance. "That's what we are here for. To learn, of course, but to do so in a supportive way. There are no incorrect answers. We learn from everything that is shared in this classroom, accurate or inaccurate. There is no room for negativity here."

Aerabelle pouted, clearly not comprehending her teacher's words, just her scolding tone. Cassie wasn't surprised. The purple-haired girl was part of a group of first years whose ringleader was a student named Vivica, who had been particularly rude to the Star Darlings from day one at Starling Academy. Aerabelle was just as kind and understanding as her pale blue friend, Vivica—which is to say not at all.

Cassie watched as Gloryah's face burned brightly with embarrassment. Cassie felt sorry for the girl but was quick to notice that she flushed a very pretty shade. Whenever Cassie blushed, her cheeks turned a silvery shade that she thought was very unflattering.

Professor Lucretia Delphinus pointed to the glow-fur, who gazed at the class serenely. "Class, please say hello to Mica," the professor instructed.

"Star greetings, Mica," said the class, and Mica rewarded them with a few notes from the "Song of Meeting New People." His singing was very pretty, though slightly muffled thanks to his bulging cheeks, stuffed with Green Globules. Cassie smiled. Glowfurs were notoriously greedy. The golden star on Mica's belly glowed in greeting.

The students all oohed and aahed, as you would do if you didn't have a pet glowfur who lived in your room and glowed its starbelly at you every morning. The creature blinked its large eyes at the students. A sigh went up.

"She's so cute!" Aerabelle cried.

"Actually, she's a he," corrected Cassie gently. But really, how could the girl not see that his belly star was half the size of a female's, the surest indicator?

"Whatever," said Aerabelle with a shrug.

Cassie shook her head. Some Starlings!

"So what is this glowfur wishing for?" the professor asked the class. "Concentrate and pay attention to the signals. This will be the most challenging part of your Wish Missions. Wishlings make many wishes, sometimes several a day. The key is to deduce their special wish."

The students all stared at the glowfur, who looked right back at them, his large eyes serious, his little paws buried in the fur on top of his head. *So that's it!* thought Cassie. His wish was suddenly so apparent to her it was like it was stamped on the middle of his furry little forehead. She felt a rush of positive energy flow through her.

Piece of pie, she thought, using a Wishworld expression her roommate had taught her. She looked around, waiting for someone to pick up on the obvious clue.

"He's hungry!" called out a girl named Tansy.

"Yes, that's it. Mica wants his breakfast!" a blue-tinged classmate chimed in.

"That's not it," said the professor. "Try again. When you figure it out, you may feel a burst of energy. But unfortunately, that doesn't happen for everyone."

Cassie yawned. With a quick glance to make sure that her professor's attention was focused elsewhere, she slipped her Star-Zap into her lap and flipped it open. She began composing a holo-text message to Vega and Scarlet.

 Do either of you have early lunch? We could meet up.

 Second lunch.

  No, last lunch. And I'm already hungry!

 Then meet after SD class? What a mess in the caf this morning, huh?

 That was crazy! Sounds good.

Okay with me.

 We have to figure out how to get our hands on those flowers! Any ideas?

 Vega?

 Scarlet?

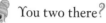 You two there?

 Hello?

Still no response. Cassie tried to keep an eye on her screen as well as on her teacher. She stole a glance at Mica, whose pink fur was now standing up on his head in his obvious irritation. She was about to raise her hand to reveal the wish and help put the glowfur out of his misery when her Star-Zap began to vibrate and beep loudly. She scrambled to silence it and dropped her Star-Zap on the floor. It landed with a loud clatter and slid to the middle of the classroom, out of her reach.

Starf! She thought she had put it in silent mode.

Her classmates stared at her, openmouthed. The room was so still you could have heard a glowfur gasp. With as much dignity as she could muster, she walked over to pick up her Star-Zap. The tiny professor glided over and held out her hand. Shamefaced, Cassie placed the Star-Zap in her palm.

"Star apologies," muttered Cassie. For a girl who hated to call attention to herself, this was an extraordinarily mortifying moment. She stood in front of her teacher, unsure what to do next.

"Outside," the professor said sternly, turning and heading toward the classroom door, which opened smoothly. As Cassie followed the teacher out of the room, she was well aware that all eyes, including Mica's, were on her.

To Cassie's dismay, the professor began to lecture her in front of the open doorway, in view of the entire class, which seemed to be hanging on every word. "Now, Cassie, I am very disappointed in you," the professor said sternly. "You know that there is no holo-texting allowed in the classroom. Your behavior was disrespectful and inexcusable."

Cassie shut her eyes. This was her worst nightmare. More than once she had dreamed of being humiliated in front of her class. And it was even more distressing and embarrassing than she had imagined it would be. *What is going to happen to me?* she wondered. *Will she keep my Star-Zap to teach me a lesson? Give me an extra holo-report assignment on wish identification? Or could it be something worse?* She had heard rumors of a double secret detention room for badly misbehaving students that featured uncomfortable chairs and a special light that masked everyone's glow, leaving them looking like dull Wishlings. She was sure it was a star legend that upperclassmen told to scare unsuspecting first years, but she certainly didn't want to find out.

She braced herself for the punishment that was no doubt to come. The classroom door slid shut behind her silently and ominously.

Cassie gulped.

CHAPTER 4

"How was that?" said the professor.

Cassie was confused. "Star-starscuse me?" she stammered. She looked up to see her that her teacher was grinning down at her.

"I was just putting on a show for the rest of the students," Professor Lucretia Delphinus explained, handing Cassie her Star-Zap. "You know, make them think I was really annoyed with you. I didn't want to blow your cover." She put a hand on Cassie's shoulder. "Pretty convincing, huh?"

Cassie nodded. She was still so tense she was unable to speak. Professor Lucretia Delphinus had been convincing, all right!

"Look, I realize how boring these introductory classes can be for you when your studies have already taken you so much further," the professor continued.

Cassie nodded again. Relief flowed over her and she was finally able to give the teacher a shaky smile.

"For the rest of these girls," Professor Lucretia Delphinus explained, "wish identification is something that will happen staryears from now. For you, it could happen any starmin."

Cassie felt her stomach give a little flip of anxiety. Professor Lucretia Delphinus's words brought her both extreme excitement and crippling terror. Each time another Star Darling was chosen to go on a mission, she could see the looks of disappointment on the other girls' faces and realized they did not experience the same overwhelming feeling of relief that swept through her.

Professor Lucretia Delphinus raised a finger as an idea came to her. "I know! I'm going to go inside and tell the rest of the class that I sent you to Lady Stella's office for a chat. That will keep them on their toes!" She laughed a conspiratorial laugh as she smoothed her skirt. "Why don't you go to the Illumination Library and relax until your next class?" She paused for a moment as if she was considering whether to say something else. "Cassie, maybe you could spend some time mulling over what's been bothering you."

Cassie looked at the teacher quizzically.

"You look like you have the weight of Starling Academy on your shoulders," the teacher explained. She looked deep into Cassie's eyes. "Is there anything you want to talk about?"

Cassie felt her chest expand for a moment when she thought of the possibility of having an adult ally. A grown-up to trust? An authority figure to share her worries with? It was like being presented with an unexpected but extremely valuable gift. But she couldn't get rid of the feeling that she just shouldn't trust anyone. She shook her head. "Actually, everything's fine," she fibbed. "I'm just worried about my Wish History assignment. Star salutations for understanding what happened in class. I'm really sorry."

The teacher nodded. "Now I'd better get back inside and help poor Mica," she said. "Of course, as you probably already figured out, he's wishing . . ."

"For a mirror so he can begin his daily grooming," finished Cassie. She could tell by the irritated way he had been preening his whiskers.

Her teacher smiled. "That he is, the vain little thing!"

The thought of having forty starmins to herself before her next class put a little bounce in Cassie's step. She walked down the hall, her footfalls echoing, as she considered her options. She could go to the Lightning Lounge and clear her mind in a meditation room and possibly come up with a clever idea for disposing of Astra and Clover's flowers. Since those two had had their flowers the longest, she thought that they could certainly put up a fight to keep them. She might have to do some fancy footwork. Or she could steal some time for herself and finish the last chapter of the holo-book she was reading. It was her uncle's latest thriller, which would definitely relax her. (It wasn't even available to the public yet, but she was certain it would be another runaway best seller.) She was pretty sure she had the mystery all figured out, but Uncle Andreas often threw a few misleading clues (also known as drifting moonbugs) into his stories, so she was really interested to find out if her hunch was correct. Not wanting to waste any of her free time, she sat on a nearby starmarble bench and pulled out her holo-book.

The words leapt into the air and she began to

read eagerly. Her uncle's books used IMT, the new Illuminated Manuscript Technology: anytime the reader wanted to see the action unfold, she just needed to push a button and the animated holo-scene would play, with the text read aloud as it happened. It was a thrilling way to experience a story, especially a mystery. She got to a particularly exciting passage and pressed the IMT button.

She held her breath as Detective Marmaduke Carbuncle stepped out of the shadowy recesses of a dark alley in Starland City. "Hold it right there, NT-96," he called.

"I . . . um . . . This does not compute!" Bot-Bot NT-96 barked. And suddenly it began to go berserk, ramming its metal body against the wall, sparks flying. Detective Carbuncle dove for cover as the Bot-Bot burst into—

"Um, starscuse me?" someone said meekly.

Cassie turned the book off with an irritated swipe. She turned to the figure that stood in front of her. "Yes?" she said through gritted teeth. There was nothing Cassie hated as much as being interrupted when she was reading.

"Um, hi, Cassie. Sorry for bothering you."

Cassie blinked. It was Ophelia. Her bright yellow hair hung on either side of her face in two pigtails. She wore a plain yellow T-shirt and a pair of overalls, which were a little short, so her yellow-and-white-striped socks peeked out. She was so tiny and frail that she made Cassie feel tall, an unfamiliar sensation for her. When she gazed down at the girl, she realized the height difference made her feel motherly and protective.

"Oh, hi," Cassie replied. "I was just talking about you with Leona."

The girl's wide ochre eyes filled with liquid-glitter tears. "Oh, Leona," she said. "I miss her so much. She was a wonderful roommate."

"Really?" said Cassie, who imagined that sharing a room with Leona would involve a large amount of appreciative observation. And applause.

"Oh, yes," she breathed. "She was so entertaining! Always putting on such fun shows. It was like going to the theater! Every day!"

"So where are you living now?" Cassie asked.

"I have a single room in the Little Dipper Dorm," said Ophelia sadly. "It's pretty lonely. I really miss Leona and also being a . . ." She looked around, saw that the hallway was deserted, and lowered her voice anyway. "A Star Darling."

Cassie nodded.

Ophelia leaned her head to one side, thinking. "I know I had some trouble fitting in. And my Wish Mission was a disaster, of course. But I really tried. Because I . . . I liked it. I finally felt like I belonged somewhere. Now I just feel kind of lost."

Cassie understood completely. "It was nice to belong to something special," she said. "Now you're just another Starling Academy student."

"That's right," said Ophelia. "That's exactly right."

"I understand you more than you know," said Cassie. She was starting to feel even more protective toward the girl. "I don't tell a lot of people about this, but I'm an orphan, too."

Ophelia gulped and looked away. "I'm sorry," she said. She let her eyes wander around the hallway, unable make eye contact with Cassie for a moment.

Cassie was touched. "Girls like us, we need to stick together," she said. She was overwhelmed with an unfamiliar desire to hug Ophelia and make her feel better. Let her know that she wasn't alone. She felt ashamed for the unkind thoughts she had had about the girl before.

"It's just so . . . hard here," said Ophelia.

Cassie nodded. "It *is* hard," she said. "It's so big and there's so much to learn and so many new people. It's difficult to be away from home. . . ." Her voice trailed off as she realized her slip. How thoughtless of her! Ophelia didn't have a home; what had she been thinking?

But Ophelia leaned forward eagerly. "I know!" she said. "My mom says . . ."

Cassie looked at the girl in sympathy. "I used to do the same thing right after my parents began their afterglow," she said. "It's hard to talk about someone you love so much in the past tense, since they're still so present for you."

"What?" said Ophelia. Her eyes widened and she shifted in place. "Oh, yeah," she said. "What I meant was that my mom *used* to tell me that you need to find a group of friends who make you sparkle. And I thought I found it with you Starlings."

"Just because you're not an official Star Darling, it doesn't mean we can't help to make you sparkle," Cassie told the girl gently.

Ophelia's face lit up. "Star salutations, Cassie," she said.

The bell rang and girls began to swarm out of their classrooms. Ophelia was jostled a bit. "I'll holo-text you later," said Cassie as she turned to head down the hallway toward her next class. "I'll see you again soon. Cross my stars and hope to shine," she promised.

Ophelia smiled wanly. "I'd like that," she said softly.

She then turned and merged into the current of students, her small yellow-pigtailed head disappearing almost immediately.

Cassie stared after her, a smile on her face. All Ophelia needed was some friends, poor thing. She started toward the science stellation for her next class, then stopped in her tracks.

"Watch it!" said a blue-haired girl. "First year!" she remarked to a friend.

A sudden thought crossed Cassie's mind. She knew why *she* was roaming the hallways during first period. But why hadn't Ophelia been in class?

CHAPTER
5

"I'm sorry," said Vega. "I never got your holo-text. Scarlet and I have band practice right now, anyway. We can't go with you."

Cassie smiled at Scarlet. Despite her disappointment, she was glad to hear that the girl was back in the band.

Most of the Star Darlings were standing in the Star Quad, the area in the middle of campus. Their secret S.D. lessons, the last class of the day, had just let out. The girls usually chatted outside a bit before they headed off to their respective clubs, sports, lessons, studies, and other leisure activities before dinnertime.

"What time will it be over?" Cassie asked. "Maybe we could do it afterwards?" She really didn't feel confident confronting the two roommates by herself.

"No, then I'm meeting Professor Elara Ursa to talk about an extra-credit assignment," Vega explained.

Cassie wanted to ask if that couldn't wait until the next starday, but she saw the determined look in Vega's eyes. She knew that Vega's dream was to be the top student at Starling Academy and that she would do whatever it took to get there. She turned to Scarlet.

"And I have an Intuition study group," offered Scarlet. "I've really got to go since I missed all those classes. Star apologies."

"So I have to go get the flowers alone?" Cassie asked.

"Can't it wait till tomorrow?" asked Vega.

Cassie glanced at Astra and Clover, who were arguing again. She gasped as Astra snatched the hat off Clover's head and tossed it into the air, levitating it with wish energy in a cruel game of keep-away.

"I guess you're right," said Vega. "The sooner, the better."

"And this is the only afternoon Astra has off from practice this week," Cassie explained. "I overheard her saying she was going back to her room to watch old holovids of the team they are playing on Bopday."

Vega considered this. "You'll have to convince only her," she said. "Clover will be at band practice with us."

"That's a plus," said Cassie, her mood lightening a bit.

"So what's your plan?" Scarlet asked.

"Oh, look!" shouted someone. Cassie turned around and gasped. The nimble Clover had scrambled up the trunk of a nearby ballum-blossom tree and now stood on a sturdy branch, her arms held out to the sides. She didn't hesitate for even a moment before walking its length like a tightrope. Clover paused for a starsec, then leapt off, plucking the hat out of the air. She landed neatly, not a hair out of place. With a smirk at Astra, who looked like she was fuming, Clover jauntily placed the hat on her head and gave a deep bow. The rest of the Star Darlings applauded.

Vega shook her head. "I keep forgetting that she's one of the Flying Molensas," she said, referring to the most well-known circus family on Starland. "That girl is a born acrobat!"

"Impressive," Cassie said, turning back to Vega and Scarlet.

"So, your plan?" Vega prompted her.

"Right," said Cassie. "My plan is . . ." She sighed. "Actually, my plan is to come up with a plan on my way to their room."

Scarlet snorted.

Vega sucked in her cheeks. "Not much of a plan," she said.

"You're telling me," Cassie replied.

"Well, good luck with that!" Vega said, grimacing. "If it doesn't happen, we can always try again tomorrow."

Scarlet nodded. "I'm free."

"Star salutations," replied Cassie. She was determined to put an end to the nonsense that day.

She watched as the two girls headed to the Lightning Lounge with Sage, Leona, and Libby. That was good. Sure, Scarlet was straggling behind, keeping apart from everyone, but she was getting back into the swing of things and that was what mattered.

Cassie turned around, looking for Astra, but she had already left. Cassie hopped on the Cosmic Transporter, hoping that the girl had gone straight back to her room. The flower business needed to end that day. She had a bigger dish to dry. She grinned as she recalled another Wishling expression one of the Star Darlings had shared with her. *I'm going to knock their clocks off when it's my turn to go down to Wishworld,* she thought. Her words were brave but her stomach flipped at the very thought.

Cassie took a deep breath and knocked on Astra and Clover's door. Her mind was a complete blank and she noticed that her hands were trembling a bit out of sheer nervousness. She pulled a piece of boingtree gum out of her pocket. She found its mellow taste soothed her nerves. Then she unwrapped another for good measure and shoved it into her mouth. A vanishing garbage can stood nearby and Cassie tossed her wrappers into it. She wondered how she was going to connect with Astra. The Starling was a total sports fanatic and Cassie didn't know a star ball from a star . . . a star something.

She was chomping away, still hoping for some stellar inspiration, when the door slid open. Cassie's head snapped up. Astra stood there, a star ball tucked under her arm.

"Cassie!" said Astra. "I have the star ball game on. But I thought I heard something."

"Um, do you mind if I come in?"

"Of course not," said Astra, stepping aside. She slid the door closed behind them.

Cassie was so keyed up she was practically vibrating with nervous energy. She was certain that Astra would notice and get suspicious. But the girl turned back to her star ball game without another glance. Cassie looked around the room, which was both sporty and sleek, reflecting the personalities of the two roommates. It was her first visit to their room, and her eyes took in Astra's side, with its star ball court and shelves lined with sporting equipment and startrophies of all shapes and sizes. The star ball game Astra was watching was playing on a screen that took up an entire wall. Clover's side had an extra-high ceiling and was filled with musical instruments and some technical-looking machines. Cassie noted with interest a terrarium, lush and green, built right into the floor.

"That's Stellar School playing Comet Prep a couple of weeks ago," said Astra, her eyes never leaving the screen. "We're playing Stellar on Bopday. They're really good, so I'm watching a holo-vid of their last couple of games to get some pointers on how to approach the game."

Cassie nodded. Sounded good.

"Just let me watch this last play and I'm all yours," said Astra.

"VALENCIA DODGES THE ONCOMING CENTER AND PIVOTS. SHE JUMPS! SHE SHOOTS! SHE SCORES!" the announcer shouted. The crowd went wild. Astra turned back to Cassie. "This game is over," she said, even though Comet Prep now had the ball. "It's all over but the sparkling."

"Oh," said Cassie, not understanding.

"There's not enough time left for them to tie," Astra explained. "So how can I help you?" she asked, cradling the star ball in the crook of her arm as if it was a baby.

Cassie wandered to the vase of glittery flowers, which never faded or lost their bloom, sitting on a table right between the two girls' sides of the room. She thought she'd try the direct approach one more time. "You know we all got these flowers, right?" she began.

Astra nodded distractedly.

"Well, Vega and I took one of the bouquets to the botany lab and found out that they are full of negative energy. Like off the charts. They were grown on the Isle of Misera. Everyone has gotten rid of their flowers but you. We think they are causing you and Clover to fight all the time." She paused to gauge Astra's reaction.

"That's ridiculous," Astra laughed. "They're so beautiful. And they smell so amazing. Like florafierces." She laughed again. "Though that crazy roommate of mine thinks they smell just like purple piphanies."

Cassie sighed. The flowers had worked their intoxicating magic on Astra. She had to come up with another plan. She had come to realize that these strange flowers smelled different to everyone. For example, she could only smell the strong odor of silverbellas. She figured that the blooms, perhaps to entice you into not discarding them, gave off the smell of your own favorite flower. And she also knew from experience that it was impossible to convey that to someone who hadn't figured it out on her own. The silverbella odor was actually so strong to Cassie that it was overwhelming and very distracting. She found herself wanting to lean over and bury her nose in the blossoms. She countered this by taking a step back and concentrating on breathing only through her mouth.

Suddenly, she had a startacular idea. Okay, maybe it was a startacularly crazy idea. She'd find out soon enough.

"I just read this amazing holo-article about keeping flowers in your room," she fibbed. "It involves sports, so I thought you'd want to be the first to know."

"Really?" said Astra, leaning forward. She knew that Cassie read more than all the other Star Darlings put together, so it was perfectly reasonable that she would have seen a holo-article Astra had missed.

"Three . . . two . . . one," the announcer counted down, and a buzzer went off. "STELLAR SCHOOL WINS AGAIN! AND THE CROWD GOES WILD!"

Astra lowered the volume with a wave of her hand and turned toward Cassie with interest. Behind her, Cassie could see the players jumping up and down, huge grins on their faces, but she tried not to let it distract her from her mission.

"Well, the holo-article said that athletes should avoid having fresh flowers in their room before a big event," Cassie said. "Apparently, it weakens their powers of concentration."

Astra stared at her. "Really?" she said. She gave the flowers a quizzical look. "That's terrible! And here I have that big game coming up."

Cassie nodded sympathetically, biting her lip.

Astra tossed the star ball onto a chair and picked up the vase of flowers. With a confused expression on her face, she held them out to Cassie, whose heart skipped a beat. *Is my crazy idea actually going to work?* she thought.

Suddenly, Astra closed her eyes and brought the flowers to her nose. She took a deep sniff and her face grew serious. "I don't know," she said, hugging the flowers to her chest. "They just smell so good. . . ."

Cassie stole a glance at the wall and spotted a holo-poster of a sporty-looking woman with her name emblazoned underneath. She winked at Cassie, as if in encouragement. Cassie hated to lie; in fact, it pained her to do so. *But this is for Astra and Clover's own good,* she thought. *They'll be grateful when the flowers are gone and things can go back to normal.*

She took a deep breath and spoke. "Um, as a matter of fact, they interviewed a top athlete named Saturnia, who said as soon as she threw out a bouquet of flowers she had in her house, she felt so much better."

"Really?" said Astra, her eyes narrowing. "And they interviewed her recently?"

Cassie nodded. "Just this morning," she said. "This news is hot off the holo-presses."

"Aha!" Astra said with a laugh as she put down the flowers (but not before taking another long, deep sniff). "Good joke, Cassie!" she said. "You had me going until you brought up Saturnia. She's in training for the Starlympics and she's in a remote mountain location. She won't be giving any interviews for starmonths."

Oh, starf! thought Cassie. "Ha-ha, I almost got you!" she said weakly. "Good joke, huh?" Her heart sank. What was she going to do now? She had to come up with something—and quick. She scanned the room, looking for something—anything—that would give her some inspiration. Her eyes fell on a stick with a star-shaped net on its end propped up in the corner, and she picked it up. "The real reason I came over was to ask you for help. Believe it or not, I'm not doing very well in P.E."

"Physical Energy?" asked Astra, a shocked look on her face.

"Yes, Physical Energy," said Cassie. "I was wondering if you could teach me how to handle this star . . ." Her mind raced. What was that thing called, anyway?

"Starstick," said Astra. "It's called a starstick. You know, for playing Star-Away. It's an important skill to master. You've come to the right place." She raced to a closet, threw open the door, and started tossing sports equipment behind her. "There it is," she said, pulling out another starstick and a medium-sized ball. She tossed the ball into the net at the end of her stick and began to bounce it up and down. "You know, where you have to get the ball into your opponent's basket to score a point? It's a lot of fun."

"Riiiight," said Cassie, nodding. All these star sports were so similar to her she could never keep them straight.

After showing Cassie how to hold the starstick properly, Astra tossed her the ball. But Cassie's initial instinct was to duck. The ball hit the wall and bounced to the floor.

Astra shook her head. "You're supposed to *catch* it, silly," she explained. "Hand me the ball." Cassie did and Astra placed it in her net and tried again. That time Cassie bobbled the ball for a moment but held on to it.

"Great job!" said Astra encouragingly. "Now toss it back to me."

Cassie did. Her throw was off target and Astra had to lunge sideways. Still, she caught it neatly.

Toss after toss, Cassie began to fall into the rhythm. Scoop and toss, scoop and toss. "Hey, this is kind of fun!" she said.

"It is," Astra agreed. "Just wait till you try star ball," she added.

Cassie could see the flowers out of the corner of her eye, mocking her with their mere existence, their presence intensified by the cloying smell of silverbellas. Suddenly, she had another crazy idea. She had no idea if it would work. But she kept moving closer and closer to the vase of flowers. The two girls tossed the ball back and forth, back and forth as she made her way across the room.

She was within arm's reach of the blooms. And suddenly, the front door slid open. Clover was standing there. Cassie saw her chance. She tossed the ball as far past Astra as she could, then scooped up the vase of flowers in the net of her starstick.

Astra jumped over her round red couch and made a flying leap, catching the ball.

"Duck!" Cassie cried to Clover. Looking puzzled, Clover did. And Cassie hurled the vase of flowers as hard as she could. Astra turned around, obviously pleased with her stellar catch. When she saw her beloved flowers hurtling through the air toward the open door, her mouth opened in shock. It seemed to Cassie as if everything was happening in slow motion: Astra's loud "Noooooo!" and her desperate lunge for the flowers. But she was too late, for miraculously, Cassie's aim was true. The flowers landed right inside the mouth of the waiting disappearing garbage can and then they were gone—instantly.

Cassie was panting hard as Clover straightened up. The roommates were both staring at Cassie in shocked silence. Astra scowled at her. "Cassie!" she shouted. "Why in the stars did you . . ." Then she noticed her roommate. "Clover!" she said pleasantly. "There you are! How did band practice go?"

"It was great," said Clover. "Star salutations for asking. Did you have a fun time with Cassie?"

"I did," said Astra. "Who knew Cassie was such a natural Star-Away player? Did you see that throw? I'm going to tell the coach we've got a brand-new hurler!"

And Cassie began to laugh. The last of the flowers were gone. Sure, she was still worried. There was still the question of who had sent them—and why. But she laughed anyway—with relief that the flowers were finally gone, with happiness that the roommates were back to normal, and also with pleasure that she had actually discovered a sport she enjoyed!

CHAPTER
6

 Operation: Flower Disposal a success! The S.D. are now flower-free. Let's meet after dinner to talk about next steps!

 Vega?

 Scarlet?

No answer. Again. This was getting weird. Something must be wrong with the Star-Zaps' holo-connections, Cassie decided. There were a lot of missed messages lately. Cassie's stomach rumbled. She had worked up quite an appetite playing starstickball—or whatever it was called. She checked her Star-Zap. It wasn't quite dinnertime, but she didn't feel like being in her room any longer. She decided to take a stroll in the ozziefruit orchard before dinner.

Cassie meandered through the trees, which were heavy with fruit. The smell of ripe ozziefruit was mouth-watering. Flutterfocuses wafted among the trees, and glimmerbees darted about, on a mission. She took a seat on a low stone wall and closed her eyes, enjoying the slight breeze and the gentle warmth of the late-afternoon sun on her upturned face.

"Cassie! What a nice starprise!" said someone with a familiar voice.

Cassie's eyes snapped open. A shadowy figure stood in front of her, blocking the sun. She squinted, but it wasn't until she shielded her eyes that she could see who it was. She gave an involuntary gasp.

"Lady Stella!" she said. "What are you doing here?"

Lady Stella laughed. "Just enjoying a pre-dinner stroll through the ozziefruit orchard, same as you," she answered. She motioned her head toward the stone wall. "Mind if I join you?" she asked.

"Not at all," said Cassie. She sat up straight and smoothed her skirt. She hadn't been alone with the headmistress since the day of her Starling Academy interview, many starmonths earlier. Truth be told, she found the headmistress, as lovely and kind as she was, a little intimidating.

Lady Stella smiled and sat down next to her. "I love the light this time of day," she said. "It's not as stunning as lightfall, but it has its own stark beauty. Everything looks so sharp and focused, you know?"

Cassie nodded. She did know. She felt the same way.

"And it's the perfect time to come to the orchards. Most people are getting ready for dinner, so you have them all to yourself."

Cassie nodded again. "Yes," she managed to say in agreement. She felt tongue-tied around the headmistress. She yearned to say something intelligent and thoughtful, but couldn't think of anything at the moment. Her face became warm and she knew that her cheeks were turning that unflattering shade of silver she so disliked.

"May I be frank with you, Cassie?" Lady Stella asked.

Cassie nodded nervously.

"You've been on my mind recently."

Cassie gulped. She had?

"I've been wanting to ask you a question. Why do you think you are here at Starling Academy? Why do you think you were chosen to be a Star Darling?"

Cassie took off her glasses and peered through them to grab a starmin to think. She had an idea, but she felt nervous about saying it aloud. She didn't want to seem like a braggart. So she shrugged.

"I only ask because you don't seem as confident as you should be. Take it from me, Cassie. You know that you and your fellow Star Darlings were chosen for your strengths, and what you bring to the group, each something different. You are one of the most intuitive students I have ever come across in my career. You scored off the charts on the entrance exams." Lady Stella gave her a sympathetic look. "You must learn to recognize your strengths and trust yourself."

"St-star salutations," said Cassie. She was both happy to have her suspicions confirmed and disappointed that she hadn't spoken up for herself. It was an odd mix of emotions.

Lady Stella stood and turned to go, then turned back. "I know you are dreading your mission, Cassie," she said. "I'd be a fool not to see it. But I am telling you that you have nothing to fear. You're going to be a natural."

"Star salutations, Lady Stella," Cassie repeated. She watched the headmistress's retreating back. Again she felt a rush of different feelings—embarrassment at being so transparent, relief that Lady Stella had faith in her, and hope that she would be successful when her mission actually happened. With a sigh, she headed to the Celestial Café for dinner. On her way, she thought she heard a rustling in the branches behind her. She turned around sharply, but no one was there.

When she walked into the bustling cafeteria and made her way to the Star Darlings' table, she was struck by the sinking sun, which lit up the sky with its warm rosy tones. She knew that as soon as the beams hit the Crystal Mountains, the view would be even more spectacular, as prisms of rainbow light would begin to appear. But what really caught her attention was the fact that Astra and Clover were sitting side by side, looking quite chummy. As Cassie pulled out a chair and sat down, she saw the Bot-Bot waiter from that starmorning zoom up with the roommates' drinks. He hesitated for a moment before placing them on the table.

Clover threw her arms up in front of Astra. "Don't worry SL-D9," she cried. "I've got you covered!" The two girls cracked up.

"Star salutations," said the Bot-Bot sincerely as he carefully placed the drinks out of Astra's reach.

Vega raised her eyebrows at Cassie, who nodded.

Vega gave her a triple wink, the Starlandian way of silently telling someone "Good job!"

Scarlet came in and sat down next to Cassie. "All good?" she asked quietly.

Across the table, Clover laughed out loud. "Oh, Astra, you're so funny!" she said.

Cassie grinned. "All good," she said.

Dinner, for the first time in more than a double starweek, was extremely pleasant—argument- and drama-free. The girls talked and laughed and joked and traded bites of their dishes. Even Leona and Scarlet seemed to be getting along, or at least not fighting with each other, which was good enough in Cassie's holo-book. Cassie had a huge smile on her face for the entire meal.

The Bot-Bot waiter came over to take their dessert order.

Tessa ordered first, as usual. "I'll have an ozziefruit parfait and a mug of hot—" she began. Just then, their Star-Zaps chimed, all twelve at the same time. It made a pleasant, musical sound to Cassie's ears.

Adora read the holo-text first. "Starmendous!" she said. She looked up. "Hey, everybody, listen to this! We're invited to a party!"

The table started to buzz. A party! How fun! *It's just*

what we all need, thought Cassie. *A chance to relax and just enjoy ourselves for a couple of hours.* All the girls flipped open their Star-Zaps as the Bot-Bot waiter hovered nearby, forgotten. Gemma read the invitation out loud. "'You are invited to a Star Mani/Pedi Party tonight after dinner in the Lightning Lounge's party room. Hydrongs of polish colors to choose from, state-of-the-art star-beautychambers, music, dancing, a floating dessert bar . . .'" She paused. "What's a floating dessert bar? We don't have those in Solar Springs."

Libby, who lived in a mansion and had been to too many fancy parties to count, supplied the answer. "Oh, you'll love it! It's a levitating cloudcandy table covered with every light-as-air dessert you've ever heard of," she said. "You know—Aeropuffs, Floating Wisps, Featherwhispers. They're so startastically delicious they just melt in your mouth. There are cocomoon star-pillows and . . ."

"Say no more. I'm in," said Tessa. She canceled her dessert order and stood up. The rest of the girls followed suit.

On her way out the door, Cassie spotted Ophelia sitting alone at a table, idly twirling a noddlenoodle on her fork and staring into space.

"I hope it's not too crowded," said Vega worriedly as they approached the Lightning Lounge. But when they pushed open the doors to the party room, they discovered they were the first to arrive.

"Oh, my stars!" said Sage, taking in the shifting, shimmering multicolored stars that were projected on the walls, floor, and ceiling; the multileveled dance floor; the colorful starbeautychambers, round and shiny; and the floating dessert bar, which was even better than it sounded, with edible fluffy pastel pink, blue, and yellow clouds of spun sugar candy suspended in the air. Nestled in the candyfloss were sweet little confections in all the colors of the rainbow. Tessa made a glitter-beeline for the sweets and loaded up a sparkling crystal plate with some carefully selected treats. The rest of the girls did the same. After eating three jujufruit gossamer-wisps, which, she was pleased to discover, were as light and airy as they were delicious, Cassie's mind returned to Ophelia, who'd been sitting all by herself in the cafeteria. She flipped open her Star-Zap and started typing.

Ophelia, we're all at the Lightning Lounge, at a mani/pedi party. The desserts are out of this world! Come join us!

That sounds startacular! I'll be right over!

 We're downstairs in the party room. See you soon!

Cassie smiled as she shut her Star-Zap. Her good deed for the day was done. Now she was ready for some beauty time.

"I don't know why the rest of the students aren't here," said Adora as she reached up to grab a hunk of pale blue spun sugar candy, as fluffy as a cloud. "But that just means more dessert for us!"

Cassie walked across the room and hesitated in front of a silvery chamber, unsure what to do next. Libby appeared at her side. "Let me help you," she said. "My mom has one," she explained. "Starbeautychambers can give you manicures, pedicures, haircuts and styles, facials, body scrubs, face sparklings, you name it." She pressed a round button on the side and the chamber opened like a flower, revealing a holo-screen, a fluffy white seat, and four covered pods. "That's where you put your hands and feet," she explained. Cassie took off her silver slippers and lowered herself onto the cozy-looking seat. She gasped at how luxuriously soft it was.

Libby nodded. "Amazing, right?"

The holo-screen slid into place at lap level. The shape of a hand appeared on the screen, and Cassie hovered her palm over it, looking to Libby for confirmation. Libby nodded. "Put your hand right on it," she said encouragingly. Cassie obliged and a list of nail polish colors in her signature shade appeared on the right-hand side of the screen. When she touched the name of the polish with her free hand, an image of the color was projected on her nails so she could make a well-informed decision. Cassie considered them all. Silver Streak was pretty-ish; Icicle a bit too frosty; Sassy Sparkles not quite as tasteful as she'd like; Time of Shadows White too austere; and Storm Queen a little too gray. She thought she'd love Pink Snowflake but was just lukewarm about it. Finally, Magic and Moonbeams came up. She gasped with delight. It was pure perfection. Sparkly, iridescent, and silvery white, it glowed with the promise of stardust and enchantment. She chose it for both her fingers and toes and slipped her hands and feet inside the pods. They were immediately enveloped in warm lotion that smelled just like glimmerdrop cookies. Cassie closed her eyes and a scene came flooding back: a day she had come home from school to find her mom, her cheeks flushed and her silvery hair escaping from her bun and framing her face. She had been baking all day and presented Cassie with a plate of warm cookies, which Cassie munched as she told her mom all about her day. It brought a sweet smile to her face and Cassie pressed the memory function on her Star-Zap to record it so she'd be able to watch it on-screen whenever she liked. A Bot-Bot masseuse zoomed up and began to knead her shoulders, which were slightly achy from the vigorous game of Star-Away she had played earlier. Ah, that was heavenly. Her chamber began to softly play "Brighter Than a Comet," one of her favorite songs, and she hummed along. Once her hands and feet were sufficiently moisturized, they were massaged. Then the nails were trimmed and shaped, and finally the polish was applied.

Vega, who had gone back to the floating dessert bar for seconds, was on her way to get her own mani/pedi. She scanned the room and leaned over Cassie's chamber to talk to her privately. "If the whole school was invited, why are there only twelve chambers?" she asked. "That's not even close to enough."

That's a good question, Cassie thought, but then the pods released her hands and feet and she saw her fingers and toes, polished to a silvery perfection. "Oh," she breathed. "I picked the most perfect color ever."

Vega shrugged and headed to a shiny blue starbeauty-chamber.

"Cassie, let me see," called Adora from a sky-blue starbeautychamber nearby.

Cassie stood and walked to her. She considered putting her shoes back on but didn't want to cover up her sparkling toes. Adora leaned over to take a look. "Pretty," she said. A Bot-Bot masseuse was giving her a neck massage as she picked her polish color. "I can't decide between Cerulean Circus for my fingers," she said, clicking on it, "or Starbeam Dream." She looked up to Cassie for help. "Oh . . . um," said Cassie. They looked exactly the same to her. "Definitely Starbeam Dream," she finally said.

"You're right," said Adora. "It's much prettier." She didn't seem to need any help choosing Indigo Spell for her toes.

When everyone's nails were done, the girls reclined on overstuffed couches and admired each other's fingers and toes as they sipped tall sparkling drinks brought to them by hovering Bot-Bot waiters. Then the lights dimmed. The starlight show began to flash faster and the music got louder. Cassie was pleased to note that Leona was the first to jump up and begin to dance—barefoot, of course. Her fingers and toes sparkled in the dim light; she had chosen a polish that made her nails look as if they had been dipped in liquid gold, which Cassie took as another sign that she was improving. Leona crooked her finger, beckoning to Cassie, who began to shake her head, her usual self-conscious response. But the idea of everyone's eyes on her as she moved to the beat, which usually unnerved her, suddenly seemed like an appealing one. She jumped up and bopped over to Leona, who grinned and grabbed her hands. The two began to spin around and around, then broke apart and twirled in the empty space. Cassie closed her eyes and moved to the music, freely and joyously. She didn't worry that she looked silly, and she didn't care what anyone was thinking of her. All she knew was that she felt beautiful, and fluid, and natural—and like she never wanted to stop moving to the music. After a few minutes, the rest of the girls joined in. They were a jumping, twirling, grinning mass. They danced until they couldn't dance anymore, then flopped onto the couches in happy exhaustion.

Cassie closed her eyes, breathing hard. She opened her eyes to see Sage leaning over her. She was still laughing.

"Cassie, get up, it's time for bed," she said.

"All right, all right." Cassie swung her feet to the floor and reluctantly slipped on her shoes. With a sigh, she stood up. She admired her fingernails again under the flashing lights. "Wow," Cassie said. "I really picked the best color."

Adora grabbed her arm. "I thought you liked Starbeam Dream," she said almost inaudibly.

"The music's too loud," said Cassie. "What did you say?"

"I said, I thought you liked Starbeam Dream."

Cassie shrugged. "Glad you like it, too," she said. She looked at Vega. "Are you coming with us?" she asked.

"You should go, you shouldn't wait," Vega said, pointing to Piper, who was sipping a sea-green beverage through a straw. "I will wait for my roommate."

Cassie was sleepy. "Okay, I'll see you all in the . . ."

"Morning," finished Piper.

Clover stood and threw her arms around Cassie.

"See you at breakfast, Clover," Cassie said.

"Wait for me," said Leona. But then she never got up, so Cassie and Sage shrugged and headed back to their room. They chatted and giggled all the way back to the dorm. Cassie tumbled into bed, fully intending to get up in a starsec to use her toothlight and sparkle her face, but she found she was so tired she couldn't move. She couldn't even muster the energy to ask Sage to please quiet down. The girl was still giggling.

Weird, she thought. *Ophelia never showed up at the party. Something better must have come up. Maybe she's not as lonely as Leona thinks she is.*

Sage rolled over, trying, and failing, to muffle a laugh.

I am so much better at falling asleep than Sage, Cassie thought. And she was right. She drifted off to sleep.

CHAPTER
7

When Cassie awoke the next morning, she felt starmendous—so much so that she said it out loud. "I feel starmendous," she said. No, that wasn't quite right. "I *am* starmendous," she tried. Yes, that was much better.

She stepped out of bed and stubbed her toe. "Moons and stars!" she cried. "That hurt!"

She looked to her roommate, whose head was resting on her lavender pillowcase, for sympathy. Sage looked back at her and giggled.

"Sage!" said Cassie with a scowl. "I hurt myself!"

"I know," said Sage, trying to make a sad face and failing miserably. "But something about it is pretty funny."

"No," said Cassie earnestly. "It's actually not."

But apparently that was very amusing to Sage, too.

With as much dignity as she could muster, Cassie hobbled her way to the sparkle shower room. Even though her toe was throbbing, she couldn't help admiring herself in the mirror, her gossamer silvery-pink hair looking so, well, gossamery and lovely around her pale face.

Cassie stood on the Cosmic Transporter, on her way to breakfast, staring into space. Suddenly, she was startled by someone skipping by, almost knocking her over. She peered after her. *Was that Scarlet?* she wondered.

When Cassie arrived in the cafeteria, she found Scarlet and Piper already sitting at the table. Piper's amazingly long seafoam green hair was pulled back into a rippling ponytail. Cassie chose the seat next to her. "Good . . ." she started.

"Morning," Piper said pleasantly.

Leona and Adora arrived next. "I'm not hungry," Leona said. "I ran into Ophelia this morning and she gave me this delicious zoomberry turnover from the huge care package she just got. So I'm just going to get a cup of hot . . ."

"Zing," said Piper.

Leona gave her a funny look. "Ozziefruit tea," she said, correcting her.

Vega arrived next and sat on the other side of Cassie. She was followed by Astra and Clover, who sat on the other side of the table.

"Last night was so much fun," said Clover.

Vega nodded. "We did our nails, had snacks, and more."

Clover nodded. "Yes, we did!"

"It certainly was not a bore," Vega finished.

The Bot-Bot waiter arrived and began to take their breakfast orders. Cassie ordered a bowl of druderwomp flakes with starberries.

Moons and stars, that was a good order, Cassie thought. She addressed Adora, who sat across from her. "I hope you don't have breakfast envy!"

"I think I'll like mine better," said Adora.

"Starscuse me?" said Cassie.

"I think I'll like mine better," repeated Adora.

"Um . . . what?" said Cassie.

"I said I think I'll like mine better," Adora said patiently.

"Uh . . . that's great," said Cassie, who still couldn't understand what the girl was saying but was too embarrassed to ask her to repeat it a third time.

When it was Leona's turn, she thought for a moment

and ordered starcakes and tinsel toast with a slice of mooncheese.

Sage giggled. "I thought you said you weren't hungry!"

"What are you talking about?" said Leona.

Breakfast arrived in record time. Tessa took a bite, then got a confused look on her face. "Starscuse me," she said politely to the Bot-Bot, "but I asked for starberry waffles. These are moonberry."

"Star apologies," said the Bot-Bot waiter. "That is highly irregular. I'll fix that right away." He zoomed back to the kitchen and returned a few starmins later.

Tessa dug in to her new breakfast excitedly, took a bite, then shook her head. "Moonberries again!" she exclaimed. "How . . ."

"Delightful," finished Piper.

"No, how odd," she said.

"I hate moonberries," said Sage disgustedly. But she punctuated her statement with a delighted laugh.

Sage's giggle is really annoying, thought Cassie. *It would be so much less annoying if she had a sweet, tinkling laugh. Kind of like . . .* She thought for a minute. *Kind of like mine,* she decided. She practiced it, putting her hand over her mouth and tittering. She nodded. It was musical and quite pleasant.

Cassie's day went on starmendously. She felt emboldened enough to raise her hand in every class, even when she wasn't quite sure of the answer. And when every eye in the class was focused on her, somehow it didn't feel intimidating at all. *That was some pep talk Lady Stella gave me yestarday*, she thought.

At the end of the day it was time for their Star Darlings lessons. Cassie settled into her usual seat in the soundproof classroom. She was starprised to see a new, unfamiliar teacher in front of the room. She was one of the youngest teachers Cassie had ever seen, with super-short magenta hair that stuck up from her head in tiny spikes. She wore swirly leggings in shades of pink, red, and orange, a fitted jacket (which the Star Darlings would soon discover, as the class went on, changed color every ten starmins), and shiny orange boots.

"Hello, class," she said, standing and walking up and down the aisles as she spoke. "I am Kiri Lillibelle and I am thrilled to be your guest lecturer today. You may not know me, but I am certainly familiar with each and every one of you. I am the researcher who hand-selects all of your—"

"Outfits," offered Piper.

Kiri gave her a quizzical look. "No, Mirror Mantras," she said. "A Mirror Mantra is a very important part of a successful Wish Mission. By repeating your Mirror Mantra while gazing into a mirror, you will receive strength and centeredness. When you recite it together with your Wisher down on Wishworld, you can bring clarity and focus to her that will aid in wish fulfillment."

She began to walk around the room as she spoke. "Mirror Mantras used to be presented to Starling Academy students upon graduation. We had four star-years to determine the perfect message for each student. The timing was a little tighter for you Star Darlings," she said with a laugh. "But we were able to determine the correct mantras for each of you."

"How do you choose them?" asked Libby with a yawn.

"An excellent question," said Kiri. "They were carefully selected based on each of your personalities, strengths, and challenges."

"Challenges?" asked Astra.

"Yes, challenges," said Kiri. "It is not just your strengths that make you the special person you are, but also your challenges and how you face them."

"But we already know our mantras," said Leona. "They were assigned to us as soon as we found out we were Star Darlings."

"Yes," said Kiri patiently. "But we've determined that the more you use them before your Wish Mission, the more their strength will increase. We want you to become as familiar with your mantra as you are with your own name. We want to make sure that they become second nature to you, and that you use them to their fullest potential. We want you to know your mantras forwards and backwards."

The girls nodded.

"So let's begin!" The classroom door opened and a bevy of Bot-Bot assistants flew into the room, each holding a floating holo-mirror, which it placed in front of a student. Cassie gazed at herself and found herself taking off her starglasses to get a closer look at her eyelashes. They were so thick and lush! How had she never noticed them before? They were pretty starmazing, actually. She was about to lean over and ask Leona if she had noticed her lashes before—and, if so, why she had never called them to Cassie's attention—when Kiri began to speak again.

"Okay," she said. "Now let's go around the room and recite your mantras for each other. Why don't you start?" she asked, pointing to Sage, who sat in the front of the room.

Sage giggled nervously and cleared her throat. She gazed into the mirror levelly. "I believe in you," she said. "Glow for it!"

Even from the back of the room, Cassie could see that Sage's reflection took on a brilliant glow.

"Look at her reflection!" Kiri cried to the class. "Her glow is intensifying even here on Starland! This is some pretty powerful stuff!"

She turned back to Sage. "Okay," said Kiri. "How did that make you feel?"

"I felt really energized," Sage said with a laugh. "While I definitely felt the power of the mantra when I used it on Wishworld, I felt something extra just now. Maybe my mantra has even more power than I realized."

Kiri nodded enthusiastically. "That's exactly it. We're thinking that we have not yet taken full advantage of the power of the mantras. And we think that you as Star Darlings may have even greater mantra powers than the other students."

The room began to buzz with excitement. When they quieted down, Kiri went around the room and had the rest of the Star Darlings recite their mantras, one by one.

"It's all in the balance. Glimmer and shine!" said Libby, her pink ponytail shimmering.

Leona said: "You are a star. Light up the world!"

Scarlet reached into her back pocket for her drumsticks and beat out a drumroll on top of her desk before stating: "Abracadabra—time for some star power!" And even she looked impressed by the burst of sparkle in her reflection.

"Dreams can come true," said Piper when it was her turn. "It's your time to shine!"

"Stronger you make challenges," said Astra with a wide grin. "Glowin' get to time!"

"Huh?" said Kiri.

Astra blinked at Kiri innocently. "I thought you said you wanted us to know our mantras forwards and backwards!"

Kiri shook her head and moved on to the next Star Darling.

"Let your heart lead the way," Tessa said, smiling at her reflection.

Her little sister went next. "Make up your mind to blaze like a comet!" Gemma shouted.

Clover adjusted her purple hat and said, "Keep the beat and shine like the star you are!"

Hmmm, thought Cassie. *That's not a bad mantra at all. Maybe Clover got mine by mistake?* She hesitated. She knew that Kiri was waiting for her to speak, but for some reason she just didn't want to say her mantra out loud. She had gladly accepted it when she had first received it, but it suddenly didn't seem right to her at all.

Kiri smiled at her encouragingly. "Come on, Cassie, let's hear it," she said.

Cassie sighed. "Listen to your feelings. Let your inner light sparkle," she said in a monotone. She was surprised to see that her reflection got extra sparkly even though her heart wasn't in it.

"What's wrong, Cassie?" Kiri asked. "That's a lovely mantra, if I do say so myself."

Cassie shrugged. Suddenly, she had an idea—a brilliant one, in fact. "Do you ever change people's mantras?" she asked.

Kiri was clearly taken aback. "Are you pulling my leg?" she said.

Gemma stood up to take a look. "No, she isn't," she told Kiri seriously. "She's not even touching you!"

Astra snorted. "Good one, Gemma!"

"I was thinking of something a little more star-forward," said Cassie slowly.

"Star-forward?" asked the teacher, her brow wrinkled.

"You know," said Cassie. "Exciting. Vibrant. Like 'You are totally startacular.' Or maybe 'You are star-mendously talented,'" she suggested.

Kiri was frowning as she studied Cassie. "But the Mirror Mantras are carefully chosen to reflect each student's personality," she said. "A lot of work went into each one. I don't think I've ever heard of a student requesting a new mantra in Starling Academy history."

Cassie shrugged. It just didn't seem like such a great fit anymore. It was kind of . . . boring.

Kiri opened her mouth as if she was going to say something, clearly thought better of it, and turned to the next student. "Adora?" she said. "It's your turn."

And Adora said, "Use your logic. You are a star!"

Kiri shook her head. She was clearly getting frustrated. "Well, apparently Adora is not ready to share yet. We'll get back to you la—"

And that was when all the Star-Zaps went off. Cassie looked down at the message: SD WISH ORB IDENTIFIED. PROCEED TO LADY STELLA'S OFFICE IMMEDIATELY. The girls all shot each other quick looks, then began to make their way out of the classroom. It was time.

CHAPTER
8

Usually, when Cassie headed to Lady Stella's office
for the Wish Orb reveal, her stomach was in knots. She
would look at her fellow Star Darlings who had not yet
been chosen for their Wish Missions and silently hope
that it was their turn, instead of hers. She'd be ready, she
would tell herself, next time. Just one more reprieve, and
she'd be ready. But then she never was.

But this time was different. Cassie knew she was
ready. And she also knew that there was no better choice
for this mission than she. In fact, she was sure of it.

Cassie calmly made her way to Lady Stella's office,
where she sat at the shiny silver table until all the Star
Darlings were gathered. Then she patiently waited her
turn as they all made their way down the hidden staircase

behind Lady Stella's desk into the cool, dark secret caves underneath Halo Hall. Scarlet was just in front of her, and in the gloom Cassie noticed a silvery white bitbat land briefly on the girl's shoulder. *That's odd*, she thought. Bitbats were notoriously skittish. Soon they entered the special Star Darlings Wish Cavern. Cassie took in the scene—sunlight shining through the glass roof, golden waterfalls of wish energy streaming down the sides, the garden they stood in green and abundant. The glowing Wish Orbs still in the ground waiting for the moment when they would be ready now numbered just six. It was clearly impossible for the place to exist deep underground, yet there it was, right in front of their eyes. The girls moved to the grass-covered platform in the middle of the Wish Cavern and waited for the chosen Wish Orb to emerge. They did not have to wait long. A shaft of sunlight lit up the center of the platform and the orb burst out. Cassie never took her eyes off the glowing globe. This time, instead of circling the room quickly, or pausing at each Star Darling as if trying to decide who it belonged to, the orb simply zoomed right up to one student: Cassie. She held out one hand confidently, motioning for the orb with the other as if to say, *Get over here right now.* The Wish Orb nestled right into her open palm. Everyone stared at Cassie in disbelief.

Even Lady Stella looked very starprised. "Cassie, the Wish Orb has chosen you," she said, which seemed unnecessary, since Cassie was already cradling the glowing orb in her hands. "Are you okay?" she asked, craning her neck to look searchingly into Cassie's eyes.

"Of course," said Cassie. "Why wouldn't I be?"

★

As Cassie sat on her bed the morning of her mission, finalizing her arrival outfit with the help of the Wishworld Outfit Selector function on her Star-Zap, she wondered why she had feared that day so much. Everyone acted like being picked to go on a Wish Mission was such a big deal, and now that Cassie was the chosen one, it didn't seem monumental at all. For stars' sake, even Ophelia had gone on a mission. (Granted hers had been a startacularly terrible mess.) Cassie couldn't understand it. She flipped through the Wishworld outfits she had picked for the rest of her trip. They were all perfectly coordinated, down to the shoes and socks. She said her mantra to herself, annoyed that she hadn't been able to change it. "Listen to your feelings. Let your inner light sparkle," she repeated unenthusiastically. Her mantra was a dud; there was no doubt about that.

She glanced at her Star-Zap. It was time to head to the

Wishworld Surveillance Deck. She picked up her Star-Zap, then decided to send a quick holo-text to Ophelia, who she hadn't seen since that day in the Celestial Café.

> Hey! I enjoyed our talk. Let's get together soon so we can start making you sparkle! I'll be in touch. . . .

She snapped her phone shut. "Time to go?" she said to Sage, who chuckled as if Cassie had said something amusing.

"Time to go!" Sage said. "Is there any last-minute advice I can give you?"

Cassie shook her head. "No, I'm good."

Cassie paused for a minute in front of the glass doors that led to the Wishworld Surveillance Deck. "You go ahead," she said to Sage. She slipped a pair of safety star-glasses over her own star-shaped glasses and took stock of herself. Though she would soon be taking off into the heavens attached to a wild shooting star and landing in an unfamiliar world, she didn't feel any flutterfocuses taking flight in her belly. She looked down at her hands, which were not even close to trembling; they were as still as a piece of starmarble. She was cool, calm, and collected.

She pushed open the door and was immediately mobbed by Star Darlings wearing safety starglasses in a rainbow of colors. She looked around at everyone. Someone was missing. "Where's Libby?" she asked.

"She was still sleeping," offered Gemma. "I couldn't get her out of bed."

"Get out of here," Cassie said.

A perplexed look crossed Gemma's face. Then she shrugged. "Okay," she said. She turned around and headed inside.

Cassie started after her, but then Vega leaned in for a hug and Cassie caught a glimpse of herself in the lenses of Vega's blue safety starglasses. Cassie smiled at herself. She really did look great in white.

"So this is it," she said to Vega. "Anything to share before I go?"

"Your Wisher is now busy wishin'," Vega replied.

"That's true," said Cassie.

"Lots of luck upon your mission," Vega concluded.

"Thanks," said Cassie.

Clover stepped up and threw her arms around Cassie, nearly knocking her over. "Good luck, Cassie!" she cheered.

Adora was next. "Are you nervous, Cassie?" she said.

Huh? "Um . . . thanks," replied Cassie. She was suddenly surrounded by a group all eager to say their good-byes—Tessa, Scarlet, Leona, and then Astra. Finally, Piper stepped forward.

"Wish me luck," Cassie said to her. "Not that I—"

"Will listen!" said Piper.

"Need it," finished Cassie.

The last people to bid farewell to her were Lady Cordial and Lady Stella. Lady Cordial handed Cassie her silver backpack, and Cassie slipped it over her arm, giving the silver stuffed star a squeeze. "Star salutations," she told Lady Cordial.

Cassie stepped forward to join Lady Stella on the edge of the surveillance deck and found she couldn't move. She looked down in confusion. That's when she realized that someone had tied her shoelaces together!

"Really, Starlings?" she said as bent down to tie them properly. "That is so not funny." *Someone must be very jealous of me and my Wish Mission*, she thought. But everyone looked back at her innocently.

Lady Stella helped her to her feet and put her arm around Cassie's shoulder She pointed to the Star Wranglers throwing out their lassos made of wish energy. "You'll be on your way any starmin now," she said. She turned so she could look directly at Cassie. "And now some last-minute advice," she said, her eyes shining. "It's to trust your instincts. As I mentioned to you, your intuitive powers are startacular. And also recognize that you have the power to shape your feelings. Feeling nervous? Use your energy to turn it into excitement. But most of all, believe in yourself."

Cassie nodded. "I'm going to do a startastic job," she said.

Lady Stella nodded. "Of course you are." But Cassie thought she saw a look of starprise in her eyes. She gave Cassie a searching look that made her feel like a starquark under a holo-scope.

"You seem a little different today," Lady Stella said, a look of concern on her usually serene face.

"I am," said Cassie. "I am."

CHAPTER
9

Cassie stood in front of a large, long building, knowing that her Wisher was somewhere inside, feeling utterly miserable. It was cold, it was muddy, and it was rainy. And rain on Wishworld was nothing like the rain back home. It was decidedly unsparkly and rather than being a gentle refreshing mist it was actually quite, well, *wet*. Her clothes were soaked clean through.

With a sigh she accessed her Wishworld Outfit Selector and changed from the adorable but now sopping silver platform sandals (for height as well as fashion), light floaty white top with spaghetti straps, and pair of pink-and-white wide-legged pants that ended just below the knee into a more weather appropriate ensemble—cozy leggings; an oversized pale pink sweater, toasty as a blanket; and rubber boots. She also added a waterproof coat with a hood which she pulled up to cover her now platinum-blond hair with pale pink tips. Then she bent to fish the shooting star out of the brown muck, gave it a shake, folded it up, and placed it in her backpack, right next to her safety starglasses.

She made her first observation, which she knew would be recorded in her Cyber Journal. *Wish Mission 6, Wishworld Observation #1: Be sure to be fully prepared for all Wishworld weather conditions because you never know what you might need. You'll save yourself some time and annoyance.*

She took another deep breath and exhaled, marveling at the billowing white cloud she created. Then she squared her shoulders and marched forward in her rubbery boots. After waiting a moment for the heavy-looking metal door to slide open, she realized she had to push it to get inside. *Look out, Wisher, here I come,* she thought.

The hallway was long and appeared to be empty. Cassie stood dripping on the floor, her glasses foggy from the sudden warmth. She sighed. Wishworld was one annoyance after another so far.

"Well, hello there, young lady."

Cassie turned around quickly in the direction of the voice, and the combination of her quick movement, her slippery boots, and the wet floor caused her feet to slide right from underneath her. *Moons and stars!* she thought as her feet scrabbled on the floor, looking for purchase. The next thing she knew, she was flat on her back, staring up at the ceiling. *Oof.*

A face appeared in her line of vision—a woman's face, staring down at her and looking concerned. "Oh, my goodness, are you okay?" she asked.

"I'm fine," said Cassie with a sigh. This was not a stellar way to begin her first Wish Mission! Luckily, the only thing that was bruised was her dignity.

The woman squinted at Cassie through a small pair of glasses perched on her nose. She was clearly trying to place her—and failing. "I'm sorry," she said. "But I don't recognize you. Who are you?" She sniffed the air. "And why does it smell just like my mother's hummingbird cake?" she mused. "Boy does that take me back."

Now was as good a time as any. Cassie took off her foggy glasses and stared up into the woman's eyes. "My name is Cassie. I am the new student in school," she said. *Will it work upside down?* she wondered.

It did. "Your name is Cassie, you are the new student in school," the woman repeated as she helped Cassie to her feet. "There you go!" she said, drying her wet hands on her pant legs. "Welcome to Mountain View School, Cassie. I am Principal McIlhenney."

"Thank you," said Cassie, mentally congratulating herself for remembering the Wishling phrase for gratitude. She bent down, pretending to tuck her leggings into her boots, and stole a glance at her Star-Zap for directions to her Wisher's location. "I belong in room 261," she told the woman as she straightened up.

"You belong in room 261," the woman echoed with a nod. "That's Ms. Olds's room. I'll take you right there." She paused. "But we'll go to your new locker so you can store your things."

Cassie followed the woman down the hallway and was delighted with the small metal closet—or "locker"—she was given. There was just enough room for her dripping coat, which she was happy to dispose of. She envisioned the small top section of the locker filled with books. Paper books. *I can hardly wait to get my hands on them*, she thought.

"Ready?" asked Principal McIlhenney.

"Ready!" said Cassie, slamming her locker shut with a clang.

Cassie slung her silver backpack over her shoulder and followed the principal down the hallway. The woman paused in front of a display opposite the stairwell. Cassie looked up. There was a photo of a serious-looking girl with straight dirty-blond hair pulled back in a headband. STUDENT OF THE MONTH, it said below her photo. "Each month a student is chosen to be honored in this way," the principal said. She turned to Cassie and smiled. "Annabel here has received the award for three months running. It's awarded to a very special student who not only excels academically but also sets an example for the other students with words and actions. Maybe someday it will be you." Cassie felt a rush of warmth to her face. *Well, of course I'd be Student of the Month if I attended your school,* Cassie thought. *I'd probably be Student of the Year if that was possible!* She nodded politely and they continued up the stairs and down the hall, then stopped at the door of her new classroom. Principal McIlhenney turned to her and gave her a reassuring smile. "You'll like Ms. Olds," she said. "She's really kind and she's a good teacher."

Cassie nodded, recognizing the symbols on the classroom door from her Wishers 101 class when they had studied Wishworld holidays. They were bright green stemmed leaves with an interesting shape. "I like those . . . valentines!" she said. "Is it Halloween already?"

The principal chuckled. "Good one, Cassie!" She leaned toward her. "But Ms. Olds already has one class clown. She doesn't need another!" She rapped on the door, then turned to Cassie and smiled again. "Are you ready? Don't be nervous, now."

"Oh, I'm not nervous at all," said Cassie, giving the principal an odd glance for suggesting such a thing.

The woman looked surprised. "Good for you!" she said.

The door was opened by a kind-looking woman with medium-length brown hair. She wore a bright red sweater with white flowers on it. "Principal McIlhenney!" she said. "To what do I owe the pleasure?"

Cassie immediately filed that Wishling expression away as *Mission 6, Wishworld Observation #2. I have a great ear for charming Wishling expressions,* she thought.

The principal stepped through the doorway and a hush fell over the classroom, just like when Lady Stella made a surprise visit to a Starling Academy classroom or appeared as a multi-classroom holo-image to make an announcement. Principal McIlhenney introduced Cassie to her new teacher. While the adults talked, Cassie looked around the classroom, trying to see if she could pick out her Wisher. The students all looked back at her curiously. *Get ready, Wisher,* thought Cassie. *This is your lucky day. Your wish is about to be granted!* But although she knew the student had to be somewhere in the room, there wasn't even the tiniest flicker in her glasses—her Wish Pendant.

As Ms. Olds walked Cassie to her new desk, remarking that the air suddenly smelled like deep-dish blueberry pie, Principal McIlhenney said her good-byes and left. The class relaxed visibly after she was gone. Cassie scanned the room again. Still no glow. *That's odd*, she thought. *Could I be in the wrong classroom?* She looked at the directions on her Star-Zap. Classroom 261, just like the sign on the door. *Could my Wisher be absent?* There was one empty seat in the row next to hers in the back of the room. . . .

"Cell phones are not allowed in class," said someone in a snippy voice.

Cassie smiled at the girl, who sat in the first seat in the row next to hers. She was wearing a pale pink sweater and a plaid skirt. She was neat and tidy, not a dirty-blond hair on her head out of place.

"Thanks for the tip," said Cassie, slipping her Star-Zap into her sweater pocket. The girl stared back, unsmiling. Cassie took a closer look. "Aren't you the Student of the Month?" she said to her.

"That's me," the girl said. "Annabel Victor. And I'm going to be Student of the Month this month, too. It'll be announced at the end of the day tomorrow."

"Well, good for you," said Cassie. The girl was obnoxious, but she certainly was sure of herself; Cassie had to give her that. She sat back in her decidedly uncomfortable Wishworld seat. *I guess I'll just sit back and observe,* thought Cassie. *Blend in and get to the bottom of this Wish Mission.* She knew that she'd have it all figured out by lunchtime. She was sure of it.

She sat patiently as Ms. Olds took attendance and then asked everyone to take out their science books. Cassie was thrilled when the teacher handed her her very own copy, and she flipped through the pages excitedly. A quick glance told her that some of the information inside was hopelessly out of date, but she loved the book anyway—the weight of it in her hands, the slickness of the paper, the colorful illustrations and photographs on every page.

"Class, it's time to get out your homework," Ms. Olds said. Just as the students began to reach into their backpacks, the door burst open. There stood a tall, thin girl with long shiny black hair, clutching her books to her chest. She had a wide pleasant face and bright blue eyes that sparkled with mischief.

Cassie's glasses immediately began to glow. So this was her Wisher!

CHAPTER
18

Annabel scowled at her. "Those glasses have to be against the rules!" she said. "They're very distracting!"

"Lila, you're late," Ms. Olds scolded gently. "What happened?"

Lila looked around the room. Cassie noticed that almost all the students were staring at her with great interest, waiting to see what happened next. She shook her head dramatically, clearly enjoying the spotlight. "It was the sign!" she said. "The one down the block, at the crosswalk." She had a wide grin, and Cassie saw a flash of silver when she spoke. *Interesting,* she thought. *Could that be a clue?*

Ms. Olds shook her head, but there was a smile on

her face. "And tell us, Lila. How did a sign manage to make you late for school today?"

Lila grinned, clearly relishing the line she was about to deliver. "It said 'School Zone. Slow down.' So I did!"

The rest of the class laughed. They obviously liked Lila a lot.

"Sit down, Lila," said Ms. Olds, but in a kind way. "It's time to turn in your homework."

Lila still stood in the aisle. "Ms. Olds, would you ever get mad at me for something I didn't do?" she asked.

Ms. Olds frowned. "Of course not, Lila," she said.

"That's good, because I didn't do my homework!" said Lila. "Just kidding!"

The class burst into laughter.

"It's time to sit down, Lila," the teacher repeated.

Lila paused next to Cassie's desk on her way down the aisle. "Hey, new girl," she said. "What's your name?"

"Cassie," she replied.

"What school did you come from?" Lila asked.

That was a tough one. "Star . . . Starfield Preparatory School of . . . um . . . Preparedness," Cassie heard herself saying. *Ugh.* Why had she said that? What a ridiculous name.

But the girl laughed. "You're funny!"

Lila sat down, and the homework was collected.

Students passed their papers up the row and then the first person in each row passed them across. Ms. Olds noticed that one boy's homework was missing, though he insisted he had turned it in. But it was nowhere to be found. Finally, Ms. Olds turned on a monitor and three images were projected onto the whiteboard in the front of the room.

"Today we are going to discuss gravity. Now, who can tell me which of these photos illustrates this force?"

Several hands shot up.

"Yes, Kristie?" Ms. Olds said. "Come show us."

Kristie stood and walked to the front of the room. She pointed to a picture of a ball going through a basketball hoop. "Gravity is what pulls the ball back to the ground so it doesn't go shooting off into space," she said.

"That's right," said Ms. Olds. "Thank you, Kristie."

Kristie returned to her seat, stumbling on her way down the aisle. Cassie noticed that she gave Annabel a dirty look.

"You tripped me!" she hissed.

"Why are you looking at me?" said Annabel innocently. "I didn't do anything!"

"Settle down class," said Ms. Olds. "Now who can tell me who *discovered* gravity?"

Lila raised her hand. "I can, I can!" she said.

"Yes, Lila?" asked Ms. Olds.

"Kristie did!"

Ms. Olds sighed. "Anyone else?"

"Actually, it was . . ." Lila started.

But Annabel spoke over her. "It was Sir Isaac Newton," she said, giving Lila a disgusted look. "He published his finding in 1687," she added.

"That is correct, Annabel," said Ms. Olds. "Nicely done."

"As usual," muttered the boy who sat behind Annabel. She turned around and gave him a smirk.

Ms. Olds continued with a discussion of the force of gravity and Cassie tuned out, choosing to spend the rest of the class trying to figure out what Lila could be wishing for. She considered the evidence. She was clearly well liked by most of her classmates and she was certainly very funny. So Cassie could probably rule out a friendship wish. Could it have something to do with her family? A friend? A pet? Cassie sighed. It could be practically anything at that point.

Finally, it was time for lunch. "Annabel," said Ms. Olds. "Will you please show Cassie to the lunchroom?"

"Of course, Ms. Olds," said Annabel with a sweet smile.

Cassie followed her out of the classroom and they walked to the cafeteria in silence. Annabel paused at the entrance and turned to Cassie. Her sweet smile was gone.

"I hope you don't plan on sitting with me and my friends," she said. "Because you are definitely not invited." She turned and flounced off, waving to a group of girls already at a table.

Cassie stared after her, a look of disgust on her face. "That girl deserves a bowl of—" she looked at the menu offerings displayed on the wall behind the ladies of lunch—"vegetable chili on her head."

A voice came from beside her. "Turkey tetrazzini would be better."

Cassie spun around. It was Lila, grinning at her. "Or mac and cheese, alphabet soup, sloppy joes. But it's not worth it. You'll just get detention."

"She's so awful," said Cassie. She brightened. Maybe Lila's wish was to get even with Annabel. But how could that possibly be a good wish?

"Yeah, and the worst part is she has all the teachers fooled," said Lila. "She's been the Student of the Month three times in a row."

Cassie felt her face get warm. "That's so unfair," she said.

"Tell me about it, sister," said Lila. "Now let's get some lunch. You can sit at my table. Just keep that chili to yourself, please."

Cassie got in line behind Lila and took a closer look at the cafeteria. It was just as bad as Sage had said—smelly, uncomfortably warm, and filled with lots of unidentifiable food you were expected to eat.

"Do you wish to get even with Annabel?" she asked Lila.

Lila shrugged. "I wouldn't waste a wish on that. I save my wishes for important things."

Aha! thought Cassie. She grabbed a tray and a bowl of the chili. She followed Lila to a table in the back of the cafeteria, close to the windows. They had a lovely mountain view, though it wasn't quite as spectacular as the Crystal Mountains.

One by one they were joined by other girls and a couple of boys, Lila's friends. Lila introduced her to them all, and Cassie recognized several of them from room 261. They seemed like a nice bunch of kids. Cassie dug in to her chili, which was actually not inedible.

Lila told the group the story from that morning. She

was a great storyteller, and even her friends from class laughed as if they were hearing it for the first time.

"So why *were* you late this morning?" Cassie asked. Lila made a sad face and said, "It's so hard, Cassie, you wouldn't believe it if I told you. It's just so terrible. My mother . . ."

Cassie leaned forward, almost placing her chin in her pudding cup. "Yes," she breathed. She was *this close* to finding out Lila's wish; she was sure of it.

"My mother"—her voice cracked—"forgot to set the alarm last night!"

Her friends all burst into laughter. "I hate it when that happens!" a blond girl cried.

Cassie tried again. "I see your teeth are silver. Do you wish they were white?" But that got a laugh from Lila.

"You don't like my braces?" she said, baring her teeth. "Well, neither do I, but they're coming off soon."

Cassie tried again. She looked out the window at the driving rain. "Perhaps you wish for this rain to end?"

"No way," said Lila. "It's good for the plants."

She leaned back and looked at Cassie. "You ask some crazy questions, new girl," she said. "How about this one? What do you call cheese that isn't yours?"

"I have no idea," Cassie replied.

"Nacho cheese!" said Lila.

Cassie didn't get it, though the rest of the students at the table howled with laughter. "Oh," said Cassie. Another joke. She was beginning to realize that it was going to be very difficult to get Lila to be serious. How was she ever going to get the truth out of her? Just before classes began, Cassie stood up from the table and dumped her tray. She was really starting to worry and needed a moment to think, so she headed to the girls' bathroom, where she stood in front of the mirror, staring at her pale, non-sparkling reflection in the mirror. Was it time to use her underwhelming Mirror Mantra already? She pulled out her Star-Zap instead and accessed her Countdown Clock. She looked at the time remaining and gasped. It had to be broken! Could she really only have twenty-seven hours left to make Lila's wish come true? Was that even possible? Even for someone as determined and talented as she was, this was going to be tight.

★

There were no other clues for Cassie for the rest of the afternoon. And as the time came to pack up their bags, Cassie was in a bit of a panic. She couldn't let Lila out of her sight; she had to be sure to stick to her like sparkleglue for the rest of the day—and somehow wrangle an invitation to stay at her house overnight. That way she'd get extra time with her. *And I also won't have to sleep in an invisible tent in this weather,* thought Cassie. While she was pretty sure the tent was waterproof and would be warm and toasty inside, she didn't want to take any chances.

The bell rang for the end of the day and Cassie pushed into the hallway, determined not to lose sight of Lila. Luckily, the girl's locker was only a couple away from hers.

"Good first day?" Lila asked, unzipping her backpack.

"It was good," said Cassie. She decided to plunge right in. "So, um, do you want to hang out after school? Do homework together?"

"Can't," said Lila. "After-school club. Ice-dating." Or at least that was what Cassie thought she said. Her words were muffled by the arrival of a noisy bunch of kids who opened the lockers that stood between them. Cassie quickly grabbed her things, but by the time she slammed her locker shut, Lila was gone. Cassie felt her heart beat faster and her pulse race. She had to find Lila immediately.

Ice-dating? What could that be? She turned to the

girl next to her, who was staring into a mirror on the inside of the top of her locker, putting a glossy-looking substance from a tube on her lips. It smelled a bit like starberries to Cassie.

"I need to find the ice-dating club," she said.

"Ice-dating?" said the girl. "What in the world are you talking about?" Then she thought for a moment and laughed. "You mean ice-skating! Yeah, the rink is right at the bottom of the hill. Go out the front door of the school and make a left. You can't miss it."

Cassie thanked her and took off down the hall.

"It's pretty cold in there," the girl called out after her. "Don't forget your gloves!"

On the run, Cassie accessed her Wishworld Outfit Selector and made her choice. She waved her mittened hand at the girl and ran out of the school as fast as she could, whipping right past Annabel. "No running in the halls!" Annabel yelled after Cassie. "Do you hear me, new girl? Do you want a detention?"

Cassie pushed open the door to the ice rink. The girl had been right; it was just as cold inside as it was out. The room was huge, and a large shiny white oval stood in the middle. After some searching, Cassie found a group of students sitting on a bench, taking off their shoes. "Hey, Cassie!" said Lila with a smile. "I didn't know you were joining the ice-skating club. That's so cool!" Then she laughed at her accidental joke.

"I am!" said Cassie.

Lila introduced her to the club moderator, a teacher named Mr. Thompson. He told Cassie to take off her shoes and go get a pair of skates.

"What size?" asked the bored-looking boy behind the counter.

"One thirty-seven G," said Cassie, giving her Starland size without thinking.

The boy's eyes nearly bugged out of his head. He stared at Cassie for a minute, then grabbed her boot off the counter and turned it over. "Size five," he said, shaking his head. "Everyone's a comedian."

It took a while for Cassie to force her feet into the stiff white boots and even longer to lace them up. She stood up and quickly realized how hard it was to balance on the thin metal blades as her legs bowed first in, then out. She took a few shaky steps toward the rink, where Lila was already zipping around. A few more and she was clutching the rink wall for support. *Whew!* She made it to the entrance. The rink was a vast, intimidating expanse of white, not a sparkle in sight. Gingerly,

Cassie placed one foot on the ice, then the other. She was standing! She pushed forward confidently. While she had never skated before, she was sure that with her inherent nimbleness and ability to master new things, she'd be a natural on the ice. She glided forward and . . . *whoosh!* Within an instant she was flat on her back, looking up at the rafters. *This is the second time I've fallen since I arrived on Wishworld*, she thought. *Must be a record.*

Cassie put her hands to the ice and struggled to her feet, happy she was wearing mittens. *Moons and stars!* she thought. *This Wish Mission is more dangerous than I thought.* She somehow managed to make it to the waist-high wall that ran around the rink, and she slowly circled the rink with short, choppy steps, her hand in an iron grip on the railing. Any time she tried to let go of it, she lost her balance. She started to get hot, sweaty, and annoyed. She could see Lila zooming around the ice with her hands behind her back, then skating backward and even doing some spins. Cassie was impressed by how graceful she was.

Lila swooped toward Cassie, then turned away and sharply doubled back, sliding to a quick stop in front of her. Cassie was so startled she lost her balance. Luckily, Lila reached out a red-gloved hand and grabbed her arm in time.

"I'm sorry," Lila said. "The ice is slippery, isn't it?"

Cassie scowled at her.

"I'm not joking," she said. "It's not easy. You've got to take it slow, and pay attention. And practice."

Then, Cassie's hand firmly in hers, Lila showed her how to keep her knees bent, which dramatically improved Cassie's balance. She began to relax, a tiny bit.

"Take little steps," said Lila. "There you go. It's all about keeping your ankles steady."

Cassie wobbled forward.

"And if you think you're going to fall, make your hands into fists," she suggested. "Don't want to lose a finger under a sharp blade!"

Lila next taught Cassie how to push off and glide. And before Cassie knew it, she had navigated one full turn around the ice without falling. At the end of the hour, the girls were laughing and joking. Cassie had made it three times around the rink without falling.

She really is kind and helpful, thought Cassie. *But unfortunately I still have no idea what her wish could be.*

After the girls left the ice and had returned their skates, they put on their boots and stood outside waiting for Lila to be picked up.

"Who are you waiting for?" Cassie asked.

"My dad," said Lila.

Cassie had an idea. She hoped it would work. "Um . . . maybe you could come to my house tonight for dinner. My mom's making . . ." she searched her memory for a Wishling dinner option. "Grilled cheese pizza burgers" was what she came up with.

Lila burst out laughing. "I'd love to find out exactly what that is, but my dad is on his way to get me."

"Oh, that's too bad," said Cassie sadly. Would Lila take the bait?

She did. "Hey, why don't you come to my house for dinner instead? And sleep over, too?" she suggested. "Maybe you can have grilled cheese pizza burgers another night."

"Okay!" said Cassie quickly. Her plan had worked!

"What would you girls like to drink with dinner?" Lila's mother asked. She had the same black hair and easy grin as her daughter.

"Sparkling water for me," said Lila.

Cassie's eyes lit up. "Oh, yes, for me, too!" she exclaimed. Why hadn't she heard about this delightful beverage in Wishers 101? It would be a tiny reminder of home. She was missing the colors and the sparkle of Starland. It really helped to keep your spirits up, she realized. Her non-glittery surroundings were starting to get her down.

Lila's mom returned with two glasses of clear liquid, which she set on the table. A few bubbles rose to the top of each glass and popped joylessly on the surface. Cassie looked at Lila. That was it? "Um, I thought you said sparkling water," she said.

"This is sparkling water," replied Lila, taking a sip.

Cassie stared at the glass. "So where are the sparkles?" she asked.

Lila laughed. "Oh, Cassie, you crack me up!"

After dinner there were chocolate ice cream sundaes for dessert, which were startastic. But even more wonderful was that Cassie finally figured out Lila's wish.

Once the table was cleared, Cassie and Lila spread out their books on the dining room table and did their homework together. Cassie did her reading comprehension homework, reading a long passage and then answering ten multiple choice questions, and her science assignment, then dawdled over the math homework, trying to look like a normal Wishling who couldn't add, subtract, divide, and multiply huge sums instantly in her head. She stole a glance over at Lila's math book. She was pleasantly surprised to see that every answer was correct.

"Hey, you're good at math!" Cassie said admiringly.

"I am," said Lila. "Very good."

Cassie next leaned over to take a look at Lila's reading comprehension answers.

"Um," Cassie began, not sure how to broach the subject "You might want to take another look at those first . . . um . . . ten answers," she said.

Lila sucked in her cheeks and looked for a moment like she might cry. Then she glared at Cassie and slammed the book shut. "It's fine," she said tersely.

"But . . ." began Cassie.

"Just leave me alone, all right," Lila said. She stormed off and Cassie was left sitting at the dining room table by herself. She could hear Lila stomping up the stairs.

Well, this is awkward, she thought.

After giving the girl a couple of minutes to cool down, Cassie walked up the stairs, which creaked under her feet. After first opening the doors to two closets and a bathroom, she spotted a door with a sign on it that said LILA'S ROOM.

She grinned. "I'm a regular Detective Marmaduke Carbuncle," she said to herself. She took a deep breath and knocked on Lila's door.

"Come in," said a muffled voice.

Cassie opened the door. Lila was lying on her bed, her face buried in a pillow.

Cassie sat gingerly on the edge of the bed. "Do you want to talk?" she said.

With a heavy sigh, Lila flipped over on her back and stared at the ceiling, unable to make eye contact with Cassie.

"So now you know," she said. "I'm great at math but I'm terrible at reading," she said. "It's so humiliating. Ms. Olds must think I'm so dumb."

Cassie felt a sudden tingly rush of energy. She shivered with excitement. "You wish Ms. Olds would appreciate you," she said, her eyes shining.

Lila sat up, clutching the pillow to her chest. "I want her to like me," she said. "So to get her attention, I try to make her laugh. But she ends up getting mad at me." She sighed. "Meanwhile, people like Annabel Victor get all the attention. It's not fair."

"Well, I have a suggestion," said Cassie. "Save the jokes for lunch and recess. Just be your smart, kind, helpful self during the school day. Like when you helped me today at the ice rink. Ms. Olds is sure to notice and appreciate you."

Lila got a hopeful look on her face. "You really think so?"

"I do," replied Cassie. "And here's another thing. I'm pretty good at reading. I can give you some tips to help with this reading comprehension stuff. You might never be as good at it as math, but you could get better," she told her. "It's kind of like ice skating. Take it slow. Pay attention. Practice, practice, practice. Use a dictionary when you get to words you don't know." She laughed. "Okay, that's not like ice skating, but you catch my gift."

"I catch your *drift*," corrected Lila.

"See, you're paying attention already," said Cassie. Though she thought her way made more sense.

The two girls got ready for bed.

Before Lila drifted off to sleep she asked, "Do you really think this plan to impress Ms. Olds is going to work?"

"I'm sure of it," Cassie said confidently. *With me on the case*, she thought, *how could it* not *work?*

CHAPTER
11

They had pancakes for breakfast the next morning. They looked just like starcakes to Cassie, only round. They tasted pretty similar, too. Cassie tried maple syrup for the first time and nearly poured the whole container onto her plate, it was so delicious. *Tessa would love this on her starberry waffles*, she thought.

"Do you remember the plan?" she asked Lila. "Plenty of participation, kindness, and generosity. Today and every day. There are much more positive ways of getting attention from your teacher."

Lila bit her lip. "I'm a little nervous!"

"No need to be nervous," said Cassie. "Just be yourself." Then she hastily added, "Maybe without quite as many jokes, of course!"

Lila held her glass of orange juice up to Cassie. "To participation, kindness, generosity, and no jokes," she said. Cassie stared at her blankly. "Pick up your glass," instructed Lila. "Let's make a toast!" Cassie held her juice aloft and Lila clinked hers against it. And Cassie made another Wishworld observation: *"Toast" has more than one meaning on Wishworld!*

There was just one problem with the plan—Annabel. Cassie knew that they only had six hours left to make Lila's wish come true and the girl thwarted them at every turn. When Lila patiently raised her hand to answer a difficult math problem, Annabel shouted out the answer. When Ms. Olds walked into the classroom with a big stack of books in her arms, and Lila raced to the front of the room to help her, Annabel leaned over and give Lila a little push so she accidentally knocked the books to the floor. Annabel then made a big show out of helping the teacher pick them up. And Cassie stewed when Ms. Olds gave Annabel a grateful smile.

"Class, please pass your homework forward," Ms. Olds said. Everyone reached into their folders and handed their work to the person in front of them. Ms.

Olds collected the sheets from the first person in each row and stacked them together. She flipped through the pages at her desk. "Lila, I don't see yours, did you forget to hand it in?" she asked.

Lila looked up, confused. "No," she said. "I handed it in."

Ms. Olds looked again. "I don't see it here," she said.

Lila looked at Cassie nervously. Then instinct must have kicked in. To Cassie's dismay she started to say, "Hey, Ms. Olds, would you get mad if . . ."

Cassie knew what was coming next. She shook her head at Lila. *No jokes!* she thought. Not realizing exactly what she was doing, she willed Lila's voice to lower in volume. And that's exactly what happened. Lila's mouth was moving, but no sound was coming out.

Wow, thought Cassie. I guess I found my secret talent. She practiced on the next student who raised her hand.

"Ms. Olds, may I please be excused?" the girl said, her voice increasing in volume with each word. She looked surprised.

Cassie stared daggers at Annabel, who was sitting primly at her desk, her hands clasped together. She knew the girl had to be the one who took Lila's homework. She pretended to be one thing, but was actually quite just the opposite. And she had all the grown-ups fooled.

The bell rang for lunch. Lila shook her head as she walked out of the classroom with Cassie. "Well, that didn't go so well," she said. "And what do you think happened to my homework?"

But then Lila caught a look at Cassie's disappointed face. "Come on," she said, trying to cheer Cassie up. "No need to look so upset. It's no big deal."

Cassie's Countdown Clock told her differently. She was running out of time. It really *was* a big deal. Cassie waved Lila off. "I'll see you in the cafeteria," she said. She looked around grumpily. Where was Ms. Olds now to see how sweet and understanding Lila was? But the hallway was empty. She looked again. Oh, no, it wasn't. There, across the hall, staring back at her, was Scarlet. She was still sparkly (at least to Cassie) but she was wearing leggings and a large black sweater that looked like it had been eaten by moonmoths over a bright pink shirt that peeked through all the holes. Her hair was almost entirely black (with pink bangs). But it was Scarlet just the same. And Cassie knew exactly what that meant.

"I know, I know," said Cassie, shaking her head. "My wish is in serious trouble."

"So what's going on?" asked Scarlet. "Lady Stella is really worried. You know you're running out of time on the Countdown Clock, right?"

Cassie told Scarlet the whole story.

"Oh, that Annabel sounds awful," said Scarlet. "So what are we going to do?"

"We have to figure out a way to help Lila look good in front of Ms. Olds," said Cassie. "Before the end of the school day, which is when the Countdown Clock will run out."

"Well, you'd better figure it out fast," said Scarlet.

Cassie thought for a moment. "Can you go down to the principal's office and tell her you're the new girl in class 261?"

Scarlet nodded. "And then what?"

Cassie shrugged. "And then she'll bring you upstairs and then . . ." her voice trailed off. "And then we'll figure something out."

"Okay," said Scarlet. She skipped down the hallway, then stopped and looked back. "I hope you know what you are doing," she said.

Cassie smiled and waved. She'd figure it out. She was sure of it.

"You never came to lunch," said Lila, when she found Cassie standing in the hallway outside of the classroom. "You must be hungry. I brought you a snack." She handed Cassie a bag of some odd-looking twisty brown things.

"Thank you," said Cassie eagerly, tearing open the bag. She was hungry. "So can you continue to not tell jokes in class?" she asked.

Lila stared at the floor. "It's hard," she said.

"Tell me a joke," said Cassie. "Get it out of your system!"

Lila looked up. "Why was the math book sad?" she asked.

"I don't know," said Cassie "Why?"

Lila grinned. "Because it had so many problems," she said.

The two girls laughed. Then Lila grew serious. "Cassie, I don't know if this is going to work. I don't think Ms. Olds is ever going to take me seriously as a student."

"Hey, would you humor me for a minute?' asked Cassie.

Lila nodded.

Cassie grabbed her hand. "Sometimes when I need

strength and reassurance, I say these words out loud. It just makes me feel better and gives me focus." And then, even though she was not particularly fond of her mantra, she said it out loud: "Listen to your feelings. Let your inner light sparkle." A tingle ran through Cassie. Lila must have felt it, too, because her eyes widened. "Wow," she said. "I *do* feel better."

Annabel came bustling over to them. "No eating in the hallway," she said. She grabbed the pretzels from Cassie's hand and tossed them into the trash.

"I was hungry," said Cassie. "And that was mean. I'm . . . I'm going to tell Ms. Olds."

"Like she's really going to believe you over me, three-time Student of the Month?" Annabel scoffed. She turned to Lila and gave her a cruel smile. "What ever happened to your homework?" she asked.

"I bet I can guess," said Lila.

"You'll never prove it," answered Annabel.

With a sigh, Cassie and Lila headed into the classroom. Cassie had no idea what she was going to do when Scarlet arrived. But still, she was certain it was going to be good.

CHAPTER
12

Scarlet stood in front of the class, doing her best to look like a new Wishling student. She looked at her feet and smiled shyly when the principal introduced her to Ms. Olds, who remarked (again) that she smelled deep-dish blueberry pie. Scarlet gave Cassie a look which plainly said "So, what do we do now?" Cassie was still not sure, so she shrugged. They'd have to play it by year, a new Wishling expression she had picked up on her mission. She assumed that meant they would make it up as they went along.

"Ms. Olds," said Principal McIlhenney, "will you join me outside for a moment?"

"Certainly," said Ms. Olds. "Scarlet, please take the

seat next to Annabel for today." She smiled. "Annabel, I'm sure you'll do your best to make our newest student feel welcome."

As soon as the adults stepped into the hallway, Scarlet skipped across the room to her seat. Cassie watched as Annabel's eyes lit up. Annabel turned to Scarlet, a mocking look on her face. Suddenly, Cassie knew exactly what to do. She concentrated, dialing up the volume. She just hoped it would be loud enough for the adults to hear.

"Did you just skip?" Annabel said mockingly. "What, are we in preschool?" Her amplified voice echoed in the classroom, but her eyes were flashing and she didn't seem to notice.

Scarlet stopped in her tracks. "Are you talking to me?" she said.

"Yes, I'm talking to you," Annabel replied. "Skipping like a baby."

Scarlet honestly looked confused. "I have no idea what you're talking about. I would never *skip*," she said hotly. "I was hurrying."

Annabel laughed. "Oh, yes you were. And those clothes. Did you get that sweater at a garage sale or something? I mean, really."

Scarlet was staring daggers at Annabel, looking like

she was about to start yelling at her. Then someone spoke up. It was Lila.

"Enough," she said, standing and walking up the aisle. "Leave the poor girl alone."

"Poor girl?" said Scarlet, clearly puzzled.

"Ms. Olds asked you to welcome Scarlet into our classroom," she said, two spots of pink in her cheeks. Noticing her voice was extra loud, she tried to lower it. But Cassie turned up the volume as loud as she could. "We are supposed to treat our classmates with respect. Be kind to them. And you did neither. You were just plain mean." She turned to Scarlet. "Welcome to our class, Scarlet. We're not all like Annabel," she said. "Actually, we're all pretty nice. I think you're going to like it here."

Just then there was the sound of clapping. Cassie spun around to look at the doorway. And there she saw Ms. Olds and Principal McIlhenney, applauding Lila.

"Nicely done, Lila," said Ms. Olds. "You are a wonderful example of a good citizen and supportive classmate." She turned to Annabel and shook her head. "And Annabel, I am shocked, simply shocked, by your behavior toward our newest student. It is simply unacceptable."

Annabel stared down at her desk in a furious silence. Cassie got the idea that her mean girl days were over.

The principal was beaming. "Lila, your behavior was a great example for the rest of the students. Exactly the way our new Student of the Month should act."

Lila nodded and smiled. "Lila," said Cassie. "Principal McIlhenney just said that you're the Student of the Month!"

"What?" said Lila with a gasp. "Are you serious? Me?"

The principal nodded. "Congratulations!"

The class, everyone except for Annabel that is, cheered.

"Student of the Month," Lila said to herself. "I can't believe it." Everyone could see the joy on her face, but only Cassie and Scarlet could see the glimmering rainbow waves of pure wish energy that arced through the air. Cassie almost ducked when they flew right at her face, but then she stood still as they were absorbed by her star-shaped glasses. She closed her eyes and felt the warmth and positive feelings flow through her.

When the bell rang for the end of the day, Lila rushed up to Cassie and hugged her so tightly she lifted her off the ground. "Thank you, Cassie!" she said, her eyes shining. Cassie hugged her back, which she knew would erase Lila's—and everyone's—memory of her visit.

When they broke apart, Lila had a strange, distant look on her face. She blinked and then walked out of the classroom, not turning back. They hadn't even had a chance to say good-bye. And Cassie, with a large lump in her throat, thought it was better that way.

Epilogue

"Star salutations," said Cassie as she walked into Lady Stella's office and was immediately surrounded by her fellow Star Darlings, all eager to congratulate her. "It wasn't easy, but I ended up doing a startacular job, if I do say so myself," she said.

Scarlet cleared her throat. "And?"

Cassie clapped Scarlet on the back, hoping she looked modest and generous as she did so. "Oh, yes, and of course Scarlet was really just so helpful to me. Star salutations, Scarlet."

Scarlet nodded. "You're welcome," she said. Then she smiled. "That was a pretty crazy mission. Why that girl accused me of skipping, I'll never know."

Everyone took their seats around Lady Stella's silver

table, but Cassie stayed standing, knowing what was about to happen. Lady Stella handed the Wish Orb to Cassie. Cassie felt a lump in her throat as she stared at the beautiful glowing ball of light. Then she gasped as it began to transform into a silverbella, its round blossom a cluster of tiny stars shining with moonglow. She stared at it for a moment, transfixed. Then the stars parted to reveal a stunning cluster of pale pink jewels—a lunalite, Cassie's Power Crystal.

"Oh," she breathed. "It's the most beautiful Power Crystal of them all."

"It is lovely," said Lady Stella. "But they're all beautiful, Cassie."

Cassie looked up and gave the headmistress a wink. *As if!* She turned to her fellow Star Darlings, who, she felt, all seemed to be waiting for her to say a few words. "My fellow Star Darlings," she began. "Although my mission was most probably the best one of all so far— no offense to the rest of you—I want to tell you that success did not come as easily to me as you may imagine. I think I can be a shining example to you all as I persevered—"

"Star salutations, Cassie," interrupted Lady Stella. "But I think we're done here." She was staring at her, Cassie imagined, with great admiration. After all, Cassie had taken the headmistress's words to heart. She had turned her fear into total confidence. And just in time for her mission, too.

★

Cassie stayed behind to chat a bit with Lady Stella, who kept asking her if she was okay. She was fine, she said. She was startastic. What was the problem?

When she got back to her room, she placed her hand on the palm scanner. "Welcome back, Cassie," said the Bot-Bot voice. "And good job!"

"Star salutations," she said distractedly.

Her room was filled with Star Darlings. Astra was bouncing her star ball against the wall. Tessa was braiding Gemma's hair. Adora was browsing through Cassie's huge collection of holo-books. Libby was sleeping on her window seat.

"Star greetings, everyone," said Cassie. "And star salutations for coming here today. I have some important things to discuss with you, my fellow Star Darlings. As you know, I am a very sensitive and thoughtful individual. I often see things that many of you might miss. As a matter of fact . . ."

"Get to the point!" someone called out.

"Fine," said Cassie. "I called you all here because

something weird is going on at Starling Academy. And it involves us, the Star Darlings. I told Vega I would wait until I had proof, and now I think I do."

"What is it?" asked Leona. "Does it have to do with my messed-up mission?"

"And Scarlet being kicked out of the Star Darlings?" asked Astra.

"Yes," said Cassie. "There are a lot of weird things going on around campus, and I think the clues all lead to one individual."

"Who?" said Leona.

"Yes, tell us!" Astra shouted.

"Ophelia," said Cassie.

"I knew it!" Scarlet shouted.

"Something just isn't right," said Cassie. "She talks about her mom in the present tense. She's an orphan but she gets care packages. How could she have been admitted to Starling Academy if she was so clueless? Something is off with her. I don't think she's an orphan and I don't think she's clueless at all. I didn't put it all together until my Wish Mission. I met a girl who was pretending to be something she wasn't. I think Ophelia is doing the same thing."

"Well, I don't believe it," said Leona stubbornly. "I

think you are being unfair. I'm going to her room right now to straighten this out once and for all."

"I'm coming with you," said Scarlet, scrambling to her feet.

But Leona continued to sit on the bed. After a few moments, Scarlet grabbed her hand and dragged her out the door. The rest of the Star Darlings (save the still napping Libby) were close behind.

They hopped on the Cosmic Transporter, everyone tensely silent, and made their way to Ophelia's new room. Leona knocked and knocked on the door. There was no answer.

"Ophelia!" she called. "It's Leona." She turned to Cassie, her face flushed golden. "I asked you to look out for her, not investigate her!"

There was no answer. Finally, Scarlet skipped off to get a Bot-Bot guard. When they told it that they were worried about Ophelia, it finally relented and opened the door for them.

Leona barged into the room first and let out a gasp.

"What's wrong?" Cassie shouted, pushing her way inside. She looked around, bewildered. Ophelia was gone. The room was empty. There was not a thing in it. It was as if no one had ever lived there.

But on the wall, in hastily scribbled yellow letters, were the words *I'M SORRY*.

"This is terrible," Gemma said.

"You can say that again," said Cassie.

"This is terrible," Gemma repeated.

And then nobody said anything else, because they were plunged into a sudden and total darkness. For the first time in Starland history, the lights had gone out.

Glossary

Aeropuff: A Starland dessert.

Afterglow: The Starling afterlife. When Starlings die, it is said that they have "begun their afterglow."

Age of fulfillment: The age at which a Starling is considered mature enough to begin to study wish granting.

Astromuffins: Baked breakfast treat.

Bad Wish Orbs: Orbs that are the result of bad or selfish wishes made on Wishworld. These grow dark and warped and are quickly sent to the Negative Energy Facility.

Ballum blossom tree: A Starland tree with cherry blossom–like flowers that light up at night.

Big Dipper Dormitory: Where third- and fourth-year students live.

Bloombug: A purple-and-pink-spotted bug that goes wild during the full moon in warm weather.

Bluebeezel: Delicate bright blue flowers that emit a scent that only glitterbees can detect.

Bluebubble: Vega's Wish Blossom. Deep blue gives way to icy blue in the petals of this compact illuminated flower. Glowing points of light illuminate the blossom. Its petals open and close with such regularity that you can use it to tell time.

Boingtree: A shrublike tree with tickly aromatic needles.

Boingtree gum: Starland chewing gum.

Bot-Bot: A Starland robot. There are Bot-Bot guards, waiters, deliverers, and guides on Starland.

Bright Day: The date a Starling is born, celebrated each year like a Wishling birthday.

Calliope: A glittery yellow flower with ruffly petals and a magenta center.

Callistola: A tiny green bell-like flower that emits a faint tinkling sound when shaken. They smell a lot like ripe ozziefruit.

Celestial Café: Starling Academy's outstanding cafeteria.

Cloudcandy: Name for various Starland confections.

Cocomoon: A sweet and creamy fruit with an iridescent glow.

Cosmic Transporter: The moving sidewalk system that transports students through dorms and across the Starling Academy campus.

Countdown Clock: A timing device on a Starling's Star-Zap. It lets them know how much time is left on a Wish Mission, which coincides with when the Wish Orb will fade.

Crystal Mountains: The most beautiful mountains on Starland. They are located across the lake from Starling Academy.

Cyber Journal: Where the Star Darlings record their Wishworld observations.

Cycle of Life: A Starling's life span. When Starlings die, they are said to have "completed their Cycle of Life."

Dododay: The third day of the starweek. The days in order are Sweetday, Shineday, Dododay, Yumday, Lunaday, Bopday, Reliquaday, and Babsday. (Starlandians have a three-day weekend every starweek.)

Double starweek: Sixteen stardays.

Drifting moonbug: A storytelling device meant to mislead the reader. Starland's version of a red herring.

Druderwomp: An edible barrel-like bush capable of pulling up its own roots and rolling like a tumbleweed, then planting itself again.

Featherwhisper: A Starland dessert.

Flash Vertical Mover: A mode of transportation similar to a Wishling elevator, only superfast.

Floating Wisp: A Starland dessert.

Floozel: The Starland equivalent of a Wishworld mile.

Florafierce: Glowing stardust rises from the middle of this flower's fiery-red petals.

Flutterfocus: A Starland creature similar to a Wishworld butterfly but with illuminated wings.

Galliope: A sparkly Starland creature similar to a Wishworld horse.

Garble greens: A Starland vegetable similar to spinach.

Glion: A gentle Starland creature similar in appearance to a Wishworld lion, but with a multicolored glowing mane.

Glitterbees: Blue-and-orange-striped bugs that pollinate Starland flowers and produce a sweet substance called gossamer.

Globerbeem: Large, friendly lightning bug–type insects that are sparkly and lay eggs.

Glorange: A glowing orange fruit. Its juice is often enjoyed at breakfast time.

Glowfur: A small, furry Starland creature with gossamer wings that eats flowers and glows.

Glowin' Glions: Starling Academy's champion E-ball team.

Glowsow: A large farm animal that is prized for the light it emits at night—perfect for working after dark.

Good Wish Orbs: Orbs that are the result of positive wishes made on Wishworld. They are planted in Wish-Houses.

Gossamer: A sweet and fragrant liquid made by glitterbees; often used in baking.

Gossamerwisp: A Starland dessert.

Green Globules: Green pellets that are fed to pet glowfurs. They don't taste very good to Starlings.

Half-moon pie: A Starland dessert.

Halo Hall: The building where Starling Academy classes are held.

Halo-harp: A melodious stringed instrument played by striking its strings with a small mallet.

Holo-diary: A holographic book used for jotting down thoughts and feelings. There are also holo-billboards, holo-cameras, holo-letters, holo-journals, holo-cards, holo-communications, holo-flyers, holo-texts, holo-videos, and holo-pictures. Anything that would be made of paper on Wishworld is a hologram on Starland.

Holo-dice: A holographic version of dice.

Holo-phone: A Starland game much like the Wishworld "Telephone" where a phrase is passed on from one Starling to another and the last Starling says it out loud. The final message is often markedly different from the initial one, much to everyone's amusement.

Holo-text: A message sent or received on a Star-Zap and projected into the air.

Hydrong: The equivalent of a Wishworld hundred.

Illuminated Manuscript Technology: Also known as IMT, a new technology allowing a reader to view the action in a holo-book as the book is read aloud.

Illumination Library: The impressive library at Starling Academy.

Impossible Wish Orbs: Orbs that are the result of wishes made on Wishworld that are beyond the power of Starlings to grant.

Isle of Misera: A barren rocky island off the coast of New Prism.

Jujufruit: A large purple fruit with thick skin and juicy flesh. It is bouncy and sometimes used as a ball before being peeled and eaten.

Kaleidoscope City: Where Vega is from. Its colorful downtown is a tourist destination. A factory town, it is well known for its metal production. Its motto is "If it's made right, it's made in Kaleidoscope City."

Kaleidoscope tree: A rare and beautiful tree whose blossoms continuously change color.

Keytar: An instrument that is held like a guitar but has keys instead of strings.

Lallabelles: Tiny turqoiuse flowers that grow in clusters. They do not fade and are often used in dried flower arrangements.

Lightning Lounge: A place on the Starling Academy campus where students relax and socialize.

Little Dipper Dormitory: Where first- and second-year students live.

Luminous Lake: A serene and lovely lake next to the Starling Academy campus.

Meepletile: A Starland creature closest in nature to a Wishworld reptile. It frequently sheds its skin.

Microjoule: A tiny amount.

Mirror Mantra: A saying specific to each Star Darling that when recited gives her (and her Wisher) reassurance and strength. When a Starling recites her Mirror Mantra while looking in a mirror, she will see her true appearance reflected.

Mooncheese: A mild, tasty cheese often melted in sandwiches. It is made from the milk of the moonnut tree.

Moonfeather: A common material used for stuffing pillows, coats, and toys. Moonfeathers are harvested from the moonfeather bush.

Moonium: An amount similar to a Wishworld million.

Moonmoth: Large glowing creatures attracted to light like Wishworld moths.

Moonshot: A very slight possibility.

Noddlenoodle: An extremely long, thin noodle often used in Starling soups. A single noodle can fill an entire bowl.

Old Prism: A medium-sized historical city about an hour from Starling Academy.

Ozziefruit: Sweet plum-sized indigo fruit that grows on pink-leaved trees. It is usually eaten raw, made into jam, or cooked into pies. Starling Academy has an ozziefruit orchard.

Power Crystal: The powerful stone that each Star Darling receives once she has granted her first wish.

Purple piphany: A Starland flower with a distinctive fragrance.

Queezle: Vega's Power Crystal. Sparkling crystalline blue nuggets held together by their own internal magnetic force. Their seemingly chaotic arrangement actually represents a precise mathematical equation.

Roxylinda: A coral-colored flower with a large blossom.

Safety starglasses: Worn by Starlings to protect their eyes when they are close to a shooting star.

Serenity Gardens: Extensive botanical gardens set on an island in Luminous Lake.

Shimmering Shores: The sparkly beach located on the banks of Luminous Lake.

Shooting stars: Speeding stars that Starlings can latch on to and ride to Wishworld.

Shortsnip: A tiny unit of measurement, generally referring to distance.

Silverbella: An orb-shaped Starland flower with tiny pink and white petals that radiate from its center.

Silver Blossom: The final manifestation of a Good Wish Orb. This glimmering metallic bloom is placed in the Hall of Granted Wishes.

Solar metal: A common, inexpensive kind of metal.

Solar Springs: A hilly small town in the countryside where Tessa and Gemma are from.

Sparkle Meal: A premade meal.

Sparkle-O's: A sweet, fruity cereal, not usually considered a healthy breakfast.

Sparkle shower: An energy shower Starlings take every day to get clean and refresh their sparkling glow.

Spill the stars: To tell someone everything.

Star ball: An intramural sport that shares similarities with soccer on Wishworld. But star ball players use energy manipulation to control the ball.

Starbounce: Starland's version of a trampoline.

Starcake: A star-shaped Starling breakfast item, similar to a Wishworld pancake.

Starcar: The primary mode of transportation for most Starlings. These ultrasafe vehicles drive themselves on cushions of wish energy.

Star Caves: The caverns underneath Starling Academy where the Star Darlings' secret Wish Cavern is located.

Starf!: A Starling expression of dismay.

Star flash: News bulletin, often used starcastically.

Starland: The irregularly shaped world where Starlings live. It is veiled by a bright yellow glow that from a distance makes it look like a star.

Starland City: The largest city on Starland, also its capital.

Starlicious: Tasty, delicious.

Starlight: An expression used to mean "public attention." When all eyes are on a Starling, she is said to be "in the starlight."

Starling Academy: The most prestigious all-girl four-year boarding school for wish granting on Starland.

Starlings: The glowing beings with sparkly skin who live on Starland.

Starmarble: An attractive stone used for surfaces in Starland architecture.

Starmin: Sixty starsecs (or seconds) on Starland; the equivalent of a Wishworld minute.

Starpillows: A Starland dessert.

Star Quad: The center of the Starling Academy campus. The dancing fountain, band shell, and hedge maze are located there.

Starriest: As in "I don't have the starriest idea." Used to express lack of knowledge or understanding.

Star salutations: The Starling way to say "thank you."

Starsec: A brief period of time, similar to a Wishworld second.

Star Wranglers: Starlings whose job is to lasso a shooting star, to transport Starlings to Wishworld.

Staryear: A period of 365 days on Starland, the equivalent of a Wishworld year.

Star-Zap: The ultimate smartphone that Starlings use for all communications. It has myriad features.

Stellar School: A rival of Starling Academy in star ball.

Stellation: The point of a star. Halo Hall has five stellations, each housing a different department.

Supernova: A stellar explosion. Also used colloquially, meaning "really angry," as in "She went supernova when she found out the bad news."

Time of Applying: The very busy time of year when Starlings work on and send out applications to schools.

Time of Letting Go: One of the four seasons on Starland. It falls between the warmest season and the coldest, similar to fall on Wishworld.

Time of Lumiere: The warmest season on Starland, similar to summer on Wishworld.

Time of New Beginnings: Similar to spring on Wishworld, this is the season that follows the coldest time of year; it's when plants and trees come into bloom.

Time of Shadows: The coldest season of the year on Starland, similar to winter on Wishworld.

Toothlight: A high-tech gadget that Starlings use to clean their teeth.

Violina: A pale blue cone-shaped flower with clusters of shiny dark blue leaves.

Wharfle: A round metal disk used for Winkedly Wharfles, a game similar to tiddlywinks in which you flick disks into a container.

Wish Blossom: The bloom that appears from a Wish Orb after its wish is granted.

Wish energy: The positive energy that is released when a wish is granted. Wish energy powers everything on Starland.

Wish energy manipulation: The ability to mentally harness wish energy to perform physical acts, like turning off lights, closing doors, etc.

Wisher: The Wishling who has made the wish that is being granted.

Wish-Granters: Starlings whose job is to travel down to Wishworld to help make wishes come true and collect wish energy.

Wish-House: The place where Wish Orbs are planted and cared for until they sparkle. Once the orb's wish is granted, it becomes a Wish Blossom.

Wishlings: The inhabitants of Wishworld.

Wish Mission: The task a Starling undertakes when she travels to Wishworld to help grant a wish.

Wish Orb: The form a wish takes on Wishworld before traveling to Starland. There it will grow and sparkle when it's time to grant the wish.

Wish Pendant: A gadget that absorbs and transports wish energy, helps Starlings locate their Wishers, and changes a Starling's appearance. Each Wish Pendant holds a different special power for its Star Darling.

Wish-Watcher: A Starling whose job is to observe the Good Wish Orbs until they glow, indicating that they are ready to be granted.

Wishworld: The planet Starland relies on for wish energy. The beings on Wishworld know it by another name—Earth.

Wishworld Outfit Selector: A program on each Star-Zap that accesses Wishworld fashions for Starlings to wear to blend in on their Wish Missions.

Wishworld Surveillance Deck: A platform located high above the campus where Starling Academy students go to observe Wishlings through high-powered telescopes.

Zeldabloom: Large fragrant purple flowers with yellow centers.

Zing: A traditional Starling breakfast drink. It can be enjoyed hot or iced.

Zoomberries: Small sweetly tart berries that grow in abundance on Starland.

Acknowledgments

It is impossible to list all of our gratitude, but we will try.

Our most precious gift and greatest teacher, Halo; we love you more than there are stars in the sky . . . punashaku. To the rest of our crazy, awesome, unique tribe—thank you for teaching us to go for our dreams. Integrity. Strength. Love. Foundation. Family. Grateful. Mimi Muldoon—from your star doodling to naming our Star Darlings, your artistry, unconditional love, and inspiration is infinite. Didi Muldoon—your belief and support in us is only matched by your fierce protection and massive-hearted guidance. Gail. Queen G. Your business sense and witchy wisdom are legendary. Frank—you are missed and we know you are watching over us all. Along with Tutu, Nana, and Deda, who are always present, gently guiding us in spirit. To our colorful, totally genius, and bananas siblings: Patrick, Moon, Diva, and Dweezil—there is more creativity and humor in those four names than most people experience in a lifetime. Blessed. To our magical nieces—Mathilda, Zola, Ceylon, and Mia—the Star Darlings adore you and so do we. Our witchy cuzzie fairy godmothers—Ane and Gina. Our fairy fashion godfather, Paris. Our sweet Panay. Teeta and Freddy—we love you so much. And our four-legged fur babies—Sandwich, Luna, Figgy, and Pinky Star.

The incredible Barry Waldo. Our SD partner. Sent to us from above in perfect timing. Your expertise and friendship are beyond words. We love you and Gary to the moon and back. Long live the manifestation room!

Catherine Daly—the stars shined brightly upon us the day we aligned with you. Your talent and inspiration are otherworldly; our appreciation cannot be expressed in words. Many heartfelt hugs for you and the adorable Oonagh.

To our beloved Disney family. Thank you for believing in us. Wendy Lefkon, our master guide and friend through this entire journey. Stephanie Lurie, for being the first to believe in Star Darlings. Suzanne Murphy, who helped every step of the way. Jeanne Mosure, we fell in love with you the first time we met, and Star Darlings wouldn't be what it is without you. Andrew Sugerman, thank you so much for all your support.

Our team . . . Devon (pony pants) and our Monsterfoot crew—so grateful. Richard Scheltinga—our angel and protector. Chris Abramson—thank you! Special appreciation to Richard Thompson, John LaViolette, Swanna, Mario, and Sam.

To our friends old and new—we are so grateful to be on this rad journey that is life with you all. Fay. Jorja. Chandra. Sananda. Sandy. Kathryn. Louise. What wisdom and strength you share. Ruth, Mike, and the rest of our magical Wagon Wheel bunch—how lucky we are. How inspiring you are. We love you.

Last—we have immeasurable gratitude for every person we've met along our journey, for all the good and the bad; it is all a gift. From the bottom of our hearts we thank you for touching our lives.

Shana Muldoon Zappa is a jewelry designer and writer who was born and raised in Los Angeles. With an endless imagination, a passion to inspire positivity through her many artistic endeavors, and her background in fashion, Shana created Star Darlings. She and her husband, Ahmet Zappa, collaborated on Star Darlings especially for their magical little girl and biggest inspiration, Halo Violetta Zappa.

Ahmet Zappa is the *New York Times* best-selling author of *Because I'm Your Dad* and *The Monstrous Memoirs of a Mighty McFearless*. He writes and produces films and television shows and loves pancakes, unicorns, and making funny faces for Halo and Shana.